SPECIMENS

OF

AMERICAN POETRY,

WITH

CRITICAL AND BIOGRAPHICAL

NOTICES.

IN THREE VOLUMES.

BY SAMUEL KETTELL.

VOL. I.

Benjamin Blom
New York

First Published Boston 1829
Reissued 1967, by
Benjamin Blom, Inc., New York 10452
Library of Congress Catalog Card No. 67-12457

PREFACE.

THE following work is the result of an attempt to do something for the cause of American literature, by calling into notice and preserving a portion of what is valuable and characteristic in the writings of our native poets. As a pursuit of mere literary curiosity, there exist no ordinary inducements to the prosecution of such an enterprise, but when we take into view the influence which an endeavor like this, to rescue from oblivion the efforts of native genius must necessarily have upon the state of letters among us, we shall have occasion to wonder that an undertaking of the kind has not sooner been entered upon. The truth is, that our neglect upon this point is in some degree a matter of reproach to us. The literary productions of our fathers have been held in unwarrantable disesteem by their descendants, who have reason to pride themselves upon the monuments of genius and learning left them by preceding generations. What though our early literature cannot boast of a Dante or a Chaucer, it can furnish such testimonials of talent and mental cultivation as are highly creditable

to the country, and of sufficient interest to call upon
the attention of those who are desirous of tracing the
general history of letters, and their connexion with the
development of the moral and intellectual character
of a people ; while to us, as Americans, they possess a
double value, and deserve to be cherished as the inher-
itance of a race whose virtues have consecrated whatever they have left behind them. Again, everything
published among us must have some value, if not on
account of its intrinsic merits, at least as affording some
insight into the spirit and temper of the times, and
illustrating the degree of social and mental improvement
in the community. Hitherto we have paid too little
regard to our native literature in this last relation, and
while the polite letters of foreign countries have been
studied in such a philosophical view by the most
accomplished scholars of our land, the same interesting
field of observation at home has been overlooked.
We have known men familiar with the details of
Tiraboschi, Bouterwek and Sismondi, who had hardly
bestowed a thought upon the most gifted spirits of the
soil where they were born and bred : as if the poets of
the western world could not bear some characteristic
traits of their day and generation as well as the
Minnesingers and Trouvéres ; or as if a lay of the
pilgrim fathers of New England could not illustrate a
point of national or individual character as effectually
as the Gongorism of the Castilian rhymesters of old.
This is surely a preposterous state of things. What
has been produced in the shape of literature among us
merits regard. It must furnish something worthy of

note in respect to the intellectual character of our nation. If it exhibit no marks of originality, it must show something of imitation, and it cannot but interest us to know the fact, for even that must have its significance.

The object, therefore, of the work which I here present to the public, is to answer, so far as my opportunities would enable me to do it, the demand which has already been manifested, to know in a general and comprehensive view, what has been done in the department of poetry by American writers. Thus far we have seen no such thing as a collection of American poetry designed for such a purpose, nor a treatise designating with fulness and accuracy, the character of the various performances in verse of our native authors, nor even a tolerably complete list of their names. We are now becoming a literary people, and are already inquisitive upon all matters connected with our character and prospects in that relation. We begin to show a national spirit in letters, and deem it important not only to exhibit to the world what manner of men we are, but to cast an eye upon those who preceded us in the career of literary improvement, and look seriously into the grounds of the insinuation thrown out some years ago by our neighbors across the ocean, that there was no such thing as an American book worthy of being read. Our countrymen have done sufficient since that period to free us from the apprehension that the charge will be repeated ; still it is a matter of interest to inquire whether nothing had been

A*

achieved before the days of Irving and Cooper and Pierpont and Percival, or whether, on the contrary, there were brave men living before Agamemnon.

I have endeavored to perform the task of supplying what seemed a desideratum. Whatever may be the estimation set upon my labors, I have the pleasure of presenting my countrymen with a collection of matter which no one can deny to be highly honorable to the land of our birth. The American reader will learn with surprise and gratification that a body of literature so respectable under all circumstances, as that contained in the following pages, can be gathered from the writings of our native authors. If, as I flatter myself, they may succeed so far as to make us better acquainted with the master spirits of our literature, and of consequence lead us to a more exalted appreciation of the intellectual capabilities of our countrymen, I shall reap a full reward for my exertions, in the reflection of having assisted in fostering a national spirit in a department, where, until such a spirit prevails, neither ourselves, nor the world will do full credit to the principles of our institutions, or the genius of our people.

That I have done entire justice to my task, I will not pretend. Were it allowed an author to go into a detail of the disadvantages under which he sets about his work, for the purpose of excusing its faults, I could furnish without difficulty in the present instance, a catalogue sufficient to account for the imperfections which I cannot help foreseeing, will be charged against these volumes. But with the greater part of a writer's disabilities or disadvantages, the world has no concern, and very properly will not suffer them to be pleaded in excuse for the defects which mar his productions. I shall therefore speak only of the difficulties inseparable from the present undertaking. I allude chiefly to the collection of the materials for the work. When it is considered, that nothing similar to this enterprise has ever before been attempted, the reader must be aware of the laborious nature of the researches necessary to be made. The whole collection of American literature was to be explored minutely without guide or direction, and the difficulty of such a task can be estimated only by those who have attempted something similar. There was no where, as I before remarked, even a tolerably accurate list of American authors. Their works were scattered as diversely as the leaves of the Sybil, and many of them were about as easily to be procured. We have no collections of them in public libraries,* and some had become so completely forgotten that I was indebted in many cases to accident for their discovery. The omissions therefore which may be discerned in these volumes the reader I trust will ascribe to the right cause. For inaccuracies in the biographical department, should any be discovered, I must plead for a similar indulgence. The best authorities however have been applied to for this species of information, and I feel confident in assert-

---

*The principal libraries in Boston and the neighborhood, New York, Philadelphia, and Worcester, have been examined in search of materials for the work. In neither of these does there appear to have been any attempt made at such a collection. The most valuable one is in the possession of Professor Ticknor of this city, comprising about seventy volumes of the scarce old writers. That gentleman will accept my thanks for the readiness he has manifested to afford me all such assistance as his library could furnish.

ing that it may in general be relied upon. In the case of many of the most important subjects, the facts have been furnished by the authors themselves, in others, by their relations, or intimate associates. The additions thus made to the stock of biography by this original matter, forms not the least valuable portion of the work.

The plan upon which the latter part has been executed, will, it is hoped, meet the general approbation, although, perhaps, somewhat different from what the public had been led to expect. It was thought best upon mature consideration, to extend the work down to the present day, and embrace within it every one who had written with credit. On account of the rapid extension of literature among us within a short period, a fair representation could not in any other way be given of what we are likely to accomplish.

It will be perceived that I have left out the drama. It was originally intended to include all the dramatic productions in verse, but having learnt that a History of the American Stage was preparing by one who has been long conversant with the subject, and who possesses peculiar advantages for such a business, I deemed it most advisable to leave that part of the field untouched.

It remains for me to speak of the assistance which I have received in the course of my labors, and of the obligations due from me to those gentlemen who have so kindly lent me their aid in various shapes. Some of the biography and criticism, has been furnished by other hands. This will account for those slight discrepancies of opinion, which may be detected in two or three different pieces. To Mr Frederic S. Hill, who in the outset took the editorial charge of the work, I am indebted for all which relates to Mather, Wolcott, Wigglesworth, Colman, Mrs Turell, Adams and J. Osborn. A few other articles are also the contributions of my friends. For the general character of these portions of the work, however, I hold myself responsible.

In selecting the specimens it will be observed that I have extracted pretty liberally from the volumes of some of our most distinguished writers. It seemed the most eligible method to give entire pieces of some length, when this could be done advantageously, rather than short and detached portions of different poems. I have in all cases where it was practicable, applied to the authors for permission to make such an appropriation of their writings, and this they have in every instance been so obliging as to grant.

Under the persuasion that the American public will look with indulgence upon the effort here shown to turn their attention to the literature and talent of their own country, I now submit these volumes to their inspection. The undertaking is one which I think they cannot but contemplate with interest. With what degree of credit I have acquitted myself of the charge, it remains for them to determine.

S. K.

Boston, April, 1829.

CONTENTS OF THE FIRST VOLUME.

INTRODUCTION.

———

THE early settlers of New England were no less distinguished for their attachment to letters than for their strong religious character ; and although their taste and partialities lay rather toward the substantial than the ornamental parts of literature, yet the *commune vinculum*, the natural and intimate connexion of all liberal pursuits, unavoidably turned their studies in some degree in the latter direction. A great number of the earliest emigrants were men of the first attainments in the principal sciences held in repute at that period, and their writings reflect no small honor on their character for learning and ability. Their earliest attempts in the department of polite literature, must certainly be considered rude and feeble, when compared with the contemporaneous productions of Europe, but they deserve attention from the influence which they undoubtedly exercised upon the writers who succeeded them, no less than from the light they throw upon the character of the writers and the state of society. They also possess an interest arising from the curiosity we naturally feel to view the most ancient memorials of literary effort on record among us. We shall proceed therefore to enumerate such of the first settlers of the country as were known for any productions in verse which have remained to the present day, and give a brief historical sketch of the early poetical literature of the English Colonies.

It was hardly three years from the arrival of the pilgrims that the first essay of this kind was made by *William Morell*, an episcopal clergyman, who wrote a description of New England in Latin hexameter verse. Morell came to this country in 1623 and remained about a year. Except therefore, as being the earliest attempt at versification within the present limits of the country, his performance can hardly claim any remark here. It was published in England with a translation by the author. Both have been reprinted in the collections of the Massachusetts Historical Society.

The next poetical production which offers itself to our notice is the version of the Psalms published at Cambridge in 1640, and which was the first book printed in the United States.* About the year 1639 the clergymen of New England considering that in their new residence they had been enabled to enjoy most of the ordinances of christian worship in all desirable purity, were induced to extend the reform they had thus effected, to the ordinance of the singing of psalms. The common metrical translation of the psalms was considered to deviate so far from the original as to be an unsatisfactory help to their devotions. A new version was therefore resolved upon, and the several portions of the work were assigned to the most eminent divines of the country. The principal of these whom we find mentioned were *John Eliot* of Roxbury, the celebrated Indian Apostle, *Thomas Welde* of Roxbury, and *Richard Mather* of Dorchester. The work thus produced was such as might have been expected from the plan. The main object of the translators was of course to make the version as literal as possible. An extract from their preface may serve to give the reader the views which they entertained of the nature of their task.

---

*Although this was the first *book*, it was not the first specimen of printing in the country. The year previous there was published an Almanack and The Freeman's Oath.

"If therefore the verses are not always so smooth and elegant as some may desire and expect, let them consider that God's altar needs not our polishings; for wee have respected rather a plain translation, than to smooth our verses with the sweetness of any paraphrase, and so have attended to conscience rather than elegance, fidelity rather than poetry, in translating the Hebrew words into English language, and David's poetry into English meetre."

This book was called The Bay Psalm Book. The version is exact enough in respect of adherence to the original to satisfy the scruples of the most rigid critic. But the versification is harsh and unmusical to the last degree, and it was soon found expedient to give it a little more polish. The following extract will convey some idea of the rest of the work.

PSALM CXXXVII.

1. The rivers on of Babilon,
     there when wee did sit downe,
   Yea even then wee mourned when
     wee remembered Sion.
2. Our harp wee did hang it amid,
     Upon the willow tree,
3. Because there they that us away
     led in captivitee
   Requir'd of us a song, and thus
     ask't mirth us waste who laid,
   Sing us among a Sion's song,
     unto us then they said.
4. The Lord's song sing can wee? being
     in strangers land, then let
5. loose her skill my right hand if I
     Jerusalem forget.
6. Let cleave my tongue my pallate on
     if minde thee doe not I,
   if chiefe joyes o're I prize not more
     Jerusalem my joy.
7. Remember Lord, Edoms sons' word,
     unto the ground said they,
   it rase it rase, when as it was
     Jerusalem her day.

8. Blest shall hee bee that payeth thee
    daughter of Babilon,
   who must be waste, that which thou hast
    rewarded us upon.
9. O happie hee shall surely bee
    that taketh up, that eke
   thy little ones against the stones
    doth into pieces breake.

After two editions had been printed, an improvement
of the language was declared necessary. It was therefore put into the hands of the Rev. Henry Dunster,
President of Harvard College and Mr Richard Lyon,
a tutor to a young student at Cambridge. These editors
gave the work a revision "with a special eye," as they
inform us, "both to the gravity of the phrase of sacred
writ, and sweetness of the verse." They added versifi-
cations of some other portions of scripture, entitling them
The Spiritual Songs of the Old and New Testament.
This "improved version" has gone through more than
thirty editions in this country, and has been often reprinted in Scotland and England, and used in many of
the English dissenting congregations.

The earliest poet of New England, however, was
ANNE BRADSTREET, the wife of Simon Bradstreet,
Governor of the Massachusetts colony, and daughter of
Thomas Dudley, also Governor. She was born in
1612, probably at Northampton or Boston in England.
She was married to Mr Bradstreet at the age of sixteen, and came the next year, 1630, with her husband
to this country. The preface to the second edition of
her poems published after her death, declares the volume
to be "the work of a woman honored and esteemed,
where she lives, for her gracious demeanor, her eminent
parts, her pious conversation, her courteous disposition,
her exact diligence in her place, and discreet managing
of her family occasions; and more than so these poems
are the fruit but of some few hours, curtailed from her
sleep and other refreshments." She died September

16th, 1672. One of the pieces in her volume bears the date of 1632, *Ætatis suæ* 19.

Her writings gained her great celebrity among her contemporaries. Cotton Mather is warm in her praise and declares that "her poems, divers times printed, have afforded a grateful entertainment unto the ingenious, and a monument for her memory beyond the stateliest marbles." The learned and excellent John Norton of Ipswich calls her the "mirror of her age and glory of her sex." He wrote a funeral eulogy in which he did not scruple to pun upon her name according to the fashion of the time.

> "Her breast was a brave pallace, a *broad street*,
> Where all heroic, ample thoughts did meet,
> Where nature such a tenement had tane
> That other souls to hers dwelt in a lane."

Many others wrote verses in her commendation, and it is much to their credit that they so justly appreciated her talents; for we must come down to a late period in the literary annals of the country before we find her equal, although her productions are not without the marks of the barbarous taste of the age. Her first essays in polite composition had but an untoward guidance from the authors most esteemed at that time. The models they presented were not adapted to promote either good taste or excellence of any sort, in writing. Du Bartas* was the favorite poet of the day, and his conceits seem to have been, in particular, the admiration of our author. She appears also to have caught something of his spirit.

---

*Guillaume de Salluste du Bartas was a French poet of the time of Henry IV. His chief work was a poem on the creation, stuffed with absurdities. He called the head the lodging of the understanding, the eyes the twin stars, the nose the 'gutter' or 'chimney,' the teeth a double palisade used as a mill to the open throat. This poem was as much admired as is now Pollok's Course of Time, and in five or six years passed through thirty editions. It was translated into English. The earliest writings of New England abound with allusions to this author.

The contents of her volume are a poem upon the Four Elements, upon the Four Humors in Man's Constitution, upon the Four Ages of Man, and the Four Seasons of the Year. In these we are presented with personifications of Fire, Air, Earth and Water; Choler, Blood, Melancholy and Phlegm; and Childhood, Youth, Middle Age and Old Age, each of whom comes forward with an address in which its peculiar excellences are set forth. Then follows a versified history of the Four Monarchies of the World, and some shorter pieces, one of which, for its great merit, we shall extract; it shows Mrs Bradstreet to have possessed genuine poetical feeling. This poem is entitled

CONTEMPLATIONS.

Some time now past in the Autumnal Tide,
When Phœbus wanted but one hour to bed,
The trees all richly clad, yet void of pride,
Were gilded o'er by his rich golden head.
Their leaves and fruits seem'd painted, but was true
Of green, of red, of yellow, mixed hew,
Wrapt were my senses at this delectable view.

I wist not what to wish, yet sure thought I,
If so much excellence abide below;
How excellent is He, that dwells on high!
Whose power and beauty by his works we know.
Sure he is goodness, wisdome, glory, light,
That hath this under world so richly dight:
More heaven than earth was here no winter and no night.

Then on a stately oak I cast mine eye,
Whose ruffling top the clouds seem'd to aspire;
How long since thou wast in thine infancy?
Thy strength, and stature, more thy years admire.
Hath hundred winters past since thou wast born?
Or thousand since thou brak'st thy shell of horn,
If so, all these as nought, eternity doth scorn.

Then higher on the glistering sun I gaz'd,
Whose beams were shaded by the leavie tree,
The more I look'd, the more I grew amaz'd,
And softly said, what glory 's like to thee?
Soul of this world, this Universe's eye,

No wonder, some made thee a deity;
Had I not better known, (alas) the same had I.

Thou as a bridegroom from thy chamber rushest,
And as a strong man, joyes to run a race,
The morn doth usher thee, with smiles and blushes,
The earth reflects her glances in thy face.
Birds, insects, animals with vegetive,
Thy heart from death and dulness doth revive:
And in the darksome womb of fruitful nature dive.

Thy swift annual, and diurnal course,
Thy daily straight, and yearly oblique path,
Thy pleasing fervor, and thy scorching force,
All mortals here the feeling knowledge hath.
Thy presence makes it day, thy absence night,
Quaternal seasons caused by thy might:
Hail creature, full of sweetness, beauty and delight.

Art thou so full of glory, that no eye
Hath strength, thy shining rayes once to behold?
And is thy splendid throne erect so high?
As to approach it, can no earthly mould.
How full of glory then must thy Creator be,
Who gave this bright light luster unto thee!
Admir'd, ador'd for ever, be that Majesty.

Silent alone, where none or saw, or heard,
In pathless paths I lead my wandering feet,
My humble eyes to lofty skyes I rear'd
To sing some song, my mazed Muse thought meet.
My great Creator I would magnifie,
That nature had, thus decked liberally:
But Ah, and Ah, again, my imbecility!

I heard the merry grasshopper then sing,
The black clad cricket, bear a second part,
They kept one tune, and plaid on the same string,
Seeming to glory in their little art.
Shall creatures abject, thus their voices raise?
And in their kind resound their maker's praise:
Whilst I as mute, can warble forth no higher layes.

When present times look back to ages past,
And men in being fancy those are dead,
It makes things gone perpetually to last,
And calls back months and years that long since fled.

It makes a man more aged in conceit,
Than was Methuselah, or 's grand-sire great;
While of their persons and their acts his mind doth treat.

Sometimes in Eden fair he seems to be,
Sees glorious Adam there made Lord of all,
Fancyes the Apple, dangle on the Tree,
That turn'd his Sovereign to a naked thral.
Who like a miscreant 's driven from that place,
To get his bread with pain, and sweat of face:
A penalty impos'd on his backsliding race.

Here sits our Grandame in retired place,
And in her lap, her bloody Cain new born,
The weeping Imp oft looks her in the face,
Bewails his unknown hap, and fate forlorn;
His mother sighs, to think of Paradise,
And how she lost her bliss, to be more wise,
Believing him that was, and is, Father of lyes.

Here Cain and Abel come to sacrifice,
Fruits of the earth, and fatlings each do bring;
On Abel's gift the fire descends from skies,
But no such sign on false Cain's offering;
With sullen hateful looks he goes his wayes.
Hath thousand thoughts to end his brothers dayes,
Upon whose blood his future good he hopes to raise.

There Abel keeps his sheep, no ill he thinks,
His brother comes, then acts his fratricide,
The Virgin Earth, of blood her first draught drinks,
But since that time she often hath been cloy'd;
The wretch with ghastly face and dreadful mind,
Thinks each he sees will serve him in his kind,
Though none on Earth but kindred near then could he find.

Who fancyes not his looks now at the barr,
His face like death, his heart with horror fraught,
Nor male-factor ever felt like warr,
When deep despair, with wish of life hath sought,
Branded with guilt, and crusht with treble woes,
A vagabond to Land of Nod he goes,
A city builds, that wals might him secure from foes.

Who thinks not oft upon the Fathers ages.
Their long descent, how nephew's sons they saw,
The starry observations of those Sages,
And how their precepts to their sons were law

How Adam sigh'd to see his progeny,
Clothed all in his black sinfull livery,
Who neither guilt, nor yet the punishment could fly.

Our Life compare we with their length of dayes,
Who to the tenth of theirs doth now arrive?
And though thus short, we shorten many ways,
Living so little while we are alive;
In eating, drinking, sleeping, vain delight,
So unawares comes on perpetual night,
And puts all pleasures vain unto eternal flight.

When I behold the heavens as in their prime,
And then the earth (though old) still clad in green,
The stones and trees, insensible of time,
Nor age nor wrinkle on their front are seen;
If winter come, and greenness then do fade,
A Spring returns, and they more youthfull made;
But Man grows old, lies down, remains where once he 's laid.

By birth more noble than those creatures all,
Yet seems by nature and by custome cursed,
No sooner born, but grief and care make fall
That state obliterate he had at first.
Nor youth, nor strength, nor wisdom spring again,
Nor habitations long their names retain,
But in oblivion to the final day remain.

Shall I then praise the heavens, the trees, the earth,
Because their beauty and their strength last longer?
Shall I wish their, or never to had birth,
Because they're bigger, and their bodyes stronger?
Nay, they shall darken, perish, fade and dye,
And when unmade, soever shall they lye,
But man was made for endless immortality.

Under the cooling shadow of a stately elm
Close sate I by a goodly River's side,
Where gliding streams the rocks did overwhelm;
A lonely place, with pleasures dignified.
I once that lov'd the shady woods so well,
Now thought the rivers did the trees excell,
And if the sun would ever shine, there would I dwell.

While on the stealing stream I fixt mine eye,
Which to the long'd-for Ocean held its course,
I markt nor crooks, nor rubs that there did lye
Could hinder aught, but still augment its force:

O happy Flood, quoth I, that holdst thy race
Till thou arrive at thy beloved place,
Nor is it rocks or shoals that can obstruct thy pace.

Nor is 't enough, that thou alone may'st slide,
But hundred brooks in thy cleer waves do meet,
So hand in hand along with thee they glide
To Thetis' house, where all embrace and greet:
Thou Emblem true, of what I count the best,
O could I lead my Rivulets to rest,
So may we press to that vast mansion, ever blest.

Ye Fish which in this liquid region 'bide,
That for each season, have your habitation,
Now salt, now fresh, where you think best to glide,
To unknown coasts to give a visitation,
In lakes and ponds, you leave your numerous fry,
So nature taught, and yet you know not why,
You watry folk that know not your felicity.

Look how the wantons frisk to taste the air,
Then to the colder bottome straight they dive,
Eftsoon to Neptune's glassie Hall repair
To see what trade the great ones there do drive,
Who forrage o'er the spacious sea-green field,
And take the trembling prey before it yield,
Whose armour is their scales, their spreading fins their shield.

While musing thus with contemplation fed,
And thousand fancies buzzing in my brain,
The sweet-tongued Philomel percht o'er my head,
And chanted forth a most melodious strain
Which rapt me so with wonder and delight,
I judg'd my hearing better than my sight,
And wisht me wings with her a while to take my flight.

O merry Bird (said I) that fears no snares,
That neither toyles nor hoards up in thy barn,
Feels no sad thoughts, nor cruciating cares
To gain more good, or shun what might thee harm;
Thy cloaths ne'er wear, thy meat is every where,
Thy bed a bough, thy drink the water cleer,
Reminds not what is past, nor what's to come dost fear

The dawning morn with songs thou dost prevent,*
Setts hundred notes unto thy feather'd crew,
So each one tunes his pretty instrument,

*i. e. Anticipate.

And warbling out the old, begins anew,
And thus they pass their youth in summer season,
Then follow thee into a better Region,
Where winter's never felt by that sweet airy legion.

Man's at the best a creature frail and vain,
In knowledge ignorant, in strength but weak:
Subject to sorrows, losses, sickness, pain,
Each storm his state, his mind, his body break:
From some of these he never finds cessation,
But day or night, within, without, vexation,
Troubles from foes, from friends, from dearest, near'st Relation.

And yet this sinfull creature, frail and vain,
This lump of wretchedness, of sin and sorrow,
This weather-beaten vessel wrackt with pain,
Joyes not in hope of an eternal morrow:
Nor all his losses, crosses and vexation,
In weight, in frequency and long duration
Can make him deeply groan for that divine Translation.

The Mariner that on smooth waves doth glide,
Sings merrily, and steers his barque with ease,
As if he had command of wind and tide,
And now become great Master of the seas;
But suddenly a storm spoils all the sport,
And makes him long for a more quiet port,
Which 'gainst all adverse winds may serve for fort.

So he that saileth in this world of pleasure,
Feeding on sweets, that never bit of th' sowre,
That's full of friends, of honour and of treasure,
Fond fool, he takes this earth ev'n for heav'ns bower.
But sad affliction comes and makes him see
Here's neither honor, wealth, nor safety;
Only above is found all with security.

O Time the fatal wrack of mortal things,
That draws oblivion's curtains over kings,
Their sumptuous monuments, men know them not,
Their names without a Record are forgot,
Their parts, their ports, their pomp's all laid in th' dust,
Nor wit nor gold, nor buildings scape time's rust;
But he whose name is grav'd in the white stone
Shall last and shine when all of these are gone.

The sister of Mrs Bradstreet, Mrs Woodbridge, the
wife of John Woodbridge, minister at Andover and

Newbury, was likewise an adventurer in verse. An epistle which she addressed to her sister upon the subject of her volume, is still extant. The poetry is respectable, but has no striking passages.

Governor Dudley, the father of Mrs Bradstreet, was a versifier. He wrote an epitaph on himself which was found in his pocket after his death ; it is hardly worth quoting, and we know not whether any other of his rhymes have been preserved. William Bradford, the second Gove nor of Plymouth Colony, who came over in the first ship in 1620, figured also as a poet. He died in 1657. His Descriptive and Historical Account of New England in verse, containing about three hundred lines, may be found in the Historical Collections. He is commended by the author of the Magnalia for his great learning and particularly for his skill in various languages. His verses however have little to recommend them.

JOHN COTTON, the minister of Boston, must be recorded among those who attempted poetry. Some of his verses upon the death of two of his children have been preserved, written in Greek letters upon the blank leaves of his Almanack. His elegy upon the death of Thomas Hooker, the first minister of Hartford, Connecticut, who died in 1647, has been commended as sensible and correct. We give a short extract.

> Twas of Geneva's worthies said with wonder,
> (Those worthies three) Farel was wont to thunder ;
> Viret like rain on tender grass to shower,
> But Calvin, lively oracles to pour.

> All these in Hooker's spirit did remain,
> A son of thunder and a shower of rain;
> A pourer forth of lively oracles,
> In saving soul the summ of miracles.

EZEKIEL ROGERS the minister of Rowley, who gave that town its name, and died in 1660, also ' embalmed' the memory of Hooker in the following epitaph, every

line of which, in the judgment of Cotton Mather, deserved a reward equal to that which Virgil received for
his verses upon Marcellus in the Æneid.

> America, although she do not boast
> Of all the gold and silver from that coast,
> Lent to her sister Europe's need and pride;
> (For that repaid her with much gain beside,
> In one rich pearl which heaven did thence afford,
> As pious Herbert gave his honest word;)
> Yet thinks she in the catalogue may come
> With Europe, Africk, Asia, for one tomb.

The same event was lamented in an elegy by Peter
Bulkly, the first minister of Concord, whose latin verses
written at the age of seventy-six, are preserved in the
Magnalia, along with the latin poetry of Elijah Corlet
of Cambridge upon the character of Hooker.

The death of any noted divine in those days seems
to have been very certain to arouse the muse of our
ancestors. Scarcely one of any eminence closed his
mortal career without drawing forth a profusion of
elegiac strains. When John Cotton died in 1652, the
event afforded a theme to BENJAMIN WOODBRIDGE
for a poem which contains a somewhat remarkable
passage, as it has been conjectured that it suggested
to Franklin the hint for his celebrated epitaph upon
himself. Benjamin Woodbridge was educated partly
at Oxford in England, and coming to this country
finished his studies at Harvard College, of which he
had the honor of being the first graduate. He afterwards returned to England and became one of the
chaplains of Charles II. The passage referred to is
this.

> A living breathing bible; tables where
> Both covenants at large engraven were;
> Gospel and law in 's heart had each its column,
> His head an index to the Sacred volume,
> His very name a title-page, and next
> His life a commentary on the text.

O what a monument of glorious worth,
When in a new edition he comes forth,
Without erratas, may we think he'll be,
In leaves and covers of eternity !

JOSEPH CAPEN, minister of Topsfield, wrote some
lines upon the death of Mr John Foster, a mathematician and printer, which have a still more remarkable
similarity to the epitaph of Franklin.

THY body which no activeness did lack,
Now 's laid aside like an old almanack ;
But for the present only 's out of date,
'T will have at length a far more active state :
Yea, though with dust thy body soiled be,
Yet at the resurrection we shall see
A fair edition, and of matchless worth,
Free from erratas, new in heaven set forth ;
Tis but a word from God the great Creator,
It shall be done when he saith *Imprimatur*.

John Norton also commemorated the death of Cotton
by an elegy ; his verses in praise of Mrs Bradstreet have
already been mentioned. Nathaniel Ward, the Simple
Cobler of Agawam, wrote poetry in his facetious way.
Edward Johnson the author of the Wonder Working
Providence, interspersed his history with a multitude of
verses, laudatory of the several worthy and eminent men
of whom he had occasion to speak. His poetry is to
be found in the records of Woburn, the town where he
passed the latter part of his life.

ROGER WILLIAMS wrote verses among his other works
during his banishment ; some of them have been preserved in his Key to the Indian Languages. We offer a
short specimen.

YEERES thousands since God gave command,
As we in scripture find,
That earth and trees and shrubs should bring
Forth fruits each in his kind.

The wilderness remembers this ;
The wild and howling land

Answers the toiling labour of
  The wildest Indian's hand.

But man forgets his maker who
  Fram'd him in righteousnesse
A Paradise in Paradise now worse
  Than Indian wildernesse.

JONATHAN MITCHEL, Pastor of the church in Cambridge, deserves some notice for his attempts at poetry. Upon the death of Henry Dunster, one of the translators of the Bay Psalm Book, who was dismissed from his office as President of Harvard College for his heterodox opinions upon the subject of baptism, Mitchel wrote an elegy, some stanzas of which deserve transcribing for the strain of liberal sentiment which they breathe on the subject of the President's religious notions.

WHERE faith in Jesus is sincere,
  That soul, he saving, pardoneth ;
What wants or errors else be there,
  That may and do consist therewith.

And though we be imperfect here,
  And in one mind can't often meet,
Who know in part, in part may err,
  Though faith be one, all do not see 't.

Yet may we once the rest obtain,
  In everlasting bliss above,
Where Christ with perfect Saints doth reign,
  In perfect light and perfect love.

Then shall we all like-minded be,
  Faith's unity is there full grown ;
There one truth all both love and see,
  And thence are perfect made in one.

There Luther both and Zuinglius,
  Ridley and Hooper there agree
There all the truly righteous
  Sans feud live to eternity.

John Wilson, the Paul of New England, who is celebrated by Cotton Mather as the greatest " anagramma-
tizer"* since the days of Lycophron, and who even
uttered anagrams by *improvisation*, has also left specimens of his verse behind him ; they may be found in the
Magnalia. Thomas Shepard of Charlestown, who died
in 1677, has left similar relics. He is better known by
the Elegy which URIAN OAKES, the President of Harvard College wrote upon his death. President Oakes
was styled the Lactantius of New England ; his fame
as a scholar was widely extended, and his character
pre-eminent for piety and benevolence. His elegy on
Shepard's death was printed in 1677 ; a good authority
has pronounced it a highly meritorious performance.
We give a few stanzas taken from different parts of the
poem.

> ART, nature, grace in him were all combined
>   To show the world a matchless paragon,
> In whom of radiant virtues no less shined
>   Than a whole constellation, but hee 's gone !
> Hee 's gone, alas ! down in the dust must ly
> As much of this rare person as could die !

> To be descended well, doth that commend ?
>   Can sons their fathers' glory call their own ?
> Our Shepard justly might to this pretend,
>   (His blessed father was of high renown :
> Both Englands speak him great, admire his name,)
> But his own personal worth 's a better claim.

> His look commanded reverence and awe,
>   Though mild and amiable, not austere :
> Well humour'd was he as I ever saw,
>   And ruled by love and wisdom more than fear.

*The rage for anagrams appears to have been universal in the
country at that time. The biographer of Wilson cites the criticisms
of the Jews upon the Old Testament in defence of the practice, and
declares that much devout instruction was realized from this play
upon names. He complains that there were not a greater number
of anagrams made upon the name of Wilson, and insinuates that the
muses looked very dissatisfied when they beheld the inscription
on his tomb without this customary appendage.

The muses and the graces too conspired
To set forth this rare piece to be admired.

He breathed love and pursued peace in hisday,
   As if his soul were made of harmony.
Scarce ever more of goodness crowded lay
   In such a piece of frail mortality.
Sure Father Wilson's genuine son was he,
New England's Paul had such a Timothy.

The successor of President Oakes at Harvard was
JOHN ROGERS. He came in his youth to New England
and was educated at the College over which he was
called to preside. Before he was chosen to the presidency he had been first a preacher and then a physician.
He died suddenly in 1684, having been President but
two years. His verses addressed to Mrs Bradstreet
merit an insertion here. They have more correctness
and elegance than are to be found in any we have yet
noticed except those of the writer to whom they are
addressed.

MADAM, twice through the Muses' grove I walkt,
Under your blissfull bowres, I shrowding there,
It seem'd with Nymphs of Helicon I talkt,
For there those sweet-lip'd sisters sporting were.
Apollo with his sacred lute sate by,
On high they made their heavenly sonnets flye,
Posies around they strow'd, of sweetest poesie.

Twice have I drunk the nectar of your lines,
Which high sublim'd my mean born phantasie,
Flusht with these streams of your Maronean wines
Above myself rapt to an extasie :
Methought I was upon mount Hybla's top,
There where I might those fragrant flowers lop,
Whence did sweet odors flow, and honey spangles drop.

To Venus' shrine no altars raised are,
Nor venom'd shafts from painted quiver fly :
Nor wanton Doves of Aphrodite's carr,
Or fluttering there, nor here forlornly lie :
Lorne paramours, not chatting birds tell news,

How sage Apollo Daphne hot pursues,
Or stately Jove himself is wont to haunt the stews.

Nor barking Satyrs breathe, nor dreary clouds
Exhaled from Styx, their dismal drops distil
Within these fairy, flowry fields, nor shrouds
The screeching night raven, with his shady quill :
But lyrick strings here Orpheus nimbly hitts,
Arion on his sadled dolphin sits,
Chanting as every humour, age and season fits.

Here silver swans, with nightingales set spells,
Which sweetly charm the traveller, and raise
Earth's earthed monarchs, from their hidden cells,
And to appearance summon lapsed dayes,
Their heav'nly air becalms the swelling frayes,
And fury fell of elements allayes,
By paying every one due tribute of his praise.

This seem'd the scite of all those verdant vales,
And purled springs, whereat the Nymphs do play :
With lofty hills, where Poets rear their tales,
To heavenly vaults, which heav'nly sound repay
By echo's sweet rebound : here ladye's kiss,
Circling nor songs, nor dance's circle miss ;
But whilst those Syrens sung, I sunk in sea of bliss.

Thus weltring in delight, my virgin mind
Admits a rape ; truth still lyes undescri'd,
Its singular that plural seem'd : I find
'T was fancie's glass alone that multipli'd ;
Nature with art so closely did combine,
I thought I saw the Muses treble trine,
Which prov'd your lonely Muse superiour to the Nine.

Your only hand those poesies did compose :
Your head the source, whence all those springs did flow :
Your voice, whence changes sweetest notes arose :
Your feet that kept the dance alone, I trow :
Then vail your bonnets, Poetasters all,
Strike, lower amain, and at these humbly fall,
And deem yourselves advanc'd to be her pedestal.

Should all with lowly congees laurels bring,
Waste Flora's magazine to find a wreathe,
Or Pineus' banks, 'twere too mean offering;
Your Muse a fairer garland doth bequeath
To guard your fairer front; here 't is your name
Shall stand immarbled; this your little frame
Shall great Colossus be, to your eternal fame.

PETER FOLGER, who settled at Nantucket, where he kept a school, was the author of a poetical work entitled " A Looking Glass for the Times." This was published in 1675 or 1676. Folger's daughter was the mother of Benjamin Franklin, and Franklin in his own life has given a description of the poem. We have not been able to obtain a sight of this performance. The only copy we have yet heard of, was in the possession of a friend a year or two since but is now lost. A few extracts have been published in one of our literary journals. We will quote the words of Franklin in describing the poem. " The author addresses himself to the governors for the time being; speaks for liberty of conscience, and in favor of the Anabaptist Quakers, and other sectaries who had suffered persecution. To this persecution he attributes the war with the natives and other calamities which afflicted the country, regarding them as the judgments of God in punishment of so odious an offence; and he exhorts the government to the repeal of laws so contrary to charity. The poem appeared to be written with a manly freedom and a pleasing simplicity." Folger's book we understand is accurately described in the above paragraph, and a short extract which we have at hand will give an idea of the poetry.

THE rulers in the country I
    do own them in the Lord!
And such as are for government,
    with them I do accord.
But that which I intend hereby
    is that they would keep bound,

> And meddle not with God's worship
> for which they have no ground.
> And I am not alone herein,
> there many hundreds more,
> That have for many years ago
> spoke much upon that score.
> Indeed I really believe
> it 's not your business,
> To meddle with the church of Christ
> in matters more or less.

The Rev. Samuel Danforth, of Roxbury, was a writer of verse. He was more celebrated, however, as a mathematician and astronomer. He calculated the trajectory of the great comet which appeared in 1664, and published a treatise on it entitled, " An astronomical description of the late comet with a brief theological description thereof."

JOHN DANFORTH, of Dorchester, son of the above, claims to be mentioned for his verses; he wrote against religious controversy in the following strains.

> By hot contention's thunderbolts
> Are armies rent in twain.
> Armies of Abels too advance
> Arm'd with the clubs of Cain.
>
> Batter'd and shatter'd by such storms
> Are best men's reputation.
> In vain they talk while strife is loud
> Of waking reformation.

In the following verses written in 1690, he attempted to point out the best method of christianizing the Indians.

> ADDRESS I pray, your Senate for good orders
> To *civilize* the heathen in our borders.
> Virtue must turn into necessity,
> Or this brave work will in its turn still lie.
> Till *agriculture* and *cohabitation*
> Come under full restraint and regulation,

Much you *would* do you 'll find *impracticable*,
And much you *do* will prove *unprofitable*.
In common lands that lie unfenced, you know,
The husbandman in vain doth plough and sow.
We hope in vain the plant of *grace* will thrive
In forests where *civility* can't live.

The next poet that offers himself to our notice is
BENJAMIN TOMPSON the "learned schoolmaster and
physician." By the Boston Records it appears that he
was master of the public school in Boston from 1667 to
1670, when having had and accepted a call to Charlestown, he removed thither and was succeeded by Cheever.
He was the son of William Thompson or Tompson, the
minister of Braintree, and was born at that place within
the limits of the present town of Quincy, in 1640, and
received a degree at Cambridge in 1662. To Benjamin Tompson* must therefore be awarded the distinction
of being the first native American poet. All his poetry
hitherto known, was thought to be comprised in an Elegy
upon the Rev. Samuel Whiting of Lynn, a poem addressed to Hubbard, and a few lines upon Cotton Mather.
But we have lately discovered another work of his, which
we consider the greatest curiosity as an antiquarian relic,
that the early writings of New England present to us.
It is a Poem on Philip's War, written and published,
according to undoubted internal evidence, during that
desperate struggle with the natives in which the very
existence of the New England colonies was at stake.
The poem is entitled New England's Crisis. We shall
offer the reader one or two extracts of some length, no
less to set in a fair light the merits of Tompson's poetry,
than to gratify the curious with an exhibition of the strains

*His name *B. Tompson*, is subscribed to the original edition of one
of his poems. The epitaph on his tombstone at Roxbury is as fol-
lows. SUB SPE IMMORTALI YE HERSE OF MR BENJAMIN THOM-
SON, LEARNED SCHOOLMASTER AND PHYSICIAN, AND YE RE-
NOWNED POET OF NEW ENGLAND. OBIIT APRILIS 13, ANNO
DOMINI 1714, ET ÆTATIS SUÆ 74. MORTUUS SED IMMORTALIS

in which our first native bard sung the wars which threatened the extinction of his nation.

The author begins with a " Prologue," in which he complains seriously of the great increase of luxurious habits in the country ! One would think the land of the Pilgrims stood hardly in danger from this cause in 1675, when the females personally assisted to build a fortification on Boston neck for a protection against the savages.

NEW ENGLAND'S CRISIS.

THE PROLOGUE.

The times wherein old Pompion was a saint,
When men fared hardly yet without complaint,
On vilest cates ; the dainty indian maize
Was eat with clamp-shells out of wooden trayes,
Under thatch'd hutts without the cry of rent,
And the best sawce to every dish, content.
When flesh was food and hairy skins made coats,
And men as wel as birds had chirping notes.
When Cimnels* were accounted noble bloud ;
Among the tribes of common herbage food.
Of Ceres' bounty form'd was many a knack,
Enough to fill poor Robin's Almanack.
These golden times (too fortunate to hold,)
Were quickly sin'd away for love of gold.
'T was then among the bushes, not the street,
If one in place did an inferior meet,
" Good morrow brother, is there aught you want ?
" Take freely of me, what I have you ha'nt."
Plain Tom and Dick would pass as currant now,†
As ever since " Your Servant Sir," and bow.
Deep-skirted doublets, puritanick capes,
Which now would render men like upright apes,
Was comlier wear, our wiser fathers thought,
Than the cast fashions from all Europe brought.
'T was in those dayes an honest grace would hold
Till an hot pudding grew at heart a cold.

*Simnels.   †Then.

And men had better stomachs at religion,
Than I to capon, turkey-cock, or pigeon;
When honest sisters met to pray, not prate,
About their own and not their neighbour's state.
During Plain Dealing's reign, that worthy stud
Of the ancient planters' race before the flood,
Then times were good, merchants car'd not a rush
For other fare than Jonakin and Mush.
Although men far'd and lodged very hard,
Yet innocence was better than a guard.
'T was long before spiders and worms had drawn
Their dungy webs, or hid with cheating lawne
New England's beautyes, which stil seem'd to me
Illustrious in their own simplicity.
'T was ere the neighbouring Virgin-Land had broke
The hogsheads of her worse than hellish smoak.
'T was ere the Islands sent their presents in,
Which but to use was counted next to sin.
'T was ere a barge had made so rich a fraight
As chocolate, dust-gold and bitts of eight.
Ere wines from France and Moscovadoe to,
Without the which the drink will scarsly doe.
From western isles ere fruits and delicacies
Did rot maids' teeth and spoil their handsome faces.
Or ere these times did chance, the noise of war
Was from our towns and hearts removed far.
No bugbear comets in the chrystal air
Did drive our christian planters to despair.
No sooner pagan malice peeped forth
But valour snib'd it.   Then were men of worth
Who by their prayers slew thousands, angel-like ;
Their weapons are unseen with which they strike.
Then had the churches rest ; as yet the coales
Were covered up in most contentious souls :
Freeness in judgment, union in affection,
Dear love, sound truth, they were our grand protection.
Then were the times in which our councells sate,
These gave prognosticks of our future fate.
If these be longer liv'd our hopes increase,
These warrs will usher in a longer peace.
But if New England's love die in its youth,

The grave will open next for blessed truth.
This theame is out of date, the peacefull hours
When castles needed not, but pleasant bowers.
Not ink, but bloud and tears now serve the turn
To draw the figure of New England's urne.
New England's hour of passion is at hand ;
No power except divine can it withstand.
Scarce hath her glass of fifty years run out,
But her old prosperous steeds turn heads about,
Tracking themselves back to their poor beginnings,
To fear and fare upon their fruits of sinnings.
So that the mirror of the christian world
Lyes burnt to heaps in part, her streamers furl'd.
Grief sighs, joyes flee, and dismal fears surprize
Not dastard spirits only, but the wise.
Thus have the fairest hopes deceiv'd the eye
Of the big-swoln expectant standing by :
Thus the proud ship after a little turn,
Sinks into Neptune's arms to find its urne :
Thus hath the heir to many thousands born
Been in an instant from the mother torn :
Even thus thine infant cheeks begin to pale,
And thy supporters through great losses fail.
This is the *Prologue* to thy future woe,
The *Epilogue* no mortal yet can know.

Having despatched his preliminaries the author plunges in *medias res* and gives us a representation of King Philip, who calls his warriors around him and makes to them a speech in choice Indian. We next have the incidents of the campaign, the marches of the troops, and the storming of an Indian fort. Then follow detached portions, celebrating battles, and the burning of towns, which items of intelligence appear to have come to hand while the author was writing his poem. In this manner we are presented with Marlburye's Fate; the Town called Providence, its Fate; Seaconk Plain Engagement; Seaconk or Rehoboth's Fate; Chelmsford's Fate, and lastly Lines On a Fortification at Boston begun by women. The subjoined extract will give an idea of his general manner.

MANY hot welcomes from the natives' arms
Hid in their sculking holes, many alarms
Our brethren had, and many weary trants:
Sometimes in melting heat and pinching wants.
Sometimes the clouds with sympathizing tears
Ready to burst, discharged about their ears.
Sometimes on craggy hills, anon in bogs,
And miry swamps, better befitting hogs;
And after tedious marches, little boast
Is to be heard of stew'd, or bakt, or roast.
Their beds are hurdles, open house they keep,
Through shady boughs the stars upon them peep:
Their chrystal drink drawn from the mother's breast,
Disposes not to mirth, but sleep and rest.
     Thus many dayes and weeks some months run out,
To find and quell the vagabonding rout,
Who like enchanted castles fair appear,
But all is vanisht if you come but near.
Just so we might the pagan archers track,
With towns and merchandize upon their back:
And thousands in the South who settled down,
To all the points and winds are quickly blown.
At many meetings of their fleeting crew,
From whom like haile, arrows and bullets flew,
The English courage with whole swarms dispute,
Hundreds they hack in pieces in pursuit:
Sed haud impuné, English sides do feel
As well as tawny skins, the lead and steel;
And some such gallant sparks by bullets fell.
As might have curst the powder back to hell.
Had only swords these skirmishes decided,
All pagan sculls had been long since divided.
     The ling'ring war outlives the summer sun,
Who hence departs hoping it might be done
Ere his return at spring; but ah! hee'l find
The sword still drawn, men of unchanged mind.
Cold winter now nibbles at hands and toes,
And shrewdly pinches both our friends and foes.
Fierce Boreas whips the pagan tribe together,
Advising them to fit for foes and weather.

The axe which late had tasted christian bloud,
Now sets its steely teeth to feast on wood.
The forests suffer now, by waight constrain'd
To kiss the earth with soldiers lately brain'd.
The lofty oakes and ashe doe wagge the head
To see so many of their neighbours dead.
Their fallen carcases are carried thence
To stand our enemies in their defence.
Their Myrmidons inclosed with clefts of trees,
And busie like the ants or nimble bees.
And first they limber poles fix in the ground,
In figure of the heavens convex: all round
They draw their arras-matts and skins of beasts,
And under these the elves do make their nests.
Rome took more time to grow than twice six hours,
But half that time will serve for indian bowers ;
A citty shall be rear'd in one daye's space,
As shall an hundred Englishmen out face.
Canonicus' precints these swarmes unite,
Rather to keep a winter guard than fight.
A dern* and dismal swamp some scout had found,
Whose bosom was a spot of rising ground
Hedg'd up with mighty oakes, maples and ashes,
Nurst up with springs, quick boggs and miery plashes ;
A place which nature coyn'd on very nonce,
For tygers, not for men to be a sconce ;
Twas here these monsters shapt and fac'd like men
Took up their *Rendezvouz* and brumal den.

On the whole, Tompson must be allowed considerable praise ; he is exceeded by none of his contemporaries for correct and smooth versification.

NICHOLAS NOYES is another native poet ; he was the nephew of James Noyes, the first minister of Newbury, and was born in that town December 22d, 1647. He was graduated at Cambridge in 1667, and settled in the ministry at Salem. His poem on the death of the Rev. Joseph Green, of Salem village, we have not seen. He

*Lonely.

wrote a prefatory poem to the Magnalia, from which we take the following lines complimentary of the author.

> HEADS of our tribes whose corps are under ground,
> Their names and fames in chronicles renown'd,
> Begemm'd on golden ouches he hath set
> Past envy's teeth and time's corroding fret.
> Of death and malice he's brush'd off the dust,
> And made a resurrection of the just.
>   *   *   *   *   *   *
> This well instructed scribe brings new and old,
> And from his mines digs richer things than gold ;
> Yet freely gives, as fountains do their streams,
> Nor more than they, himself, by giving, drains.
> He's all design, and by his craftier wiles
> Locks fast his reader, and the time beguiles ;
> Whilst wit and learning move themselves aright,
> Through every line and colour in our sight,
> So interweaving profit with delight,
> And curiously inlaying both together
> That he must needs find both who looks for either.
> His preaching, writing, and his pastoral care
> Are very much to fall to one man's share.
> This added to the rest is admirable,
> And proves the author indefatigable.
> Play is his toyl, and work his recreation,
> And his inventions next to inspiration.
> His pen was taken from some bird of light,
> Addicted to a swift and lofty flight.
> Dearly it loves art, air, and eloquence,
> And hates confinement, save to truth and sense.
>   *   *   *   *   *   *
> The *stuff* is true, the *trimming* neat and spruce,
> The workman's good, the work of public use ;
> Most piously design'd, a Public Store,
> And well deserves the public thanks and more.

TIMOTHY WOODBRIDGE, minister of Hartford, brother of Benjamin Woodbridge, already quoted, also complimented Mather and his book in a poetical address.

Whether he was a native of this country or England we know not. We extract a few lines from his poem.

> LET the remotest parts of earth behold
> New England's crowns excelling Spanish gold.
> Here be rare lessons set for us to read,
> That offsprings are of such a goodly breed.
> The dead ones here so much alive are made,
> We think them speaking from blest Eden's shade.
> Hark how they check the madness of this age,
> The growth of pride, fierce lust and worldly rage ;
> They tell we shall to clam-banks come again,
> If heaven still doth scourge us all in vain.
>   But Sir, upon your merits heap'd will be
> The blessings of all those that here shall see
> Virtue embalm'd : this hand seems to put on
> The laurel on your brow, so justly won.

The death of Urian Oakes in 1681 was lamented in an Elegy by DANIEL GOOKIN, jr. son of Daniel Gookin who made the valuable Historical Collections respecting the Indians of New England. Daniel Gookin, jr. was born, as we have reason to think, at Cambridge. He was ordained as a minister there, and was afterwards a missionary among the Indians. We have never met with any mention of him as a poet. The elegy above-mentioned exists only in a single manuscript, the autograph perhaps of the author. We have a quotation of two stanzas at hand.

> THIS turns our dance to halting, lames our mirth,
>   Untunes our harps, our hearts doth wound ;
>   No music 's now in any sound :
> Our hopes are cover'd o'er with clods of earth :
> 'T is this that kills the springing joys we had ;
> Not heads but hearts are now in mourning clad.
>
> The time doth signalize this fatal turn :
>   'T was when the Father of the Day
>   In haste was posting on his way
> To bury Summer in th' autumnal urn.

'T was when, as loath to see the dismal sight,
Phœbus had coffin'd up himself in night.

We know not whether JOHN HAWKINS, of Boston,
has left any other specimen of his metre behind him, but
we will introduce here his

EPIGRAM ON PROVIDENCE.

LORD are not ravens daily fed by thee?
And wilt thou clothe the lilies and not me?
Begone distrust, I shall have clothes and bread
While lilies flourish and the birds are fed.

SAMUEL SEWALL, who came to America in his youth,
was educated at Harvard College and afterwards became Chief Justice of the Supreme Court of Massachusetts, was also a poet. His Hymn for the New
Year, written Jan. 1st, 1701, "a little before break a
day, at Boston of the Massachusetts," we will cite as the
earliest specimen we have of that sort of occasional
composition.

ONCE more our God vouchsafe to shine,
Tame thou the rigour of our clime;
Make haste with thy impatient light
And terminate this long dark night.

Let the translated English vine
Spread further still, still call it thine.
Prune it with skill, for yield it can
More fruit to thee the husbandman.

Give the poor Indians eyes to see
The light of life, and set them free;
That they religion may profess,
Denying all ungodliness.

From hardened Jews the veil remove,
Let them their martyr'd Jesus love:
And homage unto him afford,
Because he is their rightful Lord.

So false religion shall decay,
And darkness fly before bright day ;
So man shall God in Christ adore,
And worship idols vain no more.

So Asia and Africa,
Europa with America,
All four in concert join'd, shall sing
New songs of praise to Christ our King.

Of the poetry of William Wetherell, of Scituate, we can offer no specimen. The same must be said of Joseph Rowlandson, of Lancaster, whose verses exist in some ancient manuscript files. There was an Indian youth by the name of Eleazar, who studied at Harvard College in 1678. He wrote Latin and Greek poetry, which has been preserved, but we have seen no verses in English from his pen.

The Rev. Nathaniel Pitcher, of Scituate, was also a versifier. An anonymous poem on his death, compares him to Pindar, Horace and Casimir. How well he deserved this praise we have no means of knowing. The Elegy just mentioned is a curiosity. It is entitled Pitchero Threnodia ; it is written in an odd metre, and with a great display of classical learning. Of the poetry nothing need be said. It was published at Boston in 1724.

An anonymous performance of contemporary date and greater merit, is the Gloria Britannorum, or the British Worthies, which appeared also at Boston. In this work the political and military events of the time are sung in the manner of Addison's Campaign, from which production the design was evidently borrowed. The versification is quite spirited and correct for the period.

We must notice in this place, although a little in antici-pation of the chronological order of persons, John Sec-comb. He was esteemed a wit, and wrote the ballad en-titled Father Abdy's Will. It is rather of the doggerel species, but was popular in the author's day, and pleased

Governor Belcher so much that he sent it to England, where it was first published in the Gentleman's Magazine, in 1732. Seccomb was also considered the author of an Eclogue on the death of Dr Colman, and some other anonymous pieces.

———

From a review of the character of these early and imperfect endeavors in the rhyming art, and of our literature generally, down to a very recent date, we perceive the perfectly spontaneous growth of every branch of polite letters among us. The common incitements to literary exertion, rivalry and the prospect of fame and emolument, cannot be said to have exerted any material influence in prompting the efforts of American writers. Authors have been too few to create competition, and the public, to whom they addressed themselves, too much occupied with matters of direct practical interest to bestow any high consideration upon the talents which are exerted only in the embellishment of life. Hence we have never known till the present day such a thing as a professed author. All the talent and industry of the people have been called into the field of active employment, and the most of what has been written among us consists of such productions as were executed in the early days of our authors, before the serious business of life was entered upon ; or in such leisure moments as were snatched from constant and laborious occupations. We have obtained therefore only the unripe fruits of their youth, or the imperfect performances of casual moments. The cultivation of literary talent has moreover been retarded by the state of dependence as to literature, in which we have continued, to the writers of Great Britain. Without searching for causes which lie deep in the character of our nation, we may assert that the " bales and hogsheads" of learning which our friends beyond the ocean speak of having sup-

plied us with, have been dealt to us in such abundance
that the great stimulus to exertion has been wanting, and
no pressing necessity has thrown us upon our own resources.   Still the feeling of patriotism must prompt the
desire that native genius should be conspicuous in every
high career of human intellect, and that a national spirit
in the liberal arts should be encouraged, as instru-
ments to nourish the civic virtues and give scope to the
energies of mind among our countrymen.   That this
has not hitherto been effected, can hardly excite surprise
in any one acquainted with our history.   While we have
been filling this wide land with people, it is not remarkable that as a nation, we should have found little
leisure to cultivate the refinements of intellectual taste,

The present state and future prospects of literature
among us offer a theme for fond anticipation and sagacious conjecture, but hardly for certain calculation.
There is a vast amount of intellect daily developing in the
community, and again absorbed in the great purposes to
which the ingenuity and enterprise of our busy popula-
tion are constantly giving birth.   The precise effect of
this power, when settled into regular channels of action in
the various departments of literature cannot be foreseen.
In the twilight of the morning of letters which now dawns
upon us, the general outline of the view is indistinct and
wavering, and the eye meets with hardly a point upon
which to rest with steadiness.   But nothing lingers;
every moment some new element is unfolding, the
shadows flee, and the hour cometh, we doubt not, which
shall usher in a new scene, and enlighten us with the
fulness and splendor of a brighter day.

SPECIMENS

OF

AMERICAN POETRY,

WITH

CRITICAL AND BIOGRAPHICAL NOTICES.

COTTON MATHER.

It is a pleasant exercise of the imagination, to wander back to the days of primitive simplicity, the annals of which are included in the early history of New England. To those who have mingled with the society of the present age, and have been amused and not bewildered by its pleasures; who have looked at its glittering outside, without being so dazzled as to require an unnatural splendor to excite their attention, the contemplation of this simplicity, merely in its contrast with modern refinement, will afford no small gratification. The casual observer, whose final judgment is based on first appearances, will find little to relieve the dreary sameness of the prospect before him, in the lives of those who were once regarded as the prodigies of their generations. To him, their wordly pilgrimage will seem only an unvaried routine of study, fasting and prayer, succeeding each other after measured intervals, and occupying almost every moment of the probationary threescore years and ten. Though he may find here and there a spot somewhat fresher than the rest,—perchance a green leaf or a delicate blossom, it will only excite a momentary surprise at its appearance in such a place, and the general aspect will be to him, that of an interminable regularity on which the eye loves not to repose. Such would be his impressions on a glance at the scanty detail of events embraced in this sketch, the subject of which we shall endeavor to place in a more favorable light. Not that we shall give to his character any coloring of the romantic,—he had not a particle of it in his composition,—or disclose any tissue of the " wild and wonderful," in the adventures of his life, for, in truth, his days were spent in the service of God and the active duties of benevolence ; but we will delineate him as the *good* man, who is always *great*.

Cotton Mather was born in Boston, on the 9th of February 1662-3. His father was the Reverend Increase Mather, pastor of the North Church, and president of Harvard College, and his mother was the daughter of John Cotton, an eminent divine. While a mere child, the subject of our narrative was distinguished for his piety, and was in the habit of writing forms of prayer for the use of his playmates, and of encouraging their devotional exercises by precept and example. After making the necessary progress in his mother tongue, he commenced the study of the ancient languages with avidity, and at the age of twelve was qualified for admission at College, having read Cicero, Terence, Ovid and Virgil, the Greek Testament, Isocrates, Homer and the Hebrew grammar. During his residence at Harvard, he was eminent for his intense and unwearied application to study, and for a scrupulous observance of those religious exercises, the performance of which he had enjoined upon himself while under the paternal roof. The systems of Logic and of Physics composed by him while a lad of sixteen, are of themselves sufficient proofs of his assiduity in the prosecution of his academical course, and the nature of the thesis, " *Puncta Hebraica sunt originis divinæ*," which he maintained on the reception of his Master's degree, when he was six months short of his nineteenth year, will give the reader some idea of the extent of his information, and of the peculiar tendency of his mind. By a reference to the ordinances of discipline enforced in our oldest university, during the earlier periods of its existence, the modern student will readily perceive how the scholars of former times accomplished the great amount of labor required of them. The peculiar habits of the age too, in discouraging all relaxation, and in rendering it necessary for every one who would appear as an accomplished member of society, to have pursued his researches into the arcana of the abstruse sciences, gave the mind the keenest relish for study. There were not then the inducements now held out for the encouragement of levity and dissipation. The country was newly settled, by a race of men exemplary in godliness, who countenanced the indulgence of no amusement ; a race of whom Oldmixon, speaking from personal observation, says, "they are severe in their laws against immorality, and so much so, as if they thought no pleasure could be innocent." And the laws of the college, besides requiring of each individual a perusal of the scriptures twice in each day, and an exercise consisting of " theoretical observations on the language and logic of the Bible, and in practical and spiritual truths," regarded, as an indispensable qualification for the Bachelor's degree, an ability " to read the originals of the old and new Testament into the Latin tongue, and to resolve them logically, the scholar, withal, *being of godly life and conversation.*"

After his graduation, Mr Mather commenced the study of theology, pursuing those inquiries for which he had now acquired a decided taste, with unabated zeal and extraordinary success. Soon after his initiation, however, into the science of divinity, he abandoned his original design of preparing himself for the pulpit, on account of a hesitation in his speech, which, as he thought, would so affect his delivery, as to unfit him for the sacred office. He relinquished his favorite pursuit, and without loss of time, directed all his energies to the study of medicine, till a friend of his, Elijah Corlet, who if we mistake not was master of the school connected with the college, gave him the following advice, a strict observance of which might perhaps be found as beneficial to the stammerer, as any series of lectures by our modern Leighs and Chapmans. " Sir," said he, "I should be glad if you would oblige yourself to a dilated deliberation in speaking; for as in singing there is no one who stammers, so by prolonging your pronunciation, you will get a habit of speaking without hesitation." The consequence was, that Mr Mather resumed the profession of his choice, and in due time attained a ready and happy delivery.

In 1680 he received a unanimous invitation from the North Church to become a colleague of his father, and during the three succeeding years, was urged repeatedly by the same society to accept their offers, all of which he declined. The reasons assigned for this conduct are "his modest opinion and low apprehension of himself and his talents." It must be confessed however, that he appeared very much in the light of him, who on the Lupercal " did thrice refuse a kingly crown," for according to the representation of his own son, he was ever influenced by the most ardent anticipations of becoming a great man. The malicious might well have said on this occasion, in the language of the sarcastic Casca, " he put it by once : but for all that, to my thinking he would fain have had it," for which supposition the sequel afforded good grounds. " At last," says his son, " he was prevailed with to accept the sacred burden, *onus angelicis humeris formidandum !*" and in May 1684 was ordained. He placed in his diary his meditations on his recent advancement, followed by the record of his affectation, and immediately after, indulging in a humorous conceit, added, in allusion to his sermons preached after his installation, his conviction that *proud thoughts had fly-blown his best performances.*

In the twentyfourth year of his age, Mr Mather married Miss Abigail Phillips, " a comely, ingenious woman, and an agreeable consort," by whom he was made the father of nine children. From this era no remarkable events occurred in his life until the wicked administration of Andros, when, for the first and only time, he became conspicuous for his ardor in the business of state. It is not often that men whose talents are devoted to the cause of literature, and whose time is consecrated and set apart for employments that divert the attention from

secular concerns, can feel a lively interest in the party strife
and divisions which are inseparable attendants on a freedom
of the press and a government with but a shadow of liberty
in its constitution. The retirement of the study is ill adapted
to the dreamer whose visions are unceasingly of the sceptre
of power, the chair of state and the sword of authority, and
who, whether toiling and sweating for their attainment, or
anxiously watching the current of popular opinion, is in an
everlasting fever of restlessness. He may, it is true, in the
midst of his books, speculate with much warmth, and work
himself into a species of poetic frenzy, as his theories assume
a shape which is to him that of perfection; yet they are only
beautiful apparitions that lose their comeliness, and vanish before the observation of the practical politician, who looks for
something tangible, that will bear the test of critical examination. The only school for politics is in the midst of bustling
life, and he only who has experienced its agitations can become
an adept in the science, or feel interested in its progress.
Hence is it that the man who is partially secluded from the
world, is not aroused by the tumults which affect the surface
merely of affairs. But when the aim of the aggressor is at the
very heart of civil liberty, the dwellers in the shades of the
Academy, and even the loiterers in the laurel groves of the
Muses have never been the last to repel the advances of the
invader. Accordingly, when the mad career of Andros had
attracted all eyes, and excited an universal indignation in the
colonies, we find Mr Mather among the first to cry aloud against
the maleadministration of the government, and of course in
the ranks of those singled out by the council as obnoxious to
their vengeance. He promoted by his voice and influence a
manly resistance to the illegal measures sanctioned by Sir Ed-
mund. He urged the people to a serious consideration of the
duties to themselves, their children and their God, devolving
upon them in consequence of those decrees which had recently
received the unholy ratification of a traitor to the trust reposed
in him by the king.

Thus encouraged to commence the labor of thrusting from

their seats those who had usurped a prerogative belonging only to the parliament of the mother country, and of purifying the high places of government from the abomination which had polluted them, the populace lost no time in giving ample proofs of their determination to assert their rights, and maintain them with heart and hand.

In the month of April 1688, the inhabitants of Boston held a meeting for the purpose of prescribing a course that should free them from the arbitrary oppression of their rulers. The proceedings of a public assembly of citizens accustomed to unrestrained freedom of speech, are not usually distinguished by a great degree of coolness or discretion, when concerns of extraordinary moment call for attention. Each individual, inflamed by the commission of some petty wrong which has made him a sufferer, infuses into the minds of his auditors a portion of his own vindictiveness, and by the exaggerated representation of his ills, excites a strong sentiment of commiseration. The natural consequence is, that the assembly loses its character as a deliberative body; the force of argument yields to the fiery impetuosity of passion, and without any violent effort of the imagination, we can conceive that an ungovernable frenzy may actuate the whole multitude. In such a state, the resolutions most readily adopted bear the impress of the spirit which called them forth, and if, in their cooler moments, the actors in the scene have a momentary impression that their proceedings seem less the result of judgment than of impetuosity, they generally choose to abide by the consequences of their own rashness, rather than acknowledge themselves in error, or retreat one step from the stand they have taken.

The meeting to which we have alluded, is said to have opened with dangerous and horrible paroxysms. Mr Mather was present, and fearful of the evil that might ensue from such a beginning, rose to address the multitude. The turbulence partially subsided, and he called all his powers into action. His affectionate speech was like oil poured on the troubled waves of the ocean. The audience listened with respect, and he perceived that the accomplishment of his object was at hand.

Yet he stayed not his efforts till he found that he could control them at will. Many were moved by his eloquence, coming as it did from the heart, even to tears, and though their determination had been to give full scope to the revengeful spirit that was abroad in the land, they yielded to his persuasion, and united in the adoption of pacific measures.

But the fury of the people, though lulled for a time, was not entirely at rest. On the 18th of the same month, in a state of exasperated feeling at some new and flagrant outrage, they rushed with one accord to avenge their wrongs in a short and summary method, unwilling to wait the tardy retribution of the laws. Arms were resorted to, and the inhabitants in the vicinity of Boston, eager to join in the affray which now appeared inevitable, hastened to town in great numbers. They were ripe for any outrage, and Mr Mather's aid was again necessary to quell the commotion. He addressed the multitude in the open street, and arrayed the whole force of his arguments against them. As in the former instance, he gained the mastery, and when he had quieted their fury by an impassioned appeal, he resorted to his pen to complete the work so happily begun. It was mainly through his influence that those anticipated excesses were prevented, which but for his intervention, would probably have terminated in a bloody civil war. Andros and his adherents, who, on the occasion of this latter rebellion, were in danger of immediate death at the hands of the colonists, were deposed, confined, and afterwards sent to England for trial.

We have now arrived at a period equally memorable in the life of Mather, and eventful in the history of New England. The days of the Salem witchcraft are a kind of landmark in our annals,—a convenient and conspicuous beacon, marking out the line of separation between "the olden times" and those sufficiently recent for the recurrence of memory. It was in the summer of 1692 that the "subtle devices of the arch enemy" first became apparent, and enkindled that flaming persecution which spread an alarm throughout the country, and threw a portentous gloom over the dayspring of its glory.

The name of Cotton Mather is generally associated with the horrors attending that spectacle of infatuation which attracted the observation of the whole civilized world. The prevalent impression is, that he was most strenuous in his exertions to convict those who were suspected of a demoniacal confederation. Yet a perusal of his letter to the public officers will lead the candid reader to the conclusion that he was less anxious for the effusion of blood, than for quieting the dissensions stirred up by the recent investigations; and more fearful that the reputation of his country would be tarnished, than that the great purposes of justice would be accomplished by awarding a capital punishment, on the feeble evidence of "a spectral representation." But the evil report has gone abroad, and Mather's belief in the demoniacal agency has been constantly misrepresented as his approval of the absurd and hasty examinations of the suspected individuals. The truth is, that in the letter to which we have referred, he besought the judges, on no consideration to sanction the condemnation of the accused, without the most satisfactory testimony,—without such testimony as they would require in a trial for murder. We would not in these remarks, insinuate his want of faith in the extravagant assertions of those who sought the gratification of personal revenge in accusing the inimical party of a league with the devil; his opinions on this subject are too strongly stated to admit a doubt. We would only explain his desire that the sentence of death should be pronounced with great caution, and in no case where there was not a palpable proof of guilt. That his earnest wish was to sacrifice his own indelible impressions, rather than hazard the life of a single human being, fully appears in a document that was addressed to the civil authorities of New England, signed by many influential individuals, and framed and presented by Mather himself. The interest however with which he listened to all the investigations that attended the charges of witchcraft, and the earnestness of his inquiries into the circumstances accompanying the alleged sufferings of the afflicted, were deemed satisfactory tokens of his determination to attain renown as the promoter of a persecution, the memory of which would live in after ages. He was immediately assailed on every side by all those arts which grovelling malice knows so well to employ, and unsatisfied with the success of their attacks upon his character in the public presses and in the various domestic circles to which they could gain access, his enemies resorted to the use of anonymous letters, filled with the bitterest imprecations, and the vilest and most abusive language. He received these epistles with no other emotions than those of pity at the folly and weakness by which they were dictated, and preserved them in a huge bundle, which was labelled on the outside, " *Libels : Father, forgive them.*"

In the year of 1703 Mr Mather was married for the second time, choosing as his future partner in life, Mrs Elizabeth Hubbard, who bore him six children. In 1710 he received the degree of Doctor of Divinity from the University of Glasgow, and in 1714 was made a Fellow of the Royal Society of London ; from which time we may date the commencement of his correspondence with Sir Richard Blackmore, Dr Watts, Whiston and Desaguliers,—the two latter among the most eminent mathematicians of the age. In 1715 he was united in wedlock to Mrs George, and from this period to his first illness in December 1727-8, we can collect little that would be interesting to the reader. He was aware that death approached, and in a note to his physician said, "My last enemy is come, I would say my best friend." He died on the 13th of the following February, one day after completing his 65th year.

We have thus summed up the principal events of Dr Mather's life, and proceed now to the consideration of his character and writings. Of the former, though seldom brought into strong relief by his assuming any extraordinary attitude in public emergencies, we shall learn something if we observe its development in the domestic circle and in his discharge of professional duties ; the merit and influence of the latter afford a subject for a more copious criticism than our limits will allow us to indulge.

Mather's character was a strange, we had almost said, an unnatural, compound. The ascetic gravity that enveloped his demeanor in his intercourse with society, was worn even in the midst of his family,—among his household gods, when, if ever, it would seem that the heart *must* leap up unconstrained, and assert its supremacy. And yet a quaint and awkward kind of humor accompanied this repulsive bearing, softening in some degree the asperity of his disposition; a humor that mingled itself with his devotional exercises and his discussions upon the attributes of divinity, more freely than with his worldly conversation. His familiar discourse, however, is represented to have been, at certain times, replete with the intrinsic wealth of mind, as well as with that which he had labored for, and dug deep to attain; to have blended instruction with entertainment, and counsel with reproof, the whole being seasoned with an ardent zeal for the advancement of religion. "His printed works," says one of his eulogists,* "will not convey to posterity a just idea of the real worth and great learning of the man. It was conversation and acquaintance with him in his *occasional discourses and private communications*, that discovered the vast compass of his knowledge and the projections of his piety."

The greatest infirmity of his nature appears in that superstition which is looked upon as the most striking peculiarity of his character. The modern philosopher smiles at the credulity of those whose imaginations could conjure up the apparitions of the departed from the flitting shadows of a cloud, and hear the wail of congregated spirits in the moanings of the night wind; and yet there have not been wanting the names of eminent men to give a semblance of authority to a belief in those spectres which have their birth in a diseased imagination. Johnson, the colossus of English literature, had implicit confidence in their existence, and Dr Watts, writing to his new correspondent, Mather, uses this language: "For my part (though I cannot believe that the spectral evidence

---

* Rev, Mr Colman.

was sufficient for condemnation) yet I am persuaded that there was much immediate agency of the devil in these affairs, and perhaps there were some real witches too." But Dr Mather's superstitious notions were apparent in other instances than the inquiry relative to the witchcraft. In his diary, that wonderful repository of his passing thoughts, it is recorded that being troubled with the toothache, which caused him "to lose more time than could well be spared," he concluded that he must have *broken* some holy law *with his teeth*, and was enduring the punishment of such aggression. "But how have I offended?" he asks. "Why, by sinful and excessive eating, and by *evil speeches*, for," he continues, "there are *literæ dentales* used in them." It may amuse the curious reader to know the method by which Dr Mather was relieved of his troublesome complaint. "By a course of washing behind his ears," says his son, "and on the top of his head, with cold water, he obtained a deliverance from the uneasiness."

Of his literary labors and the extent of his information, some idea may be formed when we are told that he wrote readily in seven languages, and was the author of three hundred and eighty three publications. Many of these, it is true, were but single sermons, (Oldmixon calls them *loose collections*,) yet the pages of the Magnalia, The Christian Philosopher, and The Wonders of the Invisible World, evince a mind of great endowments and a fancy luxuriant though grotesque. They are sufficient proofs, at least, of his incessant industry.

In his ministry he was equally indefatigable. Besides the routine of his parochial duties, he accustomed himself to make catalogues of the names of his communicants, of their occupations and wants, and of such incidental circumstances in their lives as he deemed worthy of notice in his official services. Stated periods were devoted to the remembrance of each individual in his private worship,—days were set apart in which his relatives were the special subjects of his prayers,— weeks, and sometimes months, were spent in a rigid abstinence from every thing but the bare necessaries of life, that the sins of the flesh might be properly expiated by an uninterrupted devotion of his faculties to the work of repentance. Over his study door, an inscription, BE SHORT, was placed, as a warning to visiters not to intrude at unseasonable hours, and the hours allotted to meditation and prayer, to sleep, the taking of food and of exercise, to study and social intercourse, were all observed with the most scrupulous nicety.

His custom of recording the commonplace affairs of every day, and of preparing a train of thought for every trivial occurrence in life, though but the eccentricity of a great mind, exposed him justly to ridicule. Who, for instance, can refrain from a smile, on perusing a series of cogitations upon the winding up of his watch, the knocking at a door, the mending of his fire, the drinking of his cup of tea, and the paying his debts. The last event, it is true, may very properly be classed in the list of serious things. When he pared his nails, he would think how he might lay aside all superfluity of naughtiness, and "I durst not let my mind lie fallow," says he, "as I walk the streets; but I have compelled the signs of the shops to point me unto something in my Saviour that should be thought upon." He had for many years a severe *cough*, which, he said, *raised* a proper disposition of piety in him. In his fondness for the chase of words he often sacrificed his best intentions of doing justice to the subject under consideration. His biography of Ralph Partridge, is nothing more than a string of puns upon the birth, life and burial of a very worthy divine, who had suffered persecution for righteousness' sake, and merited better treatment than he received after his death. He is represented as having been *hunted* from his home by the ecclesiastical *setters* of the old world,—as having no defence of *beak* or *claw*, but a *flight* over the ocean. He is pursued to his *covert* on these shores, (not by his enemies—they left him when he took to the water—but by our Nimrod of the Lexicon, who forgets every thing but the game he has started) from whence he *took wing*, says the Doctor, to become a *bird of Paradise*. Even over the grave of his friend, when called on for an epitaph, he will only ejaculate the brief but expressive *Avolavit!*

Charity, however, will cast the mantle of oblivion over these frailties, when she remembers his abundant labors in the cause of benevolence. He promoted societies for the suppression of civil disorders; projected an extensive association of peacemakers, for the composing and preventing of differences in private life; proposed the establishment of an Evangelical Treasury, for the maintenance of churches in destitute places; introduced into Massachusetts the method of inoculation for the small pox, and was constantly interested and zealously engaged in promoting the welfare of his country.

We can readily account for the deficiency of the imaginative power in his poetical compositions. His education had involved him in the venerable dust of antiquity, and had unfitted his mind for the luxuriant growth of fancy. The strong soil where the mountain oak has long flourished, will afford but little nourishment to the delicate exotic, and he who from infancy has been seeking for the treasures of ancient lore, is seldom willing, even in his moments of relaxation, to linger in the myrtle bower, or to listen to the murmurings of the silver fountain. Dr Mather's toil was truly of that kind which produces "weariness of flesh," and he sought for a more substantial mental aliment than that "camelion food," with which the poet could supply him. To such a one, the gathering of flowers, even though they were those of Parnassus, and the wandering on the banks of Ilissus itself, would be deemed but an indifferent amusement. The poetic specimens that we have selected from Dr Mather's works are distinguished by little else than the hardness of their style, and the want of that indescribable quality in which we recognise the spontaneous ebullitions of a mind "smit with the love" of song.

ON THE DEATH OF HIS SON.

The motto, inscribed on the grave stone, " Reserved for a glorious Resurrection."

THE exhortation of the Lord,
With consolation speaks to us;
As to his children his good word,
We must remember speaking thus:

My child, when God shall chasten thee,
His chastening do thou not contemn:
When thou his just rebukes dost see,
Faint not rebuked under them.

The Lord with fit afflictions will
Correct the children of his love;
He doth himself their father still,
By his most wise corrections prove.

Afflictions for the present here
The vexed flesh will grievous call;
But afterwards there will appear,
Not grief, but peace, the end of all.

ON THE DEATH OF HIS DAUGHTER.

The motto, inscribed on the grave stone, " Gone, but not lost."

THE dearest Lord of heaven gave
Himself an offering once for me:
The dearest thing on earth I have,
Now, Lord, I'll offer unto Thee.

I see my best enjoyments here,
Are loans, and flowers, and vanities;
Ere well enjoy'd they disappear:
Vain smoke, they prick and leave our eyes.

But I believe, O glorious Lord,
That when I seem to lose these toys,
What's lost will fully be restor'd
In glory, with eternal joys.

I do believe, that I and mine,
Shall come to everlasting rest;

Because, blest Jesus, we are Thine,
And with thy promises are blest.

I do believe that every bird
Of mine, which to the ground shall fall,
Does fall at thy kind will and word;
Nor I, nor it, is hurt at all.

Now my believing soul does hear
This among the glad angels told;
I know, thou dost thy Maker fear,
From whom thou nothing dost withhold!

———

*Some offers to Embalm the Memory of the truly reverend and
renowned* JOHN WILSON; *the first Pastor of Boston, in*
New England: *Interr'd (and a great part of his Country's
Glory with him)* August 11, 1667. *Aged* 79.

MIGHT Aaron's rod (such funerals mayn't be dry)
But broach the rock, 'twould gush pure elegy,
To round the wilderness with purling lays,
And tell the world, the great Saint Wilson's praise.
Here's one (pearls are not in great clusters found)
Here's one, the skill of tongues and arts had crown'd;
Here's one (by frequent martyrdom was tried)
That could forego skill, pelf, and life beside,
For Christ: both Englands' darling, whom in swarms
They press'd to see, and hear, and felt his charms.

'Tis one (when will it rise to number two?
The world at once can but one phœnix show:)
For truth a Paul, Cephas for zeal, for love
A John, inspir d by the celestial dove.
Abram's true Son for faith; and in his tent
Angels oft had their table and content.

So humble, that alike on's charity,
Wrought *Extract gent.* with *Extract rudii.*
Pardon this fault; his great excess lay there,
He'd trade for Heaven with all he came anear;
His meat, clothes, cash, he'd still for ventures send
Consign'd, per brother Lazarus, his friend.

Mighty in prayer, his hands uplifted reach'd
Mercy's high Throne, and thence strange bounties fetch'd,
Once and again, and oft: so felt by all,
Who weep his death, as a departing Paul.
All, yea, baptiz'd with tears, lo children come,
(Their baptism he maintain'd!) unto his tomb.

'Twixt an Apostle, and Evangelist,
Let stand his order in the heavenly list.
Had we the costly alabaster box,
What's left, we'd spend on this New-English Knox;
True Knox, fill'd with that great reformer's grace,
In truth's just cause, fearing no mortal's face.

Christ's word, it was his life, Christ's church, his care;
And so great with him his least brethren were,
Nor heat, nor cold, nor rain, or frost, or snow,
Could hinder, but he'd to their sermons go:
Aaron's bells chim'd from far, he'd run, and then
His ravish'd soul echo'd amen, amen!

He travers'd oft the fierce Atlantic sea,
But, Patmos of confessors, 'twas for thee.
This voyage lands him on the wished shore,
From whence this Father will return no more,
To sit the moderator of thy sages.
But tell his zeal for thee to after ages,
His care to guide his flock, and feed his lambs,
By words, works, prayers, psalms, alms, and anagrams:
Those anagrams, in which he made no start
Out of mere nothings, by creating art,
Whole words of counsel; did to motes unfold
Names, till they lessons gave richer than gold,
And every angle so exactly fay,
It should outshine the brightest solar ray.
Sacred his verse, writ with a cherub's quill;
But those wing'd choristers of Zion's hill,
Pleas'd with the notes, call'd him a part to bear
With them, where he his anagram did hear,
"I pray come in, heartily welcome sir."*

---

* The line is thus explained by Mather. Ward, the simple cobler of Agawam, as he called himself, " observing the great hospitality of Mr Wilson, in conjunction with his meta-grammatizing temper," said that the anagram of John Wilson was, *I pray come in, you are heartily welcome.*

REMARKS

*On the bright and the dark side of that American pillar, the
Reverend Mr William Thompson ; Pastor of the Church at
Braintree. Who triumphed on Dec. 10, 1666.*

But may a rural pen try to set forth
Such a great Father's ancient grace and worth?
I undertake a no less arduous theme,
Than the old sages found the Chaldee dream.
'Tis more than tythes of a profound respect,
That must be paid such a Melchizedeck.
Oxford this light, with tongues and arts doth trim ;
And then his northern town doth challenge him.
His time and strength he center'd there in this ;
To do good works, and be what now he is.
His fulgent virtues there, and learned strains,
Tall, comely presence, life unsoil'd with stains,
Things most on worthies, in their stories writ,
Did him to moves in orbs of service fit.
Things more peculiar yet, my muse, intend,
Say stranger things than these ; so weep and end.

When he forsook first his Oxonian cell,
Some scores at once from popish darkness fell ;
So this reformer studied ! rare first fruits !
Shaking a crab-tree thus by hot disputes,
The acid juice by miracle turn'd wine,
And rais'd the spirits of our young divine.
Hearers, like doves, flock'd with contentious wing,
Who should be first, feed most, most homeward bring.
Laden with honey, like Hyblæan bees,
They kneed it into combs upon their knees.

Why he from Europe's pleasant garden fled,
In the next age, will be with horror said.
Braintree was of this jewel then possess'd,
Until himself, he labor'd into rest.
His inventory then, with John's, was took ;
A rough coat, girdle with the sacred Book.

When reverend Knowles and he sail'd hand in hand,
To Christ espousing the Virginian land,
Upon a ledge of craggy rocks near stav'd,
His Bible in his bosom thrusting sav'd ;
The Bible, the best of cordial of his heart,
"Come floods, come flames,(cried he) we'll never part."
A constellation of great converts there,
Shone round him, and his heavenly glory were.

Gookins was one of these; by Thompson's pains,
Christ and New England, a dear Gookins gains.

With a rare skill in hearts, this doctor could
Steal into them words that should do them good.
His balsams, from the tree of life distill'd,
Hearts cleans'd and heal'd, and with rich comforts fill'd.
But here's the wo! balsams which others cur'd.
Would in his own turn hardly be endur'd.

Apollyon owing him a cursed spleen
Who an Apollos in the church had been,
Dreading his traffic here would be undone
By num'rous proselytes he daily won,
Accus'd him of imaginary faults,
And push'd him down so into dismal vaults:
Vaults, where he kept long ember-weeks of grief,
Till heaven alarmed sent him a relief.
Then was a Daniel in the lion's den,
A man, oh, how belov'd of God and men!
By his bed side an Hebrew sword there lay,
With which at last he drove the devil away.
Quakers too durst not bear his keen replies,
But fearing it half drawn the trembler flies,
Like Lazarus, new rais'd from death, appears
The saint that had been dead for many years.
Our Nehemiah said, "shall such as I
Desert my flock, and like a coward fly!"
Long had the churches begg'd the saint's release;
Releas'd at last, he dies in glorious peace.
The night is not so long, but Phosphor's ray
Approaching glories doth on high display.
Faith's eye in him discern'd the morning star,
His heart leap'd; sure the sun cannot be far.
In extacies of joy, he ravish'd cries,
"Love, love the Lamb, the Lamb!" In whom he dies.

EPITAPHIUM.

Sta viator; thesaurus hic jacet,
    Thomas Cobbetus;
    Cujus,
Nosti preces potentissimas, ac mores probatissimos,
    Si es Nov-Anglus.
Mirare, si pietatem colas;
Sequere, si felicitatem optes.

ROGER WOLCOTT.

ROGER WOLCOTT was the son of a farmer, and was born in Windsor, Connecticut, in 1679. During his childhood, schools were unknown in the neighborhood of his birthplace, for the constant irruptions of che Indian tribes rendered it necessary for every mother to retain her infant charge, literally, within her own reach. The vigilance requisite for self-preservation checked the growth of social intercourse between the scattered families of the same town, and it was found incompatible with the general safety, to maintain places set apart for the instruction of youth, and of convenient access to all. The early education of Wolcott,—if that may be called education, which was but an initiation into the rudiments of the English language,—was derived from his father, (himself an untaught man) before he had arrived at the age of twelve years. At this period he was bound apprentice to a mechanic. Hard labor and confirmed habits of frugality enabled him, while yet a young man, to establish himself on the banks of his native river, with bright prospects of future success ; and his exertions were finally rewarded by a competency of worldly possessions, the fruits of his honest industry. With strong native talents,—the rich though unwrought ore of the mind,—and a judgment matured by the reading and reflection of his leisure hours, he soon became an object of regard among his fellow citizens, who conferred on him such civil and military honors as were at their disposal. In 1711 he held a commission in the unsuccessful expedition against Canada, and was second in command, with the rank of Major General, at the capture of Louisburg, in 1745.*

* It was considered no slight degree of honor to have been concerned in this Louisburg affair. The French, after the peace of Utrecht, built this town to secure their navigation and fisheries, and the advantages it gave their privateers over the English were very great. It was surrounded with a rampart of stone, thirtyfive feet high, mounting 150 cannon, a ditch eighty feet wide, and was protected on the sea side by two batteries of 30 guns each. The entrance, on the land side,

Roger Wolcott's life is interspersed with few remarkable events. After having been installed as a member of the Legislative Council, Judge of the County Court, Deputy Governor, Chief Judge of the Superior Court, and Governor of the Colony of Connecticut,—which last office he held during three successive years,—he retired to private life in 1755, and died in May 1767, in the eightyninth year of his age.

By a careful economy and improvement of time, Wolcott gained some distinction as a literary man. His writings, it must be acknowledged, are of that homely and unpolished kind which was the fashion in his day, and display as little delicacy in the selection of images, and as slight a degree of fastidiousness in the introduction of figures and language, as the most earthly minded mortal could desire. Yet his poems give evidence of accurate observation, and his powers of description are certainly far superior to those of his contemporaries. A small volume of his poetry was published at New London in 1725, preceded by a long and pedantic preface, written by a friend.* Our extracts are from a "*Brief Account,*" as it is

was by a drawbridge overlooked by a semicircle of 16 cannon. Twentyfive years and thirty millions of livres had been expended in the erection of the city, and its capture by the New England militia, under Governor Shirley of Massachusetts, was one of the most daring exploits on the records of American history. Shirley disclosed his scheme to the General Court of Massachusetts, after they had bound themselves by an oath of secrecy, and carried the resolutions he had offered by a majority of one voice only. Circular letters were then addressed to the other colonies, requesting their assistance. All declined except Connecticut, New Hampshire, and Rhode Island, and the total amount of troops furnished by them was less than 4000, which, with twelve or thirteen small vessels, completed the armament against the Dunkirk of America. The town was attacked, the French driven from their external batteries, and for fourteen nights successively, the fortytwo pounders of the enemy were dragged through a morass by the soldiers with straps over their shoulders,—and Wolcott was with them,—they sinking to their knees in mud at every step. In six or seven weeks the city yielded, though it was fully furnished for a siege of as many months. The money, afterwards granted by Parliament to defray the cost of this wild undertaking, was brought to Boston and paraded through the streets. There were seventeen cart loads of silver, and ten of copper, amounting to £200,000.

* The poems are, oddly enough, followed by a clothier's advertisement, which is introduced in this manner. "I the subscriber having these many years, (even

called, in this collection, "*of the Agency* of the *Honorable John Winthrop, Esq. in the Court of King Charles the Second, Anno Dom.* 1662 ; *when he obtained a Charter for the Colony of Connecticut.*" The poem contains fifteen hundred lines, and the opening scene is at London. The king gives an audience to Winthrop, and, after the usual court ceremonies, addresses the agent.

> " Rise up," quoth Charles ; " my liberal hand supplies
> All needful help to every one that cries ;
> Nor shall I be illiberal to you :
> But, prithee, Winthrop, please to let me know
> By whom it was your place did first commence,
> Your patriarchs that led your tribes from hence ? "

> " If to declare their worth, is what you ask,
> Then I must beg your pardon. That's a task
> So worthy due performance, and so great,
> As goes beyond my utterance and conceit :
> But virtue never fails ; succeeding days
> Shall much regard their merits, and shall raise
> Men of bright parts and moving oratory,
> Who shall emblazon their immortal glory.
>   But if you ask to gain intelligence,
> What were the reasons why they went from hence,
> What straits they met with in their way, and there ?
> These facts I think I'm able to declare.
>   RELIGION was the cause : Divinity
> Having declar'd the gospel shine should be
> Extensive as the sun's diurnal shine ;
> This mov'd our founders to this great design.
> And sure the holy spirit from above,
> That first did quickning on the waters move,
> Inspir'd their minds, and fill'd them with intents,
> To bring to pass such glorious events.

from my youth) been employed in the making and working of cloth ; and having seen with regret the errors which some people commit in their preparations about so good and needful a work, am willing to offer a few thoughts to consideration ; *and having been something at charge in promoting the publishing the foregoing meditations*, do here take the liberty to advertise my country people of some rules which ought to be observed, in doing their part, that so the clothiers might be assisted in the better performance of what is expected of them, that the cloth which is made among us may both wear and last, better than it can possibly do, except these following directions are observed by us."

And now they wholly to this work devote,
Mind not the country they are going out:
Their ancient homes they leave, to come no more.
Their weeping friends and kindred on the shore
They bid adieu, and with an aching heart
Shake hands; 'tis hard when dearest friends must part.
But here they part, and leave their parent isle,
Their whilome happy seat.   The winds awhile
Are courteous, and conduct them on their way,
To near the midst of the Atlantic sea,
When suddenly their pleasant gales they change
For dismal storms that on the ocean range.
For faithless Æolus, meditating harms,
Breaks up the peace, and priding much in arms,
Unbars the great artillery of heaven,
And at the fatal signal by him given,
The cloudy chariots threatening take the plains;
Drawn by wing'd steeds, hard pressing on their reins.
These vast battalions, in dire aspect rais'd,
Start from the barriers—night with lightning blaz'd.
Whilst clashing wheels resounding thunder cracks,
Struck mortals deaf, and heaven astonish'd shakes.
   Here the ship captain, in the midnight watch,
Stamps on the deck, and thunders up the hatch;
And to the mariners aloud he cries,
'Now all from safe recumbency arise:
All hands aloft, and stand well to your tack,
Engendering storms have cloth'd the sky with black,
Big tempests threaten to undo the world:
Down topsail, let the mainsail soon be furl'd:
Haste to the foresail, there take up a reef:
'Tis time, boys, now if ever, to be brief;
Aloof for life; let 's try to stem the tide,
The ship 's much water, thus we may not ride:
Stand roomer then, let 's run before the sea,
That so the ship may feel her steerage way:
Steady at helm!' Swiftly along she scuds,
Before the wind, and cuts the foaming suds.
Sometimes aloft she lifts her prow so high,
As if she 'd run her bowsprit through the sky;
Then from the summit ebbs and hurries down,
As if her way were to the centre shown.
   Meanwhile our founders in the cabin sat,
Reflecting on their true and sad estate;
Whilst holy Warham's sacred lips did treat
About God's promises and mercies great.

Still more gigantic births spring from the clouds,
Which tore the tatter'd canvass from the shrouds,
And dreadful balls of lightning fill the air,
Shot from the hand of the great Thunderer.
    And now a mighty sea the ship o'ertakes,
Which falling on the deck, the bulk-head breaks;
The sailors cling to ropes, and frighted cry,
'The ship is foundered, we die! we die!'
    Those in the cabin heard the sailors screech;
All rise, and reverend Warham do beseech,
That he would now lift up to heaven a cry
For preservation in extremity.
He with a faith sure bottom'd on the word
Of Him that was of sea and winds the Lord,
His eyes lifts up to Heaven, his hands extends,
And fervent prayers for deliverance sends.
The winds abate, the threatening waves appease,
And a sweet calm sits regent on the seas,
They bless the name of their deliverer,
Who now they found a God that heareth prayer.
    Still further westward on they keep their way,
Ploughing the pavement of the briny sea,
Till the vast ocean they had overpast,
And in Connecticut their anchors cast.
    Here came Soheage, and told the company,
The garden of America did lie
Further up the stream, near fifty miles from hence,
Part of which country he himself was prince.
Much ask'd of th' soil, much of the government,
What kings were there? The land of what extent?
All which, by his free answers, when they knew,
They o'er his back a scarlet mantle threw.
    And now, invited with fresh southern gales,
They weigh their anchors, and they hoist their sails,
And northward for th' expected country stood,
Upon the smiling pavement of the flood.
At length they entered those awful straits,
Where the stream runs through adamantic gates.
'Twas strange to see the banks advanc'd so high,
As if with Atlas they bore up the sky.
But when those dismal straits were passed through,
A glorious country opens to their view,
Cloth'd all in green, and to the eye presents
Nature's best fruits and richest ornaments.
    Cheer'd with the sight, they set all sails a-trip,
And rais'd the English ensign on their ship.
Brave youths, with eager strokes, bend knotty oars,
Glad shouts bring cheerful echoes from the shores.

As when the wounded amorous doth spy
His smiling fortune in his lady's eye,
O how his veins and breast swell with a flood
Of pleasing raptures, that revive his blood!
And grown impatient now of all delays,
No longer he deliberating stays;
But through the force of her resistless charms,
He throws him, soul and body, in her arms.

So we, amazed at these seen delights,
Which to fruition every sense invites,
Our eager minds, already captive made,
Grow most impatient now to be delay'd,
This most delightful country to possess;
And forward, with industrious speed, we press,
Upon the virgin stream, who had, as yet,
Never been violated with a ship.

Upon the banks king Aramamet stood,
And round about his wondering multitude,
Greatly amaz'd at such an uncouth show:
What is 't? they cried.   Some say, a great canoe.
Others, a bird that in the air doth fly,
With her long bill, and wings up to the sky.
But other some, whom fear did terrify,
Cried, 'tis some ill-presaging prodigy.
Nothing on earth more impetuous we find
Than terror, when it seizeth on the mind.
Dreadful effects of this did soon appear,
The multitude surpris'd with chilling fear;
With looks distracted, and out staring eyes,
Each scares himself, and others terrifies;
Only the king, who had within his breast,
A heart which foolish fear could not infest,
Perceived the matter, and the ship he hails:
'Now drop your anchors, and unbend your sails;
And if for peace and friendship you are come,
And do desire this land should be your home,
Let some of your chief leaders come to land,
And now with me join their right hand to hand.

Sails lower amain, nor oars now touch the flood,
Down drop the anchors deep into the mud:
Their chiefs repair to land, and with them bring,
Obliging presents for the Indian king.
Majestic Aramamet, with his lords,
Steps forth to meet those guests without his guards;
Meeting he paus'd, astonish'd at the sight;
Such men, such airs, with countenances bright,
He ne'er had seen, nor now to see expecting;
Amaz'd he stood a while! but recollecting

His scatter'd intellect, he cries, ' Who's there?
Whence come you? Seek you with us peace or war?'
    ' Britons you see, say they, and we are come
From England, happiest seat in Christendom,
Where mighty Charles obligeth sea and land,
To yield obedience to his sceptred hand;
Nor came we here to live with you in wars,
As He knows best, that made sun, moon, and stars;
But rather here to live with you in peace,
Till day and night's successive changes cease.
This we propose; and this if you approve,
And do respect our neighborhood and love,
Then sell us land, whereon we towns may plant,
And join with us in friendly covenant.'
    ' What you propose, (quoth he,) is just and good,
And I shall e'er respect your neighborhood;
Land you may have, we value not the soil,
Accounting tillage too severe a toil.'
    Then he his own right hand to theirs doth join,
Of his sure friendship the undoubted sign;
Then brings them to his house, and from his boards
Feasts them with what his country best affords.
Whilst here they stay at Aramamet's court,
Hither the neighboring Indian kings resort,
And join with them in articles of peace,
And of their lands make firm conveyances;
And being now by deeds and leagues secure,
Their towns they build, their purchas'd land manure."

    Thus far he said; Then said his majesty,
" Methinks, I have a curiosity
To know this country, that for ages past
Lay hid, and you have now found out at last;
This new found river, is it fresh and fair?
What land adjoins to it? Has't a pleasant air?"

To this question Winthrop replies with several Scripture allusions, and presently branches off into an account of the Connecticut River.

    " This gallant stream keeps running from the head
Four hundred miles ere it with Neptune bed,
Passing along hundreds of rivulets,
From either bank its crystal waves besets,
Freely to pay their tributes to this stream,
As being chief and sovereign unto them;
It bears no torrent nor impetuous course.

As if 'twere driven to the sea by force.
But calmly on a gentle wave doth move,
As if 'twere drawn to Thetis' house by love.
  The water 's fresh and sweet; and he that swims
In it, recruits and cures his surfeit limbs.
The fisherman the fry with pleasure gets,
With seines, pots, angles, and his trammel nets.
In it swim salmon, sturgeon, carp and eels;
Above, fly cranes, geese, ducks, herons and teals;
And swans, which take such pleasure as they fly,
They sing their hymns oft long before they die.
  The grassy banks are like a verdant bed,
With choicest flowers all enameled,
O'er which the winged choristers do fly,
And wound the air with wondrous melody,
Here philomel, high perch'd upon a thorn,
Sings cheerful hymns to the approaching morn.
The song once set, each bird tunes up his lyre,
Responding heavenly music through the quire,
Within these fields, fair banks of violets grows;
And near them stand the air perfuming rose,
And yellow lilies fair enameled,
With ruddy spots here blushing hang the head.
  These meadows serve not only for the sight,
To charm the eye with wonder and delight;
But for their excellent fertility,
Transcends each spot that ere beheld Sol's eye,
Here lady Flora's richest treasure grows,
And here she bounteously her gifts bestows.
The husbandman, for all his diligence,
Receives an ample, liberal recompense,
And feasting on the kidneys of the wheat,
Doth soon his labor and his toil forget.
  After the meadows thus have took their place,
The champion plains draw up to fill the space.
Fair in their prospect, pleasant, fruitful, wide,
Here Tellus may be seen in all his pride.
Cloud-kissing pines in stately mangroves stand,
Firm oaks fair branches wide and large extend.
The fir, the box, the balm tree, here stand mute,
So do the nut trees, laden down with fruit.
In shady vales the fruitful vine o'erwhelms
The waving branches of the bending elms.
  Within the covert of these shady boughs,
The loving turtle and his lovely spouse,
From bough to bough, in deep affection move,
And with chaste joy reciprocate their love.

At the cool brooks, the beavers and the minks
Keep house, and here the hart and panther drinks.
And partridges here keep in memory,
How to their loss they soared once too high.
 Within these spacious forests, fresh and green,
No monsters of burnt Afric may be seen.
No hissing basilisk stands to affright,
Nor seps, nor hemorhus, with mortal bite;
The Lybian lion ne'er set footing here,
Nor tigers of Numidia do appear.
But here the moose his spreading antlers sways,
And bears down stubborn standels with their sprays.
These sport themselves within these woods, and here
The fatted roebuck and the fallow deer
Yield venison as good as that which won
The patriarchal benediction.
 Each plain is bounded at its utmost edge
With a long chain of mountains in a ridge,
Whose azure tops advance themselves so high,
They seem like pendants hanging in the sky.
Twentyfour miles, surveyors do account
Between the eastern and the western mount;
In which vast interspace, pleasant and fair,
Zephyrus whispers a delightful air.
These mountains stand at equidistant space
From the fair flood, in such majestic grace,
Their looks alone are able to inspire
An active brain with a mercurial fire.
The muses hence their ample dews distil,
More than was feigned from the twy-topt hill.
And if those witty men that have us told
Strange tales of mountains in the days of old,
Had they but seen how these are elevated,
We should have found them far more celebrated,
In the fine works that they have left to us,
Than high Olympus or long Caucasus;
Or Latmos, which Diana stops upon,
There to salute her dear Endymion.
 Hither the eagles fly, and lay their eggs;
Then bring their young ones forth out of those crags.
And force them to behold Sol's majesty,
In mid noon glory, with a steady eye.
Here the old eagle his long beak belays
Upon a rock, till he renews his days.
And hence they from afar behold their prey,
And with a steady pinion wing their way.
But why so excellent a land should lie
So many ages in obscurity,

Unseen, unheard of, or unthought upon,
I think there 's no good reason can be shown
Unless 'twere as it seems the mind of fate,
Your royal name long to perpetuate,
So order'd it that such a land might owe
Thanks for its liberties, great Sir, to you."

A narrative of the Pequot war is commenced, and the following account is given of a set battle between the Christian
settlers and the Aborigines.

" After devotions thus to Heaven paid,
Up to the enemy our armies led,
Silent as the riphean snow doth fall,
Or fishes walk in Neptune's spacious hall.
  Now Lucifer had just put out his head,
To call Aurora from old Tithon's bed.
Whereat the troops of the approaching light,
Began to beat the reg'ments of the night.
  But Morpheus, with his unperceived bands,
Had clos'd the Pequots' eyes, and chain'd their hands.
All lay asleep, save one sagacious wretch,
Who destin'd was to stand upon the watch.
Firm to his charge, with diligence he applies,
And looks around with fierce lyncean eyes.
When our avant couriers he espy'd,
Opening his lungs aloud, ' Auwunux ! ' cry'd."
  " Auwunux," said our king, " what does that mean ? "
" It signifies," said Winthrop, " Englishmen.
  The startling news doth every soldier rouse,
Each arms and hastens to his rendezvous.
Meantime the English did the fort attach
And in the same had opened a breach,
Through which our brave Alcides enter'd first,
In after whom his valiant soldiers thrust.
  Before the breach an unappalled band
Of warlike Pequots, with bow and arrows stand.
With cheerful accents these themselves confirm,
To die like men, or to outface the storm.
Then gallantly the English they assail,
With winged arrows, like a shower of hail.
These ours endure ; and with like violence,
Sent lead and sulphur back in recompense.
  And now the sight grew more and more intense,
Each violent death enflames the violence.
Charge answered charge, and shout reply'd to shout ;
Both parties like enraged furies fought ;

Till death, in all its horrid forms appears,
And dreadful noise keeps clamoring in our ears.
  Now as some spacious rivers in their way,
By which they travel onwards to the sea,
Meet with some mighty precipice, from whence,
Enrag'd, they throw themselves with violence
Upon the stubborn rocks that lie below,
To make disturbance in the way they go.
Here, though the fury of the fray doth make
The near adjacent rocks and mountains quake,
Still the remorseless stream keeps on its course,
Nor will abate a moment of its force,
But rather hastens by impetuous facts
To throw itself into those cataracts.
  And so it happened with our soldiers here,
Whose fortune 'twas to travel in the rear.
The combatings of these within the breaches,
With dreadful noise their listening ears attaches;
And from their foes, and from their brethren,
Loud cries of fighting and of dying men.
  Sense of the danger doth not them affright,
But rather proves a motive to excite
The martial flame in every soldier's breast,
And on they like enraged lions prest;
Determined upon the spot to die,
Or from the foe obtain the victory.
  Now fortune shows to the beholders' sight,
A very dreadful, yet a doubtful fight;
Whilst mighty men, born in far distant land,
Stood foot to foot, engaging hand to hand.
  As when some mighty tempests that arise,
Meet with embattled fury in the skies:
Fire balls of lightnings and loud thunders rend
And tear the raging parties that contend.
  So did the fury of these mighty foes,
With which they did each others' force oppose,
Bring on such ruins as might daunt with fears
The hearts of any men, excepting theirs.
  Never did Pequots fight with greater pride;
Never was English valor better tried.
Never was ground soak'd with more gallant blood
Than the aceldama whereon we stood.
Sometimes one party victory soon expect,
As soon their eager hopes are countercheck'd.
And those that seem'd as conquered before,
Repel with greater force the conqueror.
Three times the Pequots seemed to be beat:

As many times they made their foes retreat.
And now our hope and help for victory,
Chiefly depended from the arm on high.
    As when Euroclydon the forest rends,
The bigger oaks fall down, the lesser bends
The beaten limbs and leaves before him scour,
Affrighted and enforced by his power;
To some huge rock, whose adamantine brow,
Outbraves the fury of all winds that blow;
There hoping to be hid from the high charge
Of fierce pursuers, by his mighty verge.
The winds in pressing troops demand surrender,
Of the pursued, and boisterous storm and thunder;
But he browbeats, and masters all their pride,
And sends them roaring to the larboard side.
    So Mason here, most strongly dress'd in arms,
Reanimates his men, their ranks reforms;
Then leading on, through deaths and dangers goes,
And beats the thickest squadrons of the foes.
    Prince Mononotto sees his squadrons fly,
And on our general having fix'd his eye,
Rage and revenge his spirits quickening,
He set a mortal arrow in the string.

    Then to his god and fathers' ghosts he pray'd,
'Hear, O immortal powers, hear me,' he said;
'And pity Mistick, save the tottering town,
And on our foes hurl dreadful vengeance down.
Will you forsake your altars and abodes,
To those contemners of immortal gods?
Will those pay hecatombs unto your shrine,
Who have deny'd your powers to be divine?
O favor us; our hopes on you are built;
But if you are mindful of our former guilt,
Determine final ruin on us all;
Yet let us not quite unrevenged fall.
Here I devote this of our enemies
His precious life to you a sacrifice.
Nor shall I covet long to be alive,
If such a mischief I might once survive.
But, O indulgent, hearken to my prayer;
Try us once more; this once the city spare:
And take my gift, let your acceptance be
An omen we shall gain the victory.'

    That very instant Mason did advance,
Whereat rage interrupts his utterance;

Nor could he add a word to what was said,
But drew the winged arrow to the head:
And aiming right, discharg'd it; whereupon
Its fury made the piercing air to groan.

But wary Mason, with his active spear,
Glanced the prince's arrow in the air:
Whereat the Pequots, quite discouraged,
Threw down the gauntlet, and from battle fled.

Mason, swift as the chased roe on foot,
Outstrips the rest in making the pursuit.
Entering the palace, in a hall he found
A multitude of foes, who gather'd round
This mighty man, on every side engag'd
Like bears bereaved of their whelps enrag'd.

One finding such resistance where * * *
His mind, his weapons and his eyes * * *
Their boldness much his martial sprite provokes,
And round he lays his deep inveterate strokes.
Making his sword at each enforced blow
Send great soul'd heroes to the shades below.

But as when Hercules did undertake
A doubtful combat with the Lernian snake,
Fondly propos'd, if he cut off her head,
The monster might with ease be vanquished.

But when he the experiment did make,
Soon to his hazard found his dear mistake,
And that as often as he cut off one,
Another instantly sprang in its room.
  * * * *

After so many deaths and dangers past,
Mason was thoroughly enflam'd at last:
He snatch'd a blazing bavin with his hand,
And fir'd the stately palace with the brand.
And soon the towering and rapacious flame
All hope of opposition overcame.
Eurus and Notus readily subjoin
Their best assistance to this great design;
Drive pitchy flames in vast enfoldings down,
And dreadful globes of fire along the town.

And now the English army marched out,
To hem this flaming city round about;
That such as strived to escape the fire,
Might by the fury of their arms expire.

But O what language or what tongue can tell,
This dreadful emblem of the flames of hell!
No fantasy sufficient is to dream,
A faint idea of their woes extreme.

Some like unlucky comets do appear,
Rushing along the streets with flagrant hair:
Some seeking safety clamber up the wall,
Then down again with blazing fingers fall.
In this last hour of extremity,
Friends and relations met in company;
But all in vain, their tender sympathy
Cannot allay, but makes their misery.
The paramour here met his amorous dame,
Whose eye had often set his heart in flame:
Urg'd with the motives of her love and fear,
She runs and clasps her arms about her dear:
Where weeping on his bosom as she lies,
And languisheth, on him she sets her eyes;
Till those bright lamps do with her life expire,
And leave him weltering in a double fire.

The fair and beauteous bride, with all her charms,
This night lay melting in her bridegroom's arms.
This morning in his bosom yields her life,
While he dies sympathizing with his wife.
In love, relation, and in life the same,
The same in death, both die in the same flame.
Their souls united, both at once repair
Unto their place appointed through the air.

The gracious father here stood looking on
His little brood with deep affection;
They round about him at each quarter stands,
With piteous looks, each lifts his little hands
To him for shelter, and then nearer throng,
Whilst piercing cries for help flow from each tongue.
Fain would he give their miseries relief,
Though with the forfeiture of his own life:
But finds his power too short to shield off harms,
The torturing flame arrests them in his arms.
The tender mother with like woes opprest,
Beholds her infant frying at her breast;
Crying and looking on her, as it fries;
Till death shuts up its heart affecting eyes.

The conquering flame long sorrows doth prevent,
And vanquish'd life soon breaks imprisonment.
Souls leave their tenements, gone to decay,
And fly untouched through the flames away.
Now all with speed to final ruin haste,
And soon this tragic scene is overpast.
The town, its wealth, high battlements and spires,
Now sinketh, weltering in conjoining fires.
The general commands the officers with speed,

To see his men drawn up and martialed:
Which being done, they wheel the ranks,
And kneeling down, to Heaven all gave thanks.
   By this Aurora doth with gold adorn
The ever beauteous eyelids of the morn;
And burning Titan his exhaustless rays,
Bright in the eastern horizon displays;
Then soon appearing in majestic awe,
Makes all the starry deities withdraw;
Veiling their faces in deep reverence,
Before the throne of his magnificence.
   And now the English their red cross display,
And under it march bravely toward the sea;
There hoping in this needful hour to meet
Ample provisions coming with the fleet.
   Meantime came tidings to Sasacus' ears,
That Mistick town was taken unawares.
Three hundred of his able men he sent,
With utmost haste its ruin to prevent:
But if for that they chance to come too late,
Like harms on us they should retaliate.
   These, with loud outcries, met us coming down
The hill, about three furlongs from the town;
Gave us a skirmish, and then turn'd to gaze
Upon the ruin'd city yet on blaze.
   But when they saw this doleful tragedy,
The sorrow of their hearts did close their eye:
Silent and mute they stand, yet breathe out groans;
Nor Gorgon's head like this transforms to stones.
Here lay the numerous bodies of the dead;
Some frying, others almost calcined:
All dolefully imprison'd underneath
The dark and adamantine bars of death.
   But mighty sorrows never are content,
Long to be kept in close imprisonment;
When once grew desperate, will not keep under,
But break all bands of their restraint asunder.
And now with shrieks the echoing air they wound,
And stamp'd and tore and curst the suffering ground.
Some with their hands tore off their guiltless hair,
And throw up dust and cinders in the air.
Thus with strange actions and horrendous cries,
They celebrate these doleful obsequies.
At length revenge so vehemently doth burn,
As caused all other passions to adjourn.
Alecto raves and rates them in the ear,
' O sensless cowards, to stand blubbering here !

Will tears revive these bodies of the slain,
Or bring their ashes back to life again?
Will tears appease their mighty ghosts, that are
Hoping to be revenged, hovering here?
Surely expecting you will sacrifice
To them the lives of those their enemies:
And will you baffle them thus by delay,
Until the enemy be gone away?
O cursed negligence!' And then she strips,
And jirks and stings them with her scorpion whips;
Until with anger and revenge they yell,
As if the very fiends had broke up hell.
That we shall die, they all outrageous swear,
And vomit imprecations in the air:
Then, full speed! with ejulations loud,
They follow us like an impetuous cloud.

   Mason, to stop their violent career,
Rallies his company anew to war;
Who finding them within a little space,
Let fly his blunderbusses in their face.
Thick sulphurous smoke makes the sky look black,
And heaven's high galleries thunder with the crack.
Earth groans and trembles, and from underneath,
Deep vaulted caverns horrid echoes breathe.

   The volley that our men first made,
Struck down their stout file leaders dead.
To see them fall, a stupifying fear
Surpris'd and stop'd their soldiers in the rear:
The numerous natives stop'd, and fac'd about;
Whereat the conquering English gave a shout.
At which they start, and through the forest scour,
Like trembling hinds that hear the lions roar.

   Back to great Sasacus they now return again;
And of their loss they thus aloud complain,
' Sir, 'tis in vain to fight: The fates engage
Themselves for those with whom this war we wage.
We Mistick burning saw, and 'twas an awful sight;
As dreadful are our enemies in fight:
And the loud thunderings that their arms did make,
Made us, the earth, yea heaven itself, to shake.'

   Very unwelcome to Sasacus' ears
Were these misfortunes, and his subject's fears:
Yet to his men, the English he contemns,
And threats to ruin us with stratagems.
And now his thoughts ten thousand ways divide,
And swift through all imaginations glide.
Endless projections in his head he lays,
Deep policies and stratagems he weighs.

Sometimes he thinks, he 'll thus the war maintain,
Reviews the scheme, and throws it by again:
Now thus, or thus, concludes 'tis best to do;
But neither thus, nor thus, on the review.
And thus his mind on endless projects wanders,
Till he is lost in intricate meanders.
At last gives up the case as desperate,
And sinks, bewailing his forlorn estate.
  He and his people quite discouraged,
Now leave their seats, and towards Monhattons fled.
But in his way the English sword o'ertakes
His camp, and in it sad massacres makes.
Yet he escap'd, and to the Mohawks goes,
Where he to them keeps reckoning up his woes:
And they to cure the passions of his breast,
Cut off his head, and all his cares released.

MICHAEL WIGGLESWORTH.

Mr Wigglesworth was educated at Harvard College,
from which institution he received his degree of Bachelor of
Arts in 1651, soon after entering upon the twentieth year of
his age. Having completed his theological studies, he was
ordained minister of the church in Malden, Massachusetts.
Respected in the pulpit for his modest, though lucid and en-
ergetic exposition of the scriptures; esteemed in the social
circle for the suavity of his manners, and beloved by very
many to whom, in their youth, he had been the faithful friend
and counsellor, it was with deep regret that he yielded to the
necessity which demanded his temporary separation from the
people who had committed themselves to his spiritual guidance
and direction, and with whom he was linked by ties of the
most tender affection. The hand of disease was upon him,
and its blighting influence could be successfully resisted only
under a milder sky than that of his own New England. A
partial restoration to health enabled him to resume his station
at Malden, though, ever after, he was frequently obliged to
desist, for weeks in succession, from the active duties of his
profession. But these intervals were not mispent. He devo-

ted them to medical researches, and the needy found him as ready in imparting his skill for the benefit of the wasted frame, as he had been in affording relief to the mind oppressed with grief or cast down by disappointment.

When the weakness of his lungs disqualified him for preaching, he would strive, with his pen, to render truth attractive by investing her with the garb of poesy. Let not the modern reader turn with disgust from the perusal of his moral sentiments. Repugnant as they may be to our tastes, and grotesque as they appear in an age of refinement, they contributed nevertheless, mainly to the formation of that character for unbending integrity, and firmness of resolve, for which we almost venerate the old men who laid the foundations of our republic. Neither let the lover of the sacred nine despise the muse of our author. Homely and coarse of speech as she is, her voice probably sunk into the *hearts* of those who listened to her rude melody, leaving there an impression, deeper than any which the numbers of a Byron, a Southey, or a Moore may ever produce.

"The Day of Doom," is the title of Mr Wigglesworth's largest poem. It went through six editions in this country, and was republished in London. It comprises a version, after the manner of Sternhold and Hopkins, of all the scripture texts relative to the final judgment of man, and contains two hundred and twentyfour stanzas of eight lines each. Our selections from his writings are principally from this curious specimen of the antique.

Mr Wigglesworth died in 1705, at the age of seventyfour years. Cotton Mather wrote his funeral sermon and epitaph.*

* We copy this epitaph from the sixth edition of Wigglesworth's poems, printed in 1707.

EPITAPH

The excellent Wigglesworth remembered by some good tokens.

His pen did once meat from the eater fetch ;
And now he 's gone beyond the eater's reach.
His body once so thin, was next to none ;
From hence, he 's to unbodied spirits flown.
Once his rare skill did all diseases heal ;
And he does nothing now uneasy feel.
He to his paradise is joyful come ;
And waits with joy to see his Day of Doom.

VANITY OF VANITIES.

VAIN, frail, short-liv'd, and miserable man,
Learn what thou art when thy estate is best:
A restless wave o' the troubled ocean,
A dream, a lifeless picture finely dress'd.

A wind, a flower, a vapor and a bubble,
A wheel that stands not still, a trembling reed,
A trolling stone, dry dust, light chaff and stubble,
A shadow of something but truly nought indeed.

Learn what deceitful toys, and empty things,
This world, and all its best enjoyments be:
Out of the earth no true contentment springs,
But all things here are vexing vanity.

For what is beauty, but a fading flower?
Or what is pleasure, but the devil's bait,
Whereby he catcheth whom he would devour,
And multitudes of souls doth ruinate.

And what are friends, but mortal men, as we,
Whom death from us may quickly separate:
Or else their hearts may quite estranged be,
And all their love be turned into hate.

And what are riches to be doted on?
Uncertain, fickle, and ensnaring things;
They draw men's souls into perdition,
And when most needed, take them to their wings.

Ah foolish man! that sets his heart upon
Such empty shadows, such wild fowl as these,
That being gotten will be quickly gone,
And whilst they stay increase but his disease.

As in a dropsy, drinking draughts begets,
The more he drinks, the more he still requires;
So on this world, whoso affection sets,
His wealth's increase, increaseth his desires.

Oh happy man, whose portion is above,
Where floods, where flames, where foes cannot bereave him
Most wretched man that fixed hath his love
Upon this world, that surely will deceive him.

For what is honor? What is sovereignty,
Whereto men's hearts so restlessly aspire?
Whom have they crowned with felicity?
When did they ever satisfy desire?

The ear of man with hearing is not fill'd;
To see new lights still coveteth the eye:
The craving stomach, though it may be still'd
Yet craves again without a new supply.

All earthly things man's cravings answer not,
Whose little heart would all the world contain,
(If all the world should fall to one man's lot,)
And notwithstanding empty still remain.

The eastern conqueror was said to weep,
When he the Indian ocean did view,
To see his conquest bounded by the deep,
And no more worlds remaining to subdue.

Who would that man in his enjoyment bless,
Or envy him, or covet his estate,
Whose gettings do augment his greediness,
And make his wishes more intemperate.

Such is the wonted and the common guise
Of those on earth that bear the greatest sway;
If with a few the case be otherwise,
They seek a kingdom that abides for aye.

Moreover they, of all the sons of men,
That rule, and are in highest places set,
Are most inclin'd to scorn their bretheren;
And God himself (without great grace) forget.

For as the sun doth blind the gazer's eyes,
That for a time they nought discern aright:
So honor doth befool and blind the wise,
And their own lustre 'reaves them of their sight.

Great are their dangers, manifold their cares,
Through which, whilst others sleep, they scarcely nap,
And yet are oft surprised unawares,
And fall unwilling into envy's trap.

The mean mechanic finds his kindly rest,
All void of fear sleepeth the country clown:
When greatest princes often are distress'd
And cannot sleep upon their beds of down.

Could strength or valor men immortalize,
Could wealth or honor keep them from decay,
There were some cause the same to idolize,
And give the lie to that which I do say.

But neither can such things themselves endure,
Without the hazard of a change, one hour,
Nor such as trust in them can they secure,
From dismal days, or death's prevailing power.

If beauty could the beautiful defend
From death's dominion, then fair Absalom
Had not been brought to such a shameful end:
But fair and foul unto the grave must come.

If wealth or sceptres could immortal make
Then wealthy Crœsus, wherefore art thou dead?
If warlike force, which makes the world to quake,
Then why is Julius Cæsar perished?

Where are the Scipios' thunder bolts of war?
Renowned Pompey, Cæsar's enemy?
Stout Hannibal, Rome's terror known so far?
Great Alexander, what's become of thee?

If gifts and bribes death's favor might but win,
If power, if force, or threat'nings might it fray,
All these, and more had still surviving been:
But all are gone, for death will have no nay.

Such is this world with all her pomp and glory:
Such are the men whom worldly eyes admire,
Cut down by time, and now become a story,
That we might after better things aspire.

Go boast thyself of what thy heart enjoys,
Vain man! Triumph in all thy worldly bliss:
Thy best enjoyments are but trash and toys,
Delight thyself in that which worthless is.

Omnia prætereunt præter amare Deum.

THE DAY OF DOOM.

STILL was the night, serene and bright,
　　When all men sleeping lay;
Calm was the season, and carnal reason
　　Thought so 't would last for aye.
Soul, take thine ease, let sorrow cease,
　　Much good thou hast in store:
This was their song, their cups among,
　　The evening before.

Wallowing in all kind of sin,
　　Vile wretches lay secure:
The best of men had scarcely then
　　Their lamps kept in good ure.
Virgins unwise, who through disguise
　　Amongst the best were number'd,
Had clos'd their eyes; yea, and the wise
　　Through sloth and frailty slumber'd.

Like as of gold, when men grow bold
　　God's threat'nings to contemn,
Who stop their ear, and would not hear;
　　When mercy warned them:
But took their course, without remorse,
　　Till God began to pour
Destruction the world upon
　　In a tempestuous shower.

They put away the evil day,
　　And drown'd their care and fears,
Till drown'd were they, and swept away
　　By vengeance unawares:
So at the last, whilst men sleep fast
　　In their security,
Surpris'd they are in such a snare
　　As cometh suddenly.

For at midnight break forth a light,
　　Which turn'd the night to day,
And speedily an hideous cry
　　Did all the world dismay.
Sinners awake, their hearts do ache,
　　Trembling their loins surpriseth;
Amaz'd with fear, by what they hear,
　　Each one of them ariseth.

They rush from beds with giddy heads,
  And to their windows run,
Viewing this light, which shines more bright
  Than doth the noonday sun.
Straightway appears (they see 't with tears,)
  The Son of God most dread;
Who with his train comes on amain
  To judge both quick and dead.

Before his face the heavens gave place,
  And skies are rent asunder,
With mighty voice, and hideous noise,
  More terrible than thunder.
His brightness damps heaven's glorious lamps,
  And makes them hide their heads,
As if afraid and quite dismay'd,
  They quit their wonted steads.

Ye sons of men that durst contemn
  The threat'nings of God's word,
How cheer you now? your hearts I trow,
  Are thrill'd as with a sword.
Now atheist blind, whose brutish mind
  A God could never see,
Dost thou perceive, dost now believe
  That Christ thy judge shalt be?

Stout courages, (whose hardiness
  Could death and hell outface,)
Are you as bold now you behold
  Your judge draw near apace?
They cry, "no, no: alas! and wo!
  Our courage is all gone:
Our hardiness (fool hardiness)
  Hath us undone, undone."

No heart so bold, but now grows cold
  And almost dead with fear:
No eye so dry, but now can cry,
  And pour out many a tear.
Earth's potentates and powerful states,
  Captains and men of might,
Are quite abash'd, their courage dash'd
  At this most dreadful sight.

Mean men lament, great men do rent
　　Their robes, and tear their hair:
They do not spare their flesh to tear
　　Through horrible despair.
All kindreds wail: all hearts do fail:
　　Horror the world doth fill
With weeping eyes, and loud outcries,
　　Yet knows not how to kill.

Some hide themselves in caves and delves,
　　In places under ground:
Some rashly leap into the deep,
　　To 'scape by being drown'd:
Some to the rocks (O senseless blocks!)
　　And woody mountains run,
That there they might this fearful sight,
　　And dreaded presence shun.

In vain do they to mountains say,
　　Fall on us and us hide
From judge's ire, more hot than fire,
　　For who may it abide?
No hiding place can from his face,
　　Sinners at all conceal,
Whose flaming eye hid things doth spy,
　　And darkest things reveal.

*　　*　　*　　*　　*　　*

Then were brought in, and charg'd with sin,
　　Another company,
Who by petition obtain'd permission,
　　To make apology:
They argued, " We were misled,
　　As is well known to thee,
By their example, that had more ample
　　Abilities than we:

Such as profess'd they did detest
　　And hate each wicked way:
Whose seeming grace whilst we did trace,
　　Our souls were led astray.
When men of parts, learning and arts,
　　Professing piety,
Did thus and thus, it seem'd to us
　　We might take liberty.

The judge replies, "I gave you eyes,
　　And light to see your way,

Which had you lov'd, and well improv'd,
 You had not gone astray.
My word was pure, the rule was sure,
 Why did you it forsake,
Or thereon trample, and men's example,
 Your directory make?

This you well knew, that God is true,
 And that most men are liars,
In word professing holiness,
 In deed thereof deniers.
O simple fools! that having rules
 Your lives to regulate,
Would them refuse, and rather choose
 Vile men to imitate."

"But Lord," say they, "we went astray,
 And did more wickedly,
By means of those whom thou hast chose
 Salvation heirs to be."
To whom the judge; "what you allege,
 Doth nothing help the case;
But makes appear how vile you were,
 And rendereth you more base.

You understood that what was good
 Was to be followed,
And that you ought that which was naught
 To have relinquished.
Contrary ways, it was your guise,
 Only to imitate
Good men's defects, and their neglects
 That were regenerate.

But to express their holiness,
 Or imitate their grace,
You little car'd, nor once prepar'd
 Your hearts to seek my face.
They did repent, and truly rent
 Their hearts for all known sin:
You did offend, but not amend,
 To follow them therein."

"We had thy word," say some, "O Lord,
 But wiser men than we
Could never yet interpret it,
 But always disagree.

How could we fools be led by rules,
  So far beyond our ken,
Which to explain did so much pain,
  And puzzle wisest men."

"Was all my word abstruse and hard?"
  The judge then answered:
"It did contain much truth so plain,
  You might have run and read.
But what was hard you never car'd
  To know nor studied.
And things that were most plain and clear
  You never practised.

The mystery of piety
  God unto babes reveals;
When to the wise he it denies,
  And from the world conceals.
If to fulfil God's holy will
  Had seemed good to you
You would have sought light as you ought,
  And done the good you knew."

*   *   *   *   *

Then at the bar arraigned are
  An impudenter sort,
Who to evade the guilt that's laid
  Upon them thus retort;
"How could we cease thus to transgress?
  How could we hell avoid,
Whom God's decree shut out from thee,
  And sign'd to be destroy'd?

Whom God ordains to endless pains,
  By law unalterable,
Repentance true, obedience new,
  To save such are unable:
Sorrow for sin, no good can win,
  To such as are rejected;
Nor can they grieve, nor yet believe,
  That never were elected.

Of man's fall'n race who can true grace
  Or holiness obtain?
Who can convert or change his heart,
  If God withhold the same?

Had we applied ourselves and tried
   As much as who did most
God's love to gain, our busy pain
   And labor had been lost.

Christ readily makes this reply ;
   " I damn you not because
You are rejected or not elected,
   But you have broke my laws :
It is but vain your wits to strain
   The end and means to sever :
Men fondly seek to part or break
   What God hath link'd together.

Whom God will save such will he have
   The means of life to use :
Whom he 'll pass by, shall choose to die,
   And ways of life refuse.
He that foresees, and foredecrees,
   In wisdom order'd has,
That man's free will electing ill,
   Shall bring his will to pass.

High God's decree, as it is free,
   So doth it none compel
Against their will to good or ill,
   It forceth none to hell.
They have their wish whose souls perish
   With torments in hell fire,
Who rather chose their souls to lose,
   Than leave a loose desire.

*   *   *   *   *   *   *   *

Then to the bar, all they drew near
   Who died in infancy,
And never had or good or bad
   Effected personally,
But from the womb unto the tomb
   Were straightway carried,
(Or at the last ere they transgress'd)
   Who thus began to plead :

" If for our own transgression,
   Or disobedience,
We here did stand at thy left hand,
   Just were the recompense :
But Adam's guilt our souls hath spilt,
   His fault is charged on us ;

And that alone hath overthrown,
  And utterly undone us.

Not we, but he ate of the tree,
  Whose fruit was interdicted:
Yet on us all of his sad fall,
  The punishment's inflicted.
How could we sin that had not been,
  Or how is his sin our
Without consent, which to prevent,
  We never had a power?

O great Creator, why was our nature
  Depraved and forlorn?
Why so defil'd, and made so vild
  Whilst we were yet unborn?
If it be just and needs we must
  Transgressors reckon'd be,
Thy mercy, Lord, to us afford,
  Which sinners hath set free.

Behold we see Adam set free,
  And sav'd from his trespass,
Whose sinful fall hath split us all,
  And brought us to this pass.
Canst thou deny us once to try,
  Or grace to us to tender,
When he finds grace before thy face,
  That was the chief offender? "

Then answered the judge most dread,
  " God doth such doom forbid,
That men should die eternally
  For what they never did.
But what you call old Adam's fall,
  And only his trespass,
You call amiss to call it his,
  Both his and yours it was.

He was design'd of all mankind
  To be a public head,
A common root, whence all should shoot,
  And stood in all their stead.
He stood and fell, did ill or well,
  Not for himself alone,
But for you all, who now his fall
  And trespass would disown.

If he had stood, then all his brood
   Had been established
In God's true love never to move,
   Nor once awry to tread:
Then all his race, my Father's grace,
   Should have enjoy'd for ever,
And wicked sprites by subtle sleights
   Could then have harmed never.

Would you have griev'd to have receiv'd
   Through Adam so much good,
And had been your for evermore,
   If he at first had stood?
Would you have said, ' we ne'er obey'd,
   Nor did thy laws regard;
It ill befits with benefits,
   Us, Lord, so to reward.'

Since then to share in his welfare,
   You could have been content,
You may with reason share in his treason,
   And in the punishment.
Hence you were born in state forlorn,
   With nature so deprav'd:
Death was your due, because that you
   Had thus yourselves behav'd.

You think, ' if we had been as he,
   Whom God did so betrust,
We to our cost would ne'er have lost
   All for a paltry lust.'
Had you been made in Adam's stead,
   You would like things have wrought,
And so into the selfsame wo,
   Yourselves and yours have brought.

I may deny you once to try,
   Or grace to you to tender,
Though he finds grace before my face,
   Who was the chief offender:
Else should my grace cease to be grace;
   For it should not be free,
If to release whom I should please,
   I have no liberty.

If upon one what's due to none
   I frankly shall bestow,

And on the rest shall not think best,
   Compassion's skirts to throw,
Whom injure I? will you envy,
   And grudge at others' weal?
Or me accuse, who do refuse
   Yourselves to help and heal.

Am I alone for what's my own,
   No master or no Lord?
O if I am, how can you claim
   What I to some afford?
Will you demand grace at my hand,
   And challenge what is mine?
Will you teach me whom to set free,
   And thus my grace confine?

You sinners are, and such a share
   As sinners may expect,
Such you shall have; for I do save
   None but my own elect.
Yet to compare your sin with their
   Who liv'd a longer time,
I do confess yours is much less,
   Though every sin's a crime.

A crime it is, therefore in bliss
   You may not hope to dwell
But unto you I shall allow
   The easiest room in hell."
The glorious king thus answering,
   They cease, and plead no longer:
Their consciences must needs confess
   His reasons are the stronger.

Thus all men's pleas the judge with ease
   Doth answer and confute.
Until that all, both great and small,
   Are silenced and mute.
Vain hopes are crop'd, all mouths are stop'd,
   Sinners have nought to say,
But that 'tis just, and equal most
   They should be damn'd for aye.

Now what remains, but that to pains
   And everlasting smart,
Christ should condemn the sons of men,
   Which is their just desert;

Oh rueful plights of sinful wights!
  Oh wretches all forlorn:
'T had happy been they ne'er had seen
  The sun, or not been born.
   *   *   *   *   *

The saints behold with courage bold,
  And thankful wonderment,
To see all those that were their foes
  Thus sent to punishment:
Then do they sing unto their king
  A song of endless praise:
They praise his name and do proclaim
  That just are all his ways.

Thus with great joy and melody
  To heaven they all ascend,
Him there to praise with sweetest lays,
  And hymns that never end.
Where with long rest they shall be blest,
  And nought shall them annoy:
Where they shall see as seen they be,
  And whom they love enjoy.

BENJAMIN COLMAN.

Benjamin Colman was born in Boston, October 19, 1767,
and was the companion of Cotton Mather at the celebrated
school of Ezekiel Cheever.* He was admitted into Harvard
College in 1688, and after receiving his degree of Bachelor of

---

* Cheever died in 1708, at the age of ninetyfour, beloved and honored by all
who knew him. Mather wrote an elegy on his death, which runs in this manner;

> A mighty tribe of well instructed youth,
> Tell what they owe to him and tell with truth.
> All the eight parts of speech he taught to them,
> They now employ to trumpet his esteem.
> *Magister* pleas'd them well because 'twas he ;
> They say that *bonus* did with it agree.
> While they said *amo*, they the hint improve,
> Him for to make the object of their love.
> No *concord* so inviolate they knew,
> As to pay honors to their master due,
> With *interjections* they break off at last,
> But *ah* is all they use, *wo*, and *alas!*

Arts commenced the study of Theology. In July 1695, he embarked for London, with the intention of qualifying himself for his profession by an observation of men and manners in a wider sphere of action than the thinly settled and almost desolate Colonies of New England. He embarked on board " the good ship Swan," but in a few days she was found to be in a leaky condition, and the voyage was consequently prolonged to an unusual extent. Seven weeks had elapsed before the passengers could with safety indulge in the hope of a speedy relief from the tediousness of their situation, when an incident occurred which dimmed their brightest hopes. It was a fine morning in the early part of September ; the breeze was just strong enough to allow all sail to be set to advantage, and the wearied inmates of the cabin, as they came on deck and received an answer in the affirmative to their often repeated inquiry whether the wind was fair, were gaily congratulating each other on the prospect of a quick passage to the desired haven. In a few minutes the cry, " a sail," was heard, and far on the weather quarter a white spot could be seen, which before noon proved to be a light and fleet vessel bearing down upon the Swan with every yard of canvass extended. She was supposed to be a French privateer, and after the female passengers had been assisted to a place of security, the necessary arrangements were made for her reception.

There was a young man on board the English vessel who had often taken great pains to annoy his companions in the cabin by his malicious and atheistical sallies of wit. Before a gun was fired he informed Mr Colman, who was equipping himself with a musket and ammunition, that the passengers were seeking refuge below. " Sir," was the reply, " I shall use my poor endeavors in protecting this ship from the enemy." The other was so much abashed, and his shame so far surmounted his cowardice, that he determined to join in the fight. At the first discharge of small arms, however, he fell upon the deck, completely overcome by fear, and remained there till the Frenchman fell astern for a few moments to repair damages, when he lifted up his head and inquired " where is the enemy?" "He lies by," answered Mr Colman, "to charge anew with somewhat more vigor." At this the young man threw himself on his face by the hatches, and remained there till the boatswain giving him a hearty kick in the side, swore that he was in the way, whereupon our hero took refuge below and was seen no more till night.

As evening drew on, the contest ceased, and it was ascertained that the Swan had sustained great damage in her hull, masts, and rigging, and that the chance of escape from the enemy was almost hopeless. Five men were wounded,—one of them mortally,—but Mr Colman had suffered no harm. Great praise was bestowed upon him for his bravery, which was not expected in a slender youth, to whom constitutional weakness had given the appearance of effeminacy. To the encomiums bestowed on him, he replied by a frank confession that he had been in constant apprehension of danger through the day. He had been told that his courage would increase as the action grew hot, and he therefore loaded and discharged his piece with all possible despatch; yet after three or four broadsides he could not help wondering when this courage would come. The boatswain and the men who were managing the gun on the quarterdeck, often called on Mr Colman for assistance in charging, and made sport of the whole affair, forgetting, for the moment, that they were indulging their profanity in the presence of a minister. He did not cease from his labors, but reproved them for their wickedness while tugging with them at the breech of the same cannon, with his coat off, his sleeves tucked up, and his hat and wig thrown aside.

Early on the following morning the Swan was surrendered to the enemy, having maintained a long and gallant contest with a vessel of more than thrice her number of men and weight of metal. When Mr Colman was taken aboard the privateer, he was robbed of his money, left almost destitute of clothes, and thrown into the hold with the sick and dying; yet his cheerfulness and resignation not only lightened his own sufferings, but dispelled much gloom and useless repining among his companions. In a few days, having reached the shores of France, they were imprisoned at Nantz, and afterwards at Dinan. On the road to the latter place, the officer to whose care Mr Colman and the other captives were committed, halted at a little village, and the rabble immediately surrounded them, led on by their priest, who approached our young divine, and, holding up a crucifix, asked him if it were an object of worship. He was answered in the negative. The other, with genuine Catholic zeal, declared that he would *prove* it was, but here the French Provost interfered, and said his prisoner was a minister. " O diavole! " shouted one of the crowd, on hearing this intelligence; whereupon Mr Colman desired the priest to reprove the man. " No," said he, " it is too true ; all heretics are out of the holy church, and therefore belong to the devil, are going to the devil, and are devils." Mr Colman then begged that his antagonist would not undervalue himself by holding conversation with the devil, and bade him farewell.

An exchange of prisoners between the French and English took place at the expiration of two months, and Mr Colman was transported to Portsmouth. Very fortunately one of the female passengers in the Swan had concealed several pieces of gold for him; these she had conveyed to his hands at Nantz, and their amount was more than enough to carry him to London. At the city he was kindly received by his relatives and several dissenting clergymen, who rendered his abode in England both pleasant and profitable. He was appointed to take charge of a church in Bath, where he remained for two years. Here he formed an acquaintance with Miss Singer, then celebrated as a poetess, to whom, but for his assertions to the contrary, we should believe he became attached with more than a Platonic regard. His eulogies on her beauty and accomplishments, his constant mention of her in letters to his friends, and the occasional recurrence of her name in his private memoranda, evince an anxiety for her happiness more fervent and frequent than that milder solicitude which friendship excites. His first visit to her rural retreat, where she was accustomed to meditate and compose, called from him a

poem (what further proof of his affection for the lady is needed?) commencing thus:

> So Paradise was brighten'd, so 'twas blest,
> When innocence and beauty it possess'd.
> Such was its more retired path and seat,
> For Eve and musing angels a retreat.
> Such Eden's streams and banks and towering groves,
> Such Eve herself, and such her muse and loves.
> Only there wants an Adam on the green,
> Or else *all* Paradise might here be seen.

Miss Singer afterwards became Mrs Rowe, and the subject
of our sketch went thrice to the altar before the close of his
ministry, and each time, we believe, *with a widow!*

In 1699, Mr Colman returned to New England, and commenced a new career in the land of his nativity, as pastor of
the church in Boston, now called the Brattle Street Society.
In this station he remained till his death, nearly a half century
afterward.

In 1724, the corporation of Harvard College elected him
to succeed President Leverett, but he declined the honor they
wished to confer on him, alleging affection for his church, and
unwillingness to undertake an office above his capacity, as
his reasons for refusing their offer.*

He received the honorary degree of Doctor in Divinity
from the University in Glasgow in 1731, and after a long and
well spent life expired in August 1747, in the seventyfourth
year of his age.

Dr Colman was regarded in his day as a man possessing all
those traits which constitute goodness of disposition, in its
most comprehensive meaning. In the pulpit he was distinguished for his grace and dignity of manner, as well as for

---

* In a letter to Bishop Kennett on the subject, he says, " I have to plead
my long disuse of academical studies, and *also that I am not well in the opinion of our House of Representatives*, on whom the President depends for subsist-
ence."

his powers of persuasion and argument. In the private walks of life, he was hailed as one gifted in an eminent degree with the nobler qualities of our nature. His interest in public business brought upon him the blame of many, and he was charged with an officious intermeddling in civil and secular affairs. Whether an individual, capable of rendering his country a service, should withhold his efforts because he has been appointed to minister to the spiritual wants of a few, is a question that has caused much dispute. If you acknowledge him a subject to the laws, and a member of the government, which he maintains in obedience to the divine command, " Render unto Cæsar the things that are Cæsar's," you cannot but allow him to resist any infringement upon his own rights.* Dr Colman's opinion was, " that opportunities to do good not only legitimate the application of our capacities to do it, but also oblige and require us to do it."

His successor in the pulpit of the Brattle Street church,† has thus delineated Dr Colman: " Among the worthies of the Massachusetts clergy, we can perhaps select no character, which we may regard with more thorough esteem, than that of Dr Colman; and not much more may be said of any man. If his mind was not of that class, by which great revolutions are produced in the intellectual or social world, it was still one of uncommon comprehensiveness, penetration, wisdom, and activity ; and it had been cultivated by an enlarged acquaintance with books and men. His writings, besides giving token of a liberal spirit, a well disciplined understanding, various knowledge, and a warm heart, show, for the period in which they were produced, a remarkable acquaintance with the true beauties of composition. To nature and to opportunity he was probably alike indebted for a manly and winning address."

---

* " 'Tis a foolish thing," says Selden, " to say the minister must not meddle with secular matters, because his own profession will take up the whole man. May he not eat, or drink, or walk, or learn to sing ? The meaning of that is, he must seriously attend to his calling."

† Rev. J. G. Palfrey.

His poetic remains are few. Two or three letters in rhyme addressed to his daughter, and Elijah's Translation, are all that we have found ; but these place him far above his contemporaries in refinement of thought and language. His taste too, command of language, and skill in versification, are of a higher order than theirs, and incline us to the belief that had he cherished the muse with more fondness and attention, she would have bestowed her favors on him with a liberal hand.

ON ELIJAH'S TRANSLATION,

Occasioned by the death of the reverend and learned Mr Samuel Willard.

I SING the man, by heaven's peculiar grace,
The prince of prophets, of the chosen race,
Rais'd and accomplish'd for degenerate times,
To stem the ebb with faith and zeal sublime;
T' assert forsaken truth, to check the rage
Of rampant vice, and cure a wicked age.
Such times need such a prophet,—in his death
Is quench'd the light of Israel, and their breath.
Plain was the saint, his soul by grace refin'd,
His girdle mean, but much adorn'd his mind:
In face, as well as mind, above the toys
Of this vain world, and all its sensual joys:
Simple in diet, negligent of dress,
Hairy and rough his robe, meet to express
One mortify'd to things of time and sense,
To truth and things divine a love intense.
Jealous for Israel and the Lord of hosts,
Disdain'd to see Him rival'd by a post,
Mourn'd his forsaken covenant, and worship lost.
Courageous, dar'd alone to stand the shock,
Of numerous priests of Baal and to deride their stock.
Fac'd fierce tyrannous powers, told their crimes
And shames deserv'd the judgments of their times.
His and truth's triumphs glorious: strange to say !
A debauch'd nation convert in a day,
And sham'd, enrag'd imposters fled away !
A wondrous saint; inspir'd, employ'd and led
By heavenly love; by many wonders fed.
The care of heaven, the darling of his God,
Signally sav'd, cheer'd by His staff and rod.

Voracious ravens yield him up their prey :
Glad angels to his succor wing away :
And heaven, to show its empire more, commands
Hopeless relief from famishing widow's hands.
He pray'd, the sealed heavens withheld their rain ;
He pray'd, the open'd clouds discharge again.
Provok'd he ask'd ; strange blazing showers of flame
Stream down, and Sodom's day renewed came.
He struck the floods,—the refluent waves divide ;
His mantle's breath drove back the flowing tide.
What ail'd thee, O astonish'd sea, to fly ?
Jordan ! from Joshua's days thy banks not dry !
Yet greater wonders view : he spake,—the dead
In sin, or grave, lift up their fallen head :
Witness the happy mother, fully won
To heaven as she receiv'd her raised son :
Blest work of grace ! the mercy of the mean
Illustrious, as the saving change is seen.
Not less miraculous the prophet's fast,
Labors and travels gloriously surpass'd :
His strength and application, as his trust,
Noble and vast, angelic and august :
In public toils consum'd, of life profuse,
Exhausted in retired holy muse,
On the deep things of God, and mysteries abstruse.
Such labors bounteous heaven is wont to crown
With heavenly visions, light and joys unknown.
So heavenly glories dazzled Moses' eyes,
And laboring Paul was caught to paradise.
No less Elijah to his Saviour dear,
No less his cares and toils, his prayers and tears ;
Nor less would heaven his suff'ring soul to cheer.
The God of Israel pass'd before the cave,
In majesty, as erst the law he gave,
And frighten'd nature seem'd to seek a grave.
Tempests, and flames, and earthquakes march'd before,
Speaking the terrors of almighty power ;
These usher'd in the small still voice of grace ;
His soul grew calm, serene the troubled place ;
Hush'd as the winds were all his boisterous fears,
The humble saint, call'd forth by God, appears ;
With mantle wrapt about his face he stood,
Afraid to hear, nor wish'd to see his God.
Yet lest the hero as his God we show,
Or he elate with visions, vain should grow,

At times his passions did the man betray,
That saints have sin, and prophets are but clay.
Too timorous, 'midst his triumphs; left to fly
A woman's rage and threats, and wish to die.
Desponding moan'd Christ of his church bereft,
And not a single saint in Israel left.
All to hide pride from man, to show how vain
We are at best, and undue thoughts restrain.
God is the light, in whom 's no shade at all,
To him in prostrate adorations fall.
Created brightness ever has its blots,
And even Persia's idol has its spots.
Yet admiration, reverence and love
Are due to saints on earth, or those above.
Sure the curst spirit that hates is born of hell,
Nor is less monster then foul Jezebel:
She murd'rous sought his blood: Ahab his name
(Dearer than life) with slanderous lies defames:
And both invet'rate hate, and deadly war proclaim.
Yet spite of envy, spite of malice curst,
Virtue shall live: see, bloated fiend, and burst!
See the fair name immortal in my verse!
See the strew'd glories on the hero's hearse!
A name embalm'd shall be the just man's lot,
While vicious teeth shall gnash, and names shall rot.
Return, my muse, and sing his faithful care,
And noblest trust, in happy Bethel's chair.
Hail, venerable seat! from Jacob's days
Sacred to Israel's God, and to his praise!
Blest evermore with visions! the resort
Of holy angels! heaven's inferior court!
Hail dreadful place! the Eternal's blest abode!
The gate of heaven, and the house of God!
Here stood the spacious college, Israel's pride:
And here the illustrious seer did preside.
Stately the dome, worthy the beauteous train,
Religion pure devoted to maintain,
And to the age to come the laws divine explain.
Richly endow'd by every pious zeal,
Studious of Zion's glory and her weal:
Blest tribute! dear to heaven: a pious aid
Given to Christ, and liberally repaid
In richer blessings to the church and state;
So he returns us what we consecrate.
Hence Israel's chiefs, and hence our teachers came;

Hence truth and grace, hence issued light and flame;
Hence men renown'd, and of celebrious fame.
Micaiah one: from foul illusion free,
Faithful to God, and Ahab true to thee!
Kings trembled as he spake, and homage paid,
Of truth and the superior man afraid.
Elisha too, to greater glories born,
Was hence: and high exalted is his horn!
These beauteous sons were the blest prophet's pride,
Under his wing they bloom'd, and flourish'd by his side;
Paid him a reverence profound and true,
To heaven's election, Israel's suffrage due.
Them, as by office bound, he did inspect,
Taught heavenly truth, and errors did correct:
Cherish'd the good, and form'd their manners well,
But search'd out vice, th' infection to expel.
Meek and majestic, affable and grave,
Lowly and good; and all that's great and brave,
He overaw'd and charm'd: base hearts he won,
And perfected where goodness was begun.
To them, his lectures on the holy law,
Sublime they were, new mysteries they saw:
Like him with heavenly light and joys inspir'd,
Their ravish'd minds the sacred deeps admir'd.
They saw the promised Messiah's days,
And the glad schools resounded with his praise.
They sang the Baptist in their prophet's spirit,
And bless'd the saint elect that should inherit.
They sang of the transfigur'd Saviour's rays,
What favorite saints from heaven itself to gaze
On glories yet unknown; and talk of high
Mysterious truths; into which angels pry,
And pass in transports immortality.
They sang his high ascent, and gifts ineffable,
The cloven tongues of fire on Pentecost that fell,
And what great type should all these wonders figure and
　　foretel.
Thus taught, they waited long the great event,
Foresaw the day, amaz'd at the portent:
Stupendous grace and power they view'd, ador'd
The sov'reign God, and pry'd into his word.
And now the saint had his last visit made,
His solemn charge, and final blessing said.
His weeping sons receiv'd his last adieu,
With eager eyes their breath departing view,
And following far behind to Jordan's brink they drew.

Each emulous to succeed, but well prepar'd
To welcome him whom heaven had heir declar'd.
Elisha he! The wisdom of the choice
Applauded with united hearts and voice.
Unenvy'd in the schools, had long outshone
In gifts divine, and rival there was none.
Glorious the seer's fidelity was here,
And heaven's good conduct splendid did appear.
Nor blood, nor name, his upright zeal retard,
God's choice and will he simply did regard;
Whom heaven accomplishes it will reward.
The happy youth cleav'd to his father's feet,
Minist'ring to him with a duty meet;
From his oraculous lips ask'd counsel sage,
And had the prayers and blessings of his age.
Yet there remain'd the last'and dying bequest,
And the wise son had ready his request.
"Say, now at parting, what I shall bequeath!"
Trembling he fell the prophet's feet beneath,
Grieved to part, afraid to speak his thought,
Conscious how vast the blessing was he sought:
With mouth in dust he said,—"May I inherit
A double portion of thy blessed spirit!
O might my last and highest wish have place,
An em'nent measure of thy gifts and grace!"
Divine ambition! to be wise and good!
So he his fame and interest understood.
Modest his wish, he only ask'd a part,
And heaven gave all, even an equal heart:
Obvious the truth from sacred record known,
None came so near Elijah as his wondrous son.
'T was at high noon, the day serene and fair,
Mountains of lum'nous clouds roll'd in the air,
When on a sudden, from the radiant skies,
Superior light flash'd in Elisha's eyes:
The heavens were cleft, and from th' imperial throne
A stream of glory, dazzling splendor shone:
Beams of ten thousand suns shot round about,
The sun and every blazon'd cloud went out:
Bright hosts of angels lin'd the heavenly way,
To guard the saint up to eternal day.
Then down the steep descent, a chariot bright,
And steeds of fire, swift as the beams of light.
Wing'd seraphs ready stood, bow'd low to greet
The fav'rite saint, and hand him to his seat.
Enthron'd he sat, transform'd with joys his mein,

Calm his gay soul, and like his face serene.
His eye and burning wishes to his God,
Forward he bow'd, and on the triumph rode.
Saluted, as he pass'd the heavenly cloud,
With shouts of joy, and hallelujahs loud.
Ten thousand thousand angel-trumpets sound,
And the vast realms of heaven all echo'd round.
They sang of greater triumphs yet to come,
Their next descent to wait the Saviour home:
And the glad errand of the final day,
The raised dust of saints to bring away
In equal triumph, and in like array.
Thus 'midst inspir'd, sublime, prophetic songs,
(Sweet melody,) the vision pass'd along.
The prince of air accurs'd fled swift the light,
And heavenly sounds, more grating than the sight;
Blasphem'd, and rag'd, and gnash'd in furious spite,
Elisha saw: "My father," loud he cried,
"My father! Israel's safety! and her pride!
More wert thou our defence and glory far,
Than all our chariots and strong troops of war.
Thy prayers and power with God did more secure
Our tott'ring state, and naked coasts immure,
Than all our arms."—
He said: nor more could see: immense the space!
The flying glory now had gain'd the place
Of light, ne'er to be seen by mortal eye:
No longer gaz'd he on the closing sky.
With anguish seiz'd his goodly robes he rent,
Himself, the church, and schools did sore lament.
The prophet's bliss could not his tears restrain,
He wept their loss, in his eternal gain.
Nor yet in useless tears stay'd he to vent
His mighty griefs, on greater things intent:
The mantle fall'n with joy surprising spy'd,
Laid the dear pledge close to his panting side;
Sovereign receipt! his fainting heart reviv'd,
By it install'd in the blest Prophet's place!
With it receiv'd his spirit and his grace!
The sacred banner flying in his hand,
Display'd his empire, on the distant strand;
Nature obsequious, to his dread command.
Triumphant-wise, the pensive conqueror stood,
The precious relic wav'd, and smote the flood:
"Where is the Lord, Elijah's God?" he cry'd.
Th' obedient waves again in haste divide.

He pass'd : the ravish'd Prophets saw : confess'd
The miracle of grace, and thankful bless'd
Th' Eternal Spirit, and his glorious rest.
O'erjoy'd they ran the saint elect to meet,
And bow beneath the bright successor's feet.
They breathe their prayers and blessings in his arms,
Cheer his sad soul, and their own passions charm.
Their hearts within 'em glow, their graces burn ;
Each speak mysterious oracles in their turn :
Inspired their mind, transform'd their very mien,
In both superior grace and beauty seen.
In holiness and truth sweet their accord,
And faith their consolation did afford,
Elijah's more illustrious second coming with his Lord.

JANE TURELL.

Mrs Turell was the only daughter of the Rev. Dr Colman, of whom we have already spoken, and was born in Boston, A. D. 1708. Her devotedness to literary pursuits was remarkable, even in her childhood, and she was distinguished for sobriety of demeanor and sweetness of disposition, as well as for an ardent desire to attain those mental treasures which it was once deemed expedient to put beyond the reach of the gentler sex. The powers of Mrs Turell's mind were highly extolled by some of her contemporaries ; but their encomiums must be cautiously received, for educated ladies were, in her days, so rarely to be found in New England, that the results of careful tuition were generally mistaken for evidences of a brilliant genius, and as the fashionable code seemed to favor Mohammed's doctrine, that women were born without the gift of soul, every female, who, in the course of her reading, had advanced beyond the spelling-book and accidence, was regarded as little less than a prodigy.

Jane Colman, when a girl of eleven, made some feeble efforts in verse, and as her father frequently wrote to her in rhymes suited to her capacity, and encouraged her to peruse the English poets, she became ready in composition, and often employed her hours of recreation in writing humorous essays, which displayed ingenuity and quickness of comprehension. On entering her nineteenth year she was married to the Rev. Mr Turell of Medford. She had then read and digested all the works on Divinity, History and Philosophy to which she could gain access, and was familiarly acquainted with the modern literature of a lighter kind. She died in 1735, at the age of twentyseven, having faithfully fulfilled those duties which shed the brightest lustre upon woman's name—the duties of the friend, the daughter, the mother, and the wife.

Her poems are collected in a pamphlet, published by her husband immediately after her death.

A PARAPHRASE OF THE ONE HUNDRED AND THIRTY-FOURTH PSALM.

As on the margin of Euphrates' flood
We wail'd our sins, and mourn'd an angry God;
For God provoked, to strangers gave our land,
And by a righteous Judge condemn'd we stand;
Deep were our groans, our griefs without compare,
With ardent cries we rent the yielding air.
Borne down with woes no friend at hand was found,
No helper in the waste and barren ground:
Only a mournful willow wither'd there,
Its aged arms by winter storms made bare;
On this our lyres, now useless grown, we hung,
Our lyres by us forsaken and unstrung!
We sigh'd in chains, and sunk beneath our wo,
Whilst more insulting our proud tyrants grow.
From hearts oppress'd with grief they did require
A sacred anthem on the sounding lyre:
Come, now, they cry, regale us with a song,
Music and mirth the fleeting hours prolong.
Shall Babel's daughter hear that blessed sound?
Shall songs divine be sung in heathen ground?
No, Heaven forbid that we should tune our voice,
Or touch the lyre! whilst slaves we can't rejoice.
O Palestina! our once dear abode,
Thou once wert blest with peace, and loved by God!
But now art desolate, a barren waste,
Thy fruitful fields by thorns and weeds defaced.

If I forget Judea's mournful land,
May nothing prosper that I take in hand!
Or if I string the lyre, or tune my voice,
Till thy deliverance cause me to rejoice;
O may my tongue forget her art to move,
And may I never more my speech improve!
Return, O Lord! avenge us of our foes,
Destroy the men that up against us rose:
Let Edom's sons thy just displeasure know,
And, like us, serve some foreign conquering foe
In distant realms; far from their native home,
To which dear seat O let them never come!

Thou, Babel's daughter! author of our wo,
Shalt feel the stroke of some revenging blow:
Thy walls and towers be levell'd with the ground,
Sorrow and grief shall in each soul be found:
Thrice blest the man, who, that auspicious night,
Shall seize thy trembling infants in thy sight;
Regardless of thy flowing tears and moans,
And dash the tender babes against the stones.*

———

TO MY MUSE.

Come, gentle muse, and once more lend thine aid,
O bring thy succor to a humble maid!
How often dost thou liberally dispense
To our dull breast thy quick'ning influence!
By thee inspired, I 'll cheerful tune my voice,
And love and sacred friendship make my choice.
In my pleased bosom you can freely pour,
A greater treasure than Jove's golden shower.
Come now, fair muse, and fill my empty mind,
With rich ideas, great and unconfin'd.
Instruct me in those secret arts that lie
Unseen to all but to a poet's eye.

* Her father says of this Paraphrase, " The serious melancholy Psalm is well turned in the most parts of it, considering your years and advantages for such a performance. You speak of a single withered willow which they hung their harps on ; but Euphrates was covered with willows along the banks of it, so that it has been called the River of Willows. I hope, my dear, your lyre will not be hung on such a sorrowful shrub. Go on in sacred songs, and we 'll hang it on the stately cedars of Lebanon. Or let the pleasant elm before the door where you are suffice for you.''

O let me burn with Sappho's noble fire,
But not like her for faithless man expire.
And let me rival great Orinda's fame,
Or like sweet Philomela's* be my name.
Go lead the way, my muse, nor must you stop
Till we have gain'd Parnassus' shady top :
Till I have view'd those fragrant soft retreats,
Those fields of bliss, the muses' sacred seats.
I'll then devote thee to fair virtue's fame,
And so be worthy of a poet's name.

ON THE POEMS OF SIR RICHARD BLACKMORE.

BLACKMORE, thou wondrous bard ! whose name inspires
My glowing breast to imitate thy fires,
O that my muse could give a lasting fame !
Then should my verse immortalize thy name.
Thy matchless lines thy inborn worth displays,
Inspires our souls, and fills our mouths with praise.
Thou for mankind's preceptor Heaven design'd,
To form their manners, and instruct their mind.
In virtue's cause undaunted you engage,
To stem the tide of vice, reform the stage,
And place the present with the golden age.

What eyes can view thy heroes, and not find
In them the lively copy of thy mind ?
None but a soul profusely great and good,
A soul with every princely gift endow'd,
Could draw such virtues in their native light ;
Virtues in which heroic souls delight.

With what sweet majesty Eliza stands,
While valiant Vere attends her high commands ?
The vanquish'd Gauls before her cohorts fly,
And with their blood the Danube's current dye.

Here pious Arthur ploughs the watery main,
Heaven's righteous cause and worship to maintain ;
His pious deeds and his victorious arms
Are crown'd with peace, and Ethelina's charms.

The virtuous Alfred next imbark'd we find,
In quest of wisdom for a princely mind,
To empire born and for a throne design'd.
Sages and kings alike the prince admire,
The schools and courts yield him his whole desire :

---

* Philomela was the name on the title page of Miss Singer's poems. Mr Colman,
it seems, had not forgotten to discourse to his daughter of the fair maid of Bath.

His virtue, faithful Guithun, was thy care ;
Nobly he fled the lewd Sicilian fair !
Chaste he return'd, and as an angel wise,
And more than crowns he found in fair Elsitha's eyes.

Thus Arthur, Alfred, and Eliza stand,
Drawn for examples by your matchless hand.

Had but the Mantuan felt that heavenly fire,
That warms thy breast, whene'er you tune the lyre,
Rome ne'er had known a rival in her praise,
Nor to Augusta e'er resign'd the bays.

To sacred numbers next your lyre is strung,
And mysteries divine flow from your tongue.

What heart 's not sad, what eye flows not with tears,
When Job in all the pomp of grief appears ?
His learned friends in vain attempt and try
God's secret springs of acting to descry ;
And Job condemn, till God does justify.

With Israel's Psalmist next in cheerful lays,
Raptur'd in sacred love and heavenly praise,
To Israel's God your purer offerings rise,
For a sweet smell and grateful sacrifice.

No more shall Epicurean doctrine find
Belief in any but a sickly mind ;
Nor will the Stagyrite again persuade,
'Twas not in time these mighty orbs were made,
Who read creation by your wit display'd.

Nor the bold Arian, whose blasphemous breath
The impure steam of sulphurous hell and death,
Shall scan the Almighty's ways, his truths deny,
And from the Saviour tear the Deity :
No more shall he the gazing world delude,
Nor on mankind his hellish schemes obtrude :
While you Redemption sing our faith does cry,
" My God, my God, I see thy deity ! "

O happy land ! and of unrivall'd fame,
That claims thy birth, and boasts so great a name !
Albion alone is blest with such a son,
A birth to ages past, and thee, O Greece, unknown.

AN INVITATION INTO THE COUNTRY, IN IMITATION OF
HORACE.

FROM the soft shades, and from the balmy sweets
Of Medford's flowery vales, and green retreats,

Your absent Delia to her father sends
And prays to see him ere the Summer ends.

Now while the earth's with beauteous verdure dyed,
And Flora paints the meads in all her pride;
While laden trees Pomona's bounty own,
And Ceres' treasures do the fields adorn,
From the thick smokes, and noisy town, O come,
And in these plains awhile forget your home.

Though my small incomes never can afford,
Like wealthy Celsus to regale a lord;
No ivory tables groan beneath the weight
Of sumptuous dishes, served in massy plate:
The forest ne'er was search'd for food for me,
Nor from my hounds the timorous hare does flee:
No leaden thunder strikes the fowl in air,
Nor from my shaft the winged death do fear:
With silken nets I ne'er the lakes despoil,
Nor with my bait the larger fish beguile.
No luscious sweetmeats, by my servants plac'd
In curious order e'er my table grac'd;
To please the taste, no rich Burgundian wine,
In chrystal glasses on my sideboard shine;
The luscious sweets of fair Canary's isle
Ne'er fill'd my casks, nor in my flagons smile:
No wine, but what does from my apples flow,
My frugal house on any can bestow:
Except when Cæsar's birth day does return,
And joyful fires throughout the village burn;
Then moderate each takes his cheerful glass,
And our good wishes to Augustus pass.

But though rich dainties never spread my board,
Nor my cool vaults Calabrian wines afford;
Yet what is neat and wholesome I can spread,
My good fat bacon and our homely bread,
With which my healthful family is fed.
Milk from the cow, and butter newly churn'd,
And new fresh cheese, with curds and cream just turn'd.
For a dessert upon my table's seen
The golden apple, and the melon green;
The blushing peach and glossy plum there lies,
And with the mandrake tempt your hands and eyes.

These I can give, and if you'll here repair,
To slake your thirst a cask of Autumn beer,
Reserv'd on purpose for your drinking here.

Under the spreading elms our limbs we'll lay,
While fragrant Zephyrs round our temples play.
Retir'd from courts, and crowds, secure we 'll set,
And freely feed upon our country treat.
No noisy faction here shall dare intrude,
Or once disturb our peaceful solitude.

No stately beds my humble roofs adorn
Of costly purple, by carved panthers borne;
Nor can I boast Arabia's rich perfumes,
Diffusing odors through our stately rooms.
For me no fair Egyptian plies the loom,
But my fine linen all is made at home.
Though I no down or tapestry can spread,
A clean soft pillow shall support your head,
Fill'd with the wool from off my tender sheep,
On which with ease and safety you may sleep.
The nightingale shall lull you to your rest,
And all be calm and still as is your breast.

JOHN ADAMS.

OF the Rev. Mr Adams's life very little is known.   All that
we have been able to collect of his history, is embraced in the
concise summary of his birth in 1705; his graduation from
Harvard College in 1721; his settlement in the ministry at
Newport, Rhode Island, in 1728, his dismissal from his church
in 1730; and his death at Cambridge, Massachusetts, in 1740.
The confident predictions of his immortality,* recorded in the
preface to a little collection of his poems published after Mr
Adams's death, serve only to excite a desire of knowing something of a character so lauded as his, but we are furnished
with nothing that can gratify our curiosity.   The productions
in this volume have an internal evidence of the author's fervent

* " His own works," says his eulogist, " are the best encomium that can be
given him, and as long as learning and politeness shall prevail, his *Sermons* will
be his *Monument,* and his *Poetry* his *Epitaph.*" The former, alas, are forgotten,
and the labors of a second Old Mortality would hardly revive the latter.

piety, but we search in vain for those flights of the imagination and characteristics of sublimity spoken of in the introductory remarks of a too partial friend. These poems, however, give as good evidence of a cultivated mind, as any other written at that period. We quote the

ADDRESS TO THE SUPREME BEING,

For his assistance in my Poetical Compositions.

To Thee, great GOD! I lift my humble strains,
My verse inspire ; let judgment hold the reins,
And curb my fancy's fierce unruly fire,
Which else would, wild, to boundless flights aspire.
May I not write too little, or too much,
But paint with care, not with a hasty touch.
May all my thoughts be rather just than high,
And never let me rave when I should fly.
But yet secure me from the low extreme,
Of writing meaner than becomes my theme.
Through all my works, let order clearly shine,
And let me know the reason of each line.
Give me to trace out nature in each thought,
And let each piece be to perfection brought ;
A subject for my genius fit to choose,
Not vainly light, nor yet profanely loose,
But innocent, at least, if not sublime,
And let my numbers smoothly flow in rhyme.
May each production, writ with strength and ease,
The ear, the judgment, and the fancy please.
But if my soul, by a superior flame,
Was never fir'd to merit lasting fame,
Awaken'd, let me see my fond mistake,
And with just anger from my folly break.
Nor let me in the poet lose the priest,
But know both what and when to write is best ;
From wasting, to redeem my vacant hours,
And to refine the roughness of my powers.
The brightest ancients let me read and know,
And let their spirit in my numbers flow ;
And all the moderns, who, by thee inspired,
Will be, as long as nature lasts, admired :
By nobler patterns so to form my lays,
As from the thinking few to merit praise.

But most, dear God, assist my towering lyre,
To sound thy name upon its trembling wire;
Be thou the subject of my lofty verse,
And, thine unbounded work, the universe:
The streaming purple, gushing from his heart,
Which made the Saviour's suffering soul depart.
Doubly immortal, then, shall be my fame,
Heaven shall contain my soul, and earth my name.

Mr Knapp, in his Biographical Sketches, says that Adams's Paraphrase of the Revelations was a failure. We are of a different opinion, and are inclined to think that his best poetry will be found in this version of the Apocalypse. There is certainly an agreeable harmony, and a faithful observance of the original in the following extracts.

THE Sardian angel, Jesus bids attend,
Before whose throne the radiant spirits stand
And seven celestial lights adorn his hand.
" Through the thin veil of thine hypocrisy
I cast the flames of mine omniscient eye;
The form that lives, and dazzles all around,
Conceals a heart corrupt, a bleeding wound;
Through which your dying grace shall soon be spent,
Unless your care and penitence prevent.
Few are your deeds, nor will those pious acts
Atone the greater sum of your neglects.
Past admonitions present to your fear,
The lightnings seem to see, the thunders hear;
Nor let the less'ning sounds die on your ear.
Retain your former faith and former life,
Or else expect my judgments like a thief,
Shall steal in wrath on your unguarded hours,
The bolts descending while the tempest pours:
Too much like Sodom, Sardis has her lots,
Whose shining garments are distain'd with spots.
Their fairer vesture, whiten'd into snow,
Shall o'er the flowery walks of Eden flow.
The worthy victor shall be cloth'd in white;
At once the garb of innocence and light;
In heaven's fair book, in golden figures wrote,
His name shall shine, nor endless ages blot.
When heaven shall pour its angels all around,
And all the dead shall live before the sound,

And tribes unnumber'd circle round the king,
His name shall glitter in the shining ring:
The godlike man my Father, too, shall own,
My lips acquit him, and my hand shall crown:
Th' applauded saint, proclaim'd by every tongue,
The saints shall shout, while angels give their song.
Whose ears these counsels in attention bind,
The same or greater happiness shall find.

The Saviour holy, and the witness true,
O Philadelphia's Guardian, writes to you.
The scenes of joy and wo are in his hand
Who doth the keys of life and death command;
The gates of heaven, and hell's tremendous flame,
These none can open, nor can shut but him.
Thy power, in fiery persecutions show'd,
Though small thy strength, the rage of hell withstood:
Since in the storm thy growing courage rose,
The opening hours shall smiling scenes disclose;
Nor more shall shut by clouds of rising foes.
The boasted Jews, who Satan's army meet,
Shall own my love, and own it at your feet.
On nations round, discharg'd from throne to throne,
The storm shall fall, but fly from thee alone.
When all the driving tempest roars around,
The heavens serene and spotless will be found.

Behold I come, with speedy vengeance come,
Big with the joys of nations, or their doom:
Then let thy faith and constancy prepare
The golden crown and regal robes to wear.
A victor then, the palm shall grace thy hand,
And thou a pillar in the temple stand;
Secure, sublime, and beauteous thou shalt rise
To prop and grace the church within the skies.
Thy vesture, too, the name of God shall wear,
And that fair city, pendent in the air;
The offspring of the skies, and modell'd there;
And thy new title glitt'ring on thy vest,
Shall join a dazzling lustre to the rest.

Ye churches hear, and ponder what is said,
For depths are here, and boundless fields are spread
Laodicea, hear the great amen,
For ever true his witness will remain;
And rising at his word the world began:

I know your works; in vain you would conceal
Your dull indifference, and your languid zeal;
Or throw aside the form, and show the cheat,
Or let devotion raise a vital heat.
As water which is free from each excess
Breaks from the bosom which it did oppress;
My vengeance shall your lifeless forms explore,
And from my mouth the nauseous draught shall pour.
As, when distraction seizes on the brain,
The beggar with imagin'd wealth is vain;
His treasures flow, and plenty crowns his board,
He sees his servants, and he seems a lord;
Naked, the purple vestments seem to wear,
And every want is fled, and every fear;
So, in the garments of affected pride,
The poor and naked hypocrite is hid:
Blind to himself, his fancy gilds the stains
Which strike with horror, when his reason reigns.

To me thy poverty and wants impart,
My golden furniture shall grace thy heart:
Nor snow can rival the celestial vest
In which thy naked spirit shall be dress'd;
Where every virtue shall attract the eye,
And all the sister graces of the sky.
Blind as thou art, my salve can give thee light,
And pour the heavenly object on thy sight.
Repent, and kindle up a vigorous zeal,
Believe my mercy when my rod you feel.

See where I stand, and wait your open breast,
Not once invited, but a pleading guest!
Happy the man who hears the welcome sound,
The king shall enter; and, the table crown'd,
Celestial dainties shall regale his mind;
The food ambrosia, and the wine refin'd.
Though vile the man, with freedom I will sup,
The broken bread bestow, and purple cup.
Soft on his ear my milky speech shall flow,
As gentle showers, or drops of heavenly dew.
Who gives his lord a kind reception here
Shall, rapt to paradise, the bridal supper share.
The christian hero, seated on a throne,
Shall reign with me, and triumph in a crown.
My sufferings gave the empire of the skies,

And such as die like me, like me shall rise :
Happy, whose pensive mind shall make him wise."

*　　　*　　　*　　　*　　　*　　　*　　　*

Now kindled, on the vacant fields of space,
New shining worlds, and heaven renew'd its face ;
Earth, circling smooth, without an ocean rose,
With hills unwrinkled and unclouded brows.
The sacred city, modell'd in the sky,
Shot in a trail of glory from on high ;
Till resting on the floating fields of air,
Dress'd like a bride, it shone divinely fair.
Then a loud voice a sacred seraph sent,
Which rang through all th' extended firmament.
"A God, a God ! to dwell with men descends,
See where his sparkling tent sublimely stands !
His nation shall th' imperial city hold,
And God shall lead them through the streets of gold ;
Wipe every tear from every flowing eye,
And death shall from his courts for ever fly :
And pensive moans, and silent grief and pain,
And toilsome labor, sin's detested train ;
For every former shady scene is fled,
And light, eternal, lifts its cheerful head."

Then spoke th' almighty Sire of endless days,
Who sits enthron'd in light's severest blaze ;
"My forming word shall every thing renew,
And let thy pen proclaim my sayings true.
All things to a conclusion swiftly tend,
But ne'er begun, my years can never end ;
The Alpha I, who spoke the birth of things,
And the Omega who their period brings."

The translation from Horace will show, to advantage, Mr
Adams's manner in a lighter measure.

MÆCENAS, whose ennobled veins
The blood of ancient monarchs stains ;
My safeguard, beauty and delight.
Some love the chariot's rapid flight,
To whirl along the dusty ground,
Till with Olympic honors crown'd :
And if their fiery coursers tend
Beyond the goal, they shall ascend
In merit, equal to the gods,

Who people the sublime abodes;
Others, if mingled shouts proclaim
Of jarring citizens their name,
Exalted to some higher post,
Are in the clouds of rapture lost.
This, if his granary contain
In crowded heaps the ripen'd grain,
Rejoicing his paternal field
To plough, a future crop to yield;
In vain his timorous soul you 'd move
Though endless sums his choice should prove,
To leave the safety of the land,
And trust him to the wind's command.
The trembling sailor, when the blue
And boisterous deep his thoughts pursue,
Fearful of tempests, dreads his gain
To venture o'er the threatening main:
But loves the shades and peaceful town
Where joy and quiet dwell alone.
But when impatient to be poor,
His flying vessels leave the shore.
Others the present hour will seize,
And less for business are than ease;
But flowing cups of wine desire,
Which scatter grief, and joy inspire;
Joyful they quaff, and spread their limbs
Along the banks of murm'ring streams,
While trees which shoot their tow'ring heads,
Protect them with their cooling shades.
Some love the camp and furious war,
Where nations, met with nations, jar;
The noise of victors, and the cries
Of vanquish'd, which assault the skies,
While at the trumpet's piercing ring
Their mounting spirits vigorous spring;
When fainting matrons in a swound,
Receive the martial music's sound.
The morning hunter seeks his prey,
Though chill'd by heaven's inclemency
Forgets his house: with dogs pursues
The flying stag in her purlieus.
Or his entangling net contains
The foaming boar in ropy chains.
But me the ivy wreaths which spread
Their blooming honors round the head
Of learned bards, in raptures raise,

And with the gods unite in praise.
The coolness of the rural scenes,
The smiling flowers and evergreens,
And sportful dances, all inspire
My soul with more than vulgar fire.
If sweet Euterpe give her flute,
And Polyhymnia lend her lute—
If you the deathless bays bestow,
And by applauses make them grow,
Toward the stars my winged fame
Shall fly, and strike the heavenly frame.

JAMES RALPH.

THE earliest mention of this person is in the memoirs of
Franklin, who describes him as one of his youthful associates
in Philadelphia, "ingenuous and shrewd, genteel in his address, extremely eloquent, and the most agreeable speaker
he ever met with." Ralph had, at this early period of his
life shown his inclination for poetry by the production of
several small pieces, and was so bent upon the pursuit, that
he was disposed to abandon his occupation and devote himself wholly to the muses. Full of the lofty anticipations and
the confidence of youth, he dreamed of nothing but success,
and imagined both fame and fortune to be within his reach.
Franklin and his other friends endeavored to cure him of his
poetical passion, by assuring him that he had no genius for the
business, and would do much better to stick to his trade; but
the effect of these representations was totally destroyed by
the following incident. Franklin and Ralph, with two other
young men, named Watson and Osborne, had agreed each to
write a portion of verses for mutual remark, criticism, and
correction, by way of amusement and the improvement of
their style. Franklin having little inclination for the business,
neglected his, and agreed to offer Ralph's performance as his
own, in aid of a design of this last to secure the approbation

of Osborne, Ralph imagining that Osborne depreciated his talents from personal envy alone. The stratagem succeeded to his wish. Osborne and the other commended the piece in the highest terms, and Ralph had the satisfaction of hearing his verses receive the warm admiration of the person who had been the foremost to deny his poetical talent. He made known the trick, enjoyed his triumph, and was fixed in his determination to become a poet.

Shortly after this, Franklin embarked for England, and Ralph accompanied him on his voyage with the ostensible purpose of establishing himself in the mercantile commission business, but as Franklin afterwards learnt, to get away from his wife, with whose parents he had fallen out. On their arrival in London, Ralph and Franklin lived together in the strictest intimacy. Ralph met some of his relations, but none of them were able to assist him, and his money being gone he began to look about for employment. Thinking himself possessed of talents for the stage, he resolved to turn actor, but the person to whom he applied succeeded in persuading him that he had no prospect of success in such a line. He then proposed to a London bookseller to write a weekly paper in the manner of the Spectator, but without any better result. He next tried to procure employment as a copyist, of the lawyers and stationers about the Temple, in which attempt he likewise failed. Finally he succeeded in obtaining the care of a school in a small village in Berkshire, but continuing to indulge in his dreams of future greatness, he resolved upon a precaution that his exercise of what he considered so ignoble an office should not be known afterward; and therefore changed his name, and as Franklin remarks, did him the honor to assume his. He continued to correspond with Franklin at London, and sent him fragments of an epic poem he was composing, for his criticism and correction. Franklin lent him this assistance, but accompanied his good offices with the advice to give up his literary pursuits, and seconded his entreaties by transmitting him a part of one of Young's satires upon the folly of cultivating the muses with a hope of rising in the world. This had no effect; he kept on writing his poem, and sent it piece after piece by the post.

Sometime after, a breach occurred between him and Franklin, the occasion of which is related in the memoirs of the latter. No further particulars are known of him except that he became a political writer, and was patronized by some distinguished persons in public affairs. He wrote a poem called Sawney, very abusive, according to Warburton, of Swift, Gay, and Pope, for which he was put into the Dunciad. Another poem of his, entitled "Night," is mentioned in the notes to Pope. We have never seen either of these performances.

The work which he wrote upon his first arrival in England, and got Franklin to correct for him, was probably Zeuma, or the Love of Liberty, printed in London in 1729. This is an heroic poem in three books in blank verse, which celebrates the resistance of a fabulous South American chieftain against the Spanish invaders. The story has little merit on the score of invention, and is executed in a style sufficiently negligent. Warburton vilifies Ralph as a person totally illiterate, and we should judge by this production of his early years, that he had not formed his taste by a very careful study. Still there is something of a poetical spirit about him.

ZEUMA, OR THE LOVE OF LIBERTY.

FROM THE FIRST BOOK.

BEYOND the vast Peruvian realms, whose wealth
Supports the Iberian throne, and freights whole fleets
To Europe's hostile strand ; a wond'rous ridge
Of cumb'rous hills, vast, huge, and piled abrupt,
Ascend above the clouds, and bound the view
From sky to sky ; aloft bleak winter holds
Eternal reign, and from the mountain's brow,
All cover'd o'er with ice, and white with snow,
Looks hideous down, breathes out his chilling gales,
And the sad wand'rer freezes to the ground,
A ghastly statue, with the dread of death,
Still graved upon his face ; sometimes he bids
The whirlwinds roar, and with destruction wing'd

Impels it on the realms below, and oft,
Assembling clouds on clouds, draws o'er the world
A midnight darkness ; and with sudden gush
Pours down the rain in dreadful showers, and drowns
The hope of harvest on the field.   Where ends
This rocky chain, succeeds a dreary length
Of barren sands, torn up by every wind,
And roll'd in heaps, like the vex'd billows
On the stormy main: around, a frightful, wild,
And horrid prospect, tires the lab'ring eye
In gazing for its end.   No vernal green
E'er cheers the yellow waste ; no bubbling spring
Its cooling azure rolls along ; no rains,
Nor kindly dews refresh the burning soil :
But nature looks as crumbled into dust ;
And ruin, sole possessor of the void.
   Yet on the sterile desert's utmost verge,
And the rude mountain's skirt, the Spaniards found
A land of plenty, where enlivening Spring
And fruitful Autumn, with alternate change,
Rejoiced the year ; where wealth immense (the hope
And end of all their execrable deeds,)
Was found in earth's dark womb, and every joy
Invited their abode.   Such Peru was ; '
And when, subjected to their arms, its tribes
Became the vassals of their power, athwart
This ridge of mountains they pursued
Their way to conquest, and in Chili's realms,
Resolved to fix their arbitrary rule,
Though death in all its horrid forms opposed
Their common toil, and not a soul return'd
In safety from the war. There Zeuma reign'd,
A prince, who in the opening bloom of youth,
Preferr'd his country's welfare to his own.

  *   *   *   *   *   *

   Once, as with ardent zeal he urged the chase,
And press'd, with matchless swiftness, to secure
His frighted prey, through the thick wood, from far
He spied, low-bending o'er the limpid stream,
An aged hermit ; who seem'd wrapp'd in thought
And solitary muse ; behind him, arch'd
By nature in the hollow rock, appear'd
A gloomy cave, o'ergrown with moss, his calm
Abode ; above, with difficult ascent,
Arose the hill, with vivid verdure crown'd ;
Around, the forest spread its grateful shade,

And gently murmur'd to the gale ; beneath,
Spontaneous flowers adorn'd the grassy turf,
And sweeten'd every breeze : long gazed the king
On the enchanting scene, and wonder'd much
It had till then escaped his haunt; when, waked
By his approaching step, the father rose,
And with meek rev'rence thus began.   " 'T is not,
Great prince, by accident you 've stray'd to this
Sequester'd place, but by divine decree ;
That you may know what instant dangers threat
Your rule, what miseries your realms ;
That no surprise enervate your resolves
When war alarms you to the field ; no dread
Of stranger nations, or unusual arms
Confuse the combat, and in foul retreat
Disperse your routed squadrons o'er the plain."
He said, and led him, by a winding way,
To the high brow of that delightful hill,
And bid him view the prospect round.   He look'd,
And lo! the whole world's globe seem'd stretch'd along
Before his view, so far the landscape reach'd,
So many objects crowded on the eye ;
On this side cities stand, and forests wave,
Green fields extend, and gentle rivers glide ;
O'erhanging precipices frown, and hills
Ascend on high: on this the white sea foams,
And on the nearer shores, with speedy roll,
Breaks wide its hasty billows.   Zeuma starts
At the surprising roar, yet still intent,
Beholds the restless wave, when, new and strange!
High tossing on the angry surge appear
Vast floating piles, that with capacious wings
Collect the breathing gale, and by degrees
Approach the strand ; with thund'ring voice discharge
Huge streams of ruddy flame, in cloudy smoke
Involved, and fright the nations round.   Again
The monarch starts, astonish'd at the noise,
While, down their steepy sides, descend a throng
Of bearded men, of foreign look and mien;
That brighten'd o'er the plain with shining arms,
And all the pomp of war.   To them succeeds
An herd of creatures, fierce and active, train'd
To battle, and the din of arms ; on which
The warriors mounting, all proceed, in firm
And regular array, across the field ;
Then sound a charge ; and o'er the tranquil glebe
Let loose destruction, and with slaughter glut

The sword; with dirè oppressive force, and stern
Dominion fix their barb'rous rule, and lord
It o'er the groaning tribes. With horror struck,
Sad Zeuma overlook'd the scene, and mourn'd
The dire event: when thus the hoary sage
His lore renew'd. "These are the foes that now
Are marching to invade your land; and such
The ills that must afflict your tribes; see o'er
Yon ridge of hills, contemning all the force
Of freezing cold, and wintry gales, they pass
Unwearied with the toil: then haste away,
Alarm your people, and with princely care
Draw all your squadrons to the field. If aught
Of doubt yet hangs upon your mind,
Again survey the landscape, and believe
My mission from above." He look'd, and all
Th' illusive prospect vanish'd from the view,
And nought remain'd, but one vast length of wood,
That murm'ring bow'd before the wanton gale.
  So, where the setting sun, with upward ray
Adorns the evening clouds in fleecy gold,
And purple deeply dyed, th' attentive eye,
With wonder, views a maze of objects dawn
In bright confusion o'er the blue sky's edge,
And with a round of never ceasing change
Perplex the doubtful scene, till night's deep shade,
Ascending swiftly, darkens o'er the heavens,
And in grey vapors sweeps the whole away.

   *   *   *   *   *   *

FROM THE THIRD BOOK.

  —He said; and, turning swiftly round, began
His solemn charms; when sudden darkness veil'd
The starry skies, and hollow murm'ring gales
Sung dreadful in the trees; red meteors flash'd
Along the troubled air; and, from beneath,
Loud inbred thunders shook the steadfast earth;
Unnumber'd ghosts, all pale with hostile wounds,
Stalk'd o'er the green, and fill'd the night's dark gloom
With ghastly terror and distracting groans:
Silence succeeds, vanish the ghosts away,
And earth no longer shakes; the lab'ring clouds
Unveil'd the heavens, and, in their stony caves,
The slumb'ring winds their weary pinions rest.
  Then sleep's still influence seized the drowsy king,
And down he sunk, unable to resist

The pressing weight of the prevailing god:
But inspiration waked his inward powers,
And roused light fancy, in her thousand forms,
To strike the wond'rous vision on the mind.
　First his great father's shade, with glory crown'd,
Descends, and, through the fluid realms of air,
Bears the young monarch, swift as tempests fly
When the grim ruler of the raging winds,
Drives down their fury o'er the Atlantic seas,
And, in a moment, to the farthest verge
Of the vex'd ocean, heaps the roaring waves.
　The crystal gates of Cynthia's silver orb
Unfold, and, up the portals' bright ascent,
The rev'rend guardian leads his earthly charge
Entranced in raptures ; when the glorious scene,
To his attentive view, unveil'd its charms :
For there soft pleasures, in eternal rounds,
For ever circle with an easy wing ;
All that the realms of either India boast,
Or Afric's regions, or Europa's lands,
By turns delight the happy tribes, and more,
Ten thousand more, than man's experience knows,
Or fancy forms, maintain eternal rule,
And bless the immortals with continual joy.
　Music, through every shade sweet warbling breathes
Soft gladness on the soul ; the dulcet voice
Attempers the respondent lyre.
　　*　　*　　*　　*　　*　　*
—Eternal verdure cheers the gladsome green,
And odorous flowers, for ever blooming, waft
Unfading sweets, and fume the wanton gale :
From the slope hills, descend the trickling streams,
And, through the fruitful vales, o'er sands of gold,
In gentle currents, smoothly roll along ;
The mountain's brow with tufted woods is crown'd,
With sparkling gems the silent grot 's emblazed,
And luscious plenty gladdens every field :
No wintry snows, or summer suns infest
The blissful climes, nor war's destructive rage
Lays waste the regions, and deforms the plain ;
But heaven-born love and everlasting spring
Dance hand in hand, and lead the smiling hours,
All gay with newborn happiness and joy.
　Through spicy forests, and through flowery fields,
The sweet abode of souls for ever bless'd !

The princely ghost his raptured offspring led
To that sublime retreat, where patriot shades,
In matchless pleasures, and supreme delights,
Enjoy the great reward their virtues earn'd,
With long fatigue, and endless toils, below ;
There pointed, to his view, the illustrious chiefs,
Who, scorning bribes, and all the baits of sense,
Trod, with undaunted soul, the paths of death,
When freedom claim'd the sword, and honor call'd to arms.
   Zymron,* the best, and bravest of mankind,
Towers with superior glory, and presides
Amidst the noblest heroes of the globe ;
Dreadless he looks, as when his rightful arms
O'ercame the tyrants of an hundred realms,
And made that bold attempt to free the western world.
   His mighty ancestor, of deathless name,
The next in order treads the social green,
Round his distinguish'd head bright virtue ties
The laurel wreath, and glories in his deeds ;
Nations, preserved by his indulgent care,
Shout his applause, and fame's eternal trump,
Fill'd with his praises, shakes the tyrant's throne.
   Alascar, chief of Montezeuma's line,
Stands at his side, severe his awful brow,
As when, impartial to his country's laws,
He doom'd his sons to ignominious death,
And, in a patriot's zeal, restrain'd the parent's tears.
   The brave Atalgah, steadfast as the earth
Pois'd on itself, and glorious as the sun
In its meridian height, transported hears
The wonders of his toilsome march rehearsed
With loud acclaim, when, scorching in the heat,
He patient bore the raging pangs of thirst,
Till the last fainting soldier was refresh'd
With frequent draughts from the enlivening spring.
   See ! fair Amrena, with majestic front,
And eye sublime, among the mightiest stand,
Fond of the liquid death, which freed her soul
From the proud insults of the victor's rage ;
Surrounding chiefs admire the heroic deed,
And hail her dauntless mind which dared to lead
An host to war, and, by the dint of sword,
Restore lost freedom to her mourning realm.
   A thousand more, the champions of the world !
Dwell here encircled with superior bliss,
And dream of dangers and of toil no more.

* Kings of America famous for valor and virtue.

*   *   *   *   *   *

—" But now, descending to the seats of wo,
And vengeful torments, where the sons of men
Are rack'd for all the enormities of life,
We for a while must leave these happy plains."
He said ; and, plunging from the argent world,
Sails on the winds, and bears his son along :
At last upon a huge volcano's brink,
With clouds of gloomy smoke involved, they stoop,
And sink immediate down the vast profound ;
Nor stay'd till (through unnumber'd caverns pass'd,
The abodes of fear, of horror and despair,)
They reach'd the dreadful dungeons cf the great.
Where, bound in adamantine chains, they lie
On beds of raging fire, and no hope
Of comfort, or a kind reprieve from pain ;
From pain, which every hour increasing, gives
A keener twinge ; while fiercer flames prepare
Their eager vengeance, and exert their rage ;
While round, the sad companions of their crimes,
Condemn'd to endless woe, attend their lords,
And aid the furies, and increase the fires.

* Here haughty Nimroc, plunged in burning lakes,
And deeply drench'd beneath the sulphurous wave,
No longer grasps at universal rule,
Or wastes the nations with destructive arms ;
But, inly tortured with incessant pangs,
Reflects with horror on his impious schemes.

Fix'd in a ruddy car of burning steel,
With sullen sadness, proud Guascara mourns
His fond ambition to be thought a god,
While, o'er the scorching soil, he 's dragged along,
And scornful dæmons aggravate his wo,
With pageant grandeur, and disdainful state.

Tlaxcalla's† vaunt, great Zagnar's martial son,
Extended on the rack, no more complains
That realms are wanting to employ his sword ;
But, circled with innumerable ghosts,
Who print their keenest vengeance on his soul,
For all the wrongs, and slaughters of his reign,
Howls out repentance to the deafen'd skies,
And shakes hell's concave with continual groans.

Ten thousand thousand more, whom fame records
As the dread tyrants of the tortured globe,
'Midst the dire rigors of surrounding flames,
Clank their huge fetters, and, with ceaseless yell,

* Indian tyrants.   † A province bordering on Mexico.

Bewail the frantic fury of their lives,
Which forced down all the vengeance of the gods.
   This dreadful scene survey'd, again the ghost
Broke the long silence, and his lore renew'd ;
" These, these are they, the execrable souls,
Who vaunted heavenly birth, yet scorning truth,
And virtue's sacred laws, acted worse deeds
Than all the infernals could inspire ; the worst,
The basest of the sons of men, whose joy
Was murther, whose delight was death, who thought,
Mankind was destined only to adore
Their transient glories, live upon their breath ;
Who laugh'd at justice, trampled on the laws,
And gave whole armies to the rage of war!

JOHN MAYLEM.

CONCERNING this writer, we can collect no information,
except that he was graduated at Harvard College, in 1715.
He wrote two poems upon the wars with the French and Indians. These are entitled, " Gallic Perfidy," and " The Conquest of Louisbourg." The first is a narrative in blank verse.
Of the second we shall give a few passages.

THE CONQUEST OF LOUISBOURG.

NOT to Aonian spring, Parnassian mount,
Famed Helicon, nor Aganippe's fount,
For fancied fire, I aim the wonted flight,
Nor yet explore Olympus' craggy height ;
Where fabled gods in famed assembly meet,
Self-poised the globe, an atom at their feet—
But to th' empyreal Throne, for solid rhyme,
Address the Universal Cause sublime.

   O God ! Immortal Deity—Supreme !
Father of goodness ! deign a heavenly gleam.
Me with celestial ray benign inspire,
And through each vein diffuse poetic fire !

Æthereal vigor in each line display,
While I the man and glitt'ring arms essay:
Since Thou, great Parent, deign'd paternal aid,
And terrible thy mighty power display'd.
Heroic verse to noble deeds belong,
Arms and the hero claim immortal song.
These I attempt—but first the mighty cause,
And bold infringer of establish'd laws—
(How violate so beautiful a plan?)
The peace of nature, and the tie of man.

In that warm season of the rolling year,
When fields begin fresh livery to wear,
And the gay meads display their varied hue,
With all green nature open to the view;
'Twas then the winding maze of vernal trees
Deign'd a safe covert, and benignant breeze,
To the fell savage; who in skulking mood
Ranged the vast circuit of eternal wood,
Through the meanders of the forest scour,
And the long winding labyrinth explore:
By Gallia won to fell Canadian rage
With murd'rous shaft, to horrid deeds engage.
Nor frontier village, garrison, or seat,
But a dire ravage, or destruction meet.
Where fathers stabb'd, and mothers in despair,
With piteous shrieks, and cries, afflict the air,
The brother, and fond sister meet in death,
And hapless babes resign their infant breath.

   *   *   *   *   *   *   *

And now the drums beat up, and now appears
With hearts elate, twelve thousand volunteers.
Fired with ambition in their country's cause,
Resolved to purchase fame, and loud applause,
The ample sea-ports each assiduous man
Their floating bulwarks for the mighty plan.
The gather'd navy, glorious in her pride,
In Plymouth's safe, capacious harbor ride.
Till the fair summons of a genial breeze,
Call forth to weigh, and cut the briny seas.
Then for Cape Breton the Atlantic plough,
While joy sat smiling on each martial brow,
Urge their swift passage through the liquid green,
Till all Britannia sinks behind the scene.
The dancing castles, fann'd by easy gales,
Hide half the circuit with their canvass sails.

Thus forty days, the yielding deep explore,
And reach at length Acadia's distant shore ;
Where generous Lawrence, with propitious sway,
Harmonious, rules in peace the genial day ;
Whose fair metropolis, and growing town,
By Halifax in Nova-Scotia 's known.
To a safe harbor bids the welcome fleet,
And hails the heroes to his ample seat.
A spacious basin now the fleet immure
Where the tall navy rendezvous secure.

  *   *   *   *   *   *   *

 See Amhurst now his warlike squadrons range,
Portending dreadful death, and loud revenge.
Forms his fierce legions in embattled ranks
With van, and rear guard, and important flanks—
Then at their head, heroic and serene,
March'd like young Scipio to a bloodier scene,
To a high battery, or winding length,
Of double embrasures, of double strength,
Whose mighty walls the enemy immure,
And the long trenches, aid their great secure.
Now o'er the heath his brave myrmidons leads,
While the shrill music sounds to noble deeds,
And the warm sunbeams on their firelocks play,
Strike off in spires, and aid the blaze of day.
A general halt ensues—nor yet the van
Had the fierce onset of attack began,
Six deep the front a martial grace disclose,
That dared the thunder of their Gallic foes.
But lo ! while ready for the charge they stood,
Death, blunderbuss, artillery, and blood !
Blue smoke, and purple flame, around appear,
And the hot bullets hail from front to rear.
Tremendous fate by turns incessant flies,
While the black sulphur clouds the azure skies.
And ghastly savages, with fearful yell,
Invoke their kindred of profoundest hell.
Whose hoarse shrill powaws valiant Amhurst scorns,
And roars loud thunder from his dread cohorns.
Now, dire confusions on confusions rise,
And the deep conflict aids the mighty noise.
From hills of smoke see spire ascend on spire ;
And Amhurst there enveloped all in fire.
With his drawn sabre from a livid cloud,
With teeming death, emerging like a god !

Ten thousand beams spire from the flaming steel,
And Gallia's sons his weighty prowess feel.
Now the vast tumult wakes the drowsy gods,
Who all look down to see the mighty odds.
When Amhurst there, like Peleus' mighty son,
Dreadful in arms, and Tyrian scarlet shone,
Engaging here, in martial order stood
Fierce as Alcides or the Scythian god ;
Till thundering Mars no more the sight could bear,
Turn'd pale with envy, and let drop his spear.
And fame, all flaming from the imperial car,
Hail'd him sole rival of the god of war.
'Twas such inspired immortal Maro's tongue,
When Ilium's fate, " arms and the man " he sung.
Thus the long conflict, undecided held,
And each fierce veteran maintain'd the field.
The conscious hero, thoughtful of our good,
Fierce in the van, bespatter'd o'er with blood,
With mien majestic, thrice his sabre shook,
Thrice waved his arm, and thus, heroic, spoke.
" Intrepid heroes—Britain's loyal band !
Who valiant fought on this important land,
In equal poise of this exploit th' event
As yet hangs dubious—you fatigued and spent,
Like valiant boys, give three huzzas and rush
Victorious on—and give a final push."
He said—and swift as the revolving sun,
Drove rapid through, and urged his passage on ;
While mighty Wolf, in terrible array,
With dreadful phalanx, change the face of day ;
There sable chiefs and Gallic heroes yield,
And vital carnage spreads the ample field.

See ! Whetmore, yonder, moving o'er the heath,
Makes it one sad continued scene of death.
Or, bending victor o'er the ample soil,
Reaps a huge conquest with herculean toil.
With Lawrence there, whose gen'rous bosom warms,
And like Ascanius their enclosure storms.
Of the deep trenches quick essays the verge,
And deals wide slaughter with a heavy charge.
Intrepid Frazer rushes impetuous on,
Whose wielding broad-sword flames a circling sun.
And Highland heroes charge their double flanks,
Attack whole squadrons, and enclose their ranks.
And Scott with ardor penetrates the wood,
And sable warriors weep a vital flood ;

So a young lion with amazing dread,
Strews the green covert with the passive dead.

    *   *   *   *   *

  Opposed to where their famed asylum stood,
Was a fair rising by a neighb'ring wood,
An easy eminence, whose top accline,
To their strong ramparts bore a level line.
To this grand object of their martial scenes,
Through fierce encounters move the huge machines.
Now Wolf's long trenches and fascines appear,
And conquer'd batteries ope each embrasure,
With horrid mortars gaping on their tier,
And the fix'd cannon point their fatal maws,
While peals of thunder issue from their jaws.
Boscawen now his naval vengeance hurls,
And clouds of sulphur fleet away in curls;
Intrepid Hardy, from his floating force,
Wings fate on fate, with an incessant course,
And brave Durell his keen combustions throw,
While shells or break above or burst below.
Thus long the sun in his diurnal race,
Saw the dire conflict from his radiant space:
When now a bomb of huge diameter,
From a vast mortar, flamed a livid sphere,
With dire combustion fill'd, and death innate,
The last sad prelude to their final fate!
Aloft in ambient ether now it spires,
Strikes on the sunbeams, interchanging fires;
Now prone inclines in terrible display,
Like the last comet at the judgment day;
On the French admiral, tremendous cracks,
And swift as lightning drops beneath the decks.

    *   *   *   *   *

  Meanwhile, alternate deaths promiscuous fly,
And the fierce meteors blaze along the sky;
Then shiver in the air, and sudden pour
A cloud of atoms, in a sulphur shower;
Or in their city wild convulsive burst
Ten thousand ways, and mingle with the dust,
A gaping chasm in their wall disclose,
The reeking soldier at his death repose.
While fate in showers of lead connected rains,
And wings famed heroes to her dark domains;
The cutting grape-shot spatter o'er the heath,
And the fierce langrel aid the glare of death.

In such sad scenes alternately involved,
Till one fair season half her course dissolved;
Too much the odds—the Gallic ensigns struck,
By all their patron images forsook,
With drooping flag and solemn pace advance,
Their courage faints, nor more can stand the chance,
The last sad purpose of their souls impart,
And claim the mercy of a British heart.

THOMAS GODFREY.

THOMAS GODFREY was born in Philadelphia, in the year
1736. His father, Thomas Godfrey, was a glazier of that
city, and possessed a great talent for mathematics: of this he
gave a splendid and durable testimony to the world by the
invention of the quadrant now in common use, which has
been generally called Hadley's quadrant. Godfrey, the father,
died when his son was very young, and left him to the care of
his relations. By these he was placed in an English school,
and received, as we are told, "a common education in his
mother tongue." In his youth he displayed a strong inclination for poetry and painting, and was very desirous of being
bred to the latter profession. His guardians, however, wished
to dispose of him in another way, and he was put apprentice
to a watchmaker of Philadelphia. In this employment we do
not find that he evinced any of that propensity for the me-
chanical arts which had enabled his father to gain such distinction. His partialities lay in a different direction, and he
devoted himself to the study of polite letters with great zeal
and assiduity in his private hours. In the latter part of his
apprenticeship he wrote several poetical scraps, which were
published with great approbation in the American Magazine.

Upon the expiration of his apprenticeship he obtained a
lieutenant's commission in the Pennsylvania forces which
were raised in 1758, for the expedition against Fort Du
Quesne. What services he performed during the campaign

we have no means of knowing ; but it appears that his military duties did not altogether abstract his thoughts from the muses. A poetical epistle, addressed to one of his friends, was written while he was in garrison at Fort Henry, on the frontier.

At the end of the campaign, the troops were disbanded, and Godfrey went to North Carolina where he resided three years engaged in mercantile transactions. While in this employment he composed a tragedy in blank verse designed for representation at the Philadelphia theatre : what success it met with we are not informed. Godfrey's employer dying, he returned to Philadelphia, and shortly after, embarked for the island of New Providence, in which place he spent some months, but meeting with disappointments in his business, he returned to North Carolina. A few weeks after his arrival, he was attacked by a fever occasioned by riding into the country on a very hot day : of this illness he died on the third of August, 1763, in the twentyseventh year of his age. An amiable disposition, an unpretending modesty of manners, a warm heart, and spotless integrity of conduct, endeared him to all who shared his acquaintance.

If we consider the circumstances of Godfrey's youth, his employment, and his scanty education, we must allow that his works do him great credit. The Court of Fancy, his principal poem, will give the most favorable specimen of his powers. A single glance at the work will apprize the reader that the design is taken from Chaucer's House of Fame. To powers of invention Godfrey can lay no claim ; his great talent lies in description ; his images are selected with taste, and clothed in verse generally harmonious and correct.

His tragedy of the Prince of Parthia, is, we believe, the first attempt at dramatic composition which the annals of our literature can furnish, a circumstance sufficiently remarkable to entitle it to notice. The story of the piece is to this effect : Artabanes, the king of Parthia, had conquered Armenia, married the queen of that country, and bestowed the crown upon her son. The new made king revolted, and was defeated and slain by Arsaces the eldest son of the king of Parthia. The queen was inflamed with revenge, and determined upon the ruin of Arsaces, a design in which she found a ready accomplice in Vardanes, the king of Parthia's second son, who is driven by his ambition to plot against his brother. These brothers are moreover rivals in the affections of Evanthe, a captive Arabian princess, and Vardanes is heated in his enmity by scorned love as' well as incited by the thirst of dominion. Meantime the queen makes the discovery that her royal husband is also captivated by the charms of Evanthe, a piece of knowledge which inflames her lurking wish for vengeance into open rage. It must be granted that the author has furnished the personages of his drama with motives sufficient for every tragic incident. Vardanes persuades the king that the prince, his brother, is conspiring against his throne and life ; Vardanes seizes Evanthe. The king is then put to death at the instigation of the queen, who also attempts the murder of the prince, but is deterred by the appearance of the ghost of her husband, whereupon she becomes distracted. The prince arrives at the head of the army to quell the conspiracy. A battle ensues and Vardanes is killed. Evanthe during the conflict deceived by a false report of the death of Arsaces, swallows poison, but lives sufficient time to learn the victory of her love and her fatal precipitancy. She expires in his arms and the unfortunate Prince of Parthia falls by his own hand.

Godfrey was twentytwo years of age when he finished this work, and with this fact in view, we ought not to wonder at the moderate degree of taste shewn in the selection of the subject, or the want of skill manifested in the construction and developement of the story. The tragedy written by Pope in his youth would probably, had it been preserved, have done as little credit to the author, as the Prince of Parthia does to Godfrey. To write a tragedy is to attempt a species of composition for which the highest powers of human genius are requisite. That conjunction of the greatest inventive faculties with a profound knowledge of the workings of those passions and sympathies which control every variety of human action, and a skilful perception of the nice peculiarities of character, which operate unseen and unsuspected in directing the destiny of men, is a rare accomplishment even among those who possess undeniable claim to the character of true poets. It is needless to say that the Prince of Parthia is a failure. We are little moved by the incidents of the story, notwithstanding they are of the most tragic description. The characters are uninteresting, although marked by strong shades, and placed in every requisite advantage of situation. The execution is hardly more felicitous than the design. The dialogue is heavy, the sentiments commonplace, and the language stiff and prosaic.

If, however, we can find little to admire in his tragedy, his other works give us a favorable opinion of his talents. The natural powers which produced the Court of Fancy, under the disadvantages of comparative youth and a stinted education, would in maturer age, and with proper cultivation, have produced a work of high credit to American literature.

THE COURT OF FANCY.

'Twas sultry noon,—impatient of the heat
I sought the covert of a close retreat;
Soft by a bubbling fountain was I laid,
And o'er my head the spreading branches play'd;
When gentle slumber stole upon my eyes,
And busy fiction bid this vision rise.

Methought I pensive, unattended, stood,
Wrapp'd in the horrors of a desert wood;
Old night and silence spread their sway around,
And not a breeze disturb'd the dread profound.
To break the wild, and gain the neighboring plain,
Oft I essay'd, and essay'd oft in vain;
Still in intricate mazes round I run;
And ever ended where I first begun.
While thus I laboring strove t' explore my way,
Bright on my sense broke unexpected day:
Retiring night in haste withdrew her shade,
And sudden morn shone through the opening glade.

No more the scene a desert wild appear'd,
A smiling grove its vernal honors rear'd;
While sweetness on the balmy breezes hung,
And all around a joyful matin rung.
Soft was the strain of Zephyr in the grove,
Or purling streams that through the meadows rove.
Now wild in air the varying strain is toss'd,
In distant echoes then the sound is lost;
Again revived, and lo! the willing trees
Rise to the powerful numbers by degrees.
Trees now no more, robb'd of their verdant bloom,
They shine supporters of a spacious dome,
The wood to bright transparent crystal changed,
High fluted columns rise, in order ranged.

   So to the magic of Amphion's lyre
Stones motion found, and Thebes was seen t' aspire;
The nodding forests rose with the soft sound,
And gilded turrets glitter'd all around:
Each wond'ring god bent from his heavenly seat
To view what powerful music could complete.

   High on a mountain was the pile disclosed,
And spreading limes th' ascending walks composed;
While far below the waving woods declined,
Their verdant tops bow'd with the gentle wind.
Bright varying novelty produced delight,
And majesty and beauty charm'd the sight.
Such are the scenes which poets sweetly sing,
By Fancy taught to strike the trembling string.
Here Fancy's fane, near to the blest abode
Of all her kindred gods, superior stood.
Dome upon dome it sparkled from on high,
Its lofty top lost in the azure sky.
By fiction's hand the amazing pile was rear'd,
In ev'ry part stupendous skill appear'd;
In beautiful disorder, yet complete,
The structure shone irregular and great:
The noble frontispiece of antique mould
Glitter'd with gems, and blazed with burnish'd gold.

   Now through the sounding vaults, self-opening, rung
The massy gates on golden hinges hung;
All the bright structure was disclosed to view,
Magnificent with beauty ever new!
Trembling I stood absorb'd in dread surprise,
And sudden glory dimm'd my aching eyes.

Unnumber'd pillars all around were placed,
Their capitals with artful sculpture graced.
Wide round the roof a fictious sky was raised,
A glorious sun in the meridian blazed,
On the rich columns played his dazzling ray,
And all around diffused immortal day ;
A shining phœnix on the effusive rays
Fix'd his aspiring eye with steady gaze.
Beneath appear'd a chequer'd pavement, bright
With sparkling jaspanyx and chrysolite.
Round, by creating Fiction's hand renew'd
Gay visionary scenes in order stood ;
The obedient figures at her touch disclosed,
And various tales the glowing walls composed.

Here mighty Jove, amidst assembled gods,
Raised on his starry throne, majestic nods ;
On his right hand the dreadful fates are seen,
And on his left is placed his haughty queen.
There the pale tyrant of the dreary coasts
Sways with his powerful sceptre fleeting ghosts.
Blue Neptune scours along his wat'ry reign,
Now lifts the waves aloft, now stills the raging main.
Perch'd on a lofty rock Æolus stands,
And holds the winds in strong coercive bands.
Here the bright queen of beauty stands confess'd,
There angry Mars in martial honors dress'd.
Alcides here appears with warrior pride,
The lion's spoil descending o'er his side,
The watchful dragon at his feet is lain,
The Lernean Hydra and dire Centaurs slain.
Here glows Diana, eager in the chace,
And there Minerva shows with sober grace.
There with the maddening rout close at his heels,
Young Bacchus, jolly god, triumphant reels.
Gay Maia's son, high mounted on the wind,
Cuts through the air and leaves the clouds behind.

Toward the rosy east, great Mithra shone,
Bright in the glories of a rising sun.
Beneath, in solemn pomp, with hands uprear'd,
In flowing robes the Magi all appear'd ;
Here the sage* Bactrian poised his magic wand,
Obedient Genii waited his command.

* Zoroaster.

There Thammuz lay, while from the gaping wound
Pour'd the rich stream, and sanguined all the ground.
Amidst his impious votaries Chemos stood,
And horrid Moloch, smear'd with infant blood.

Northward fierce Woden stood, with terrors crown'd,
And angry Thor threw heedless thunder round.
Fair Friga with her lovely train was seen,
The beauteous rival of the Paphian queen.
Old Merlin struck the lyre, the wond'ring throng
Attended round to his prophetic song.

Southward disorder'd figures struck my eyes,
Monkeys and serpents raised to deities ;
Mad, superstitious Egypt these revered,
And to the hideous tribe their prayers preferr'd.
Maim'd Memnon there seem'd on his harp to play,
And hail Osiris bringing on the day.
Pale Isis' crescent faintly glimmer'd here,
And barking Anubis display'd the year.

Gay sportive fawns adorn'd the distant scene,
In antic measures skipping o'er the green.
There sea nymphs wanton'd on the wat'ry gleam,
Rode on the waves, or cleaved the yielding stream.
Here the pale Sybils ranged their mystic leaves,
And Ætna with the laboring Cyclops heaves.
There craggy rocks the sons of Titan tore,
And mountains shaggy roots tremendous bore,
And threaten'd Jove with the promiscuous war.

Bold Phaeton here urged his mad request,
Ambitious joy swell'd his presumptuous breast ;
Elate he mounted in the flaming car,
The sire attended with a fix'd despair ;
Nor could the parent's tears the youth restrain,
He laugh'd at fear, and daring took the rein.
The fiery steeds his feeble hand despise,
And stretch'd with glowing ardor through the skies ;
Now thunders roll'd, pale lightning play'd around,
And the rash boy soon felt the burning wound.

Pygmalion there the statue seem'd to move,
Assisted by the powerful queen of love ;
With rapture fired, to his exulting breast
The animated stone he fondly press'd ;

Transported on each shining feature gazed,
Now soften'd into life, and saw amazed,
Awaken'd into sense, her eye-balls roll,
And heaving breasts bespoke the entering soul ;
Saw on her cheek the rosy tincture burn,
And felt her lips the ravish'd kiss return.

Famed Dædalus here wing'd the midway air,
And sighing, saw his son disdain his care.
Young Icarus on spreading pinions rose,
And scorn'd the path his weary sire had chose :
For heaven the aspiring boy his flight begun,
But felt the ardor of too near a sun ;
The temper'd wax before the scorching ray
Melted, and lo! the loosen'd wings gave way ;
And while his father's name his accents gave,
Fell from the height, and sunk beneath the wave.

Diana's rage there hapless Acteon feels,
And saw his hounds pursuing at his heels ;
Changed to a stag, he swept along the plain,
In vain his speed, he flew from death in vain.

Elysium next disclosed its blissful bowers,
With heavenly fruitage deck'd, and radiant flowers ;
Celestial Amaranth eternal bloom'd,
And the bright plains with odorous scents perfumed ;
Through the gay meads an amber current roll'd,
O'er sands resplendent as Arabia's gold,
On whose green banks the happy shades reclined,
Quaff'd its sweet stream, and left their cares behind.

What ever dreamer dreamt, or poet sung,
Or lying fable with her double tongue
Told the believing world, now did appear
Delusions all, for when approaching near,
They shunn'd the view, and shrunk to empty air.

High in the midst, raised on her rolling throne,
Sublimely eminent, bright Fancy shone.
A glitt'ring* tiara her temples bound,
Rich set with sparkling rubies all around ;

* This conceit is occasioned, by the tiara's being a badge of royalty used in the east, and the oriental writers abounding much in pieces of imagination.

Her azure eyes roll'd with majestic grace,
And youth eternal bloom'd upon her face,
A radiant bough, ensign of her command,
Of polish'd gold, waved in her lily hand ;
The same the sybil to Æneas gave,
When the bold Trojan cross'd the Stygian wave.
In silver traces fix'd unto her car,
Four snowy swans, proud of the imperial fair,
Wing'd lightly on, each in gay beauty dress'd,
Smooth'd the soft plumage that adorn'd her breast.
Sacred to her the lucent chariot drew,
Or whether wildly through the air she flew,
Or whether to the dreary shades of night,
Oppress'd with gloom she downward bent her flight,
Or proud aspiring sought the bless'd abodes,
And boldly shot among the assembled gods.

On her right hand appear'd the joyful nine,
And on her left the graces all divine ;
Young infant love soft on her breast reclined,
And with his mother's glowing beauty shined.
Her favorite sons were ranged in order round ;
In three bright bands with deathless laurels crown'd ;
Great Homer here enjoy'd superior day,
Illuminated by bright fancy's ray ;
Apelles there, whose magic hand could give
Form to the mass, and bid the fiction live ;
Timotheus next, whose animated lyre
Cold grief could charm, and thoughtless rage inspire.

Close at her feet a bard in raptures lost,
Was placed, and wildly round his eyeballs toss'd ;
Great Fancy was the theme! the soothing train
In floods of pleasure thrill'd through every vein.
Thus, while the trembling notes ascend on high,
He sung ; " Indulgent queen of every joy,
What rapture fills the breast thou dost inspire,
The lover's transport, and the poet's fire !
At thy command obedient pleasure bends,
And rosy beauty to thy call attends ;
The fanning gales shall swelling spread thy fame,
And echoing groves well pleased resound thy name ! "

While thus around my eyes I wildly threw,
From charm to charm, and did each wonder view,
Pleased on the heavenly ravishment to gaze,
Rose with the strain, or wanton'd in the blaze !

Her awful silence the bright goddess broke,
And frowning, thus in angry mood she spoke:
" Com'st thou, vain mortal, here with searching eye,
Into the secrets of our court to pry ?
What rash presumption swells thy youthful breast,
That in our presence thus you 've rudely press'd ? "

Trembling I kneel'd, with fear my tongue was tied
A space, when speech regain'd, I thus replied:
" With lowly reverence I hither came,
Not to deride, but to adore thy name;
To thee I ever dedicate my song,
To hail thy glories 'midst this suppliant throng."

Then from her shining seat, the heavenly maid
In beautiful arrision, answering said ;
" Then have thy wish—here, mortal, take this lyre,
Strike bold the strings, and sing as I inspire.
Humbly I bow'd, her mild commands obey'd,
And careless o'er the lyre my fingers laid,
And soon with wild poetic rage possess'd,
All my frame shook, and laboring heaved my breast.
By Fancy fired, enraptured thus I sung,
Whilst all around redoubling echoes rung.

" Zephyr attend, or whether through the grove
Soft whisp'ring, you the leafy branches move,
Or, shaking dulcet dew-drops from each flower,
Wide through the plain you spread the fragrant shower,
Or whether Sylvia, panting in some shade,
In tender accents woos thee to her aid!
No more in amorous sporting spend the day,
No longer wanton on her bosom play;
Fancy commands! obey the regal fair,
Fancy commands! quick all your wings prepare !
From the sun's early dawn till where again
He sets his glories in the azure main ;
Through every clime her royal mandate bear,
And bid mankind to her bright court repair.
Hear, earth's inhabitants! ye mortals, hear!
And let attentive wonder fix each ear.
Fancy invites ! nor let her ask in vain,
Come, taste her heavenly sweets, and hail her reign!"

Zephyr, obedient, on his wings convey'd
The joyful summons warbling through the glade ;

Swiftly he swept along the spicy vale,
Caught all its sweets, and in a balmy gale
Gently he stole on the fond lover's ear,
And in loud accents bade the warrior hear!
From different climes the thronging nations came,
And rush'd promiscuously before the dame;
Prostrate before her throne their hands they rear,
And to the goddess loud prefer their prayer.
Confused, they all demand her promised joys,
While the long vaults resound their clamorous noise.
As when loud billows break upon the shore,
Or o'er the opposing rocks the torrents roar.
Her glittering branch impatient round she swung,
And instant silence seized each babbling tongue.
Abash'd they trembling stood, and seem'd to be
Transfix'd in mute insensibility.
Quick was dispersed each wild tumultuous sound,
And the soft breezes all were hush'd around.

Now swiftly forward false Delusion came,
Wrapt in a fulvid cloud appear'd the dame.
Thin was her form, in airy garments drest,
And grotesque figures flamed upon her vest;
In her right hand she held a magic glass,
From whence around reflected glories pass.
Blind by the subtle rays, the giddy croud
Rush'd wildly from the dome and shouted loud.
The few remain'd whom Fancy did inspire,
Yet undeceived by vain Delusion's fire.

A troop of shining forms the next came on,
Foremost bright Nature's awful goddess shone.
Fair Truth she led, in spotless white array'd,
And pleasing Beauty, sweet celestial maid;
Where Truth and Nature aid the great design,
Beauty attends, and makes it all divine.

Sweet Poesy was seen their steps behind,
With golden tresses sporting in the wind;
In careless plaits did her bright garments flow,
And nodding laurels waved around her brow;
Sweetly she struck the string, and sweetly sung,
Th' attentive tribe on the soft accents hung.
'Tis hers to sing who great in arms excel,
Who bravely conquer'd or who glorious fell;
Heroes in verse still gain a deathless name,
And ceaseless ages their renown proclaim.

Oft to philosophy she lends her aid,
And treads the sage's solitary shade;
Her great first task is nobly to inspire
The immortal soul with Virtue's sacred fire.

    Then Painting forward moved in garlånds drest,
The rainbow's varied tints adorn'd her vest.
Great Nature's rival!——quick to her command
Beauty attends, and aids her powerful hand.
At her creative touch gay fictions glow,
Bright tulips bloom, and opening roses blow.
The canvass see, what pleasing prospects rise!
What varying beauty strikes our wondering eyes!
Chill winter's wastes, or spring's delightful green,
Hot summer's pride, or autumn's yellow scene ;
Here lawns are spread, there towering forests wave,
The heights we fear, or wish the cooling lave !

    Her blooming sister in her hand she led,
Joy in her eye, fair Sculpture, heaven-taught maid.
'Tis hers to stone a mimic life to give,
Heroes and sages at her call revive ;
See flowery orators with out-stretched hand
Addressed to speak, in glowing marble stand !

    Sudden I heard soft sounds, a pleasing strain !
Music advanced with all her heavenly train.
Sweetly enraptured then my pulse beat high,
And my breast glow'd, fraught with unusual joy.
'Tis harmony can every passion move,
Give sorrow ease, or melt the soul to love ;
Exulting pleasure to her call attends,
E'en stormy rage to powerful Music bends.

    With turrets crown'd bright Architecture shone.
The lovely maid with easy steps came on ;
Graceful her mien, her looks celestial shined,
Where majesty and softening beauty join'd.
At her command see lofty piles ascend,
Columns aspire, triumphal arches bend.

    Astronomy, with proud aspiring eye,
Gazed on the glowing beauties of the sky.
Her vest with glittering stars was spangled o'er,
And in her hand a telescope she bore.
With this she marked the rolling planet's way,
Or where portentous comets dreadful stray.

Though last, not least, Philosophy was seen :
Slow was her step, and awful was her mien.
A volume open in her hand she held ;
With nature's law the ample page was fill'd.
'Tis hers great Nature's wondrous depths t' explore,
Or to the gods in heavenly rapture soar.

With these bright Fancy's sons their hours employ,
Pursue their lore, and taste each rising joy.

Now suddenly the scene was changed again,
And brought to view Delusion's spreading reign :
There intermingled hills and rocks were seen,
Here shady groves and flowery lawns between.
Full in the front a lofty pile was rear'd,
The architecture old and rude appear'd.
Delusion's residence, within confined
Gay fictions lurk, and dreams of every kind.
Constant as waters roll, or flames ascend,
Hither their course the rising vapors bend ;
Dress'd by her hand they shine with mimic bloom,
Or at her word their nothingness resume.
But still from Fancy all her power she draws,
Bows to her name, and owns her sacred laws.
Some in light dreams the sleeping senses move,
And led by them the thoughts unsettled rove,
Others, more bold, majestic portments take,
And plague delighted those who dream awake.
Such are the dreams of those who thirst for power,
The superstitious, and a thousand more.
Others usurp the features of the dead,
And shake the torch around the murderer's bed ;
Affright the vigil, or in wanton mirth,
Make fools seek hidden treasures in the earth,
Or lead the weary traveller awry,
Or rising, flame amazement in the sky.

Now with the crowd Delusion forward came,
A troop of phantoms flutter'd round the dame ;
In bands the throng she instantly divides,
A phantom over every band presides.

Foremost a bright majestic form appear'd,
And in her hand the honor'd fasces rear'd ;
Forward she strode with more than virgin pace,
And leer'd upon the crowd with haughty grace.

Power was her name ; assuming, selfish Pride
And glittering Pomp attended by her side.
Her favorite son on a high seat she placed,
With mimic gems and glassy bawbles graced ;
Close by his side was seated wrinkled Care,
While Envy view'd him with malicious stare :
Sternly he eyed around the servile throng,
While loud acclaim proceeded from each tongue ;
But from the giddy height devolving soon,
Reproach, contempt, and shame is on him thrown.
Eager another mounts the chair of power,
And shines the empty pageant of an hour.

Dame Superstition was the next came on,
Bright on her head the gilded mitre shone,
Varying her aspect, now she raised her eye,
And seem'd bewilder'd with ecstatic joy ;
Then sudden gloom her countenance depress'd,
Tears roll'd apace, and sorrow heaved her breast ;
Now calm again she silent view'd around
The prostrate crowd bent humbly to the ground :
Then, caught with sudden rage, she hurl'd about
Her thund'ring anathema 'mong the rout.

An aged, wrinkled hag the next appear'd,
Four mouldering turrets o'er her temples rear'd ;
In rows like beads the faithful medals tied,
In ornamental rust adorn'd her side.
A broken column of an ancient date
She dragg'd, and sinking seem'd beneath the weight.
The column all admired, the medals more,
" The inscription value, but the rust adore."

The next to her approach'd a reverent dame,
In trophies great, from insects torn, she came ;
With stately step she trod the plain along,
And threw her treasure 'midst the admiring throng.
Forward with joy each curious mortal sprang,
This caught a gaudy wing, and that a pointed fang.

Before the giddy throng, which now advanced,
With mincing step gay Affectation danced,
Then sudden stopp'd, and staring on the crowd,
She frown'd, then smiled, and giggled out aloud.
The numerous throng attending round the fair,
Mimic'd her gestures, and assumed her air.

A crowd of mortals here, with wondering eyes,
All pale and trembling gazed upon the skies;
Where on blue plains opposing hosts engage,
While shouts are heard and all the battle's rage.
Amidst the throng stood cold and heartless Fear,
The fall of nations whispering in each ear.

Here pallid spectres gleam'd, and there were seen
The fairy train in gambols on the green.
Through miry ways the rustic journeys round,
Nor dares presuming tread the hallow'd ground ;
Dire ills await the wretch, so fable sings,
Or pinch'd all o'er, or pierced with thousand stings.

The structure entering, as around I threw
My wondering eyes, gay forms arose to view.
False Pleasure here the borrow'd form of Joy
Assumed, and roll'd around her sparkling eye.
But who, allured by her enchanting song,
From virtue shrinks, and mingles with her throng,
Soon sees her beauties fade, and to his eyes
Deformity and sad disease arise.

In a dark corner hell-born Jealousy,
A wan and haggard sprite, I did espy ;
Watchful she roll'd her ghastly eyes around,
And cautious trod, to catch the whispering sound.
Her heart for ever deathless vultures tear,
And by her side stalk anguish and despair.
Curst is the wretch with her dire rage possess'd,
When fancied ills destroy his wonted rest.

Pale Avarice was seen with looks of care,
And clasp'd her bags with never ceasing fear.
Close following her, a wretched spectre came,
With tatter'd garments, Poverty her name.
In vain her search t' elude still Avarice strives,
Amidst her store in endless want she lives.

False Honor here I saw all gaily dress'd,
Glass were her beads, and tinsel'd was her vest;
Form'd in barbaric ages, rude her mien,
And in her hand the sanguined sword was seen.
Not stain'd like patriots in their country's cause,
To save religion, or support the laws ;
In private strife the crimson torrents flow,
Their country wounded by each fatal blow.

With chequer'd hood Dissembling stood behind,
And Falsehood, coining lies to cheat mankind;
While with smooth art deceitful Flattery
Address'd the ear of listening Vanity.

The gloom was now disclosed where Spleen remain'd:
A thousand various ills the goddess pain'd.
As powerful Fancy works, here mortals are
Transform'd to glass, or China's brittle ware;
Oppress'd by Spleen, no longer joy they know,
For ever tortured with imagined woe.

As thus I onward moved with wandering pace,
And view'd the varied wonders of the place;
"Just heaven," I cried, "Oh! give me to restrain
Imagination with a steady rein!
Though oft she leads through Pleasure's flowery ways,
In Error's thorny path she sometimes strays.
Let me my hours with solid judgment spend,
Nor to Delusion's airy dreams attend;
By Reason guided, we shall only know
Those heavenly joys which Fancy can bestow!

EPISTLE TO A FRIEND.

FROM FORT HENRY.

FROM where his lofty head Talheo rears,
And o'er the wild in majesty appears,
What shall I write that ——— wont disdain,
Or worth, from thee one moment's space to gain?
The muse,—in vain I court the lovely maid,—
Views with contempt the rude unpolish'd shade;
Nor only this, she flies fierce war's alarms,
And seeks where peace invites with softer charms;
Where the gay landscapes strike the traveller's eyes,
And woods and lawns in beauteous order rise;
Where the glad swain sings on the enamell'd green,
And views, unawed by fears, the pleasing scene.
Here no enchanting prospects yield delight,
But darksome forests intercept the sight;
Here fill'd with dread the trembling peasants go,
And start with terror at each nodding bough,
Nor as they trace the gloomy way along,
Dare ask the influence of a cheering song.
If in this wild a pleasing spot we meet,

In happier times some humble swain's retreat;
Where once with joy he saw the grateful soil
Yield a luxuriant harvest to his toil,
(Bless'd with content, enjoy'd his solitude,
And knew his pleasures, though of manners rude ;)
The lonely prospect strikes a secret dread,
While round the ravaged cot we silent tread,
Whose owner fell beneath the savage hand,
Or roves a captive on some hostile land,
While the rich fields, with Ceres' blessings stored,
Grieve for their slaughter'd or their absent lord.
   Yet would I now attempt some sprightly strain,
And strive to wake your breast to mirth again,
Yet would I call you from your Delia's urn,
But Britain's genius bids her sons to mourn;
She shows the fatal field, all drench'd in gore,
And in sad accents cries, " My Howe 's no more ! "
Then let again the briny torrents flow.
Oh ! teach your breast a nobler kind of woe !
To mourn her faded beauties now forbear,
And give the gallant chief a British tear.

NATHANIEL EVANS.

NATHANIEL EVANS was born in Philadelphia, June 8th, 1742. He was educated at the Academy in that place, but not with a view to any liberal profession on the part of his parents, who after six years spent in his studies, bound him apprentice to a merchant. The business, however, did not suit his inclination, and the muses engrossed a great portion of those hours which should have been devoted to the affairs of the counting house. When his apprenticeship expired, he entered college, and pursued his studies with such application and success, that he was rewarded with a Master's degree without passing through the intermediate gradation of academical preferment.

The society for propagating the gospel in foreign parts, which was then established in England, contemplated opening a mission in the county of Gloucester in New Jersey; and Evans was recommended as a fit person for this undertaking. He accordingly sailed for England in 1765, for the purpose of procuring the appointment. In this he was successful. The society nominated him for holy orders; and he was admitted by the lord bishop of London. He returned to Philadelphia in December of the same year, and entered immediately upon the business of his mission, but his labors were interrupted by death, ere they had completed a course of two years. He died on the 29th of October, 1767, at the age of twentyfive. He was the intimate friend of Godfrey, and after the death of that poet, prepared his works for the press.

Evans published two or three inconsiderable scraps in verse in the public prints, but gave to the world nothing during his lifetime, which could support a claim to any eminent rank as a poet. By his own directions a volume of his poems was published after his death. It is probable most of these were composed before he devoted himself to his clerical pursuits, as but a few pages among them contain anything of a devotional sort. A tone of cheerfulness and gaiety pervades the smaller pieces of the collection, which must strike the reader as a special rarity in the lucubrations of an American clergyman of that day. Evans appears to have possessed a lively temperament, with a considerable share of enthusiasm. He was evidently imbued with a strong love for poetry, and a nice conception and feeling of its beauties. The fragment of an unfinished preface to his works contains evidence that his mind was of that delicate and refined stamp, over which the imagination exercises a powerful sway.

Evans, like his friend Godfrey, was cut off at an age when few have sufficiently developed their powers to execute any work of great and permanent excellence. Yet from what he has left behind him, his poetical talent may be estimated highly. His taste was excellent, and his imagination vivid. The Ode on the Prospect of Peace is decidedly the most finished and elegant production which the literature of our country could exhibit at that date.

EPISTOLARY ODE TO A FRIEND.

LIKE as Lybia's burning sand,
　　Or the parch'd Arabian plain,
Which gentle Eurus never fann'd,
　　Would drink the unfathomable main—
So is the wretch who endless craves,
　　And restless pines in every state—
O ! place him with the worst of slaves,
　　Whether in high or low estate ;
Heap him around with massy wealth,
　　High-throne him on the seat of power ;
Each generous joy he 'll use by stealth,
　　While want shall prey on every hour ;
Let glittering pomp allure his soul,
　　Or nobler fame his mind dilate ;
Through complicated plagues he 'll roll,
　　And dire vexations still create.
The first-born mortal upon earth,
　　When round him smiling nature play'd,
With discontent was void of mirth,
　　Though he o'er every creature sway'd.

He who contented spends his days—
　　Calm as the clear unruffled stream,
His life in gentle current strays,
　　Mild as the maiden's silver dream—
　　Be he born to till the field,
　　Or in war the sword to wield ;
　　If he o'er the midnight oil
　　Wastes his life in learned toil,
　　Studious to instruct mankind
　　Where true happiness to find ;
　　Or if o'er the lawless main
　　He roams in search of sordid gain ;
　　Or sorts with nobles in proud ease,
　　Or humble swains in cottages ;
　　Be he with content but blest—
　　He 's the happy man confest !

Listen, dear Strephon, to my song—
　　O herd not with ambitious slaves,
Nor join thou with the vulgar throng—
　　Their joys unstable as the waves.
Strephon, thrice blest with fruitful plains,
　　The lover of a sapient theme ;
Strephon, whose sweetly soothing strains

Flow gently as thy native stream—
O leave the ruthless scenes of war,
  Unfit art thou for rude alarms,
Beside thy gentle Delaware,
  Come, Strephon, seek more pleasing charms.
Here, while o'er the fertile valleys
  Thou shalt tuneful stray along,
I will make repeated sallies,
  To catch the transport of thy song ;
Then mutual joy shall swell our soul,
  Attendant to bright wisdom's strain,
While we shall quaff the friendly bowl,
  Far from the noisy and the vain.

ODE ON THE PROSPECT OF PEACE. 1761.

When elemental conflicts rage,
  And heaven is wrapp'd in tempests dire,
When storms with storms dread combat wage,
  And thunders roll etherial fire ;—
Returning zephyr's odorous race,
  And radiant Sol's all-cheering face,
The trembling mortals most desire.

When Eurus, charged with livid clouds,
  Scours o'er old ocean's wild domain,
And Boreas rends the vessel's shrouds,
  And o'er her swells the raging main ;
If lighter breezes should succeed,
  And Iris sweet, of varied hue,
Lift o'er the main her beamy head,
  What raptures fill the marine crew !
Thus, when Bellona (ruthless maid !)
  Her empire through the world has spread,
And death his flag has proud display'd
  O'er legions that in battle bled ;—
If peace, bedeck'd with olive robe,
  (Resplendent nymph, sweet guest of heaven)
Transfuse her balm around the globe,
  A theme of joy to man is given.
Then wake, O muse ! thy sweetest lays—
  Returning peace demands thy praise ;
And while the notes in varied cadence sound,
Eye thou the Theban swan that soars o'er heav'nly
        ground.

If thou from Albion's sea-girt shore,
   Advent'rous muse, wilt deign to rove,
Inclined remotest realms to explore
   And soothe the savage soul to love ;
Hither wave thy wandering pinion,
Here be fix'd thy last dominion.
   Warbling in 'Sylvania's grove,
Bright-eyed Euphrosyne! attend.
If genial peace can aught avail,
With all thy graceful charms descend,
   And o'er the youthful lyre prevail.
Bounteous peace with lavish hand,
   To every shore thy blessings strew,
O veil the blood-polluted land,
   And all thy grateful joys renew.
Thy blissful pregnant reign restore,
   And calm the breasts of angry kings;
Thy horn of Amalthean store
   Ope, and expand thy golden wings ;
Till trade secure her treasure beams,
   And science reassumes her shades ;
Till shepherds quaff untainted streams,
   And hinds enjoy their native glades;
   Till the glad muses strike the lyre,
   And virtuous social deeds inspire ;
Till the loud drum no more shall bid to arms prepare,
Nor brazen trumpets breathe the horrid din of war.

Auspicious power, whose salutary ray
   Form'd this new world, and rear'd her infant fame,
Extend anew thy mitigating sway,
   And quell the hero's battle-breathing flame.
Ye fragrant myrtles, ope your peaceful bowers,
   And charm the warrior with your pleasing scenes,
Shield him with woodbine's aromatic flowers,
   And for his sopha spread your velvet greens.
For him the flute mellifluous shall blow
In Lydian music, sounding soft and low,
And blooming beauty, with attractive art,
Shall sweetly melt the tumults of his heart ;
The nectar'd bowl, with rosy garlands twined,
Shall waft his sorrows to the vagrant wind,
While the victorious laurel of renown,
In verdant wreaths his manly brows shall crown.

Too long has war's terrific train,
   (The barbed spear and reeking blade)

Made nations rue their chieftains slain,
  And sanguined every muse's shade.
From distant Volga's rapid floods,
  To Canada's high towering woods,
Has the deadly cannon bray'd.
  From whence the effulgent god of day
Impearls Arabia's spicy fields,
  To where his setting lustres play—
The world to British valor yields.
  How has bold Clive, with martial toil,
O'er India borne his conquering lance,
  For Brunswick gain'd the distant soil,
  And dash'd th' aspiring hopes of France?
Let Goree, rich with flaming ore,
  Heroic Keppel's acts proclaim,
And Senegal's Eburnean shore
  Resound to future times his name.
O'er red Germania's hostile waste,
  Britannia's chiefs have conquering shone.
Brave Elliot's warlike fates have graced
  His monarch's high illustrious throne;
And Granby's deeds the muses claim
To swell the immortal trump of fame.
But victory enough has waved her glittering wand,
With British honors graced, o'er every prostrate land!

Witness, ye plains bedew'd with gore,
  So late ambitious Gallia's boast,
Where howling o'er the desert shore,
  Was seen the genius of the coast.
Thus, leaning on her shatter'd spear,
She wildly wail'd in deep despair,
  Her fallen towers and vanquish'd host—
  "As Niobe (when Juno's hate
Pursued to death her tender care)
  I moan my offspring's hopeless fate,
And vex with sighs the passing air.
Not with less grief my bosom heaves,
  Than did the breast of Hector's sire,
When slain were all his Dardan chiefs,
  And Ilium blazed with Grecian fire.
For lo! where heap'd with slaughter'd Gauls,
  Is Louisbourg a ruin'd pile!
Her bulwarks and stupendous walls
  Are whelm'd in dust and ashes vile.
Imperial Lawrence heaves with woe,

Of many a Gallic chief the grave,
And as his purple billows flow
    To hoary Neptune's coral cave,
Tells how my vaunting troops, o'erthrown,
Britannia's matchless prowess own;
Tells how Quebec, so late for martial might
                renown'd,
Her rocky ramparts crush'd, lies smoking on the
                ground.

" What force can Albion's warlike sons dismay,
    Dauntless who mingle in the embattled plain ?
What toils dishearten, or what dangers stay ?
    Not rocks, nor deserts, nor the boisterous main !
How torn my laurels, by her Wolfe's dread arm !
    O'er mountains huge, who chased my armed band,
Roused the fierce savage with dire war's alarm,
    And hurl'd his thunder o'er my carnaged land !
No more gay trophies shall emblaze my name,
Nor Gallia's realms re-echo with my fame.
Lost are those honors which my heroes gain'd,
With blood my temples and my domes are stain'd ;
But men directed by a heavenly hand,
'Tis vain, 'tis mad, 'tis impious to withstand."—
She spoke, and mounting from a lofty height,
Westward she wing'd her solitary flight.

Thus has Britannia's glory beam'd,
    Where'er bright Phœbus, from his car,
To earth his cheerful rays hath stream'd,
    Adown the crystal vault of air.
Enough o'er Britain's shining arms,
Hath victory display'd her charms,
    Amid the horrid pomp of war—
Descend then, Peace, angelic maid,
    And smooth Bellona's haggard brow;
Haste to diffuse thy healing aid,
    Where'er implored by scenes of woe.
Henceforth, whoe'er disturbs thy reign,
    Or stains the world with human gore,
Be they from earth (a gloomy train !)
    Banish'd to hell's profoundest shore ;
Where vengeance, on Avernus' lake,
    Rages, with furious Até bound ;
And black rebellion's fetters shake,
    And discord's hideous murmurs sound;

Where envy's noxious snakes entwine
  Her temples round, in gorgon mood,
And bellowing faction rolls supine
  Along the flame-becurled flood!—
Hence, then, to that accursed place,
Disturbers of the human race!
And with you bear ambition wild, and selfish pride,
With persecution foul, and terror by her side.

Thus driven from earth war's horrid train—
  O Peace, thou nymph divine, draw near!
Here let the muses fix their reign,
  And crown with fame each rolling year.
Source of joy and genuine pleasure,
Queen of quiet, queen of leisure,
  Haste thy votaries to cheer!
Cherish'd beneath thy hallow'd rule,
  Shall Pennsylvania's glory rise ;
Her sons, bred up in Virtue's school,
  Shall lift her honors to the skies—
A state thrice blest with lenient sway,
  Where liberty exalts the mind ;
Where plenty basks the live long day,
  And pours her treasures unconfined.
Hither, ye beauteous virgins tend,
  With Arts and Science by your side,
Whose skill the untutor'd morals mend,
  And to fair honor mankind guide ;
And with you bring the graces three,
  To fill the soul with glory's blaze ;
Whose charms give charms to poesy,
  And consecrate the immortal lays—
Such as, when mighty Pindar sung,
Through the Alphean village rung ;
Or such as, Meles, by thy lucid fountains flow'd,
When bold Mæonides with heavenly transports glow'd.

To such, may Delaware, majestic flood,
  Lend, from his flowery banks, a ravish'd ear ;
Such note as may delight the wise and good,
  Or saints celestial may endure to hear!
For if the muse can aught of time descry,
  Such notes shall sound thy crystal waves along,
Thy cities fair with glorious Athens vie,
  Nor pure Ilissus boast a nobler song.
On thy fair banks, a fane to Virtue's name
  Shall rise—and justice light her holy flame.

All hail then, Peace! restore the golden days,
And round the ball diffuse Britannia's praise ;
Stretch her wide empire to the world's last end,
Till kings remotest to her sceptre bend !

———

ODE TO MY INGENIOUS FRIEND, MR THOMAS GODFREY.

WHILE you, dear Tom, are forced to roam,
In search of fortune, far from home,
 O'er bogs, o'er seas and mountains ;
I too, debarr'd the soft retreat
Of shady groves, and murmur sweet
 Of silver prattling fountains,

Must mingle with the bustling throng,
And bear my load of cares along,
 Like any other sinner :
For, where 's the ecstasy in this,
To loiter in poetic bliss,
 And go without a dinner ?

Flaccus, we know, immortal bard !
With mighty kings and statesmen fared,
 And lived in cheerful plenty :
But now, in these degenerate days,
The slight reward of empty praise,
 Scarce one receives in twenty.

Well might the Roman swan, along
The pleasing Tiber pour his song,
 When bless'd with ease and quiet ;
Oft did he grace Mæcenas' board,
Who would for him throw by the lord,
 And in Falernian riot.

But, dearest Tom ! these days are past,
And we are in a climate cast
 Where few the muse can relish ;
Where all the doctrine now that 's told,
Is that a shining heap of gold
 Alone can man embellish.

Then since 't is thus, my honest friend,
If you be wise, my strain attend,

And counsel sage adhere to ;
With me, henceforward, join the crowd,
And like the rest proclaim aloud,
   That money is all virtue !

Then may we both, in time, retreat
To some fair villa, sweetly neat,
   To entertain the muses ;
And then life's noise and trouble leave—
Supremely blest, we 'll never grieve
   At what the world refuses.

HYMN TO MAY.

Now had the beam of Titan gay
Usher'd in the blissful May,
Scattering from his pearly bed,
Fresh dew on every mountain's head ;
Nature mild and debonair,
To thee, fair maid, yields up her care.
May, with gentle plastic hand,
Clothes in flowery robe the land ;
O'er the vales the cowslips spreads,
And eglantine beneath the shades ;
Violets blue befringe each fountain,
Woodbines lace each steepy mountain ;
Hyacinths their sweets diffuse,
And the rose its blush renews ;
With the rest of Flora's train,
Decking lowly dale or plain.

   Through creation's range, sweet May !
Nature's children own thy sway—
Whether in the crystal flood,
Amorous, sport the finny brood ;
Or the feather'd tribes declare,
That they breathe thy genial air,
While they warble in each grove
Sweetest notes of artless love ;
Or their wound the beasts proclaim,
Smitten with a fiercer flame ;
Or the passions higher rise,
Sparing none beneath the skies,
But swaying soft the human mind
With feelings of ecstatic kind—

Through wide creation's range, sweet May!
All nature's children own thy sway.

Oft will I, (e'er Phosphor's light
Quits the glimmering skirts of night)
Meet thee in the clover field,
Where thy beauties thou shalt yield
To my fancy, quick and warm,
Listening to the dawn's alarm,
Sounded loud by Chanticleer,
In peals that sharply pierce the ear.
And, as Sol his flaming car
Urges up the vaulted air,
Shunning quick the scorching ray,
I will to some covert stray,
Coolly bowers or latent dells,
Where light-footed silence dwells,
And whispers to my heaven-born dream,
Fair Schuylkill, by thy winding stream!
There I 'll devote full many an hour,
To the still-finger'd Morphean power,
And entertain my thirsty soul
With draughts from Fancy's fairy bowl ;
Or mount her orb of varied hue,
And scenes of heaven and earth review.

Nor in milder eve's decline,
As the sun forgets to shine,
And sloping down the ethereal plain,
Plunges in the western main,
Will I forbear due strain to pay
To the song-inspiring May ;
But as Hesper 'gins to move
Round the radiant court of Jove,
(Leading through the azure sky
All the starry progeny,
Emitting prone their silver light,
To re-illume the shades of night)
Then, the dewy lawn along,
I 'll carol forth my grateful song,
Viewing with transported eye
The blazing orbs that roll on high,
Beaming lustre, bright and clear,
O'er the glowing hemisphere.
Thus from the early blushing morn,
Till the dappled eve's return,
Will I, in free unlabor'd lay,
Sweetly sing the charming May!

VERSES FOR THE NEW YEAR, 1762.

STILL as emerges from the womb of time,
Each circling year, you claim our humble rhyme;
But where 's the muse, whose fiery numbers best
Shall rouse heroic ardor in each breast?
To wing the flight where conquest leads the way,
Transcends our song, and mocks the feeble lay.
Such themes sublime best suit a rapturous lyre,
And bards transported with poetic fire—
Yet when inspired with Britain's glorious fame,
What bosom glows not with the hallow'd flame?

When angry Gallia pour'd her hostile train,
Intent on plunder, o'er th' Atlantic main;
Strangers to arms, we knew no murderous art,
Nor crimson falchion, nor the poisonous dart,
From earliest youth, instructed to abhor
The deadly engines of destructive war;
The cannon's sound, as dire assail'd our ears,
As Jove's red thunder, when he shakes the spheres.

Yet to our aid when mighty Brunswick came,
It kindled in each breast the martial flame;
Undaunted as our warlike troops advance,
To walls, inglorious, shrink the sons of France;
Their cities storm'd, their chiefs in fetters bound,
And their proud ramparts levell'd with the ground.

O'er this new world, thus have Britannia's arms
Restored lost peace, and exiled war's alarms;
Again rich commerce crowns the merchant's toil,
And smiling Ceres paints the pregnant soil.
Thus the good shepherd, when he views from far
The deadly wolves beset his fleecy care,
Quick to their help his guardian crook he wields,
And soon the prowling throng is scatter'd o'er the fields.
Yet not to us is Britain's care confined,
Her fame is wafted to remotest Ind;
By justice call'd, her chiefs, with matchless swords,
Have humbled mighty Asia's proudest lords;
Far distant scenes her martial deeds proclaim,
And Pondicherry bows to Britain's name.

See the sad chance of all destructive war—
See Lally captived at the victor's car;

Lally, whose soul the maddening furies claim,
And cursed with longings for the voice of fame.
So when a tyger, flush'd with reeking blood,
Ramps o'er the plains, and tears the leafy wood,
A lion spies him from his secret cave,
Bursts from his stand, to seize the insulting slave;
Then hunts him, generous, from the neighboring fields,
And peace and safety to the forest yields.

O'er Europe too, great George's arms prevail,
And on its seas his fleets triumphant sail;
Witness Belleisle, around whose wave-worn shore
His navies ride, and his loud cannons roar.
Oh! could we boast the seeds of epic song,
Immortal Frederick should the verse prolong;
The chief should shine, inclosed with fields of dead,
And guardian angels hovering round his head.
There, in dread chains the barbarous Russ should bow,
And here, submissive, kneel the Hungarian foe;
There should be seen to bend, the sons of Gaul,
Here lesser troops, his enemies, should fall.
Thus firm a rock, begirt with raging waves,
Stands the fierce charge, though all the tempest raves;
Now round his summit dash the broken tides,
And vainly beat his adamantine sides!
But these we leave to deck the historic page,
And wake the wonder of a future age.

Now let our muse the Paphian trumpet blow,
Beauty's the theme, and melting strains shall flow.
See Neptune, mounting with his nereid train,
To smooth the surface of the azure main;
As conscious of his charge, he joys to please
The beauteous Charlotte, mistress of the seas!
The jovial sailors ply their shining oars,
And now they reach fair Albion's white-cliff shores;
With warbling flutes, and hautboy's pleasing sound,
They spread sweet music's silver notes around.
On Cydnus' stream, so once array'd was seen
Fair Cleopatra, Egypt's beauteous queen.

But here we fix, rejoiced to see you bless'd,
And Britain's glory in each clime confess'd!

ELEGY TO THE MEMORY OF MR THOMAS GODFREY.

O DEATH! thou victor of the human frame!
The soul's poor fabric trembles at thy name!
How long shall man be urged to dread thy sway,
For those whom thou untimely tak'st away?
Life's blooming spring just opens to our eyes,
And strikes the senses with a sweet surprise,
When thy fierce arm uplifts the fatal blow
That hurls us breathless to the earth below.

Sudden, as darts the lightning through the sky,
Around the globe thy various weapons fly.
Here war's red engines heap the field with slain,
And pallid sickness there extends thy reign;
Here the soft virgin weeps her lover dead,
There maiden beauty sinks the graceful head;
Here infants grieve their parents are no more,
There reverend sires their children's deaths deplore;
Here the sad friend—O! save the sacred name,
Yields half his soul to thy relentless claim;
O pardon, pardon the descending tear!
Friendship commands, and not the muses, here.
O say, thou much loved, dear departed shade,
To what celestial region hast thou stray'd?
Where is that vein of thought, that noble fire,
Which fed thy soul, and bade the world admire?
That manly strife with fortune to be just,
That love of praise? an honorable thirst!
The soul, alas! has fled to endless day,
And left its house a mouldering mass of clay.

There, where no fears invade, nor ills molest,
Thy soul shall dwell immortal with the blest;
In that bright realm, where dearest friends no more
Shall from each other's throbbing breasts be tore,
Where all those glorious spirits sit enshrined,
The just, the good, the virtuous of mankind.
There shall fair angels in a radiant ring,
And the great Son of heaven's eternal King,
Proclaim thee welcome to the blissful skies,
And wipe the tears for ever from thine eyes.

How did we hope—alas! the hope how vain!
To hear thy future more enripen'd strain;
When fancy's fire with judgment had combined
To guide each effort of the enraptured mind.

Yet are those youthful glowing lays of thine
The emanations of a soul divine ;
Who heard thee sing, but felt sweet music's dart
In thrilling transports pierce his captive heart ?
Whether soft melting airs attuned thy song,
Or pleased to pour the thundering verse along,
Still nobly great, true offspring of the Nine,
Alas ! how blasted in thy glorious prime !
So when first ope the eyelids of the morn,
A radiant purple does the heavens adorn,
Fresh smiling glory streaks the skies around,
And gaily silvers each enamel'd mound,
Till some black storm o'erclouds the ether fair,
And all its beauties vanish into air.

Stranger, whoe'er thou art, by fortune's hand
Toss'd on the baleful Carolinian strand,
Oh ! if thou seest perchance the poet's grave,
The sacred spot with tears of sorrow lave ;
Oh ! shade it, shade it with ne'er fading bays.
Hallow'd 's the place where gentle Godfrey lays.
(So may no sudden dart from death's dread bow,
Far from the friends thou lov'st, e'er lay thee low,)
There may the weeping morn its tribute bring,
And angels shield it with their golden wing,
Till the last trump shall burst the womb of night,
And the purged atoms to their soul unite !

JOHN OSBORN.

JOHN OSBORN was born in the year 1713, at Sandwich,
Massachusetts. His father, an educated Scotchman, was
then a schoolmaster, but was afterward settled in the ministry
at Eastham, where he devoted as much time to the education
of his son as could be spared from his agricultural occupations, and his labors for the welfare of his little church. The
destitute state of the section of the country in which he
lived, rendered manual employment absolutely necessary for
the support of every individual, and the worthy divine used
alternately to ply his pen in the study, and his spade in the
field. His counsel, we are told, was valued quite as highly in

secular, as in spiritual affairs,—for he taught his parishioners the art of cutting and preparing peat for fuel; and under his instruction they were enabled to supply a necessity that had often been severely felt, in a region where a tree of sponta- neous growth might be sought for with as little success as in the desert of Zahara. His pupil, the poet, meanwhile, was busy one week with his Latin and Greek, and the next in the clam and cod fishery; revelling today among the trea- sures of classic lore, and storing up the wealth of mighty minds, and digging tomorrow in a sand-bank for the shelly prey that was to be his sustenance during the ensuing winter. In his aquatic excursions, he imbibed those ideas which he has thrown into his celebrated whaling song,—once on the tongue of every Cape Cod sailor. At the age of nineteen, young Osborn entered Harvard College, where he was no- ticed as a lively and eccentric genius. When his collegiate term was expired, he repaired to his father's house, at East- ham, and while yet undecided what profession to select, devo- ted a portion of his time to the study of divinity, though the levity of his disposition was such as to preclude all hopes of his prospering in a vocation that would require much gravity and self-denial. After two years spent in turning over the folios in his father's library, he submitted himself to the exami- nation of the neighboring clergy, assembled in solemn con- clave, and read a sermon of his composition before them. They praised the ingenuity of his arguments, and the ele- gance of his composition, but ventured to surmise that his sentiments, as developed in his discourse, were not *exactly* orthodox.* From their scruples on this head, they refused to grant him a recommendation as a suitable candidate for the ministry. Thus debarred from the pulpit, he turned his thoughts in another direction, and began a course of reading on medicine and surgery. He was afterwards invited to accept

* Osborn's father had been dismissed from his church, for having embraced the doctrines of Arminius. Perhaps the young man's mind was too much distorted by the heresies of his sire, to entitle him to the approbation of the examining committee.

a tutorship at Harvard College, but he declined the honor, on account of his intended matrimonial alliance, which would disqualify him for the station. He married a Miss Doane of Chatham, and removed to Middletown, Connecticut, where he commenced practice as a physician. In a letter to his sister, dated March 1753, he says, " Our family at present are in usual plight, except myself. I am confined chiefly to the house, am weak, lame, and uneasy, and never expect to be hearty and strong again. I have lingered along, almost two years, a life not worth having ; and how much longer it will last, I cannot tell. We have six children ; the eldest fourteen years old last November—the youngest two years, last January—the eldest a daughter, the next a son, and so on to the end of the chapter."—He died soon after writing the above, at the age of forty.

Mr Osborn possessed that cheerfulness of disposition, and those frank and agreeable manners which palliate many aberrations, and in some degree reconcile us to a volatile temperament. His morals were unimpeached, and his scholastic acquisitions respectable.

His poetic style is rather polished, and his diction quite correct, considering the time and circumstances in which he wrote. It is believed that he never gave but two poems to the world, but his popularity among the people of a soil that has never been remarkably fruitful in poets, entitles him to a place in our collection.

A WHALING SONG.

When spring returns with western gales,
  And gentle breezes sweep
The ruffling seas, we spread our sails
  To plough the wat'ry deep.

For killing northern whales prepared,
  Our nimble boats on board,
With craft and rum (our chief regard)
  And good provisions stored,

Cape Cod, our dearest, native land,
  We leave astern, and lose
Its sinking cliffs and lessening sands,
  While Zephyr gently blows.

Bold, hardy men, with blooming age,
  Our sandy shores produce ;
With monstrous fish they dare engage,
  And dangerous callings choose.

Now towards the early dawning east
  We speed our course away,
With eager minds, and joyful hearts,
  To meet the rising day.

Then as we turn our wondering eyes,
  We view one constant show ;
Above, around, the circling skies,
  The rolling seas below.

When eastward, clear of Newfoundland,
  We stem the frozen pole.
We see the icy islands stand,
  The northern billows roll.

As to the north we make our way,
  Surprising scenes we find ;
We lengthen out the tedious day,
  And leave the night behind.

Now see the northern regions, where
  Eternal winter reigns ;
One day and night fills up the year,
  And endless cold maintains.

We view the monsters of the deep,
  Great whales in numerous swarms ;
And creatures there, that play and leap,
  Of strange, unusual forms.

When in our station we are placed,
  And whales around us play,
We launch our boats into the main,
  And swiftly chase our prey.

In haste we ply our nimble oars,
    For an assault design'd ;
The sea beneath us foams and roars,
    And leaves a wake behind.

A mighty whale we rush upon,
    And in our irons throw :
She sinks her monstrous body down
    Among the waves below.

And when she rises out again,
    We soon renew the fight ;
Thrust our sharp lances in amain,
    And all her rage excite.

Enraged, she makes a mighty bound ;
    Thick foams the whiten'd sea ;
The waves in circles rise around,
    And widening roll away.

She thrashes with her tail around,
    And blows her redd'ning breath ;
She breaks the air, a deaf'ning sound,
    While ocean groans beneath.

From numerous wounds, with crimson flood
    She stains the frothy seas,
And gasps, and blows her latest blood,
    While quivering life decays.

With joyful hearts we see her die,
    And on the surface lay ;
While all with eager haste apply,
    To save our deathful prey.

———

ELEGIAC EPISTLE,

ADDRESSED TO ONE OF HIS SISTERS ON THE DEATH OF ANOTHER.

DEAR sister, see the smiling spring
    In all its beauties here ;
The groves a thousand pleasures bring,
    A thousand grateful scenes appear.
With tender leaves the trees are crown'd,
And scatter'd blossoms all around,

Of various dyes
Salute your eyes,
And cover o'er the speckled ground.

Now thickets shade the glassy fountains;
Trees overhang the purling streams;
Whisp'ring breezes brush the mountains,
Grots are fill'd with balmy steams.

But, sister, all the sweets that grace
The spring and blooming nature's face;
The chirping birds,
Nor lowing herds;
The woody hills,
Nor murm'ring rills;
The sylvan shades,
Nor flowery meads,
To me their former joys dispense,
Though all their pleasures court my sense.
But melancholy damps my mind,
I lonely walk the field,
With inward sorrow fill'd,
And sigh to every breathing wind.

I mourn our tender sister's death,
In various plaintive sounds;
While hills above, and vales beneath,
The faltering notes rebound.

Perhaps when in the pains of death,
She gasp'd her latest breath,
You saw our pensive friends around,
With tears bedew the ground.
Our loving father stand,
And press her trembling hand,
And gently cry, "My child, adieu!
We all must follow you."

Some tender friend did then perhaps arise,
And close her dying eyes:
Her stiffen'd body, cold and pale,
Was then convey'd within the gloomy vale
Of death's unhallow'd shade.

Weak mortals, Oh! how hard our fate;
How sure our death,—how short our date,

How quickly sets our day!
We all are doom'd to lay our heads
Beneath the earth in mournful shades,
  To hungry worms a prey.

But, loving sister, let's prepare
    With virtue's steady feet,
    That we may boldly meet
The *rider of the pale horse* void of fear.

But why should you and I for ever mourn
Our dear relation's death? She's gone—
    We 've wept enough to prove
    Our grief and tender love.
    Let joy succeed, and smiles appear,
    And let us wipe off every tear.
    Not always the cold winter lasts,
    With snow and storms, and northern blasts.
    The raging seas with fury tost,
    Not always break and roar;
    Sometimes their native anger 's lost.
And smooth hush'd waves glide softly to the shore.

MATHER BYLES.

The Rev. Mather Byles was the son of an English gentleman, and descended on the maternal side from the Rev.
Richard Mather of Dorchester, and the Rev. John Cotton of
Boston. He was born in Boston on the 15th day of March
1706 old style. He was educated at Harvard University, and
received a Bachelor's degree in 1725. He made choice of
theology for his profession, and was ordained over the church
in Hollis street, Boston, in 1732. Possessed of sound talents,
aided by a wide course of general reading, besides his theological studies, he soon became very favorably known as a
preacher, and a man of literature, not only at home, but in
Europe. He was a person of wit and sociality, and the agree-
ableness of his conversation gained him a ready welcome

among society in Boston; notwithstanding the rigorism and
staidness of ancient puritanism had maintained itself in a
great measure among the members of the clergy up to that
period. The whim and facetiousness of Byles, his turn for
raillery, sarcasm, and repartee, displayed on almost every occasion, and often with a reckless unconcern as to the consequences, might have seemed unnatural adjuncts of the priestly
character, to a people accustomed to an almost overstrained
sobriety of demeanor in persons of that rank. A rhyming
catalogue of the principal church dignitaries of Boston and
the neighborhood, which we have met with in manuscript,
thus introduces him.—

> There's punning Byles, provokes our smiles,
>   A man of stately parts.
> He visits folks to crack his jokes,
>   Which never mend their hearts.
>
> With strutting gait, and wig so great,
>   He walks along the streets;
> And throws out wit, or what's like it,
>   To every one he meets.

It does not appear, however, that the colloquial vagaries of
the facetious parson at all diminished his reputation as a sound
divine, or in the least injured the gravity or effect of his pulpit
discourses.

Byles wrote verses and essays in the journals, and on incidental occasions, for his own amusement and the gratification
of his friends, but never attempted any work of magnitude,
or exercised his pen on any subject with a view to literary
reputation. He became known, however, to many persons of
eminence and talents in England, who corresponded with him
and sent him their works. Pope, Landsdowne, and Watts,
are mentioned among these. His professional attainments
were sufficiently prized by the king's college at Aberdeen, to
obtain for him the degree of Doctor of Divinity from that
seminary.

The breaking out of the revolutionary troubles, involved
him in difficulties with the civil authority, which resulted in

separating him from his parish, and finally debarring him from
the exercise of his profession. From the beginning of the
contest, he appears to have inclined to the side of the British.
He remained in Boston during the occupation of that town
by the enemy, and associated familiarly with the British officers,
a course of conduct which drew upon him the dislike of the
people, among whom party animosities were sufficiently violent
to sunder the most intimate ties. Byles was denounced as a
person disaffected to the cause of the revolution, and dismissed from his parish. In June 1777 he underwent a public trial
before a special court, when charges of hostility to the country were exhibited against him. He was pronounced guilty,
and sentenced to be imprisoned on board a guard ship, and in
forty days to be sent with his family to England. The board
of war took his case into consideration, and remitted most of
the sentence. He was confined to his own house, and kept
under a guard for some time. After being set at liberty, he
continued to lead a private life, incapacitated by the imputation
he lay under, of being a tory, for the exercise of any pastoral
charge. In 1783, he was attacked by a paralytic disorder,
under which he labored some years. He died July 5th, 1788,
in his eightysecond year.

Byles's reputation among the people of his own town and
neighborhood, has been mostly owing to his performances, as
a wit. His pleasantries were current in every social circle,
and obtained him such a notoriety in that character, as to beget
a practice of ascribing every bon mot in vogue to the Doctor,
in the manner that jokes are fathered upon Joe Miller. Such
of his poems as we have been able to collect (for the few he
has written are very scarce) show him to have been possessed of
a good degree of poetical talent. Evidences of a rich fancy
are perceptible in them, and the versification is polished and
spirited.

THE CONFLAGRATION.

In some calm midnight, when no whispering breeze
Waves the tall woods, or curls the undimpled seas,

Lull'd on their oozy beds, the rivers seem
Softly to murmur in a pleasing dream ;
The shaded fields confess a still repose,
And on each hand the dewy mountains drowse:
Meantime the moon, fair empress of the night !
In solemn silence sheds her silver light,
While twinkling stars their glimmering beauties shew,
And wink perpetual o'er the heavenly blue;
Sleep, nodding, consecrates the deep serene,
And spreads her brooding wings o'er all the dusky scene ;
Through the fine ether moves no single breath ;
But all is hushed as in the arms of death.
  At once, great God ! thy dire command is given,
That the last tempest shake the frame of heaven.
Straight thickening clouds in gloomy volumes rise,
Gather on heaps, and blacken in the skies;
Sublime through heaven redoubling thunders roll ;
And gleaming lightnings flash from pole to pole.
Old ocean with presaging horror roars,
And rousing earthquakes rumble round the shores;
Ten thousand terrors o'er the globe are hurl'd,
And general dread alarms a guilty world.
  But Oh ! what glory breaks the scattering glooms ?
Lo ! down the opening skies, he comes ! he comes!
The Judge descending flames along the air;
And shouting myriads pour around his car :
Each ravish'd seraph labors in his praise,
And saints, alternate, catch the immortal lays :
Here in melodious strains blest voices sing,
Here warbling tubes, and here the vocal string,
Here from sweet trumpets silver accents rise,
And the shrill clangor echoes round the skies.
  And now, O earth ! thy final doom attend,
In awful silence meet thy fiery end.
Lo ! rising radiant from his burning throne,
The Godhead, thundering, calls the ruins on.
" Curst earth ! polluted with the prophets' blood,
Thou, the vile murderer of the Son of God,
Full ripe for vengeance, vengeance be thy due,
Perish in flames, refine, and rise anew ! "
Thus as he speaks, all nature owns the God,
Quiver the plains, the lofty mountains nod.
The hollow winding caverns echo round,
And earth, and sea, and air, and heaven resound.
  Now rattling on, tremendous thunder rolls,
And loudly crashing, shakes the distant poles ;

O'er the thick clouds amazing lightnings glare,
Flames flash at flames, and vibrate through the air
Roaring volcanoes murmur for their prey,
And from their mouth curls the black smoke away ;
Deep groans the earth, at its approaching doom,
While in slow pomp the mighty burnings come.
As when dark clouds rise slowly from the main,
Then, in swift sluices, deluge all the plain,
Descending headlong down the mountain's sides,
A thousand torrents roll their foamy tides,
The rushing rivers rapid roar around,
And all the shores return the dashing sound :
Thus awful, slow, the fiery deluge lowers,
Thus rushes down, and thus resounding roars.
  But O ! what sounds are able to convey
The wild confusions of the dreadful day !
Eternal mountains totter on their base,
And strong convulsions work the valley's face ;
Fierce hurricanes on sounding pinions soar,
Rush o'er the land, on the toss'd billows roar,
And dreadful in resistless eddies driven,
Shake all the crystal battlements of heaven.
See the wild winds, big blustering in the air,
Drive through the forests, down the mountains tear,
Sweep o'er the valleys in their rapid course,
And nature bends beneath the impetuous force.
Storms rush at storms, at tempests tempests roar,
Dash waves on waves, and thunder to the shore.
Columns of smoke on heavy wings ascend,
And dancing sparkles fly before the wind.
Devouring flames, wide-waving, roar aloud,
And melted mountains flow a fiery flood :
Then, all at once, immense the fires arise,
A bright destruction wraps the crackling skies ;
While all the elements to melt conspire,
And the world blazes in the final fire.
  Yet shall ye, flames, the wasting globe refine,
And bid the skies with purer splendor shine,
The earth, which the prolific fires consume,
To beauty burns, and withers into bloom ;
Improving in the fertile flame it lies,
Fades into form, and into vigor dies :
Fresh-dawning glories blush amidst the blaze,
And nature all renews her flowery face.
With endless charms the everlasting year
Rolls round the seasons in a full career ;

Spring, ever-blooming, bids the fields rejoice,
And warbling birds try their melodious voice ;
Where'er she treads, lilies unbidden blow,
Quick tulips rise, and sudden roses glow :
Her pencil paints a thousand beauteous scenes,
Where blossoms bud amid immortal greens ;
Each stream, in mazes, murmurs as it flows,
And floating forests gently bend their boughs.
Thou, autumn, too, sitt'st in the fragrant shade,
While the ripe fruits blush all around thy head :
And lavish nature, with luxuriant hands,
All the soft months, in gay confusion blends.
   The holy nation here transported roves
Beneath the spreading honors of the groves,
And pleased, attend, descending down the hills,
The murmuring music of the running rills.
Anthems divine by every harp are played,
And the soft music warbles through the shade.
   Hither, my lyre, thy soft assistance bring,
And let sweet accents leap from string to string :
Join the bright chorus of the future skies,
While all around loud Hallelujah's rise,
And to the tuneful lays the echoing vault replies.
This blessed hope, my ravish'd mind inspires,
And through my bosom flash the sacred fires :
No more my heart its growing joy contains,
But driving transports rush along my veins ;
I feel a paradise within my breast,
And seem already of a heaven possess'd.

THE GOD OF TEMPEST AND EARTHQUAKE.

THY dreadful power, Almighty God,
   Thy works to speak conspire ;
This earth declares thy fame abroad,
   With water, air, and fire.

At thy command, in glaring streaks,
   The ruddy lightning flies,
Loud thunder the creation shakes,
   And rapid tempests rise.

Now gathering glooms obscure the day,
   And shed a solemn night ;
And now the heavenly engines play,
   And shoot devouring light.

The attending sea thy will performs,
　Waves tumble to the shore,
And toss, and foam amidst the storms,
　And dash, and rage, and roar.

The earth, and all her trembling hills,
　Thy marching footsteps own ;
A shuddering fear her entrails fills,
　Her hideous caverns groan.

My God ! when terrors thickest throng,
　Through all the mighty space,
And rattling thunders roar along,
　And bloody lightnings blaze :

When wild confusion wrecks the air,
　And tempests rend the skies,
Whilst blended ruin, clouds and fire
　In harsh disorder rise :

Amid the hurricane I 'll stand
　And strike a tuneful song ;
My harp all trembling in my hand,
　And all inspired my tongue.

I 'll shout aloud, " Ye thunders ! roll,
　And shake the sullen sky ;
Your sounding voice from pole to pole
　In angry murmurs try.

" Thou sun ! retire, refuse thy light,
　And let thy beams decay ;
Ye lightnings, flash along the night,
　And dart a dreadful day.

" Let the earth totter on her base,
　Clouds heaven's wide arch deform ;
Blow, all ye winds, from every place,
　And breathe the final storm.

" O Jesus, haste the glorious day,
　When thou shalt come in flame,
And burn the earth, and waste the sea,
　And break all nature's frame.

" Come quickly, blessed hope, appear,
　Bid thy swift chariot fly :
Let angels warn thy coming near,
　And snatch me to the sky.

" Around thy wheels, in the glad throng,
  I'd bear a joyful part ;
All Hallelujah on my tongue,
  All rapture in my heart."

ELEGY,

ADDRESSED TO GOVERNOR BELCHER ON THE DEATH OF HIS LADY.

BELCHER, once more permit the muse you loved,
By honor, and by sacred friendship moved,
Waked by your woe, her numbers to prolong,
And pay her tribute in a funeral song.

From you, great heaven with undisputed voice,
Has snatch'd the partner of your youthful joys.
Her beauties, ere slow hectic fires consumed,
Her eyes shone cheerful, and her roses bloom'd :
Long lingering sickness broke the lovely form,
Shock after shock, and storm succeeding storm,
Till death, relentless, seized the wasting clay,
Stopp'd the faint voice, and catch'd the soul away.

No more in converse sprightly she appears,
With nice decorum, and obliging airs :
Ye poor, no more expecting round her stand,
Where soft compassion stretch'd her bounteous hand
Her house, her happy skill no more shall boast ;
" Be all things plentiful, but nothing lost."
Cold to the tomb, see the pale corpse convey'd,
Wrapt up in silence, and the dismal shade.

Ah ! what avail the sable velvet spread,
And golden ornaments amidst the dead ?
No beam smiles there, no eye can there discern
The vulgar coffin from the marble urn :
The costly honors, preaching, seem to say,
" Magnificence must mingle with the clay."

Learn here, ye fair, the frailty of your face,
Ravish'd by death, or nature's slow decays :
Ye great, must so resign your transient power,
Heroes of dust, and monarchs of an hour !
So must each pleasing air, each gentle fire,
And all that's soft, and all that's sweet expire.

But you, O Belcher, mourn the absent fair,
Feel the keen pang, and drop the tender tear :
The God approves that nature do her part,
A panting bosom, and a bleeding heart.
Ye baser arts of flattery, away !
The virtuous muse shall moralize her lay.
To you, O favorite man, the power supreme,
Gives wealth, and titles, and extent of fame ;
Joys from beneath, and blessings from above ;
Thy monarch's plaudit ; and thy people's love :
The same high power, unbounded, and alone,
Resumes his gifts, and puts your mourning on.
His edict issues, and his vassal, death,
Requires your consort's,—or your flying breath.
Still be your glory at his feet to bend,
Kiss thou the Son, and own his sovereign hand ;
For his high honors all thy powers exert,
The gifts of nature, and the charms of art ;
So, over death, the conquest shall be given,
Your name shall live on earth, your soul in heaven.

Meantime my name to thine allied shall stand,
Still our warm friendship, mutual flames extend ;
The muse shall so survive from age to age,
And Belcher's name protect his Byles's page.

———

HYMN WRITTEN DURING A VOYAGE.

GREAT God thy works our wonder raise ;
    To thee our swelling notes belong ;
While skies and winds, and rocks and seas,
    Around shall echo to our song.

Thy power produced this mighty frame,
    Aloud to thee the tempests roar,
Or softer breezes tune thy name
    Gently along the shelly shore.

Round thee the scaly nation roves,
    Thy opening hands their joys bestow,
Through all the blushing coral groves,
    These silent gay retreats below.

See the broad sun forsake the skies,
    Glow on the waves and downward glide,
Anon heaven opens all its eyes,
    And star-beams tremble o'er the tide.

Each various scene, or day or night,
    Lord! points to thee our nourish'd soul;
Thy glories fix our whole delight;
    So the touch'd needle courts the pole.

JOSEPH GREEN.

JOSEPH GREEN was born in Boston, A. D. 1706. He was educated at Harvard College, and received a degree in 1726. On leaving college, he entered into mercantile pursuits in Boston, to which he continued to devote himself for the greater part of his life. He possessed a lively temperament with a copious vein of humor and satire, and became the master spirit of a club of wits who entertained themselves with turning to ridicule the political freaks of the government, and the follies in vogue among the society of Boston. Green wrote satires, epigrams, and parodies upon every matter which offered scope for his powers of sarcasm and drollery. His wit was without malignity or peevishness, and never degenerated into abuse. He made no attempt at any work of magnitude, but contented himself with short and occasional sallies. Governor Belcher and the most noted public characters offered a theme for his pleasantry, which he vented in many a political diatribe, for Green, though not in the early part of his life placed in any public station, was a sagacious and interested observer of political events. Retiring and unambitious in his personal character, he was a firm opposer of arbitrary power.

Green's lampooning contest with Mather Byles afforded much entertainment to the people of Boston. Governor Belcher being about to sail to the eastern part of the province, upon a visit to the Indian tribes, invited Byles to accompany him, which he declined. But the Governor, who valued the pleasure of his company upon such an expedition too highly to forego it upon a slight consideration, made use of a stratagem to obtain his object. He embarked on board the Scarborough man of war, on Saturday. The ship dropped down the harbor and anchored near the castle. On Sunday Belcher prevailed with the chaplain of the castle to exchange pulpits with Byles, and in the afternoon invited the doctor on board to drink tea. While they were at table the ship weighed anchor and put to sea, and Byles upon making the discovery, found himself too far from land to think of returning. The governor had provided everything necessary for him, and he was easily reconciled to the voyage. The next Sunday, on making arrangements for divine service, it was found there was no hymn-book on board, and to supply the defect, Byles wrote the hymn which we have given among his pieces.

This incident was too broad a mark for Green's ridicule to escape notice. He made it the subject of a jeu d'esprit, in which he burlesqued the matter in a truly farcical strain. Byles did not think it beneath him to parody Green's burlesque, and turned the ridicule against his rival wit with great spirit and vehemence. In this "keen encounter" Green excelled his opponent in the weapons of light agreeable raillery. Byles's retort is too splenetic and coarse to be fully relished as a piece of humorous sarcasm.

Green passed the most of a long life in Boston, and acquired a good fortune by his business. In 1774, the British parliament took away the charter of Massachusetts, and one of the new political regulations thereby introduced was the appointment of the Counsellors of the Province by the royal authority instead of popular election. General Gage, the governor, nominated Green a counsellor under the new administration, but he refused the office. What were his political principles at this time we are not informed. His age and infirmities caused him to view the approaching convulsion in public affairs with dread, and he sought an asylum in England. He left this country in 1775, and died in 1780, at the age of seventyfour.

He wrote the "Entertainment for a Winter's Evening," a ridicule upon the free-masons: "The Land Bank," a personal

satire : " A True and Exact Account of the celebration of St.
John the Baptist," and the pieces which follow in this work.
As no collection of his poems has ever been printed, there
are many, probably, which have not come to our knowledge.
Two of those named above, exist only in manuscript, and
abound too much in personal allusions to interest the reader
at the present day.

In David's Psalms an oversight
   Byles found one morning at his tea,
Alas ! that he should never write
   A proper psalm to sing at sea.

Thus ruminating on his seat,
   Ambitious thoughts at length prevail'd.
The bard determined to complete
   The part wherein the prophet fail'd.

He sat awhile and stroked his muse,*
   Then taking up his tuneful pen,
Wrote a few stanzas for the use
   Of his seafaring brethren.

The task perform'd, the bard content,
   Well chosen was each flowing word ;
On a short voyage himself he went,
   To hear it read and sung on board.

Most serious Christians do aver,
   (Their credit sure we may rely on,)
In former times that after prayer,
   They used to sing a song of Zion.

Our modern parson having pray'd,
   Unless loud fame our faith beguiles,
Sat down, took out his book and said,
   " Let's sing a psalm of Mather Byles."

* Byles's favorite cat, so named by his friends.

At first, when he began to read,
　　Their heads the assembly downward hung.
But he with boldness did proceed,
　　And thus he read, and thus they sung.

THE PSALM.

With vast amazement we survey
　　The wonders of the deep,
Where mackerel swim, and porpoise play,
　　And crabs and lobsters creep.

Fish of all kinds inhabit here,
　　And throng the dark abode.
Here haddock, hake, and flounders are,
　　And eels, and perch, and cod,

From raging winds and tempests free,
　　So smoothly as we pass,
The shining surface seems to be
　　A piece of Bristol glass.

But when the winds and tempests rise,
　　And foaming billows swell,
The vessel mounts above the skies,
　　And lower sinks than hell.

Our heads the tottering motion feel,
　　And quickly we become
Giddy as new-dropp'd calves, and reel
　　Like Indians drunk with rum.

What praises then are due that we .
　　Thus far have safely got,
A.narescoggin tribe to see,
　　And tribe of Penobscot.

———

A MOURNFUL LAMENTATION FOR THE DEATH OF MR OLD TENOR.*

A DOLEFUL tale prepare to hear,
　　As ever yet was told :
The like, perhaps, ne'er reach'd the ear
　　Of either young or old.

* A New England currency.

'T is of the sad and woeful death
  Of one of mighty fame,
Who lately hath resign'd his breath;
  Old Tenor was his name.

In vain ten thousands intercede,
  To keep him from the grave;
In vain, his many good works plead;
  Alas! they cannot save.
The powers decree, and die he must,
  It is the common lot,
But his good deeds, when he 's in dust,
  Shall never be forgot.

He made our wives and daughters fine,
  And pleased everybody:
He gave the rich their costly wine,
  The poor their flip and toddy.
The laborer he set to work;
  In ease maintain'd the great:
He found us mutton, beef, and pork,
  And everything we eat.

To fruitful fields, by swift degrees,
  He turn'd our desert land:
Where once nought stood but rocks and trees,
  Now spacious cities stand.
He built us houses, strong and high,
  Of wood, and brick, and stone;
The furniture he did supply;
  But now, alas! he 's gone.

The merchants too, those topping folks,
  To him owe all their riches;
Their ruffles, lace, and scarlet cloaks,
  And eke their velvet breeches.
He launch'd their ships into the main,
  To visit distant shores;
And brought them back, full fraught with gain,
  Which much increased their stores.

Led on by him our soldiers bold,
  Against the foe advance;
And took, in spite of wet and cold,
  Strong Cape Breton from France.

Who from that fort the French did drive,
    Shall he so soon be slain?
While they, alas! remain alive,
    Who gave it back again.

From house to house, and place to place,
    In paper doublet clad,
He pass'd, and where he show'd his face,
    He made the heart full glad.
But cruel death, that spareth none,
    Hath robbed us of him too;
Who through the land so long hath gone,
    No longer now must go.

In senate he, like Cæsar, fell,
    Pierced through with many a wound,
He sunk, ah, doleful tale to tell!
    The members sitting round:
And ever since that fatal day,
    Oh! had it never been,
Closely confined at home he lay,
    And scarce was ever seen,

Until the last of March, when he
    Submitted unto fate;
In anno regis twentythree,
    Ætatis fortyeight.
For ever gloomy be that day,
    When he gave up the ghost;
For by his death, oh! who can say,
    What hath New England lost?

Then, good Old Tenor, fare thee well,
    Since thou art dead and gone;
We mourn thy fate, e'en while we tell
    The good things thou hast done.
Since the bright beams of yonder sun,
    Did on New England shine,
In all the land, there ne'er was known
    A death so mourn'd as thine.

Of every rank are many seen,
    Thy downfal to deplore;
For 't is well known that thou hast been
    A friend to rich and poor.

We 'll o'er thee raise a silver tomb,
  Long may that tomb remain,
To bless our eyes for years to come,
  But wishes, ah ! are vain.

And so God bless our noble state,
  And save us all from harm,
And grant us food enough to eat,
  And clothes to keep us warm.
Send us a lasting peace, and keep
  The times from growing worse ;
And let us all in safety sleep,
  With silver in our purse.

———

LAW bears the name, but money has the power.
The cause is bad whene'er the client 's poor.
Those strict-lived men, who seem above our world,
Are oft too modest to resist our gold ;
So judgment like our other wares is sold.
And the grave knight, that nods upon the laws,
Waked by a fee, hems and approves the cause.

———

EXTEMPORE ON THE FOURTH LATIN SCHOOL BEING TAKEN DOWN TO MAKE ROOM FOR ENLARGING THE CHAPEL CHURCH.

A FIG for your learning, I tell you the town,
To make the church larger must pull the school down.
" Unluckily spoken," replied Master Birch,
" Then learning, I fear, stops the growth of the church."

———

WILLIAM LIVINGSTON.

WILLIAM LIVINGSTON, governor of New Jersey, was descended from a Scotch family which settled in New York. He was born in New York about the year 1723, and studied at Yale college, where he received a degree in 1741. He afterwards became a distinguished lawyer, and upon his re-

moval to New Jersey, was chosen a member of the first
Congress in 1774, having previously signalized himself by
his public writings against the encroachments of Britain.   In
1776 the inhabitants of New Jersey deposed their colonial
governor, and formed a new constitution, under which Livingston was chosen first chief magistrate, and continued to be
re-elected to the office till his death.   He was a delegate in
1787 to the grand convention which formed the constitution
of the United States.   He died at his seat near Elizabethtown
July 25th, 1790, aged 67.

Governor Livingston, besides his political writings, was
the author of various essays upon miscellaneous topics: a
poem entitled " Philosophic Solitude, or the choice of a Rural
Life," published in 1747, when he was about 24 years of age ;
and a few short poetical effusions of a subsequent date.

———

PHILOSOPHIC SOLITUDE.

LET ardent heroes seek renown in arms,
Pant after fame, and rush to war's alarms ;
To shining palaces let fools resort,
And dunces cringe to be esteem'd at court :
Mine be the pleasure of a rural life,
From noise remote, and ignorant of strife ;
Far from the painted belle, and white-gloved beau,
The lawless masquerade, and midnight show,
From ladies, lap-dogs, courtiers, garters, stars,
Fops, fiddlers, tyrants, emperors, and czars.

Full in the centre of some shady grove,
By nature form'd for solitude and love ;
On banks array'd with ever blooming flowers,
Near beauteous landscapes, or by roseate bowers ;
My neat, but simple mansion I would raise,
Unlike the sumptuous domes of modern days ;
Devoid of pomp, with rural plainness form'd,
With savage game, and glossy shells adorn'd.

No costly furniture should grace my hall ;
But curling vines ascend against the wall,
Whose pliant branches should luxuriant twine,
While purple clusters swell'd with future wine :

To slake my thirst a liquid lapse distil
From craggy rocks, and spread a limpid rill.
Along my mansion spiry firs should grow,
And gloomy yews extend the shady row;
The cedars flourish, and the poplars rise
Sublimely tall, and shoot into the skies;
Among the leaves refreshing zephyrs play,
And crowding trees exclude the noon-tide ray;
Whereon the birds their downy nests should form,
Securely shelter'd from the battering storm;
And to melodious notes their choir apply,
Soon as Aurora blush'd along the sky;
While all along the enchanting music rings,
And every vocal grove responsive sings.

Me to sequester'd scenes, ye muses, guide,
Where nature wantons in her virgin pride;
To mossy banks edged round with opening flowers,
Elysian fields, and amaranthine bowers,
T' ambrosial founts, and sleep-inspiring rills,
To herbaged vales, gay lawns, and sunny hills.

Welcome, ye shades! all hail, ye vernal blooms!
Ye bowery thickets, and prophetic glooms!
Ye forests, hail! ye solitary woods!
Love-whispering groves, and silver-streaming floods!
Ye meads, that aromatic sweets exhale!
Ye birds, and all ye sylvan beauties, hail!
Oh how I long with you to spend my days,
Invoke the muse, and try the rural lays!

No trumpets there with martial clangor sound,
No prostrate heroes strew the crimson'd ground;
No groves of lances glitter in the air,
Nor thundering drums provoke the sanguine war:
But white-robed peace, and universal love,
Smile in the field, and brighten every grove.
There all the beauties of the circling year,
In native ornamental pride appear.
Gay, rosy-bosom'd spring, and April showers
Wake from the womb of earth the rising flowers:
In deeper verdure summer clothes the plain,
And autumn bends beneath the golden grain;
The trees weep amber, and the whispering gales
Breeze o'er the lawn, or murmur through the vales.
The flowery tribes in gay confusion bloom,
Profuse of sweets, and fragrant with perfume.

On blossoms blossoms, fruits on fruits arise,
And varied prospects glad the wand'ring eyes.
In these fair seats I 'd pass the joyous day,
Where meadows flourish and where fields look gay ;
From bliss to bliss with endless pleasure rove,
Seek crystal streams, or haunt the vernal grove,
Woods, fountains, lakes, the fertile fields, or shades,
Aerial mountains, or subjacent glades.

* * * * *

When rising Phœbus ushers in the morn,
And golden beams the impurpled skies adorn ;
Waked by the gentle murmur of the floods ;
Or the soft music of the waving woods,
Rising from sleep with the melodious choir,
To solemn sounds I 'd tune the hallow'd lyre.
Thy name, O God ! should tremble on my tongue,
Till every grove proved vocal to my song :
(Delightful task ! with dawning light to sing
Triumphant hymns to heaven's eternal King.)
Some courteous angel should my breast inspire,
Attune my lips, and guide the warbled wire,
While sportive echoes catch the sacred sound,
Swell every note, and bear the music round ;
While mazy streams meandering to the main,
Hang in suspense to hear the heavenly strain,
And hush'd to silence all the feather'd throng,
Attentive listen to the tuneful song.

Father of Light ! exhaustless source of good !
Supreme, eternal, self-existent God !
Before the beamy sun dispensed a ray,
Flamed in the azure vault, and gave the day ;
Before the glimmering moon with borrow'd light
Shone queen amid the silver host of night,
High in the heavens, thou reign'dst superior Lord,
By suppliant angels worshipp'd and adored.
With the celestial choir then let me join
In cheerful praises to the power divine.
To sing thy praise, do thou, O God ! inspire
A mortal breast with more than mortal fire.
In dreadful majesty thou sitt'st enthroned,
With light encircled, and with glory crown'd :
Through all infinitude extends thy reign,
For thee, nor heaven, nor heaven of heavens contain;
But though thy throne is fix'd above the sky
Thy omnipresence fills immensity.

Saints robed in white, to thee their anthems bring,
And radiant martyrs hallelujahs sing :
Heaven's universal host their voices raise
In one eternal chorus to thy praise ;
And round thy awful throne with one accord
Sing, holy, holy, holy is the Lord.
At thy creative voice, from ancient night
Sprang smiling beauty, and yon worlds of light :
Thou spak'st—the planetary chorus rolled,
And all the expanse was starr'd with beamy gold ;
"Let there be light," said God,—light instant shone,
And from the orient burst the golden sun ;
Heaven's gazing hierarchies with glad surprise
Saw the first morn invest the recent skies,
And straight the exulting troops thy throne surround
With thousand thousand harps of heavenly sound ;
Thrones, powers, dominions, (ever-shining trains !)
Shouted thy praises in triumphant strains :
" Great are thy works," they sing, and all around
" Great are thy works," the echoing heavens resound.
The effulgent sun, insufferably bright,
Is but a beam of thy o'erflowing light ;
The tempest is thy breath : the thunder hurl'd,
Tremendous roars thy vengeance o'er the world ;
Thou bow'st the heavens ; the smoking mountains nod,
Rocks fall to dust, and nature owns her God ;
Pale tyrants shrink, the atheist stands aghast,
And impious kings in horror breathe their last.
To this great God, alternately I 'd pay
The evening anthem, and the morning lay.

For sovereign gold I never would repine,
Nor wish the glittering dust of monarchs mine.
What though high columns heave into the skies,
Gay ceilings shine, and vaulted arches rise,
Though fretted gold the sculptured roof adorn,
The rubbies redden, and the jaspers burn !
Or what, alas ! avails the gay attire
To wretched man, who breathes but to expire !
Oft on the vilest riches are bestow'd,
To show their meanness in the sight of God.
High from a dunghill, see a Dives rise,
And Titan-like insult the avenging skies :
The crowd in adulation calls him lord,
By thousands courted, flatter'd, and adored :
In riot plunged, and drunk with earthly joys,
No higher thought his grovelling soul employs ;

The poor he scourges with an iron rod,
And from his bosom banishes his God.
But oft in height of wealth and beauty's bloom,
Deluded man is fated to the tomb !
For, lo, he sickens, swift his color flies,
And rising mists obscure his swimming eyes :
Around his bed his weeping friends bemoan,
Extort the unwilling tear, and wish him gone ;
His sorrowing heir augments the tender shower,
Deplores his death—yet hails the dying hour.
Ah, bitter comfort ! sad relief to die !
Though sunk in down, beneath a canopy !
His eyes no more shall see the cheerful light,
Weigh'd down by death in everlasting night :
And now the great, the rich, the proud, the gay,
Lies breathless, cold—unanimated clay !
He that just now was flatter'd by the crowd
With high applause, and acclamation loud ;
That steel'd his bosom to the orphan's cries,
And drew down torrents from the widow's eyes ;
Whom, like a God, the rabble did adore—
Regard him now—and lo ! he is no more.

My eyes no dazzling vestments should behold,
With gems instarr'd, and stiff with woven gold ;
But the tall ram his downy fleece afford,
To clothe in modest garb his frugal lord.
Thus the great father of mankind was dress'd,
When shaggy hides composed his flowing vest ;
Doom'd to the cumbrous load for his offence,
When clothes supplied the want of innocence ;
But now his sons (forgetful whence they came,)
Glitter in gems, and glory in their shame.

Oft would I wander through the dewy field,
Where clustering roses balmy fragrance yield ;
Or in lone grots for contemplation made,
Converse with angels, and the mighty dead :
For all around unnumber'd spirits fly,
Waft on the breeze, or walk the liquid sky,
Inspire the poet with repeated dreams,
Who gives his hallow'd muse to sacred themes,
Protect the just, serene their gloomy hours,
Becalm their slumbers, and refresh their powers.
Methinks I see the immortal beings fly,
And swiftly shoot athwart the streaming sky :

Hark! a melodious voice I seem to hear,
And heavenly sounds invade my listening ear.
" Be not afraid of us, innoxious band,
Thy cell surrounding by divine command;
Erewhile like thee we led our lives below,
(Sad lives of pain, of misery, and woe!)
Long by affliction's boisterous tempests tost,
We reach'd at length the ever-blissful coast:
Now in the embowering groves and lawns above,
We taste the raptures of immortal love,
Attune the golden harp in roseate bowers,
Or bind our temples with unfading flowers.
Oft on kind errands bent, we cut the air
To guard the righteous, heaven's peculiar care!
Avert impending harms, their minds compose,
Inspire gay dreams, and prompt their soft repose.
When from thy tongue divine hosannas roll,
And sacred raptures swell thy rising soul,
To heaven we bear thy prayers like rich perfumes,
Where, by the throne, the golden censer fumes.
And when with age thy head is silver'd o'er,
And cold in death, thy bosom beats no more,
Thy soul exulting shall desert its clay,
And mount triumphant to eternal day."

BENJAMIN CHURCH.

Dr Benjamin Church was born in Boston, in 1739, and
studied at Harvard College, where he was graduated in 1754.
He chose the profession of medicine, which he exercised for
many years in his native town, and rose to great eminence as
a physician. He appears to have cultivated literary studies
with considerable attention, and was the most distinguished
among his contemporaries in Boston as a poet. A great number of prose writings also from his pen, upon subjects relating
to politics, philology and the like, as well as of a lighter description, attest the versatility of his talent, and the extent of
his acquirements. These casual performances are extant for
the most part only in newspapers, and other periodical works,

and we know of but one of his effusions either in prose or verse, which has occupied a more imposing or durable shape than that of a pamphlet.

Although the general estimation in which his abilities were held, and his own decided taste for letters, might be supposed to have inclined him to strive for eminence as a literary man, yet it does not appear that his labors were directed to this point with any very powerful endeavor. His poetical effusions were indebted for their origin on most occasions, to occurrences of local and temporary interest, and never appear to have been put forth in anticipation of the reward of public applause. They were all, we believe, published anonymously.

Dr Church had a high reputation as a poet and political writer previous to the revolution, but his treachery in deserting the American cause has contributed to throw a shade over his talents, and few have since thought of him as a man of science and letters, but only as the recreant to the cause of freedom and his country. His writings, therefore, have fallen into neglect, although his most spirited performance was executed before his political backslidings, and breathes a purely patriotic feeling.

At the commencement of the revolutionary troubles, Church was a staunch whig. His poem upon the Times, as just observed, is perfectly in accordance with the popular feeling at that period. His oration upon the massacre of the fifth of March, is distinguished for its patriotic sentiments, as well as elegance of style. His political essays, no less than his conversation, were in the same strain, and this unreserved devotion to the cause of his country, with his known talents, made him one of the leading politicians of the popular party. He was chosen a member of the Massachusetts Legislature, and on the beginning of hostilities, received the appointment of physician general of the American army. Although he was known to have kept up a strict intimacy with some of the British officers before this period, yet the reasons he assigned for this, by stating it to be done with a view of obtaining their secrets, removed all suspicion of his insincerity, and at the time of the battle of Lexington, he was one of the committee of safety. But with all this seeming attachment to the American cause, Church was partial to the British interest, and while openly professing the strongest zeal for the popular measures, he was laboring in secret against them. The patriotic songs current among the people were parodied by him in favor of the British. The political essays which he wrote on the popular side received answers from the same pen in a tory print.* In 1775, shortly after the battle of Lexington, he visited the enemy in Boston upon pretence of an errand after medicines for the use of the army; according to the account he gave of his journey after his return, he was made prisoner by the British on entering the town, and carried before General Gage, where he underwent an examination, but it came to be known afterwards, that he visited the British general's house voluntarily, and held a long conference with him.

In October of the same year, his dealings with the enemy were discovered. A letter was intercepted, written in cipher by him to a British officer in Boston, and containing statements of the force of the American army, the designs of the government, the prevailing opinions of the people, conjectures on their ability to resist the British arms, and other varieties of the like intelligence. Church was arrested by order of Washington, and confined till the meeting of the General Court, of which he was then a member. On his examination he did not deny the letter, but endeavored to defend himself by asserting that he gave the information contained therein to the enemy, with a view to impress them with a high opinion of the strength of the Americans, in order that the meditated attack might be delayed till the continental army was stronger.

* The *Censor.* The author of a tract in the fifth volume of the Massachusetts Historical Collections, has affirmed that there is no evidence that Church was a writer in this paper, or that he abandoned the whigs before the breaking out of hostilities. Circumstances, however, have been related to us by a person now living in Boston, who was familiar with the events of that period, which remove all doubts as to the fact stated above.

The mode by which this intelligence was transmitted, he had adopted as a means of obtaining knowledge of the British, and he had on several former occasions, he averred, succeeded in thus getting possession of much important information which he had improved to the advantage of the Americans.

This explanation did not avail him, any more than the ardent and unreserved professions of attachment to the cause of the country, which he did not spare during his defence. The House of Representatives declared him guilty of holding a traitorous correspondence with the enemy, and deprived him of his seat. A court of inquiry at Cambridge, consisting of the officers of the army, passed the same judgment upon him, and referred the question of his punishment to Congress. A resolve of that body sentenced him to close confinement, and he was imprisoned some months in a jail in Connecticut, but his health suffering in this state, he was allowed occasional enlargement, and finally set at liberty. He went to Newport in Rhode Island, where he embarked in 1776 for the West Indies. The vessel in which he sailed was never heard from.

Some writers, struck with the bold strain in which he protested his innocence during his trial, and the ingenuity he displayed in coloring the circumstances which had brought the charges upon him, have been inclined to doubt any treacherous intention on his part, and represent him as having been sacrificed to the blind and headlong jealousy of party, which swept away, with inconsiderate rashness, every object touched by the slightest taint of suspicion. But the facts brought against him at the time, regarded in connexion with what has been before alluded to of his writing secretly on the tory side in the early part of the contest, seem to afford no room for doubt in the matter. Church, we may reasonably suppose, was well affected to the country, and was ready to lend his influence and exertions to secure its ultimate welfare; so far his professions of patriotism and honesty were sincere. But he was led to believe that this object would be most effectually secured by making the sway of the mother country predominant, an error of the understanding which could have been pardoned him, had he not followed it up by playing a scheme of double dealing, at variance with every principle of political honesty. To have been a partizan of the British crown, would have subjected him only to the fate of being pitied for his misguided zeal, and classed among hundreds of others, who gave equally small proof of sagacity in political affairs without any abandonment of moral principle. But the duplicity of openly espousing an interest which he was practising every art underhand to defeat, brings him under a much severer censure than we feel called upon to bestow on the ordinary disaffected to the cause of independence.

The poetical works of Dr Church which were the most widely known during his lifetime, are The Times, The Choice, An Elegy on the death of Dr Mayhew, An Elegy on the death of George Whitefield, An Address to a Provincial Bashaw, and a portion of the volume entitled *Pietas et Gratulatio Collegii Cantabrigiensis apud Novanglos*. This last was a poetical offering to George II, upon his accession to the throne, and consists of above thirty different pieces in Latin, Greek, and English, furnished chiefly by the officers of Harvard University. The part written by Church, may claim a just preeminence among them. The Times is a satirical piece, written just after the passing of the Stamp Act. The objects of the writer's denunciation are in some parts not very clearly manifest to the modern reader, but the general scope of the performance is sufficiently intelligible to those familiar with the history of the period, while the polish and spirit of the verse recommend it very favorably to our notice.

THE TIMES.

Pollio, be kind! nor chide an early crime,
Spawn of chagrin, and labor'd waste of time;
This heart misguides me with a bent so strong,
It mocks restraint, and boldly errs in song:
Thus crimes indulged, such vigorous growth obtain,
Your friendly caution frowns rebuke in vain.

'T is not great Churchill's ghost that claims your ear
For even ghosts of wit are strangers here;
The patriot-soul to other climes removed,
Well-pleased enjoys that liberty he loved;
No pang resents for W—— to exile driven,
Exults that worth and Pratt are dear to heaven:
Young sure it is not, from whose honey'd lays
Streams a rank surfeit of redundant praise;
For guilt like his what genius shall atone?
Curse the foul verse that daubs a Stuart's throne.

    Cursed lack of genius, or thou soon should'st know,
This humble cot conceals a tyrant's foe;
By nature artless, unimproved by pains,
No favor courts me, and no fear restrains,
Wild as the soil, and as the heavens severe,
All rudely rough, and wretchedly sincere;
Whose frowning stars have thrown me God knows where,
A wild exotic neighbor to the bear;
One glebe supports us, brethren cubs we run,
Shoot into form, as fostered by the sun;
No tutoring hand the tender sapling train'd
Through walks of science, nor his growth sustain'd;
Such fruit he yields, luxuriant wildings bear,
Coarse as the earth, and unconfined as air:
No muse I court, an alien to the Nine,
Thou chaste instructress, Nature! thou art mine;
Come, blessed parent, mistress, muse, and guide,
With thee permit me wander, side by side;
Smit with thy charms, my earliest joy I trace,
Fondly enamor'd of thy angel face;
Succeeding labors smother not the flame,
Still, still the dear attachment lives the same.

    No idle task the earliest muse began,
But mark'd the morals, e'er she praised the man;
To struggling worth supplied no feeble aid,
And wove the honest wreath for virtue's head,
Uncourtly grave, or through the lessen'd page
Shed wisdom's lore, and humanized the age;
Pour'd wholesome treasures from her magic tongue,
Instructed, ruled, corrected, blest, by song:
How changed! how lost! in these degenerate days,
She stuns me with the clamor of her praise:
Is there a villain eminent in state,
Without one gleam of merit?—she 'll create;

Is there a scoundrel, has that scoundrel gold?
There the full tide of panegyric 's roll'd;
From venal quills shall stream the sugar'd shower,
And bronze the wretched lordling—if in power:
Stamp me that blockhead, which (kind heaven be blest!)
My Maker form'd my temper to detest,
If sacred numbers I again desert,
The native bias of an honest heart,
Basely to truckle to a wretch in rule,
Or spread a feast for gods, to cram a fool.
Not for a monarch would I forge a lie,
To nestle in the sunshine of his eye.
The paths of error if in youth I trod,
Dress'd a gay idol in the garb of God,
The pageant shrinks, I weep my folly past,
Heaven frown me dead, but there I 've sinn'd my last.
George, scarce one lustrum numbers out its days,
Since every tongue was busy in thy praise;
(O make it nameless in the tale of time,
Nor consecrate to ages such a crime ;
We loved him, love him still, by heavens do more,
But make us British subjects, we 'll adore.)
Successful war has added wide domain,
And crowded oceans scarce his fleets sustain.
United Gaul and Spain his easy prey,
And but compact to give their realms away;
Where'er he bids, consenting Britons fly,
For George they conquer, or for George they die ;
Bless the glad hour, the glorious strife approve,
That sounds his glory, and proclaims their love ;
Ah, sad reverse ! with doubling sighs I speak,
A flood of sorrow coursing down my cheek,
The salient heart for George forgets to bound,
Dark disaffection sheds her gloom around ;
Fair liberty, our soul's most darling prize,
A bleeding victim flits before our eyes:
Was it for this our great forefathers rode
O'er a vast ocean to this bleak abode!
When liberty was into contest brought,
And loss of life was but a second thought ;
By pious violence rejected thence,
To try the utmost stretch of providence ;
The deep, unconscious of the furrowing keel,
Essay'd the tempest to rebuke their zeal;
The tawny natives and inclement sky
Put on their terrors, and command to fly ;

They mock at danger ; what can those appal ?
To whom fair liberty is all in all.
See the new world their purchase, blest domain,
Where lordly tyrants never forged the chain ;
The prize of valor, and the gift of prayer,
Hear this and redden, each degenerate heir !
Is it for you their honor to betray,
And give the harvest of their blood away ?
Look back with reverence, awed to just esteem,
Preserve the blessings handed down from them ;
If not, look forwards, look with deep despair,
And dread the curses of your beggar'd heir :
What bosom beats not, when such themes excite ?
Be men, be gods, be stubborn in the right.

Where am I hurried ? Pollio, I forbear,
Again I 'm calm, and claim thy sober ear ;
To independence bend the filial knee,
And kiss her sister sage economy.
Economy, you frown ! " O hide our shame !
'T is vile profusion's ministerial name,
To pinch the farmer groaning at the press,
Commission leeches to adopt the peace ;
That peace obtain'd Scotch armies to augment,
And sink the nation's credit two per cent ;
With barren Scottish bards the lists to load,
Both place and pension partially bestowed ;
Nay more, the cave of famine to translate
Within the purlieus of the royal gate ;
While brats from northern hills, full, battening lie,
Their meagre southern masters pining by."
Peace, peace, my Pollio ! sluice thy sorrows here ;
Thy country's ghost now points thee to its bier.
Of foreign wrongs, and unfelt woes no more,
While dogs cry havock on thy natal shore ;
Yon funeral torch that dimly gilds my cell,
Comes fraught with mischiefs, terrible to tell ;
It dawns in sables——too officious ray !
Yet, yet compassionately roll away ;
All, all is o'er, but anguish, slavery, fear,
The chains already clanking in my ear ;
O death ! though awful, but prevent this blow,
No more thou 'rt censured for the human foe ;
O'er life's last ebbs, thy dregs of sorrow fling,
Point all my pangs, and stab with every sting ;
I 'll bless the alternative, if not a slave,
And scorn the wretch who trembles at the grave.

Art thou persuaded, for a moment cool,
That nature made thee slave, and mark'd thee fool,
That what we won by hardy war, was given,
That non-resistance is secure of heaven ;
That persecution in our infant state,
Was nursing kind compassion in the great ;
That emigration was not to secure
Our liberties, but to enslave the more ;
That charters, privileges, patents, powers,
Were ours till now, and now no longer ours ;
To claim exemption by the charter seal,
Will rashly violate the common weal ;
Juries are nuisances, and traffic worse,
And to be blind, sagacity of course ;
The stamp and land tax are as blessings meant,
And opposition is our free consent ;
That where we are not, we most surely are,
That wrong is right, black white, and foul is fair ;
That Mansfield's honest, and that Pitt's a knave,
That Pratt's a villain, and that Wilkes's a slave ;
That godlike Temple is not greatly good,
Nor Bute a rigid jacobite by blood ;
That sordid Grenville lately is become
The patron of our liberties at home,
(For whom, now hear me, gods ! be hell inflamed,
And murderers of their country doubly d——d)
Now stretch thy pliant faith, adopt this creed,
And be a J-r-d Ing-rs-l indeed ;
If thou art wretched, crawling in the dust,
Condemn'd, despised, and herded with the just :
Frown, honest Satire ! menace what you will,
Rogues rise luxuriant, and defeat you still ;
Fatigued with numbers, and oppress'd with gall,
One general curse must overwhelm them all :
But O ye vilest vile, detested few !
Eager, intent, and potent to undo ;
Come out, ye parricides ! here take your stand,
Your solemn condemnation is at hand ;
Behold your crimes, and tremblingly await
The grumbling thunder of your country's hate ;
Accursed as ye are ! how durst ye bring
An injured people to distrust their king ?
Accursed as ye are, how could ye dare,
To lisp delusion in your monarch's ear ?
How do I laugh, when such vain coxcombs lower,
Some grave pretence of dread, from lawless power ;
To hear a scribbling fry, beneath my hate,
Adopt the fraud, and sanctify deceit ;

With mean importance, point regardless stings,
To aid injustice, menace mighty things;
Nay to such height of insolence they 're flown,
The knaves crave shelter underneath a throne;
A throne all-gracious, such is George's praise,
Nor shall oppression blast his sacred bays.

Witness, ye fathers! whose protracted time,
Fruitful of story, chronicles the clime;
These howling deserts, hospitably tame,
Erst snatch'd ye, martyrs, from the hungry flame;
'T was heaven's own cause, beneath whose sheltering power,
Ye grew the wonder of the present hour;
With anxious ear we 've drank your piteous tale,
Where woes unnumber'd long and loud prevail;
Here savage demons, sporting with your pains,
There boding mischief in a Stuart reigns;
Mark the glad era, when prevailing foes,
The state's fell harpies, doubling woes on woes,
Had wing'd destruction—vengeance slept no more,
But flung the tyrant from the British shore:
Learn hence, ye minions! reverence to the law,
Salvation died not with the great Nassau.
And shall such sons, from such distinguished sires,
Nurtured to hardships, heirs of all their sires,
Shall they, O pang of heart! thus tamely bear,
Who stalk erect, and toss their heads in air?
Let beasts of burthen meanly woo the chain,
We talk of masters with a proud disdain.
" Prythee forbear, rash youth! conceal thy fears,
A modest silence best becomes thy years;
Submit, be prudent—in some future hour,
You 'll feel the iron-gripe of ruthless power : "
Truce, spawn of phlegm! thy frozen heart conceal,
Benumb'd, unerring, and unapt to feel;
No deed of glory can that soul entice,
Involved in adamantine walls of ice;
Within that bosom is a nook so warm,
That vice or virtue kindles to a storm?
Could nature ever lure thee into sin?
Or bursts of passion thaw the frost within?
Thou happy cynic! still thy senses lull,
Profoundly cautious, and supinely dull;
And should some hero start his rash career,
Eccentric to thy lazy, drowsy sphere;
Be wondrous wise, thy frigid temper bless,
That never wrought thee to a bold excess:

Call truth a libel, treason, honest zeal,
So strange is virtue, and so few can feel ;
Call Churchill blockhead, Freedom, madness, rage,
Call injured Wilkes a monster of the age ;
To make me blest, unite this lay with those,
And then, then kindly rate yourselves my foes.

Fop, witling, favorite, stampman, tyrant, tool,
Or all those mighty names in one, thou fool !
Let mean ambition, sordid lust of pride,
League thee, vile pander ! to a tyrant's side.
Sport with thy country's groans, and be the first
To stab the bosom which a traitor nursed ;
Rifle the womb, and on those bowels prey,
To plague mankind, that spawn'd thee into day ;
Be eminent, thy little soul exert,
And call forth all the rancor of thy heart :
But should the eye of merit on thee lower,
(Though lowly crush'd beneath the wheel of power,)
Thou art my pity, monster ! I forgive,
And beg one only curse, that thou mayst live.

Where lies our remedy, in humble prayer ?
Our lordly butchers have forgot to hear ;
'T is rank rebellion, rashness to complain,
And all submission tighter tugs the chain :'
Go ask your heart, your honest heart regard,
And manumission is your sure reward ;
Would'st thou be blest, thy sovereign pride lay by,
To tyrant custom give the hardy lie ;
Yon shag will warm thee, in thy country fleece
Sleeps independence lined with balmy peace ;
Would'st thou be blest? be diligent ! be wise !
And make a chaste sufficiency suffice :
Ye lovely fair ! whom heaven's blest charms array,
The proud Sultanas of some future day ;
Sweet as ye are, complete in every grace,
That spreads angelic softness o'er the face ;
Go ply the loom—there lies the happy art,
By new avenues to attack the heart ;
With labors of your own, but deck those charms,
We 'll rush with transport to your blissful arms.
Amid this wreck——from all aspersions clear,
Nay blush not, Peter, honest truths to hear ;
Base adulation never stain'd my lay,
But modest merit must be brought to day ;

What though thy great desert mounts far above
The mean expression of thy country's love ;
In praise like thine the rustic muse will soar,
Then damn'd to endless silence sing no more.
" With great contempt of power, alone to stand,
Thy life, and spotless honors in thy hand ;
To wage unequal wars—and dare the worst,
And if thy country perish, perish first ;
With pious vigilance the state to guard,
And eminent in virtue, shun reward ;
No force of avarice warps thy steady heart,
To meanness, falsehood, or dishonest art ;
A tyrant's mandate, thy supreme disdain,
Our last, best bulwark in a Scottish reign."
These are the honors we to fame consign,
Nay blush not, Peter—these are surely thine.

To close—dread sovereign at whose sacred seat,
Justice and mercy, spotless maidens meet ;
George ! parent ! king ! our guardian, glory, pride,
And thou, fair regent ! blooming by his side !
Thy offspring pleads a parent's fostering care,
Reject not, frown not, but in mercy spare ;
Besprent with dust, the lowly suppliant lies,
A helpless, guilty, injured sacrifice :
If e'er our infant efforts could delight,
Or growing worth found favor in thy sight,
If warm affection due returns may plead,
Or faith unshaken ever intercede ;
With modest boldness we thy smiles demand,
Nor wish salvation from another hand ;
Depress'd, not helpless, while a Brunswick reigns,
Whose righteous sceptre, no injustice stains.

LINES ON THE ACCESSION OF GEORGE II.

WHERE thick embowering shades, and clustering trees,
Form soft recess, and shed poetic ease ;
Inarching boughs embrown the silent way,
Fan breezy cool, and half exclude the day :
A moss-clad rock here spread its bulky base,
Where the lithe ivy winds its close embrace ;
Beneath its slope—grey parent of the wood,
A mouldering oak, grotesque and naked, stood ;

From its chafed root, a gurgling rivulet strays,
And through the forest worms its sparkling maze:
Here his sluiced eyes, the pensive Pollio led,
And lo his anguish utter'd, " George is dead."

The swift wing'd breeze, excursive, wafts the sound,
The cloud-topp'd forest nodded to the ground;
The bellying clouds, with sable skirts advance,
And a dun horror shrouds the blue expanse;
Slow swells the blast, the transient gusts arise,
And grumbling thunders roll along the skies;
The storm collects, in dusky clouds array'd,
And brooding tempest frowns the deepest shade.
Involved in glooms, reclined upon the oak,
In faltering accents, Pollio sobb'd and spoke.

" Lower on, ye sables, shed a tenfold gloom!
George is deceased, and earth is but his tomb;
The heavens were deaf, when Albion pour'd her cries:
Ah fruitless anguish! ah relentless skies!
War on, ye elements, ye tempests sweep
The heaving bosom of the hoary deep;
Ye trembling forests hide your faded green,
May darksome horrors wrap the saddening scene;
Ye verdant walks a sicklier face shall wear,
No flowers, to breathe soft incense through the air;
Their savory banquets shall the flocks refrain,
Nor crop the velvet of the pasturing plain;
No fostering showers from hence refresh the lawn,
No pearly blessings cheer the parching dawn;
The widow'd groves lost foliage shall deplore,
And balmy zephyrs gather sweets no more:
Thy George, O Albion! Heaven declines to spare,
Bestow'd too long to prevalence of prayer;
Albion! thy parent dies!—as bless'd a mind,
As heaven could furnish to exalt mankind;
Religion, mercy, peace, his steps attend,
And numerous virtues all their lustres lend;
His guide was truth, benevolence his road,
His life, one effort of redundant good;
No sword of violence protects a crime,
Stains the clear page, or dims the golden time;
No vice illustrious stalk'd behind the king,
No shelter'd folly fledged beneath his wing;
No ravenous grasp, no lawless lust of power,
Sullies his life, or stains a single hour;

So kindly just, the parent monarch sighs,
And greatly pities, while the laws chastise:
When Albion's safety would, how swift to save ?
(A deed for gods) he pitied and forgave :
Large as his heart, the blessings he design'd ;
His godlike bounty deluged all mankind :
Here he restrain'd the Indian's thirst of gore,
And bid the murderous tomax drink no more ;
Crush'd faithless Gallia, with her savage train,
Who foster factions, to disturb his reign ;
Stretch'd through these haunts the blessings of his sway,
And pour'd on pagan darkness, beamy day ;
'T is from his hand this tide of plenty flows,
Thence learning buds, the infant of repose ;
'T is he, whose wisdom crown'd the happiest reign,
When patriots only, equal honors gain ;
Where all distinction was to vice denied,
And patriot virtue spread its influence wide :
No sons but virtue's, shone among the great,
Nor less than Pitt, the pilot of the state.
Nor civil virtues were his only claim,
His early prowess won a martial fame :
The victor wreath in dreadful fields he twined,
And valor throned him monarch of mankind ;
Germania's realms his matchless courage boast,
And clustering glories in his name are lost.
Long was the blessing spared to Albion's cries,
Loved by his realms, and ripening for the skies ;
In his full orb of majesty complete,
He quits his earthly for a heavenly seat :
Death, and death only, to such kings imparts
A kingdom equal to their great deserts."

   Here the full tide of grief his song suppress'd,
And sighs and tears, instructive, spoke the rest.
Amid the instant wreck, the laboring sigh,
What glorious form commands the weeping eye ?
Pierced with a kingdom's woes, she leads the tear,
The infections drop our lids are proud to wear ;
'T is Albion's guardian ! see, her glossy plume
Darts a keen radiance through the withering gloom !
Not Cynthia's beams with such effulgence flow,
When her full disk gives all its broad below :
High o'er the silver-skirted main she rose,
And o'er a world in anguish smiled repose :
She waves her hand, and points to Britain's throne,
" George still survives, O Albion ! all thy own :

From deep despair, redemption he commands,
And guides the sceptre with instructed hands."

New flush'd with life, the blooming forests rise,
Shine with fresh green, and climb to taller skies ;
The warbling wantons through the dusky grove,
Sweetly conspiring pour a waste of love ;
Perfumes from every breathing flower exhale,
And balmy incense loads the fragrant gale ;
Their savory banquet lowing herds regain,
Ranged on the velvet of the pasturing plain :
On the bless'd theme the bard indulged him long,
Then thus his raptures he attuned to song :
" Thrice bless'd Britannia ! heaven's peculiar care !
Oft rescued in the moment of despair ;
Pangs but arrive e'er blessings swift pursue,
We scarcely tremble, e'er we triumph too.
How scourged ! how lost ! let Albion's groans inform ;
This western empire scarce survived the storm :
Our ague fears, and enervating woe,
Edged the keen vengeance of the insulting foe ;
But—snatch'd from fate, when to its stroke resign'd—
Who dares despair ? for heaven and George were kind.
Then whilst with Albion we our joys contest,
And pour our raptures in the monarch's breast ;
The distant blessing honor and approve,
With secret avarice dwell upon his love ;
To listening skies our laboring breasts unload,
And wrest new blessings from his conscious God ;
He dies.   At this our bursting bosoms rave,
And pain'd remembrance envied George his grave.

" What kindly God presides ? the tumults cease,
This hour all tempest, and the next all peace ;
We smile, bless'd heaven ! a George upon the throne,
Another George, O Albion ! all thy own ;
From deep despair a nation to redeem,
And check our sorrows in their midway stream :
He sways the sceptre, takes the glorious charge ;
Unbounded goodness now shall lord at large :
His virtues blazon'd wide as fame can wing,
And proud Britannia glories in her king.
Blush, grandeur ! blush, in all thy purple pride,
True greatness is to goodness close allied :
The worthy heart will ever claim esteem ;
O prince, thy virtue is thy brightest gem :

Food for applause to distant realms dispense,
Beyond the reach of poor magnificence ;
Blessings are tongued, and ever on the wing—
A wondering world 's a circle for a king.
Joy to the realms where slavery was design'd,
A Brunswick reigns, the guardian of mankind.
While gay-eyed conquest rears his banners high,
A flaming meteor in the Gallic sky.
He bids his bolted thunders cease their roar ;
And offers peace to Gallia's faithless shore.
Bless'd prince ! whose unexampled goodness charms,
Thy people's blessings be thy brightest arms :
The base of empire is the king's desert,
And merit is the monarch of the heart.
Nor hostile worlds shall favorite George dethrone ;
Each Briton's breast 's a barrier to his own.
May one clear calm attend thee to thy close,
One lengthen'd sunshine of complete repose :
Correct our crimes, and beam that christian mind
O'er the wide wreck of dissolute mankind ;
To calm brow'd peace, the maddening world restore,
Or lash the demon thirsting still for gore ;
Till nature's utmost bound thy arms restrain,
And prostrate tyrants bite the British chain.

JAMES ALLEN.

JAMES ALLEN was born in Boston, July 24th, 1739. His
father was a merchant of considerable wealth, and wished to
make him a scholar, but the youth, although possessed of good
natural parts, was too averse to study to make any great progress with his books. The resolution and assiduities however,
of his tutor, carried him through his preparatory studies in a
short space, after the pupil had spent most of the time allotted
to that purpose in slothful inactivity. He entered Harvard College, but his inattention to his books, and his free notions
upon religion, hindered his attaining to the honors of the
University. He spent but three years at College, and then
abandoned his scholastic pursuits altogether. His life offers

nothing of interest or vicissitude. He continued to reside in Boston, without applying himself to regular business of any sort. Inheriting a comfortable patrimony, and naturally inclined to repose, he felt none of those stimulants to exertion, which in other circumstances might have effected the full development of his powers. His occupations, or more properly, amusements, were writing essays and verses upon the political affairs of the times ; but he was too fond of his ease to become individually a partizan in public disputes, or load himself with the cares of any official station. The career of hardly any man of letters (if Allen's disinclination for study, and the small degree of care he bestowed upon his works, can allow him any claim to that title) is less diversified by any striking event. He led the noiseless easy life of a bachelor, and though a person of considerable whim and eccentricity of character, passed his days in the pleasures of a cheerful intimacy with a circle of friends. He died in 1808, in his 70th year.

Mr Allen was the author of a great number of poems, but few of them have been published. The lines on the massacre of the fifth of March are the best known. These were first printed in 1772. The performance was written at the request of Dr Warren, and designed to be published as a companion to the oration on the same subject which the Doctor had been appointed by a committee of the town of Boston to deliver. Allen's poem struck the committee so favorably that they voted it to be printed with the oration, but insinuations being thrown out that the political principles of the writer were unsound, that body thought fit to suppress it. Mr Allen seems to have been not very solicitous to disabuse the public respecting the matter, and prized his literary fame too little to make any exertion for the purpose of bringing his poetry into notice. The work might therefore have been neglected and finally lost like the greater part of his writings, but for the endeavors of some of his friends, who procured the manuscript and published it, accompanied by specimens of another poem of his, called " The Retrospect," which the editors offered their comments upon, with the object of clearing the author's

character as to his politics, no less than to commend his poetical abilities. We believe nothing of his besides these two
pieces has been made public, save a few short scraps in the
magazines.

He wrote an epic with the title of "Bunker Hill," and
went so far as to make arrangements for its publication, but
his indolent habits soon mastered this resolution, and the poem
we think is now lost. No inducement could prevail upon
him to bestow any pains upon the correction of his writings,
or make any resolute effort to extend his reputation as a poet.
He cared nothing for fame, and though an author's rank
must be awarded him according to the merits of what he has
executed, we should form too low an estimate of Allen's
powers, from performances which display so little care and
application, as those which he has given to the world. His
verses are not wanting in poetical spirit, but they do not bear
the marks of finished elaboration.

LINES ON THE MASSACRE.

From realms of bondage, and a tyrant's reign,
Our godlike fathers bore no slavish chain.
To Pharaoh's face the inspired patriarchs stood,
To seal their virtue, with a martyr's blood :
But lives so precious, such a sacred seed,
The source of empires, heaven's high will decreed ;
He snatch'd the saints from Pharaoh's impious hand,
And bid his chosen seek this distant land :
Thus to these climes the illustrious exiles sped,
'T was freedom prompted, and the Godhead led.
Eternal woods the virgin soil defaced,
A dreary desert, and a howling waste ;
The haunt of tribes no pity taught to spare,
And they opposed them with remorseless war,
But heaven's right arm led forth the faithful train,
The guardian Godhead swept the insidious plain,
Till the scour'd thicket amicable stood,
Nor dastard ambush trench'd the dusky wood :
Our sires then earn'd no more precarious bread,
Nor 'midst alarms their frugal meals were spread.

Fair boding hopes inured their hands to toil,
And patriot virtue nursed the thriving soil,
Nor scarce two ages have their periods run,
Since o'er their culture smiled the genial sun;
And now what states extend their fair domains,
O'er fleecy mountains, and luxuriant plains!
Where happy millions their own fields possess,
No tyrant awes them, and no lords oppress;
The hand of rule, divine discretion guides,
And white-robed virtue o'er her path presides,
Each policed order venerates the laws,
And each, ingenuous, speaks in freedom's cause;
Not Spartan spirit, nor the Roman name,
The patriot's pride, shall rival these in fame;
Here all the sweets that social life can know,
From the full fount of civil sapience flow;
Here golden Ceres clothes th' autumnal plain,
And art's fair empress holds her new domain;
Here angel Science spreads her lucid wing,
And hark, how sweet the new-born muses sing;
Here generous Commerce spreads her liberal hand,
And scatters foreign blessings round the land.
Shall meagre mammon, or proud lust of sway,
Reverse these scenes—will heaven permit the day?
Shall in this era all our hopes expire,
And weeping freedom from her fanes retire?
Here shall the tyrant still our peace pursue,
From the pain'd eyebrow drink the vital dew?
Not nature's barrier wards our father's foe,
Seas roll in vain, and boundless oceans flow.

Stay, Pharaoh, stay, that impious hand forbear,
Nor tempt the genius of our souls too far;
How oft, ungracious! in thy thankless stead,
'Mid scenes of death, our generous youth have bled;
When the proud Gaul thy mightiest powers repell'd,
And drove your legions trembling from the field,
We rent the laurel from the victor's brow,
And round your temples taught the wreath to grow,
Say, when thy slaughter'd bands the desert dyed,
Where lone Ohio rolls her gloomy tide,
Whose dreary banks their wasting bones inshrine,
What arm avenged them?—thankless! was it thine?
But generous valor scorns a boasting word,
And conscious virtue reaps her own reward,
Yet conscious virtue bids thee now to speak,
Though guilty blushes kindle o'er thy cheek:

If wasting wars, and painful toils at length,
Had drain'd our veins, and wither'd all our strength,
How couldst thou, cruel, form the vile design,
And round our necks the wreath of bondage twine!
And if some lingering spirit roused to strife,
Bid ruffian murder drink the dregs of life?
Shall future ages e'er forget the deed?
And shall n't for this imperious Britain bleed?
When comes the period heaven predestines must,
When Europe's glories shall be whelm'd in dust,
When our proud fleets the naval wreath shall wear,
And o'er her empires hurl the bolts of war,
Unnerved by fate, the boldest heart shall fail,
And 'mid their guards auxiliar kings grow pale;
In vain shall Britain lift her suppliant eye,
An alien'd offspring feels no filial tie,
Her tears in vain shall bathe the soldier's feet,
Remember, ingrate, Boston's crimson'd street;
Whole hecatombs of lives the deed shall pay,
And purge the murders of that guilty day.

But why to future periods look so far,
What force e'er faced us, that we fear'd to dare?
Then, canst thou think, e'en on this early day,
Proud force shall bend us to a tyrant's sway?
A foreign foe opposed our sword in vain,
And thine own troops we 've rallied on the plain,
If then our lives thy lawless sword invade,
Think'st thou, enslaved, we 'd kiss the pointed blade?
Nay, let experience speak—be this the test,
'T is from experience that we reason best.
When first thy mandate show'd the shameless plan,
To rank our race beneath the class of man,
Low as the brute to sink the human line,
Our toil our portion, and the harvest thine,
Modest but firm, we plead the sacred cause,
On nature based, and sanction'd by the laws;
But your deaf ear the conscious plea denied,
Some demon counsel'd—and the sword replied;
Your navy then our haven cover'd o'er,
And arm'd battalions trespass'd on our shore.
Through the prime streets, they march'd in war's array,
At noon's full blaze, and in the face of day:
With dumb contempt we pass'd the servile show,
While scorn's proud spirit scowl'd on every brow;
Day after day successive wrongs we bore,
Till patience, wearied, could support no more,

Till slaughter'd lives our native streets profaned,
And thy slave's hand our hallow'd crimson stain'd,
No sudden rage the ruffian soldier tore,
Or swam the pavement with his vital gore.
Deliberate thought did all our souls compose,
Till veil'd in glooms the lowery morning rose ;
No mob then furious urged the impassion'd fray,
Nor clamorous tumult dinn'd the solemn day.
In full convene the city senate sate,
Our fathers' spirit ruled the firm debate ;—
The freeborn soul no reptile tyrant checks,
'T is heaven dictates when the people speaks ;
Loud from their tongues the awful mandate broke,
And thus inspired, the sacred senate spoke ;
" Ye miscreant troops, begone ! Our presence fly,
Stay, if ye dare, but if ye dare, ye die ! "
" Ah ! too severe," the fearful chief replies,
" Permit one half—the other instant flies."—
" No parle, avaunt, or by our fathers' shades,
Your reeking lives shall glut our vengeful blades,
Ere morning's light begone,—or else we swear,
Each slaughter'd corse shall feed the birds of air ! "
Ere morning's light had streak'd the skies with red,
The chieftain yielded, and the soldier fled.
'T is thus experience speaks—the test forbear,
Nor show these states your feeble front of war,
But still your navies lord it o'er the main,
Their keels are natives of our oaken plain ;
E'en the proud mast that bears your flag on high,
Grew on our soil, and ripen'd in our sky :
" Know then thyself, presume not us to scan,"
Your power precarious, and your isle a span.

Yet could our wrongs in just oblivion sleep,
And on each neck revived affection weep,
The brave are generous, and the good forgive,
Then say you 've wrong'd us, and our parent live ;
But face not fate, oppose not heaven's decree,
Let not that curse, our mother, light on thee.

———

THE RETROSPECT.

Her warlike sons the palm of victory bore,
Where hoary Neptune's utmost billows roar,
More far than Rome who ruled unnumber'd kings,
Where Cæsar's eagles never stretch'd their wings,

From Polar climes where daylight scarcely gleams,
To where full Phœbus pours his torrid beams,
Where gorgeous Asia spreads the sumptuous loom,
Or stately nabobs rear the princely dome,
Where arid Afric gives to foreign toil
Her pearly rivers and her golden soil,
Far as the sachem roams the loneliest wood,
Or tempts with venturous barque Ontario's flood,
To where fair Europe's vernal regions rise
In medial climates, and in temperate skies.
The British powers for seven successive years,
Had thus triumphant circled both the spheres,
O'er the whole globe their course of glory run
Whence day emerges to where sets the sun.
No waste of life pollutes the soldier's deed,
Nor wanton spoliage bids reflection bleed.

** * * * * *

 Barbarian ravage hung the pagan car,
The spoils of empires, and the waste of war,
In fields of death did Cæsar's laurels bloom,
And shamed the triumphs of imperial Rome,
Whose wreath renown'd to mightier Timur yields,
Famed for the feats of more illustrious fields.
He, half the world in one great day withstood,
And bid the rising crescent set in blood.
From tyrant power preserved the realms of Greece,
And o'er Byzantium stretched the palm of peace.
Yet conquer'd kings in chains inglorious led,
And captive queens with sordid offal fed.
Not so the Briton gleans the field of war,
Nor such the trophies of a Brunswick's car ;
No frown of danger daunts his fearless eye,
Where the fight storms, and where the bravest die.
But when the thunder of the battle 's o'er,
And adverse legions tempt their fate no more,
His heart humane regrets a hero's deeds,
And for the foe his generous bosom bleeds !
A sanguine spirit fires the soldier slave,
But manly pity ever warms the brave.
Say ! round the circuit of this spacious earth,
What barbarous act degrades the warrior's worth ?
Through the vast regions stretch'd from either pole,
What aching bosom, or what anguish'd soul ?
Doth hoary age a single solace mourn,
Or from whose breasts are tender nurslings torn ?

What spouse bewails the bridal bed profaned,
Or what fond youth the plighted virgin stain'd ?
What hostile fires the rural works consume,
Or waste the labors of the ingenious loom?
Still the blithe swain enjoys his fleecy care,
And still the lover woos the spotless fair,
Still nuptial life connubial virtues bless,
And parent bosoms the sweet babe compress.

* * * * *

Her hallow'd courts no vulgar trophy soils,
No rapined gold, nor unillustrious spoils ;
Great Brunswick's eye dejected Bourborn waits,
And India's monarchs throng Augusta's gates,
Whole maps of conquest all the war reveal,
And at her side the vanquish'd princes kneel,
Till peace, fair goddess, spreads her balmy wings,
And grace benignly lifts the prostrate kings :
The kings arise, the gates of Janus close,
And Britain gives the weary world repose ;
Now casts her eye through every various zone,
And counts a hundred different climes her own.
Here, right of conquest pleads a boon to fame,
And here, the sword prescribes the sovereign's claim.
Not so, endear'd by nature's kindly tie,
Beloved Columbia meets her parent's eye,
Pleased she surveys her darling's fair domains,
Her fleecy mountains, and her bearded plains,
Where peace and plenty rule with union sway,
Where Britain's genius beams politic day.

* * * * *

Ah ! seats of Eden, nature's care in vain !
Bright as thy sons, and as thy heavens serene !
Unbless'd, amid the circling course of clime,
In spring's fair bloom, or autumn's golden prime,
Though fruits luxuriant crown the reaper's toil,
Or flowers spontaneous deck the enamel'd soil,
Though flocks and herds innumerable teem,
And silver Naiads sport in every stream,
Did Britain now a mother's aid deny,
Or Brunswick pass thee with regardless eye?
When peopling regions wear a various face,
And laws ill-system'd ask a broader base,
When thoughtful senates feel a patriot's care,
And lift to gracious George the wishful prayer,
When some ill genii, guised in friendly form,
Might dark and subtile mix the civil storm,

With specious art aerial codes prepare,
And in the senate stretch the stygian snare;
The infernal magic spell her palsied voice,
Perplex'd—confounded, 'midst a maze of choice;
Whilst all without to heights anarchial wrought,
The pomp of passion, or the pride of thought,
Till vulgar councils sit in bold debate,
And votes plebeian awe the wayward state,
Then factious fires the impassion'd heart might feel,
And rage delirious with fantastic zeal.
Till civil fury give the impious blow,
And brother's blood in mingling currents flow!
Till kindred carnage heap the humid vale,
And loathed effluvia taint the passing gale:
But days so dire no son of thine shall see,
So George resolves, and such is heaven's decree.
O! precious offspring of the queen of Isles,
Nursed in the sunbeam of thy mother's smiles.

*   *   *   *   *   *   *

Henceforth no vulgar tongue profanely dare
The bench to dictate or control the bar!
On adamantine base the Judge shall stand,
And deal out justice with a fearless hand;
Each villain's heart the dread tribunals awe,
And nature's sanctions form the sageful law,
The sovereign's fiat guide the policed poise,
As life grows social, and new interests rise.
Through the mixt mazes of contingent cause
Dart the keen glance and spirit all the laws.
The state's great genius, whose magnific soul
Conducts, protects, and constitutes the whole.

Hail, times illustrious! blissful era, hail!
When patriot princes hold the public scale,
With eye judicious range the walks of state,
From the coarse peasant to the purpled great.

Shall base-born faction, nurtured up in crimes,
Malign the laws, or fault the halcyon times?
Against the throne uprear the factious brand,
And bid the vulgar madden round the land?
With black illusion pest the public ear,
And spread his spells infectious demon here?
Still o'er thy realms, paternal prince, preside,
The sovereign reason, and thy people's guide.

Aloft in air the golden standards play,
Standards erst spread to many a glorious day,
When Britain's host the illustrious Marlborough led,
When Tallard yielded, or when Berwick bled,
Standards, no hostile hand shall dare profane,
Nor e'er be trampled on the carnaged plain,
Their sacred shade the soldier's soul inspires,
Nerves his whole heart, and kindles all his fires.
The embattled war to martial music moves
Through long known vales, and oft frequented groves,
To the clift skirt coast that girds fair Albion's reign,
On whose broad margin swells the ambient main.

*   *   *   *   *   *

Here the big heart is seen to breathe a sigh,
And the salt tear to scald the soldier's eye;
Not that his sire betrays a parent's pangs,
Or round his neck the spoused virgin hangs ;
To these, to all, he freely bids adieu,
But every fear, Columbia, is for you.
For you he braves the storm, with dauntless soul,
Sees the surge burst, or mountain billow roll,
Through the long voyage unnumber'd perils past,
Safely he makes Cape Breton's coast at last:
Ah! Lewis, start, dire dreams thy sleep invade,
Here falls thy favorite, here thy lilies fade.
A mint of cost in vain her ramparts rear'd,
And her proud walls thy best battalions guard.
Thy name, presumptuous prince, in vain she wears,
And heaves her haughty bulwarks to the stars.
Her period 's come, now shines the fated day,
When all her glories in the dust shall lay.
But ah ! what havock strews her stormy shore,
And floats her flowery fields with floods of gore?
Ere the last gasp, ere the decisive groan,
When British valor wins the important town.

Ye youth, who glorious to the battle bled,
And you by fate to future fame decreed,
Now from the roving corsair's ravage free,
The rich fraught vessels course the peaceful sea ;
On the broad bank the fisher feels no fear,
New Albion thanks ye with a grateful tear.

*   *   *   *   *   *

" You whom the duties of the day can spare,
In manly mirth the grateful banquet share,

Nor bids your chief refrain the rustic's toil,
What generous victor stains his hands with spoil?
A deed so base may suit the armed slave,
But piteous pillage misbecomes the brave."
The general thus, the troops in shouts reply,
The echoing plaudit thunders to the sky.

    *   *   *   *   *   *   *

The genial supper spreads the unsullied green,
The bowl convivial crowns the festive scene.
In pleasing talk the guiltless eve they pass,
In social circles on the fragrant grass,
Till soft each eye salubrious slumbers close,
They sink unconscious in serene repose.
No dreary dream, nor morphean dozes steep
The soldiers' senses in abortive sleep.
Soon as the cheerly goddess of the morn
From her light pinion sheds the silver dawn,
Each placid brow the kind oblivion flies,
And fresh as day the invigor'd warriors rise.

AN INTENDED INSCRIPTION FOR THE MONUMENT ON BEACON-HILL, IN BOSTON.

Where stretch'd your sail, beneath what foreign sky
Did lovelier landscape ever charm your eye?
Could fancy's fairy pencil, stranger! say,
E'en dipt in dreams, a nobler scene pourtray?

Behold yon vales, whose skirts elude your view,
And mountains fading to aerial blue!
Along their bowery shades how healthy toil
Alternate sports, or tends the mellow soil.
See rural towns 'mid groves and gardens rise,
And eastward,—where the stretching ocean lies,
Lo! our fair capital sublimes the scene,
New Albion's pride, and ocean's future queen;
How o'er the tradeful port august she smiles,—
Her sea-like haven boasts an hundred isles,
When hardy commerce swell the lofty sails
O'er arctic seas, and mocks the polar gales;
Thence tides of wealth the wafting breezes bring,
And hence e'en culture feels its vital spring.

These scenes our sires from rugged nature wrought,
Since—what dire wars their patriot race have fought!
Witness yon tract, where first the Briton bled,
Driven by our youth redoubted Percy fled :
There Breed ascends, and Bunker's bleeding steeps,
Still o'er whose brow abortive victory weeps ;
What trophies since ! the gaze of after times,
Rear'd freedom's empire o'er our happy climes!

But hence, fond stranger, take a nobler view,
See yon shorn elm,* whence all these glories grew.
Here, where the armed foe presumptuous trod,
Trampled our shrines, and even mouth'd our God,
His vengeful hand, deep as the parent root,
Lopt each grown branch, and every suckling shoot ;
Because beneath her consecrated shade
Our earliest vows to liberty were paid.
High from her altar blew the heaven-caught fire,
While all our wealth o'erhung the kindling pyre.
How at the deed the nations stood aghast,
As on the pile our plighted lives we cast!

O! if an alien from our fair domains,
The blood of Britain, hapless, taint your veins,
Pace o'er that hallow'd ground with awful tread,
And tears, atoning, o'er yon relic shed ;
But if, American ! your lineage springs,
From sires, who scorn the pedigree of kings,
A Georgian born, you breathe the tepid air,
Or on the breezy banks of Delaware,
Or hardy Hampshire claim your haughty birth,
Revere yon root, and kiss its nurturing earth :
O be its fibres fed by flowing springs,
Whence rose our empire o'er the thrones of kings :
E'en now descend, adore the dear remain,
Where first rear'd liberty's illumin'd fane.
There all her race, while time revolves, shall come,
As pilgrims flock to Mecca's idol'd tomb.

ON WASHINGTON'S VISIT TO BOSTON. 1789.

Did human eye e'er see so fair a day ?
Behold thy genius, freedom, lead the way.
Rude kings of old did Russian armies wait,
And swell with barb'rous port the pomp of state.

*The stump of liberty tree.

While the proud car, bedeck'd with guilty gold,
On freedom's writhing neck triumphant roll'd.
The nobles proud, who led the gorgeous train,
Wore slavery's badge and drew a gilded chain,
While the loud shouts which pierced the troubled air,
The tongue of nations, only thrilled with fear.
The eye adoring, scarce could check its flow,
For all their trophies swell'd but human wo.
The paths of triumph thus the nations trod,
And thought the sovereign power derived from God.
Hence o'er the historic roll what hateful crimes
Were wrought, the model of succeeding times.
But now fair liberty illumes the age,
And reason tints renown's recording page,
Blots from her eye the fierce barbarian's name,
And even Cæsar blurs the page of fame.
Who wrought the wond'rous change ? what power divine ?
The wond'rous change, O Washington ! was thine.
'T is thine own era graced the radiant page,
The fostering parent of a filial age.
        Thou too, illustrious Hancock, by his side
In every lowering hour of danger tried,
With him conspicuous o'er the beamy page,
Descend the theme of every future age.
When first the sword of early war we drew,
The king presaging fix'd his eye on you.
T was your dread finger press'd the sacred seal,
Whence rose to sovereign power the public weal.
Then, Washington ! Oh dearly honor'd name,
From callow youth the favorite of fame,
When hovering navies, haughty Albion's boast,
Pour'd her dread armies o'er our trembling coast,
Your country beck'd you from the rural bower,
And nerved your mighty arm with all her power.
The tyrant saw, and sickening at the view,
In fancy bade his frantic hopes adieu.
But urged by fate, still bade his armies dare,
Blew the vain trump, and waged abortive war.
At length you drew the tyrant from his throne,
And bade his seal your course of glory crown.
        When polish'd wisdom seem'd her seats to fly,
On thee again the public cast her eye.
How rose the model from your forming hand ! .
The proud palladium of our happy land.
        Ah ! gentle parent of the cradled states,
On whose fond eye an infant nation waits,
While now affection seems your steps to stay,
And swarming concourse checks your laboring way ;

Perhaps among the loud acclaiming throng,
Your ear may heed the muse's transient song ;
The high-born muse from adulation free,
Attunes, Oh chief! her haughty lyre to thee.
No vulgar theme could ever tempt her strain,
Perhaps the proudest of the tuneful train.
Apart from busy life her hours are led,
And her lone steps the shades of science tread.
Her years revolving roll a playful flow,
Nor ever care o'erhung the muse's brow.
From the recess where her own roses twine,
How oft her fancy drew a form like thine.
Ere morning waked she wing'd her early way
To hail the dawn of this auspicious day.

BENJAMIN FRANKLIN.

Born 1706.—Died 1790.

PAPER.

Some wit of old—such wits of old there were—
Whose hints show'd meaning, whose allusions care,
By one brave stroke to mark all human kind,
Call'd clear blank paper every infant mind ;
Where still, as opening sense her dictates wrote,
Fair virtue put a seal, or vice a blot.

The thought was happy, pertinent, and true ;
Methinks a genius might the plan pursue.
I (can you pardon my presumption?) I—
No wit, no genius, yet for once will try.

Various the papers various wants produce,
The wants of fashion, elegance, and use.
Men are as various ; and if right I scan,
Each sort of *paper* represents some *man*.

Pray note the fop—half powder and half lace—
Nice as a band-box were his dwelling-place :

He 's the *gilt paper*, which apart you store,
And lock from vulgar hands in the 'scrutoire.

Mechanics, servants, farmers, and so forth,
Are *copy-paper*, of inferior worth ;
Less prized, more useful, for your desk decreed,
Free to all pens, and prompt at every need.

The wretch, whom avarice bids to pinch and spare,
Starve, cheat, and pilfer, to enrich an heir,
Is coarse *brown paper;* such as pedlars choose
To wrap up wares, which better men will use.

Take next the miser's contrast, who destroys
Health, fame, and fortune, in a round of joys.
Will any paper match him ? Yes, throughout,
He 's a true *sinking-paper*, past all doubt.

The retail politician's anxious thought
Deems *this* side always right, and *that* stark naught ;
He foams with censure ; with applause he raves—
A dupe to rumors, and a tool of knaves ;
He 'll want no type his weakness to proclaim,
While such a thing as *foolscap* has a name.

The hasty gentleman, whose blood runs high,
Who picks a quarrel, if you step awry,
Who can't a jest, or hint, or look endure :
What is he ? What ? *Touch-paper* to be sure.

What are our poets, take them as they fall,
Good, bad, rich, poor, much read, not read at all ?
Them and their works in the same class you 'll find ;
They are the mere *waste-paper* of mankind.

Observe the maiden, innocently sweet,
She 's fair *white-paper*, an unsullied sheet ;
On which the happy man, whom fate ordains,
May write his *name*, and take her for his pains.

One instance more, and only one I 'll bring ;
'T is the *great man* who scorns a little thing,
Whose thoughts, whose deeds, whose maxims are his own,
Form'd on the feelings of his heart alone :
True genuine *royal-paper* is his breast :
Of all the kinds most precious, purest, best.

———

JOHN TRUMBULL.

JOHN TRUMBULL, the author of M'Fingal, was born on the 24th day of April, 1750, in the parish of Westbury, then a part of the town of Waterbury, in New Haven county, Connecticut. The place is now called Watertown, and is included in the county of Litchfield. His father was the first minister of the congregational church in that town, a man of good classical attainments and for many years one of the trustees of Yale College. The subject of this memoir was an only son, and of a very delicate and sickly constitution. He received the strictest care from his mother, who was a woman of superior education for those 'of her day. Young Trumbull gave early manifestations of his poetical turn by studying and committing to memory all the verses contained in the Spectator and Watts's Lyric Poems, which comprised the department of English literature in his father's library. This slight initiation into the rudiments of polite letters enabled him to exert his propensity to verse by making rhymes of his own, an exercise in which he was encouraged by his parents. His father, in conformity to a practice common at that time, had taken under his tuition a youth of seventeen years of age for the purpose of directing his studies previous to his entering college. Trumbull took notice of the student's method of learning Latin, and unaided and unperceived by any one except his mother, set about the study of the language himself. His father after some time discovered it, and finding he made a more rapid progress than his fellow student, encouraged him to proceed. He was examined and admitted at the college in 1757, but owing to his extreme youth and ill health, was not sent to reside there till 1763.

He employed this interval of time in the study of the Greek and Latin classics, and such English writers as were to be procured in his native village, consisting of few beside Milton, Dryden, Pope and Thomson. Upon entering college he found little attention paid to polite literature, except in the department of the ancient languages, and as his proficiency in this branch of learning was such that the ordinary duties of his class required but a trifling portion of his time, he turned his attention to Algebra, Geometry, and Astronomy, sciences newly introduced to the notice of the students. After receiving his degree, he continued three years longer at college, occupied in a general course of literary study.

At this time he began his acquaintance with Dr Dwight, who was also pursuing his studies at the college. This young poet, who had already attracted notice by some elegant translations from Horace, became an intimate associate of Trumbull, and the two friends exerted their talents and industry in conjunction, to promote the taste for elegant letters among the inmates of the college. These pursuits were then looked upon as idle and worthless: nothing was held in high repute but the learned languages, mathematics, logic, and scholastic theology. The wit of Trumbull, who summoned the aid of his muse to root out this remnant of puritanical barbarism, seconded by the efforts of others who joined his party, effected in the end a material change in the taste and pursuits of the students. He attracted further notice by engaging with the assistance of his friends, in the publication of a series of essays in the manner of the Spectator; these were printed in a newspaper, first at Boston, and afterwards at New Haven. In 1771, Trumbull and his friend Dwight were chosen tutors at the college. In 1772, appeared the first part of his poem, The Progress of Dulness, which he wrote with a view to help the cause of education by exposing the absurdities then prevalent in the system; the work was completed the following year. Dwight was at this time busy upon his great poem, the Conquest of Canaan, in the composition of which he was assisted with the criticism and advice of Trumbull.[*]

During the exercise of his college duties, Trumbull found leisure to devote himself to the study of the law, and in 1773,

---

[*] We have heard an anecdote which illustrates Trumbull's turn for wit, as well as for just criticism. Dwight had crowded into his poem several descriptions of thunder storms. Trumbull having read a part of it, sent him word that when he forwarded the remainder, he wished him also to send a *lightning rod*.

he was admitted to the bar in Connecticut, where however, he did not pursue the profession, but removed his residence to Boston, and continued his studies in the office of John Adams, afterwards President. The revolutionary struggle was then just commencing, and Trumbull entered with great warmth and enthusiasm into the political controversies which then monopolized the public attention, and displayed himself as a strenuous partizan of the cause of liberty. Many of his political essays were published in the gazettes. He returned to Connecticut, and began practice at the bar in New Haven in 1774. In 1775, he wrote the first part of his M'Fingal, which was immediately published at Philadelphia, where Congress was then sitting.

In 1776 he married, and in 1781 removed to Hartford, where he fixed his residence. His friends at this time requested him to finish M'Fingal, and set on foot a subscription for the work. With this prospect he applied himself to the revision of the first part, and the composition of another canto. The poem was completed and published at Hartford, in 1782. No legal provision existed at that period to secure to an author his own literary property, and in consequence, this work, which had an immense popularity, became the prey of hawkers and pedlars, without bringing any profit to the writer beyond the first edition. More than thirty editions of the poem were published.

Upon the return of peace, the country remained in an unsettled condition, without any bond of union among the several states, except the articles of confederation. This loose and insecure system of government was attended by a copious train of evils. No harmony of plan or policy existed among the different state governments. The country was impoverished; great dissatisfaction and clamor arose at the extra pay granted to the revolutionary army, and at the formation of the society of the Cincinnati, while the national debt pressed heavily upon the people. The insurrection of Shays burst forth in Massachusetts, mobs were raised in Connecticut, and violent efforts were made to stir up the people in opposition to the general government and kindle a civil war. The exertions of all who were attached to peace, good order, and regular authority, were called for at this crisis to save the country from impending ruin. All the efforts of persuasion, eloquence, argument, ridicule, and satire, were put forth on the occasion, and the tempest of popular discontent was allayed. Trumbull lent his pen to the cause, and in conjunction with several gentlemen at Hartford, produced a poem called the Anarchiad, which we shall notice hereafter.

In 1789, Trumbull was appointed Attorney to the state of Connecticut for the County of Hartford, which office he held till 1795. He has also several times represented the town of Hartford in the state Legislature, and in 1801, was appointed a Judge of the Superior Court of the State of Connecticut. He received the additional appointment in 1808, of a Judge of the Supreme Court of Errors, which he held till the organization of the courts in 1819, under the new constitution of the state.

In 1820 he made a collection of his poems, to which he prefixed a memoir and added notes, and they were published in a handsome style in two vols. 8vo. On announcing the work, the public voice was warmly expressed in favor of it, and consequently a large edition was published. After a great effort, however, a small subscription only could be obtained, and the enterprise proved unfortunate to the publisher. Trumbull realized one thousand dollars, and a gratuity of one hundred copies of the work. This statement is made to correct an error prevalent at the time, that the author derived no benefit from the publication.

In 1825 he removed, at the age of seventyfive to Detroit, where he has continued to reside with his daughter to the present day.

Although Trumbull's fame as a poet has rested mainly upon M'Fingal, yet the modern reader would probably assign as high a rank to his earliest piece, "The Progress of Dulness." This is a satire in Hudibrastic verse upon the errors and absurdities which were then prevalent in the literature and manners of the author's neighborhood. The pedantry and ignorance of the members of the learned professions, the preposterous customs on the subject of education, the coxcombry and conceit of fashionable life, are handled with a felicitous power of sarcasm. Had he produced no other work than this, it would have sufficed to bring him into distinguished notice. But it has attracted little regard compared to the more popular and national work, M'Fingal.

M'Fingal has had a greater celebrity than any other American poem, owing partly to its intrinsic merit, but more, doubtless, to the time and circumstances which gave it birth. It was written, at the request of some members of the American Congress, in 1775, with a view to aid the struggle for independence, which had then just begun. The period had arrived when England and America were to be separated. Reflecting men saw the necessity of this, long before it was visible to the common people. A redress of grievances had been the end of their views; the thought of independence was forbidden by their reverence for their king, their love of England, and their respect for its power.

It was a task no less difficult than necessary for the crisis, that the American people should be roused to active and bloody resistance ; that the breasts which had been accustomed to glow with loyalty should burn with indignation; that the filial feeling should give place to resentment; and that the language of prayer and petition should be laid aside for the accents of hostility.

In this critical moment the keen sighted politicians of the day did not overlook the influence, which the still lingering respect toward England, and the deep sense of her power, must exert over the colonists. They understood the advantage which would be gained, if this respect and dread of power could be made to give place to scorn and contempt. They foresaw that if the Americans could despise the English, they would more boldly face them in battle ; that if they could once laugh at them by their firesides, and in the camp, at night, they would beat them in the field on the morrow.

The wit of Trumbull was in this extremity a better rein-forcement than regiments. He had been an attentive specta-tor of the events which had preceded, and which opened the war; he had watched with a satirical eye, the errors and follies of England and her officers; and felt with indignation the wrongs which had been inflicted on his country. He had already drawn more than one keen shaft from his quiver, and found, with unerring aim, the vital part of his country's ene-mies. But there was now a requisition for help on all who could give it; and while others, at the earliest call of a suffer-ing country, drained their purses and their veins in her behalf, Trumbull could not refuse the contribution of such timely aid as he had to bestow.

It was at this moment, and to serve this emergency, that M'Fingal was written. Its direct object was to pour contempt upon the British and their Tory friends, and consequently to inspire the lovers of liberty with confidence, and give point and efficacy to their indignation. It is probable that the author, now but twentyfive years of age, appearing on the stage when everything was turned to politics, educated in a country where the taste for the luxuries of literature was either not formed, or was absorbed in more stirring excitements, and when literary competition did not yet exert much influence in stimulating to effort, had little in view, in composing M'Fin-gal, beyond the immediate political effect. His purpose was, to influence immediately and strongly the common people. The style and subject of his work were therefore prescribed to him by the occasion which he was to serve; the one must be coarse and familiar, adapted to the plain apprehension of common minds; the other must be the British and the Tory party. He was not at liberty to choose, even if his taste had inclined him, to the higher and more inspired language of the muse; nor might he seize upon some great event, over which distance had thrown its mist, and to which time had lent its enchantment. He must be popular, at the risk of being short lived; he must serve his country, and take the chance of being remembered as a patriot, and forgotten as a poet.

In truth, we suspect if M'Fingal had not lived beyond the war, and, after having answered its immediate design, had passed with other productions of the day into oblivion; that the author had not been disappointed. Such must have been the fate of a work written in the heat of party excitement, and possessing in its very constitution the elements of decay, if, indeed, the breathing of genius may not have endowed it with immortality.

M'Fingal is a burlesque poem, directed against the enemies of American liberty, and holding up to particular scorn and contempt, the tories and the British officers, naval, military, and civil, in America. It is a mercile satire throughout: whatever it touches, it transforms; kings, ministers, lords, bishops, generals, judges, admirals, all take their turn, and become in the light or associations in which they are exhibited, alternately the objects of our merriment, hatred, or scorn. So wedded is the author to his vein of satire, that even M'Fingal, the friend of England, and the champion of the tories, is made the undisguised scoffer of both them and their cause.

The story of M'Fingal is this: the hero, a Scotchman, and justice of the peace in a town near Boston, and who had two gifts by virtue of his birth, " rebellion and the second sight," goes to a town meeting, where he and one Honorius, make speeches at each other through two whole cantos. At the end of the second canto, the town meeting breaks up tumultuously; and the people gather round a liberty pole erected by the mob. Here M'Fingal makes a virulent speech of near two hundred lines, at the end of which he is pursued, and brought back to the liberty pole, where the constable is swung aloft, and M'Fingal tarred and feathered. M'Fingal is set at liberty; he goes home, and at night makes a speech to some of his tory friends in his cellar, extending through the rest of the poem, leaving only room to tell that the mob broke off his address in the middle by assaulting the house, and that M'Fingal escaped to Boston. These are all the incidents, and this the whole story of a poem of four cantos, and consisting of some thousands of lines.

The work is written after the manner of Hudibras, sometimes affecting the carelessness of its versification and the
drollery of its rhymes, and occasionally verging into the more
artificial and dignified manner of Pope. It often condescends
to deal in the coarse language and revolting images of its
prototype, and even surpasses it, we think, in free allusions to
scripture. In its general manner, it is characterized by less of
levity than Hudibras, and more of vivacity than the Dunciad.
It frequently and happily imitates them both, sometimes in the
quaint humor of Butler, exhibiting new and striking analogies
between images altogether remote and dissimilar ; and sometimes in the unrelenting manner of Pope, holding up the objects of its satire to hatred and abhorrence. If it seldom or
never rivals the more exquisite passages of either, we are almost ready to admit that it is because they are inimitable.

The gifts of the author seem to lie in a keen perception of
the ridiculous, and a ready talent for seizing upon the true point
of humor. The excellencies of the poem therefore are found
in the address with which a satirical light is made to play
upon the objects of the writer's fancy, and that power of ridicule, which like an uneven glass, throws everything that is
seen through it, into absurd and ridiculous positions. The
principal defects of the work, considered without relation
to the objects for which it was written, are a want of creative imagination; a barrenness of incident and consequent
deficiency of interest in the story; a cast of extravagance
and a tone of bitterness in the sentiments, which, however
natural for the time and fitting to the occasion, must ever after
be beyond the sympathy of the reader.

There is another weighty deduction to be made from the
merit of the work. Burlesque poetry is but an inferior species
of composition, and the masters of it can claim but a second
place in the temple of the muses. We may admit with Johnson that Hudibras has made Butler immortal, but we wish
with Dryden, that he had written a different work. We feel
it to be in some sense a prostitution of poetry, to busy it with
the faults and follies of men. The free and chosen haunts

of the muse are in the lofty mountains, along the margin of the silver rivulet, through silent valleys, in solitary woods, on the sea-shore, in the blue sky, on the sailing cloud. Here she communes with nature, and discourses of loveliness and beauty. It is not willingly, but by compulsion, that she leaves these scenes for the crowded haunts of men, to deal with vice and deformity. The change is almost fatal to her charms. In the narrow streets of the city we hardly recognise the enchantress. Her white wing becomes soiled and drooping; her brow furrowed with indignation; her lip curled in scorn; a quiver of poisoned arrows is at her back; a whip of scorpions in her hand. The silver music of her voice is gone; her inspired language is exchanged for the vulgar speech of men; her fancy is filled with images of deformity! Who that has been her companion in the lone mountain, by the wild waterfall, and in the trackless wood; when weary, has reposed on beds of wild roses, when thirsty, has kissed the lip of a virgin fountain, that ever before has flowed untouched in its secret bower—who, that has lived and communed with her thus, would wish to see her degraded to the business of a satirist and scourge?

Yet in contemplating M'Fingal, if we cannot admire the poet, we must acknowledge the debt we owe the patriot. It is in the light of history and not by the tests of literary criticism, that we would estimate the value of the work. Let it be tried by the stern question, why was it written, and what has it done? the answer is a proud one.—It was dictated by patriotism, and served efficiently the cause it was designed to promote. While most satires have originated in personal malice, or feelings nearly allied to it, this was written in an hour of national trial, to serve the cause of justice and humanity. The Dunciad was designed to blast the enemies of Alexander Pope; M'Fingal to confound the enemies of liberty. The higher motives which gave birth to the last, cannot indeed elevate it to the literary rank of the other; yet while critics deny to M'Fingal a place among the English classics, the name of Trumbull is honorably registered in the annals of American Independence.

M'FINGAL.

CANTO III.

Now warm with ministerial ire,
Fierce sallied forth our loyal 'squire,
And on his striding steps attends
His desperate clan of tory friends.
When sudden met his wrathful eye
A pole ascending through the sky,
Which numerous throngs of whiggish race
Were raising in the market-place.
Not higher school-boys' kites aspire,
Or royal mast, or country spire;
Like spears at Brobdignagian tilting,
Or Satan's walking-staff in Milton.
And on its top, the flag unfurl'd
Waved triumph o'er the gazing world,
Inscribed with inconsistent types
Of *liberty* and *thirteen stripes*.
Beneath, the crowd without delay
The dedication-rites essay,
And gladly pay, in ancient fashion,
The ceremonies of libation;
While briskly to each patriot lip
Walks eager round the inspiring flip :
Delicious draught! whose powers inherit
The quintessence of public spirit;
Which whoso tastes, perceives his mind
To nobler politics refined;
Or roused to martial controversy,
As from transforming cups of Circe;
Or warm'd with Homer's nectar'd liquor,
That fill'd the veins of gods with ichor.
At hand for new supplies in store,
The tavern opes its friendly door,
Whence to and fro the waiters run,
Like bucket-men at fires in town.
Then with three shouts that tore the sky,
'T is consecrate to liberty.
To guard it from the attacks of tories,
A grand committee cull'd of four is;
Who foremost on the patriot spot,
Had brought the flip, and paid the shot.
　　By this, M'Fingal with his train
Advanced upon the adjacent plain,
And full with loyalty possess'd,
Pour'd forth the zeal that fired his breast.

" What mad-brain'd rebel gave commission,
To raise this May-pole of sedition ?
Like Babel, rear'd by bawling throngs,
With like confusion too of tongues,
To point at heaven, and summon down
The thunders of the British crown ?
Say, will this paltry pole secure
Your forfeit heads from Gage's power ?
Attack'd by heroes brave and crafty,
Is this to stand your ark of safety ;
Or driven by Scottish laird and laddie,
Think ye to rest beneath its shadow ?
When bombs, like fiery serpents, fly,
And balls rush hissing through the sky,
Will this vile pole, devote to freedom,
Save like the Jewish pole in Edom ;
Or like the brazen snake of Moses,
Cure your crack'd sculls and batter'd noses ?
" Ye dupes to every factious rogue
And tavern-prating demagogue,
Whose tongue but rings, with sound more full,
On the empty drumhead of his scull ;
Behold you not what noisy fools
Use you, worse simpletons, for tools ?
For liberty, in your own by-sense,
Is but for crimes a patent license,
To break of law the Egyptian yoke,
And throw the world in common stock ;
Reduce all grievances and ills
To Magna Charta of your wills ;
Establish cheats, and frauds, and nonsense,
Framed to the model of your conscience ;
Cry justice down, as out of fashion,
And fix its scale of depreciation ;
Defy all creditors to trouble ye,
And keep new years of Jewish jubilee ;
Drive judges out, like Aaron's calves,
By jurisdiction of white staves,
And make the bar, and bench, and steeple,
Submit t' our sovereign lord, the people :
By plunder rise to power and glory,
And brand all property, as tory ;
Expose all wares to lawful seizures
By mobbers or monopolizers ;
Break heads, and windows, and the peace,
For your own interest and increase ;

Dispute, and pray, and fight, and groan,
For public good, and mean your own;
Prevent the law by fierce attacks
From quitting scores upon your backs;
Lay your old dread, the gallows, low,
And seize the stocks, your ancient foe,
And turn them to convenient engines
To wreak your patriotic vengeance;
While all, your rights who understand,
Confess them in their owner's hand;
And when by clamors and confusions,
Your freedom's grown a public nuisance,
Cry 'liberty,' with powerful yearning,
As he does 'fire!' whose house is burning;
Though he already has much more
Than he can find occasion for.
While every clown, that tills the plains,
Though bankrupt in estate and brains,
By this new light transform'd to traitor,
Forsakes his plough to turn dictator,
Starts an haranguing chief of whigs,
And drags you by the ears, like pigs,
All bluster, arm'd with factious license,
New-born at once to politicians.
Each leather-apron dunce, grown wise,
Presents his forward face t' advise,
And tatter'd legislators meet,
From every workshop through the street.
His goose the tailor finds new use in,
To patch and turn the Constitution;
The blacksmith comes with sledge and grate
To iron-bind the wheels of state;
The quack forbears his patient's souse,
To purge the council and the house;
The tinker quits his moulds and doxies,
To cast assembly-men and proxies,
From dunghills deep of blackest hue,
Your dirt-bred patriots spring to view,
To wealth and powers and honors rise,
Like new-wing'd maggots changed to flies,
And fluttering round in high parade,
Strut in the robe, or gay cockade.
See Arnold quits, for ways more certain,
His bankrupt-perj'ries for his fortune,
Brews rum no longer in his store,
Jocky and skipper now no more:
And cleansed by patriotism from shame,

Grows General of the foremost name.
For in this ferment of the stream
The dregs have work'd up to the brim,
And by the rule of topsy-turvies,
The scum stands foaming on the surface.
You 've caused your pyramid t' ascend,
And set it on the little end.
Like Hudibras your empire 's made,
Whose crupper had o'ertopp'd his head.
You 've push'd and turn'd the whole world up-
Side down, and got yourselves at top,
While all the great ones of your state
Are crush'd beneath the popular weight;
Nor can you boast, this present hour,
The shadow of the form of power.
For what 's your Congress or its end ?
A power t' advise and recommend ;
To call forth troops, adjust your quotas—
And yet no soul is bound to notice ;
To pawn your faith to the utmost limit,
But cannot bind you to redeem it ;
And when in want, no more in them lies,
Than begging from your state assemblies ;
Can utter oracles of dread,
Like friar Bacon's brazen head,
But when a faction dares dispute 'em,
Has ne'er an arm to execute 'em :
As though you chose supreme dictators,
And put them under conservators.
You 've but pursued the self-same way
With Shakespeare's Trinc'lo in the play ;
" You shall be viceroys here, 't is true,
But we 'll be viceroys over you."
What wild confusion hence must ensue ?
Though common danger yet cements you :
So some wreck'd vessel, all in shatters,
Is held up by surrounding waters,
But stranded, when the pressure ceases,
Falls by its rottenness to pieces.
And fall it must ! if wars were ended,
You 'll ne'er have sense enough to mend it :
But creeping on, by low intrigues,
Like vermin of a thousand legs,
'T will find as short a life assign'd,
As all things else of reptile kind.
Your Commonwealth 's a common harlot,
The property of every varlet ;

Which now in taste, and full employ,
All sorts admire, as all enjoy:
But soon a batter'd strumpet grown,
You'll curse and drum her out of town.
Such is the government you chose;
For this you bade the world be foes;
For this, so mark'd for dissolution,
You scorn the British Constitution,
That Constitution form'd by sages,
The wonder of all modern ages;
Which owns no failure in reality,
Except corruption and venality;
And merely proves the adage just,
That best things spoil'd corrupt to worst:
So man supreme in earthly station,
And mighty lord of this creation,
When once his corse is dead as herring,
Becomes the most offensive carrion,
And sooner breeds the plague, 't is found,
Than all beasts rotting on the ground.
Yet with republics to dismay us,
You've call'd up Anarchy from chaos,
With all the followers of her school,
Uproar, and rage, and wild misrule:
For whom this rout of whigs distracted,
And ravings dire of every crack'd head;
These new-cast legislative engines
Of county meetings and conventions;
Committees vile of correspondence,
And mobs, whose tricks have almost undone 's:
While reason fails to check your course,
And loyalty's kick'd out of doors,
And folly, like inviting landlord,
Hoists on your poles her royal standard;
While the king's friends, in doleful dumps,
Have worn their courage to the stumps,
And leaving George in sad disaster,
Most sinfully deny their master.
What furies raged when you, in sea,
In shape of Indians, drown'd the tea;
When your gay sparks, fatigued to watch it,
Assumed the moggison and hachet,
With wampum'd blankets hid their laces,
And like their sweethearts, primed their faces:
While not a red-coat dared oppose,
And scarce a tory showed his nose
While Hutchinson, for sure retreat,
Manœuvred to his country seat,

And thence affrighted, in the suds,
Stole off bareheaded through the woods.
"Have you not roused your mobs to join,
And make Mandamus-men resign,
Call'd forth each duffil-dress'd curmudgeon,
With dirty trousers and white bludgeon,
Forced all our councils through the land,
To yield their necks at your command;
While paleness marks their late disgraces,
Through all their rueful length of faces?
"Have you not caused us woful work
In our good city of New York,
When all the rabble, well cockaded,
In triumph through the streets paraded,
And mobb'd the tories, scared their spouses,
And ransack'd all the custom-houses;
Made such a tumult, bluster, jarring,
That 'mid the clash of tempests warring,
Smith's weather-cock, in veers forlorn,
Could hardly tell which way to turn?
Burn'd effiges of higher powers,
Contrived in planetary hours;
As witches with clay-images
Destroy or torture whom they please:
Till fired with rage, the effulgent club
Spared not your best friend, Beelzebub,
O'erlook'd his favors, and forgot
The reverence due his cloven foot,
And in the selfsame furnace frying,
Stew'd him, and North, and Bute, and **Tryon**?
Did you not, in as vile and shallow way,
Fright our poor Philadelphian, Galloway,
Your Congress, when the loyal ribald
Belied, berated and bescribbled?
What ropes and halters did you send,
Terrific emblems of his end,
Till, lest he'd hang in more than effigy,
Fled in a fog the trembling refugee?
Now rising in progression fatal,
Have you not ventured to give battle?
When treason chased our heroes troubled,
With rusty gun, and leathern doublet;
Turn'd all stone walls, and groves, and bushes,
To batteries arm'd with blunderbusses;
And with deep wounds, that fate portend,
Gall'd many a Briton's latter end;
Drove them to Boston, as in jail,

Confined without mainprize or bail.
Were not these deeds enough betimes,
To heap the measure of your crimes:
But in this loyal town and dwelling,
You raise these ensigns of rebellion ?
'T is done ! fair mercy shuts her door ;
And vengeance now shall sleep no more.
Rise then, my friends, in terror rise,
And sweep this scandal from the skies.
You 'll see their Dagon, though well jointed,
Will shrink before the Lord's anointed ;
And like old Jericho's proud wall,
Before our ram's horns prostrate fall."
　　This said, our 'Squire, yet undismay'd,
Call'd forth the constable to aid,
And bade him read, in nearer station,
The riot-act and proclamation.
He swift, advancing to the ring,
Began, " Our sovereign lord, the king"—
When thousand clamorous tongues he hears,
And clubs and stones assail his ears.
To fly was vain, to fight was idle ;
By foes encompassed in the middle,
His hope, in stratagems, he found,
And fell right craftily to ground ;
Then crept to seek an hiding place,
'T was all he could, beneath a brace ;
Where soon the conquering crew espied him,
And where he lurk'd, they caught and tied him.
　　At once with resolution fatal,
Both whigs and tories rush'd to battle.
Instead of weapons, either band
Seized on such arms as came to hand.
And as famed Ovid paints the adventures
Of wrangling Lapithæ and Centaurs,
Who at their feast, by Bacchus led,
Threw bottles at each other's head ;
And these arms failing in their scuffles,
Attack'd with andirons, tongs and shovels,
So clubs and billets, staves and stones
Met fierce, encountering every sconce,
And covered o'er with knobs and pains
Each void receptacle for brains,
Their clamors rend the skies around,
The hills rebellow to the sound ;
And many a groan increased the din
From batter'd nose and broken shin.

M'Fingal, rising at the word,
Drew forth his old militia-sword ;
Thrice cried " King George," as erst in distress,
Knights of romance invoked a mistress ;
And brandishing the blade in air,
Struck terror through the opposing war.
The whigs, unsafe within the wind
Of such commotion, shrunk behind.
With whirling steel around address'd,
Fierce through their thickest throng he press'd,
(Who roll'd on either side in arch,
Like Red Sea waves in Israel's march)
And like a meteor rushing through,
Struck on their pole a vengeful blow.
Around, the whigs, of clubs and stones
Discharged whole volleys in platoons,
That o'er in whistling fury fly ;
But not a foe dares venture nigh.
And now perhaps with glory crown'd
Our 'Squire had fell'd the pole to ground,
Had not some power, a whig at heart,
Descended down and took their part ;
(Whether 't were Pallas, Mars or Iris,
'T is scarce worth while to make inquiries)
Who at the nick of time alarming,
Assumed the solemn form of chairman,
Addressed a whig, in every scene
The stoutest wrestler on the green,
And pointed where the spade was found,
Late used to set their pole in ground,
And urged, with equal arms and might,
To dare our 'Squire to single fight.
The whig thus arm'd, untaught to yield,
Advanced tremendous to the field :
Nor did M'Fingal shun the foe,
But stood to brave the desperate blow ;
While all the party gazed, suspended
To see the deadly combat ended ;
And Jove in equal balance weigh'd
The sword against the brandish'd spade :
He weigh'd ; but lighter than a dream,
The sword flew up, and kick'd the beam.
Our 'Squire on tiptoe rising fair
Lifts high a noble stroke in air,
Which hung not, but like dreadful engines,
Descended on his foe in vengeance.
But ah ! in danger, with dishonor

The sword perfidious fails its owner;
That sword, which oft had stood its ground,
By huge trainbands encircled round;
And on the bench, with blade right loyal,
Had won the day at many a trial,
Of stones and clubs had braved the alarms,
Shrunk from these new Vulcanian arms.
The spade so temper'd from the sledge,
Nor keen nor solid harm'd its edge,
Now met it, from his arm of might,
Descending with steep force to smite;
The blade snapp'd short—and from his hand,
With rust embrown'd the glittering sand.
Swift turn'd M'Fingal at the view,
And call'd to aid the attendant crew,
In vain; the tories all had run,
When scarce the fight was well begun;
Their setting wigs he saw decreased
Far in the horizon toward the west.
Amazed he view'd the shameful sight,
And saw no refuge, but in flight;
But age unwieldly check'd his pace,
Though fear had wing'd his flying race;
For not a trifling prize at stake;
No less than great M'Fingal's back.
With legs and arms he work'd his course,
Like rider that outgoes his horse,
And labor'd hard to get away, as
Old Satan struggling on through chaos;
Till looking back, he spied in rear
The spade-arm'd chief advanced too near:
Then stopp'd and seized a stone, that lay
An ancient landmark near the way;
Nor shall we, as old bards have done,
Affirm it weigh'd an hundred ton;
But such a stone, as at a shift
A modern might suffice to lift,
Since men, to credit their enigmas,
Are dwindled down to dwarfs and pigmies,
And giants exiled with their cronies
To Brobdignags and Patagonias.
But while our hero turn'd him round,
And tugg'd to raise it from the ground,
The fatal spade discharged a blow
Tremendous on his rear below:
His bent knee fail'd, and void of strength
Stretch'd on the ground his manly length.

Like ancient oak o'erturn'd, he lay,
Or tower to tempests fallen a prey,
Or mountains sunk with all his pines,
Or flower the plough to dust consigns,
And more things else—but all men know 'em,
If slightly versed in epic poem.
At once the crew, at this dread crisis,
Fall on, and bind him, ere he rises;
And with loud shouts and joyful soul,
Conduct him prisoner to the pole.
When now the mob in lucky hour
Had got their enemies in their power,
They first proceed, by grave command,
To take the constable in hand.
Then from the pole's sublimest top
The active crew let down the rope,
At once its other end in haste bind,
And make it fast upon his waistband;
Till like the earth, as stretch'd on tenter,
He hung self-balanced on his centre.
Then upwards, all hands hoisting sail,
They swung him, like a keg of ale,
Till to the pinnacle in height
He vaulted, like balloon or kite.
As Socrates of old at first did
To aid philosophy get hoisted,
And found his thoughts flow strangely clear,
Swung in a basket in mid air:
Our culprit thus, in purer sky,
With like advantage raised his eye,
And looking forth in prospect wide,
His tory errors clearly spied,
And from his elevated station,
With bawling voice began addressing.
    "Good gentlemen, and friends, and kin,
For heaven's sake hear, if not for mine!
I here renounce the Pope, the Turks,
The king, the devil, and all their works;
And will, set me but once at ease,
Turn whig or Christian, what you please;
And always mind your rules so justly,
Should I live long as old Methus'lah,
I'll never join in British rage,
Nor help Lord North, nor General Gage;
Nor lift my gun in future fights,
Nor take away your charter-rights;
Nor overcome your new-raised levies,

Destroy your towns, nor burn your navies;
Nor cut your poles down while I 've breath,
Though raised more thick than hatchel-teeth:
But leave king George and all his elves
To do their conquering work themselves."
    This said, they lower'd him down in state,
Spread at all points, like falling cat;
But took a vote first on the question,
That they 'd accept this full confession,
And to their fellowship and favor,
Restore him on his good behaviour.
    Not so our 'Squire submits to rule,
But stood, heroic as a mule.
" You 'll find it all in vain," quoth he,
" To play your rebel tricks on me.
All punishments, the world can render,
Serve only to provoke the offender ;
The will gains strength from treatment horrid,
As hides grow harder when they 're curried.
No man e'er felt the halter draw,
With good opinion of the law ;
Or held in method orthodox
His love of justice, in the stocks ;
Or fail'd to lose by sheriffs' shears
At once his loyalty and ears.
Have you made Murray look less big,
Or smoked old Williams to a whig ?
Did our mobb'd Oliver quit his station,
Or heed his vows of resignation?
Has Rivington, in dread of stripes,
Ceased lying since you stole his types ?
And can you think my faith will alter,
By tarring, whipping, or the halter ?
I 'll stand the worst ; for recompense
I trust king George and Providence.
And when with conquest gain'd I come,
Array'd in law and terror home,
Ye 'll rue this inauspicious morn,
And curse the day when ye were born,
In Job's high style of imprecations,
With all his plagues, without his patience."
    Meanwhile, beside the pole, the guard
A bench of justice had prepared,
Where sitting round in awful sort
The grand committee hold their court ;
While all the crew, in silent awe,
Wait from their lips the lore of law.

Few moments with deliberation
They hold the solemn consultation;
When soon in judgment all agree,
And clerk proclaims the dread decree;
" That 'Squire M'Fingal having grown
The vilest tory in the town,
And now in full examination
Convicted by his own confession,
Finding no tokens of repentance,
This court proceeds to render sentence :
That first the mob a slip-knot single
Tie round the neck of said M'Fingal,
And in due form do tar him next,
And feather, as the law directs;
Then through the town attendant ride him
In cart with constable beside him,
And having held him up to shame,
Bring to the pole, from whence he came."
  Forthwith the crowd proceed to deck
With halter'd noose M'Fingal's neck,
While he in peril of his soul
Stood tied half-hanging to the pole;
Then lifting high the ponderous jar,
Pour'd o'er his head the smoking tar.
With less profusion once was spread
Oil on the Jewish monarch's head,
That down his beard and vestments ran,
And cover'd all his outward man.
As when (so Claudian sings) the gods
And earth-born giants fell at odds,
The stout Enceladus in malice
Tore mountains up to throw at Pallas ;
And while he held them o'er his head,
The river, from their fountains fed,
Pour'd down his back its copious tide,
And wore its channels in his hide :
So from the high-raised urn the torrents
Spread down his side their various currents;
His flowing wig, as next the brim,
First met and drank the sable stream;
Adown his visage stern and grave
Roll'd and adhered the viscid wave ;
With arms depending as he stood,
Each cuff capacious holds the flood;
From nose and chin's remotest end,
The tarry icicles descend ;
Till all o'erspread, with colors gay,

He glitter'd to the western ray,
Like sleet-bound trees in wintry skies,
Or Lapland idol carved in ice.
And now the feather'd bag display'd
Is waved in triumph o'er his head,
And clouds him o'er with feathers missive,
And down, upon the tar, adhesive:
Not Maia's son, with wings for ears,
Such plumage round his visage wears;
Nor Milton's six-wing'd angel gathers
Such superfluity of feathers.
Now all complete appears our 'Squire,
Like Gorgon or Chimæra dire;
Nor more could boast on Plato's plan
To rank among the race of man,
Or prove his claim to human nature,
As a two-legg'd, unfeather'd creature.
Then on the fatal cart, in state
They raised our grand Duumvirate,
And as at Rome a like committee,
Who found an owl within their city,
With solemn rites and grave processions
At every shrine perform'd lustrations;
And lest infection might take place
From such grim fowl with feather'd face,
All Rome attends him through the street
In trumph to his country seat:
With like devotion all the choir
Paraded round our awful 'Squire;
In front the martial music comes
Of horns and fiddles, fifes and drums,
With jingling sound of carriage bells,
And treble creak of rusted wheels.
Behind, the crowd, in lengthen'd row
With proud procession closed the show.
And at fit periods every throat
Combined in universal shout;
And hail'd great liberty in chorus,
Or bawl'd ' confusion to the tories.'
Not louder storm the welkin braves
From clamors of conflicting waves;
Less dire in Lybian wilds the noise
When ravening lions lift their voice;
Or triumphs at town-meetings made,
On passing votes to regulate trade.
　　Thus having borne them round the town,
Last at the pole they set them down;

And to the tavern take their way
To end in mirth the festal day.
   And now the mob, dispersed and gone,
Left 'Squire and constable alone.
The constable with rueful face
Lean'd sad and solemn o'er a brace ;
And fast beside him, cheek by jowl,
Stuck 'Squire M'Fingal 'gainst the pole,
Glued by the tar t' his rear applied,
Like barnacle on vessel's side.
But though his body lack'd physician,
His spirit was in worse condition.
He found his fears of whips and ropes
By many a drachm outweigh'd his hopes.
As men in jail without mainprize
View everything with other eyes,
And all goes wrong in church and state,
Seen through perspective of the grate :
So now M'Fingal's second-sight
Beheld all things in gloomier light;
His visual nerve, well purged with tar,
Saw all the coming scenes of war.
As his prophetic soul grew stronger,
He found he could hold in no longer.
First from the pole, as fierce he shook,
His wig from pitchy durance broke,
His mouth unglued, his feathers flutter'd,
His tarr'd skirts crack'd, and thus he utter'd.
   " Ah, Mr Constable, in vain
We strive 'gainst wind, and tide, and rain,
Behold my doom ! this feathery omen
Portends what dismal times are coming.
Now future scenes, before my eyes,
And second-sighted forms arise.
I hear a voice, that calls away,
And cries, 'the whigs will win the day.'
My beck'ning genius gives command,
And bids me fly the fatal land;
Where changing name and constitution,
Rebellion turns to revolution,
While loyalty, oppress'd, in tears,
Stands trembling for its neck and ears.
   " Go, summon all our brethren, greeting,
To muster at our usual meeting ;
There my prophetic voice shall warn 'em
Of all things future that concern 'em,
And scenes disclose on which, my friend,

Their conduct and their lives depend.
There I—but first 't is more of use,
From this vile pole to set me loose ;
Then go, with cautious steps and steady,
While I steer home and make all ready.

JONATHAN MITCHEL SEWALL

Was born at Salem, Massachusetts, in 1748. He lost his
parents at an early age, and was adopted by his uncle, Stephen
Sewall, Chief Justice of the Supreme Court of Massachusetts.
He studied at Harvard College, and afterwards entered into
mercantile business, which he finally abandoned for the profession of the law, and settled in Portsmouth New Hampshire,
where he passed the remainder of his life, with a high character for integrity and disinterestedness. He died March 29th,
1808, in his sixtieth year.

Mr Sewall applied himself to poetry in his youth, and many
of his pieces were made public previous to the revolution.
Ossian charmed his juvenile fancy to such a degree, that he
versified nearly the whole work. Specimens of this performance, with other miscellaneous pieces, were published in a
volume in 1801. It was his custom, when confined to his bed
by long indisposition, to beguile the wearisomeness of his
sleepless nights, by the composition of verses, which, when he
had sufficiently recovered to handle a pen, he committed to
writing.

The piece best entitled to our regard among his productions,
is the ode of War and Washington, a patriotic Tyrtæan strain,
which was sung throughout the country during the revolutionary war, and served to inspire zeal and courage in the
cause of independence. No national lyric ever aroused more
enthusiasm, or was chanted with better effect than this war
song of the American revolution. It was the favorite strain
throughout the ranks of the army in every part of the country,

and kindled the martial ardor and patriotic feelings of all. Such relics are the most precious and interesting which can be gathered from the literature of the times.

WAR AND WASHINGTON.

Vain Britons, boast no longer with proud indignity,
By land your conquering legions, your matchless strength at
    sea,
Since we, your braver sons, incensed, our swords have girded
    on,
Huzza, huzza, huzza, huzza, for war and Washington!

Urged on by North and vengeance, those valiant champions
    came,
Loud bellowing Tea and Treason, and George was all on
    flame,
Yet sacrilegious as it seems, we rebels still live on,
And laugh at all their empty puffs,—huzza for Washington!

Still deaf to mild entreaties, still blind to England's good,
You have for thirty pieces betray'd your country's blood.
Like Esop's greedy cur you'll gain a shadow for your bone,
Yet find us fearful shades indeed, inspired by Washington.

Mysterious! unexampled! incomprehensible!
The blundering schemes of Britain, their folly, pride, and zeal.
Like lions how ye growl and threat! mere asses have you
    shown,
And ye shall share an ass's fate, and drudge for Washington!

Your dark, unfathom'd counsels our weakest heads defeat,
Our children rout your armies, our boats destroy your fleet,
And to complete the dire disgrace, coop'd up within a town,
You live, the scorn of all our host, the slaves of Washington!

Great heaven! is this the nation whose thundering arms were
    hurl'd,
Through Europe, Afric, India? whose navy ruled a world?
The lustre of your former deeds, whole ages of renown,
Lost in a moment, or transferred to us and Washington!

Yet think not thirst of glory unsheaths our vengeful swords,
To rend your bands asunder, and cast away your cords.
'T is heaven-born freedom fires us all, and strengthens each
    brave son,
From him who humbly guides the plough, to godlike Wash-
    ington.

For this, Oh could our wishes your ancient rage inspire,
Your armies should be doubled, in numbers, force, and fire.
Then might the glorious conflict prove which best deserved
    the boon,
America, or Albion; a George, or Washington!

Fired with the great idea, our fathers' shades would rise;
To view the stern contention, the gods desert their skies.
And Wolfe; 'mid hosts of heroes, superior bending down,
Cry out with eager transport, God save great Washington!

Should George, too choice of Britons, to foreign realms
    apply,
And madly arm half Europe, yet still we would defy
Turk, Hessian, Jew, and Infidel, or all those powers in one,
While Adams guides our senate, our camp great Washington!

Should warlike weapons fail us, disdaining slavish fears,
To swords we'll beat our ploughshares, our pruninghooks to
    spears,
And rush, all desperate! on our foe, nor breathe till battle
    won;
Then shout, and shout America! and conquering Washing-
    ton!

Proud France should view with terror, and haughty Spain
    revere,
While every warlike nation would court alliance here.
And George, his minions trembling round, dismounting from
    his throne,
Pay homage to America, and glorious Washington!

FRANCIS HOPKINSON.

JUDGE HOPKINSON, was born in Philadelphia, in 1737. He was the son of Thomas Hopkinson, an English gentleman who filled a considerable office in the government of Pennsylvania. Thomas Hopkinson was a man of respectable attainments in science, and was associated with Franklin in his experiments upon electricity. He died early in life, and left his son at the age of fourteen to the direction of a very affectionate and attentive mother, who spared no exertion in the care of his morals and education. He was sent to the college of Philadelphia, after which he devoted himself to the study and practice of law. He visited England in 1765, where he remained above two years. At the commencement of the revolution he represented the state of New Jersey in Congress, a post which gave him the distinction of affixing his signature to the Declaration of Independence. He distinguished himself very early in the contest, by his writings against the designs of the British government, and possessing great powers of humor and command of language, his pieces were extensively circulated, and contributed not a little to the support of the cause which he had embraced. His judicious selection of topics, and his skill in handling them, procured his writings a ready acceptance with all classes of people. The versatility of his powers may be attested by the readiness with which he wielded the weapons of satire, wit, or argumentation, and drew upon every department of the human faculties for materials in the warfare ; now declaiming against the encroachments of Britain with the skill and eloquence of a statesman, and now framing a satirical ballad, or quaint allegory, seasoned with the accompaniment of humor and sarcasm to the popular relish. The elegance and politeness which marked his writings had a considerable effect in improving the manner of most of the publications of the day. His satire was pointed at the follies and impertinences current among those with which he was familiar, as well as against the political enormities of his country's enemies, and contributed equally to help the cause of public morals, promote good breeding in polite society, and soften the asperity of party rage.

Although drawn within the circle of politics at a period of great events, the course of his life is not marked with any remarkable vicissitude or striking incident. He held an appointment in the loan office for some years, and was afterwards made Judge of the Admiralty for the state of Pennsylvania. In 1790, he was appointed Judge of the District Court in Pennsylvania. He died on the 8th of May, 1791.

Hopkinson applied himself to the law with assiduity, and his acquirements in that branch of learning were such as to gain him a high reputation among his contemporaries. With general science too, he was well acquainted. His powers of wit and satire shine in various parts of his lighter performances, and notwithstanding the zest has in many instances evaporated by time, there are some in which the humor preserves all its original freshness. The Essay on Whitewashing is deservedly celebrated as a *morceau* of spirited pleasantry. His manners were the counterpart of his writings; polished, lively, and engaging, and without any stiffness or rigor, under the guidance of the strictest decorum.

His works embrace quite a miscellaneous collection, mostly of prose. They were published shortly after his death, in three volumes.

THE BATTLE OF THE KEGS.*

GALLANTS attend, and hear a friend,
  Trill forth harmonious ditty,
Strange things I 'll tell which late befell
  In Philadelphia city.

* This ballad was occasioned by a real incident. Certain machines, in the form of kegs, charged with gunpowder, were sent down the river to annoy the British shipping then at Philadelphia. The danger of these machines being discovered, the British manned the wharves and shipping, and discharged their small arms and cannons at everything they saw floating in the river, during the ebb tide.

'T was early day, as poets say,
  Just when the sun was rising,
A soldier stood on a log of wood,
  And saw a thing surprising.

As in amaze he stood to gaze,
  The truth can't be denied, sir,
He spied a score of kegs or more
  Come floating down the tide, sir.

A sailor too, in jerkin blue,
  This strange appearance viewing,
First damn'd his eyes, in great surprise,
  Then said, " Some mischief 's brewing.

" These kegs, I 'm told, the rebels bold,
  Pack'd up like pickled herring ;
And they 're come down t' attack the town,
  In this new way of ferrying."

The soldier flew, the sailor too,
  And scared almost to death, sir,
Wore out their shoes, to spread the news,
  And ran till out of breath, sir.

Now up and down, throughout the town,
  Most frantic scenes were acted ;
And some ran here, and others there,
  Like men almost distracted.

Some fire cried, which some denied,
  But said the earth had quaked ;
And girls and boys, with hideous noise,
  Ran through the streets half naked.

Sir William he, snug as a flea,
  Lay all this time a snoring,
Nor dream'd of harm, as he lay warm,
  In bed with Mrs L——g.

Now in a fright he starts upright,
  Awaked by such a clatter ;
He rubs both eyes, and boldly cries,
  " For God's sake, what 's the matter ?'

At his bedside he then espied
　　Sir Erskine at command, sir,
Upon one foot he had one boot,
　　And the other in his hand, sir.

" Arise, arise," Sir Erskine cries,
　　" The rebels—more 's the pity,
Without a boat are all afloat,
　　And ranged before the city.

" The motly crew, in vessels new,
　　With Satan for their guide, sir.
Pack'd up in bags, or wooden kegs,
　　Come driving down the tide, sir.

" Therefore prepare for bloody war,—
　　These kegs must all be routed,
Or surely we despised shall be,
　　And British courage doubted."

The royal band now ready stand,
　　All ranged in dread array, sir,
With stomach stout to see it out,
　　And make a bloody day, sir.

The cannons roar from shore to shore,
　　The small arms make a rattle;
Since wars began I 'm sure no man
　　E'er saw so strange a battle.

The rebel dales, the rebel vales,
　　With rebel trees surrounded;
The distant wood, the hills and floods,
　　With rebel echoes sounded.

The fish below swam to and fro,
　　Attack'd from every quarter;
Why sure, thought they, the devil 's to pay,
　　'Mongst folks above the water.

The kegs, 't is said, though strongly made,
　　Of rebel staves and hoops, sir,
Could not oppose their powerful foes,
　　The conquering British troops, sir.

From morn to night these men of might
  Display'd amazing courage;
And when the sun was fairly down,
  Retired to sup their porridge.

An hundred men with each a pen,
  Or more, upon my word, sir.
It is most true, would be too few,
  Their valor, to record, sir.

Such feats did they perform that day,
  Against these wicked kegs, sir,
That years to come, if they get home,
  They 'll make their boasts and brags, sir.

SONG.

Soft ideas love inspiring,
  Every placid joy unite;
Every anxious thought retiring,
  Fill my bosom with delight.

Soft ideas, gently flowing,
  On your tide, so calm and still;
Bear me where sweet zeyphrs blowing,
  Wave the pines on Borden's Hill.

Where the breezes odors bringing,
  Fill the grove with murmuring sound;
Where shrill notes of birds, sweet singing,
  Echo to the hills around.

To the pleasing gloom convey me,
  Let my Delia too be there;
On her gentle bosom lay me,
  On her bosom soft and fair.

Whilst I there, with rapture burning,
  All my joy in her express,
Let her, love for love returning,
  Me with fond caresses bless.

On his little wings descending,
　Bring the god of soft delight:
Hymen too, with torch attending,
　Must our hands and hearts unite.

She the source of all my pleasure
　Shall my breast with transport fill;
Delia is my soul's best treasure,
　Delia, pride of Borden's Hill.

———

SONG.

Come, fair Rosina, come away,
　Long since stern winter's storms have ceased!
See! Nature, in her best array,
　Invites us to her rural feast:
The season shall her treasure spread,
　Her mellow fruits and harvests brown,
Her flowers their richest odors shed,
　And every breeze pour fragrance down.

At noon we 'll seek the wild wood's shade,
　And o'er the pathless verdure rove;
Or, near a mossy fountain laid,
　Attend the music of the grove.
At eve, the sloping mead invites
　'Midst lowing herds and flocks to stray;
Each hour shall furnish new delights,
　And love and joy shall crown the day.

———

SONG.

O'er the hills far away, at the birth of the morn,
I hear the full tone of the sweet sounding horn;
The sportsmen with shoutings all hail the new day,
And swift run the hounds o'er the hills far away.
Across the deep valley their course they pursue,
And rush through the thickets yet silver'd with dew;
Nor hedges nor ditches their speed can delay—
Still sounds the sweet horn o'er the hills far away.

———

SONG.

My generous heart disdains
　　The slave of love to be,
I scorn his servile chains,
　　And boast my liberty.
　　　　This whining
　　　　And pining
And wasting with care,
Are not to my taste, be she ever so fair.

Shall a girl's capricious frown
Sink my noble spirits down?
Shall a face of white and red
Make me droop my silly head?
Shall I set me down and sigh
For an eyebrow or an eye?
For a braided lock of hair,
Curse my fortune and despair?
　　My generous heart disdains, &c.

Still uncertain is tomorrow,
Not quite certain is today—
Shall I waste my time in sorrow?
Shall I languish life away?
All because a cruel maid
Hath not love with love repaid.
　　My generous heart disdains, &c.

———

LINES ON THE QUARREL AMONG THE STUDENTS IN ANATO-MY IN PHILADELPHIA.

Friends and associates! lend a patient ear,
Suspend intestine broils and reason hear.
Ye followers of —— your wrath forbear—
Ye sons of ——— your invectives spare;
The fierce dissension your high minds pursue
Is sport for others—ruinous to you.

Surely some fatal influenza reigns,
Some epidemic *rabies* turns your brains;
Is this a time for brethren to engage
In public contest and in party rage?
Fell discord triumphs in your doubtful strife,
And, smiling, whets her anatomic knife;

Prepared to cut our precious limbs away
And leave the bleeding body to decay.

Seek ye for foes ? alas, my friends, look round,
In every street, see numerous foes abound!
Methinks I hear them cry, in varied tones,
" Give us our father's—brother's—sister's bones."
Methinks I see a mob of sailors rise—
" Revenge!—revenge ! " they cry, and damn their eyes—
" Revenge for comrade Jack, whose flesh they say,
You minced to morsels and then threw away."
Methinks I see a black infernal train—
The genuine offspring of accursed Cain—
Fiercely on you their angry looks are bent,
They grin and gibber dangerous discontent,
And seem to say—" Is there not meat enough ?
Ah! massa cannibal, why eat poor Cuff? "
Even hostile watchmen stand in strong array,
And o'er our heads their threatening staves display :
Howl hideous discord through the noon of night,
And shake their dreadful lanthorns in our sight.

Say, are not these sufficient to engage
Your high wrought souls eternal war to wage?
Combine your strength these monsters to subdue,
No friends of science and sworn foes to you ;
On these—on these, your wordy vengeance pour,
And strive our fading glory to restore.

Ah ! think how, late, our mutilated rites
And midnight orgies, were by sudden frights
And loud alarms profaned—the sacrifice,
Stretch'd on a board before our eager eyes,
All naked lay—even when our chieftain stood
Like a high priest, prepared for shedding blood ;
Prepared, with wonderous skill to cut or slash,
The gentle sliver or the deep drawn gash ;
Prepared to plunge even elbow deep in gore,
Nature and nature's secrets to explore—
Then a tumultuous cry—a sudden fear—
Proclaim'd the foe—the enraged foe is near—
In some dark hole the hard-got corse was laid,
And we, in wild conclusion, fled dismay'd.

Think how, like brethren, we have shared the toil,
When in the Potter's field we sought for spoil,

Did midnight ghosts and death and horror brave—
To delve for science in the dreary grave.—
Shall I remind you of that awful night
When our compacted band maintained the fight
Against an armed host?—fierce was the fray,
And yet we bore our sheeted prize away.
Firm on a horse's back the corse was laid,
High blowing winds the winding sheet display'd ;
Swift flew the steed—but still his burthen bore—
Fear made him fleet, who ne'er was fleet before ;
O'er tombs and sunken graves he coursed around,
Nor aught respected consecrated ground.
Meantime the battle raged—so loud the strife,
The dead were almost frighten'd into life—
Though not victorious, yet we scorn'd to yield,
Retook our prize, and left the doubtful field.

In this degenerate age, alas ! how few
The paths of science with true zeal pursue ?
Some trifling contest, some delusive joy
Too oft the unsteady minds of youth employ.
For me—whom Esculapius hath inspired—
I boast a soul with love of science fired ;
By one great object is my heart possess'd—
One ruling passion quite absorbs the rest—
In this bright point my hopes and fears unite ;
And one pursuit alone can give delight.

To me things are not as to vulgar eyes,
I would all nature's works anatomize—
This world a living monster seems, to me,
Rolling and sporting in the aerial sea ;
The soil encompasses her rocks and stones
As flesh in animals encircles bones.
I see vast ocean, like a heart in play,
Pant *systole* and *diastole* every day,
And by unnumbered *venous* streams supply'd
Up her broad river force the *arterial* tide.
The world's great lungs, monsoons and tradewinds show
From east to west, from west to east they blow
Alternate respiration——
The hills are pimples which earth's face defile,
And burning Ætna, an eruptive bile :
From her vast body perspirations rise,
Condense in clouds and float beneath the skies :
Thus fancy, faithful servant of the heart,
Transforms all nature by her magic art.

E'en mighty love, whose power all powers controls;
Is not, in me, like love in other souls—
Yet I have loved—and Cupid's subtle dart
Hath through my *pericardium* pierced my heart.
Brown Cadavera did my soul ensnare,
Was all my thought by night and daily care—
I long'd to clasp, in her transcendant charms,
A living skeleton within my arms.

Long, lank, and lean, my Cadavera stood,
Like the tall pine, the glory of the wood—
Oft times I gazed, with learned skill to trace
The sharp edged beauties of her bony face—
There rose *os frontis* prominent and bold,
In deep sunk orbits two large eye-balls roll'd,
Beneath those eye-balls, two arch'd bones were seen
Whereon two flabby cheeks hung loose and lean;
Beneath those cheeks, proturberant arose,
In form triangular, her lovely nose,
Like Egypt's pyramid it seem'd to rise,
Scorn earth, and bid defiance to the skies;
Thin were her lips, and of a sallow hue,
Her open'd mouth exposed her teeth to view;
Projecting strong, protuberant and wide
Stood *incisores*—and on either side
The *canine* ranged, with many a beauteous flaw,
And last the grinders, to fill up the jaw—
All in their *alveoli* fix'd secure,
Articulated by *gomphosis* sure.
Around her mouth, perpetual smiles had made
Wrinkles wherein the loves and graces play'd;
There, stretch'd and rigid by continual strain,
Appear'd the *zygomatic* muscles plain,
And broad *montanus* o'er her peaked chin
Extended to support the heavenly grin.
Long were her fingers and her knuckles bare,
Much like the claw-foot of a walnut chair.
So plain was complex *metacarpus* shown
It might be fairly counted bone by bone.
Her slender *phalanxes* were well defined,
And each with each by *ginglymus* combined.
Such were the charms that did my fancy fire,
And love—chaste, scientific love inspire.

ANN ELIZA BLEECKER.

Mrs Bleecker was the daughter of Mr Brandt Schuyler, and was born in New York in 1752. In 1769 she was married to John J. Bleecker Esq. of New Rochelle, and removed to Poughkeepsie, and shortly after to Tomhanick, a beautiful solitary village eighteen miles above Albany. Here she passed several years in the unbroken quiet of the wilderness, and although accustomed to move in the busy and gay throngs of the metropolis, her love for rural scenery, and the endearments of her domestic circle, rendered her life in this retirement a scene of unalloyed tranquillity and happiness. The repose of this beautiful and romantic spot, was at length broken by the clamors of war. In 1777 the approach of Burgoyne's army from Canada spread terror and consternation throughout the back settlements, in that quarter. The horrors of military rapine were augmented by the fierce cruelties of savage warfare, and the dread of the British general's Indian ally frightened the peaceful inhabitants of the forest from their dwellings. Mr Bleecker's residence lay directly in the march of the invading foe, and he hastened to Albany to prepare a shelter for his family. But a few hours after his departure, Mrs Bleecker, as she sat at table, received intelligence that the enemy was within two miles of the village, burning and slaughtering all before him. In unspeakable terror at this information, she started up, and taking one of her daughters under her arm, and seizing the other by the hand, set off on foot, attended only by a young mulatto girl, leaving her house and all its contents a prey to the savages. The roads were incumbered with carriages loaded with women and children, and no assistance could be obtained; nothing but confusion and distress prevailed. After travelling on foot four or five miles, she procured a seat for the children in a wagon, and walked onward to the village of Stony Arabia, where after much difficulty she obtained shelter in a garret. Her husband returning from Albany, met her the next morning, and they proceeded to that city, from which place they departed down the Hudson by water.   Twelve miles below Albany, her youngest daughter was taken so ill, that they were forced to go on shore, where shortly after she died.   From hence they proceeded to Red Hook, where they considered themselves in safety .

The capture of Burgoyne soon after allowed them to return to their retreat in the country, but the loss of her daughter made so deep an impression upon her mind, that she never recovered her former happiness.   She was naturally of a pensive turn, and brooded over her griefs with too free an indulgence.   She lived, however, in tolerable tranquillity till the year 1781, when, as Mr Bleecker was assisting in the harvest one day in August, he was surprised by a party of the enemy from Canada, and carried off prisoner with two of his men. Mrs Bleecker, unknowing of the circumstance, continued to expect him home till late in the day, at which time, growing apprehensive, she despatched a servant in search of him, who returned without making any discovery.   As a number of parties from Canada were known to be prowling about in the woods for the purpose of seizing and carrying off the most active citizens, she began to conjecture what had become of him.   The neighborhood was raised, and the forest searched for him, but without effect; not a trace could be discovered of the party.   Mrs Bleecker, completely overcome with grief, gave him up for lost, and set out for Albany, although it was near night.   Mr Blecker however, had the good fortune to be rescued from his captors, just at the time when they had proceeded so far as to imagine themselves in perfect security. He was retaken by a party of Americans from Bennington, and returned to his wife, after an absence of six days.   The joy she experienced on again beholding him, so far overpowered her, as to bring on a fit of sickness, which nearly proved fatal.

After the peace, she returned to New York for the purpose of revisiting the scenes and associates of her childhood, but the loss of her friends, and the ruinous condition of her native city, preyed so powerfully upon her, that her spirits were unequal to the burden. She returned to her cottage at Tomhanick where she died on the 23d of November, 1783, at the age of 31.

Mrs Bleecker's poetry is not of that high order which would sustain itself under any very bold attempt; but the events of her life confer a degree of interest upon the few productions which she has left behind her. A female cultivating the elegant arts of refined society at the *ultima Thule* of civilized life, in regions of savage wildness, and among scenes of alarm, desolation, and bloodshed, is a spectacle too striking not to fix our attention.

TO MISS TEN EYCK.

Dear Kitty, while you rove through sylvan bowers,
Inhaling fragrance from salubrious flowers,
Or view your blushes mantling in the stream,
When Luna gilds it with her amber beam;
The brazen voice of war awakes our fears,
Impearling every damask cheek with tears
The savage, rushing down the echoing vales,
Frights the poor hind with ill portending yells;
A livid white his consort's cheeks invest;
She drops her blooming infant from her breast;
She tries to fly, but quick recoiling sees
The painted Indian issuing from the trees;
Then life suspensive sinks her on the plain,
Till dire explosions wake her up again.
Oh, horrid sight! her partner is no more;
Pale is his corse, or only tinged with gore;
Her playful babe is dash'd against the stones,
Its scalp torn off, and fractured all its bones.
Where are the dimpling smiles it lately wore?
Ghastly in agony it smiles no more!
Dumb with amaze, and stupefied with grief,
The captured wretch must now attend her chief:
Reluctantly she quits the scene of blood,
When lo! a sudden light illumes the wood;
She turns, and sees the rising fires expand,
And conflagration roll through half the land;
The western flames to orient skies are driven,
And change the azure to a sable heaven.

Such are our woes, my dear, and be it known
Many still suffer what I tell of one:
No more Albania's sons in slumber lie,
When Cynthia's crescent gleams along the sky;
But every street patrole, and through the night
Their beamy arms reflect a dreadful light.

Excuse, dear girl, for once this plaintive strain;
I must conclude, lest I transgress again.

TO MR BLEECKER, ON HIS PASSAGE TO NEW YORK.

SHALL fancy still pursue the expanding sails,
Calm Neptune's brow, or raise impelling gales?
Or with her Bleecker ply the laboring oar,
When pleasing scenes invite him to the shore,
There with him through the fading valleys rove,
Bless'd in idea with the man I love?
Methinks I see the broad majestic sheet
Swell to the wind; the flying shores retreat:
I see the banks, with varied foliage gay,
Inhale the misty sun's reluctant ray:
The lofty groves stripp'd of their verdure, rise
To the inclemence of autumnal skies.

Rough mountains now appear, while pendant woods
Hang o'er the gloomy steep and shade the floods;
Slow moves the vessel, while each distant sound
The cavern'd echoes doubly loud rebound:
A placid stream meanders on the steep,
Till tumbling from the cliff, divides the frowning deep.

Oh tempt not fate on those stupendous rocks,
Where never shepherd led his timid flocks;
But shagged bears in those wild deserts stray,
And wolves, who howl against the lunar ray:
There builds the ravenous hawk her lofty nest,
And there the soaring eagle takes her rest;
The solitary deer recoils to hear
The torrent thundering in the midway air.
Ah! let me intercede—Ah! spare her breath,
Nor aim the tube charged with a leaden death.

But now advancing to the opening sea,
The wind springs up, the lessening mountains flee;
The eastern banks are crown'd with rural seats,
And nature's work the hand of art completes.
Here Philips' villa, where Pomona joins
At once the product of a hundred climes;

Here, tinged by Flora, Asian flowers unfold
Their burnish'd leaves of vegetable gold.
When snows descend, and clouds tumultuously fly
Through the blue medium of the crystal sky,
Beneath his painted mimic heaven he roves
Amidst the glass-encircled citron groves;
The grape and luscious fig his taste invite,
Hesperian apples glow upon his sight;
The sweet auriculas their bells display,
And Philips finds in January, May.

　But on the other side the cliffs arise,
Charybdis like, and seem to prop the skies:
How oft with admiration have we view'd
Those adamantine barriers of the flood?
Yet still the vessel cleaves the liquid mead,
The prospect dies, the aspiring rocks recede;
New objects rush upon the wondering sight,
Till Phœbus rolls from heaven his car of light,
And Cynthia's silver crescent gilds the night.

　I hear the melting flute's melodious sound,
Which dying zephyrs waft alternate round,
The rocks in notes responsive soft complain,
And think Amphion strikes his lyre again.
Ah! 'tis my Bleecker breathes our mutual loves,
And sends the trembling airs through vocal groves.

　Thus having led you to the happy isle
Where waves circumfluent wash the fertile soil,
Where Hudson, meeting the Atlantic, roars,
The parting lands dismiss him from their shores;
Indulge the enthusiast muse her favorite strain
Of panegyric, due to Eboracia's plain.

　There is no land where heaven her blessings pours
In such abundance, as upon these shores;
With influence benign the planets rise,
Pure is the ether, and serene the skies;
With annual gold kind Ceres decks the ground,
And gushing springs dispense bland health around:
No lucid gems are here, or flaming ore,
To tempt the hand of avarice and power:
But sun-burnt labor, with diurnal toil,
Bids treasures rise from the obedient soil,
And commerce calls the ships across the main,
For gold exchanging her superfluous grain;
While concord, liberty, and jocund health
Sport with young pleasure 'mid the rural wealth.

AN EVENING PROSPECT.

Come, my Susan, quit your chamber,
  Greet the opening bloom of May,
Let us up yon hillock clamber,
  And around the scene survey.

See the sun is now descending,
  And projects his shadows far,
And the bee her course is bending
  Homeward through the humid air.

Mark the lizard just before us,
  Singing her unvaried strain,
While the frog abrupt in chorus,
  Deepens through the marshy plain.

From yon grove the woodcock rises,
  Mark her progress by her notes,
High in air her wings she poises,
  Then like lightning down she shoots.

Now the whip-o-will beginning,
  Clamorous on a pointed rail,
Drowns the more melodious singing
  Of the catbird, thrush, and quail.

Pensive Echo, from the mountain,
  Still repeats the sylvan sounds,
And the crocus-border'd fountain
  With the splendid fly abounds.

There the honeysuckle blooming,
  Reddens the capricious wave ;
Richer sweets—the air perfuming,
  Spicy Ceylon never gave.

Cast your eyes beyond this meadow,
  Painted by a hand divine,
And observe the ample shadow
  Of that solemn ridge of pine.

Here a trickling rill depending,
  Glitters through the artless bower ;
And the silver dew descending,
  Doubly radiates every flower.

While I speak, the sun is vanish'd,
　All the gilded clouds are fled,
Music from the groves is banish'd,
　Noxious vapors round us spread.

Rural toil is now suspended,
　Sleep invades the peasant's eyes,
Each diurnal task is ended,
　While soft Luna climbs the skies.

Queen of rest and meditation,
　Through thy medium I adore
Him—the author of creation,
　Infinite, and boundless power.

'T is he who fills thy urn with glory,
　Transcript of immortal light;
Lord! my spirit bows before thee,
　Lost in wonder and delight.

PEACE.

ALL hail, vernal Phœbus! all hail, ye soft breezes!
　Announcing the visit of spring;
How green are the meadows! the air how it pleases!
　How gleefully all the birds sing!

Begone, ye rude tempests, nor trouble the ether,
　Nor let blushing Flora complain,
While her pencil was tinging the tulip, bad weather
　Had blasted the promising gem.

From its verdant unfoldings, the timid narcissus
　Now shoots out a diffident bud;
Begone ye rude tempests, for sure as it freezes
　Ye kill this bright child of the wood:

And peace gives new charms to the bright beaming season:
　The groves we now safely explore,
Where murdering banditti, the dark sons of treason,
　Were shelter'd and awed as before.

The swain with his oxen proceeds to the valley,
   Whose seven years sabbath concludes,
And blesses kind heaven, that Britain's black ally
   Is chased to Canadia's deep woods.

And Echo no longer is plaintively mourning,
   But laughs and is jocund as we ;
And the turtle-eyed nymphs, to their cots all returning,
   Carve " Washington," on every tree.

I 'll wander along by the side of yon fountain,
   And drop in its current the line,
To capture the glittering fish that there wanton ;
   Ah, no ! 't is an evil design.

Sport on, little fishes, your lives are a treasure
   Which I can destroy, but not give ;
Methinks it 's at best a malevolent pleasure
   To bid a poor being not live.

How lucid the water ! its soft undulations
   Are changeably ting'd by the light ;
It reflects the green banks, and by fair imitations
   Presents a new heaven to sight.

The butterfly skims o'er its surface, all gilded
   With plumage just dipp'd in rich dies ;
But yon infant has seized the poor insect, ah ! yield it ;
   There, see the freed bird how it flies !

But whither am I and my little dog straying ?
   Too far from our cottage we roam ;
The dews are already exhaled ; cease your playing,
   Come, Daphne, come let us go home.

———

RETURN TO TOMHANICK.

Hail, happy shades ! though clad with heavy snows,
At sight of you with joy my bosom glows ;
Ye arching pines, that bow with every breeze,
Ye poplars, elms, all hail my well known trees !
And now my peaceful mansion strikes my eye,
And now the tinkling rivulet I spy ;
My little garden, Flora, hast thou kept,
And watch'd my pinks and lilies while I wept ?

Or has the grubbing swine, by furies led,
The enclosure broke, and on my flowrets fed?
  Ah me! that spot with blooms so lately graced,
With storms and driving snows is now defaced;
Sharp icicles from every bush depend,
And frosts all dazzling o'er the beds extend:
Yet soon fair spring shall give another scene,
And yellow cowslips gild the level green;
My little orchard sprouting at each bough,
Fragrant with clustering blossoms deep shall glow:
Ah! then 't is sweet the tufted grass to tread,
But sweeter slumbering is the balmy shade;
The rapid humming bird, with ruby breast,
Seeks the parterre with early blue-bells drest,
Drinks deep the honeysuckle dew, or drives
The laboring bee to her domestic hives:
Then shines the lupine bright with morning gems,
And sleepy poppies nod upon their stems;
The humble violet and the dulcet rose,
The stately lily then, and tulip blows.
  Farewell, my Plutarch! farewell, pen and muse!
Nature exults—shall I her call refuse?
Apollo fervid glitters in my face,
And threatens with his beam each feeble grace:
Yet still around the lovely plants I toil,
And draw obnoxious herbage from the soil;
Or with the lime-twigs little birds surprise,
Or angle for the trout of many dyes.
  But when the vernal breezes pass away,
And loftier Phœbus darts a fiercer ray,
The spiky corn then rattles all around,
And dashing cascades give a pleasing sound;
Shrill sings the locust with prolonged note,
The cricket chirps familiar in each cot.
The village children, rambling o'er yon hill,
With berries all their painted baskets fill.
They rob the squirrel's little walnut store,
And climb the half exhausted tree for more;
Or else to fields of maize nocturnal hie,
Where hid, the elusive water-melons lie;
Sportive, they make incisions in the rind,
The riper from the immature to find;
Then load their tender shoulders with the prey,
And laughing bear the bulky fruit away.

MARGARETTA V. FAUGERES.

This lady was the daughter of Mrs Bleecker, and her poems were published in the same volume with those of her mother, in 1793.

THE HUDSON.

Nile's beauteous waves, and Tiber's swelling tide
   Have been recorded by the hand of Fame,
And various floods, which through earth's channels glide,
   From some enraptured bard have gain'd a name;
E'en Thames and Wye have been the poet's theme,
   And to their charms hath many an harp been strung,
Whilst, Oh! hoar genius of old Hudson's stream,
   Thy mighty river never hath been sung:
Say, shall a female string her trembling lyre,
   And to thy praise devote the adventurous song?
Fired with the theme, her genius shall aspire,
   And the notes sweeten as they float along.
Where rough Ontario's restless waters roar,
   And hoarsely rave around the rocky shore;
Where their abode tremendous north-winds make,
   And reign the tyrants of the surging lake;
There, as the shell-crown'd genii of its caves
Toward proud Lawrence urged their noisy waves,
A form majestic from the flood arose;
A coral bandage sparkled o'er his brows,
A purple mantle o'er his limbs was spread,
And sportive breezes in his dark locks play'd:
Toward the east shore his anxious eyes he cast,
And from his ruby lips these accents pass'd:
"O favor'd land! indulgent nature yields
Her choicest sweets to deck thy boundless fields;
Where in thy verdant glooms the fleet deer play,
And the hale tenants of the desert stray,
While the tall evergreens that edge the dale
In silent majesty nod to each gale:
Thy riches shall no more remain unknown,
Thy wide campaign do I pronounce my own;
And while the strong arm'd genii of this lake
Their tributary streams to Lawrence take,
Back from its source my current will I turn,
And o'er thy meadows pour my copious urn."

He said, and, waving high his dripping hand ;
Bade his clear waters roll toward the land.
Glad they obey'd, and struggling to the shore,
Dash'd on its broken rocks with thundering roar :
The rocks in vain oppose their furious course ;
From each repulse they rise with tenfold force ;
And gathering all their angry powers again,
Gushed o'er the banks, and fled across the plain
Soon as the waves had pressed the level mead,
Full many a pearly-footed Naiad fair,
With hasty steps, her limpid fountain led,
To swell the tide, and hail it welcome there :
Their busy hands collect a thousand flowers,
And scatter them along the grassy shores.
There, bending low, the water-lilies bloom,
And the blue crocus shed their moist perfume ;
There the tall velvet scarlet lark-spur laves
Her pale green stem in the pellucid waves ;
There nods the fragile columbine, so fair,
And the mild dewy wild-rose scents the air ;
While round the trunk of some majestic pine
The blushing honeysuckle's branches twine :
There too Pomona's richest gifts are found,
Her golden melons press the fruitful ground ;
The glossy crimson plums there swell their rinds,
And purple grapes dance to autumnal winds ;
While all beneath the mandrake's fragrant shade
The strawberry's delicious sweets are laid.

   *   *   *   *

Through many a "blooming wild" and woodland green,
 The Hudson's sleeping waters winding stray ;
Now 'mongst the hills its silvery waves are seen,
 And now through arching willows steal away :
Then bursting on the enamor'd sight once more,
 Gladden some happy peasant's rude retreat ;
And passing youthful Troy's commercial shore,
 With the hoarse Mohawk's roaring surges meet.
Oh, beauteous Mohawk ! 'wildered with thy charms,
 The chilliest heart sinks into rapturous glows ;
While the stern warrior, used to loud alarms,
 Starts at the thunderings of thy dread Cohoes.
Now more majestic rolls the ample tide,
 Tall waving elms its clovery borders shade,
And many a stately dome, in ancient pride,
 And hoary grandeur, there exalts its head.

There trace the marks of culture's sunburnt hand,
　The honeyed buck-wheat's clustering blossoms view,
Dripping rich odors, mark the beard-grain bland,
　The loaded orchard, and the flax field blue.
Albania's gothic spires now greet the eye;
　Time's hand hath wiped their burnish'd tints away,
And the rich fanes which sparkled to the sky,
　'Reft of their splendors, mourn in cheerless grey.
There many an ancient structure tottering stands;
　Round the damp chambers mouldy vapors creep,
And feathery-footed Silence folds her hands,
　While the pale genii of the mansion sleep.
Yet thither Trade's full freighted vessels come;
　Thither the shepherds mercantile resort:
There Architecture late hath raised her dome,
　And Agriculture's products fill her port.
The grassy hill, the quivering poplar grove,
　The copse of hazle, and the tufted bank,
The long green valley, where the white flocks rove,
　The jutting rock, o'erhung with ivy dank;
The tall pines waving on the mountain's brow,
　Whose lofty spires catch day's last lingering beam;
　The bending willow weeping o'er the stream,
The brook's soft gurglings, and the garden's glow.

　　*　　　*　　　*　　　*　　　*　　　*

Low sunk between the Alleganian hills,
　For many a league the sullen waters glide,
　And the deep murmur of the crowded tide,
With pleasing awe the wondering voyager fills.
On the green summit of yon lofty clift
　A peaceful runnel gurgles clear and slow,
Then down the craggy steep-side dashing swift,
　Tremendous falls in the white surge below.
Here spreads a clovery lawn its verdure far,
　Around it mountains vast their forests rear,
And long ere day hath left his burnish'd car,
　The dews of night have shed their odors there.
There hangs a louring rock across the deep;
　Hoarse roar the waves its broken base around;
Through its dark caverns noisy whirlwinds sweep,
　While Horror startles at the fearful sound.
The shivering sails that cut the fluttering breeze,
　Glide through these winding rocks with airy sweep:
Beneath the cooling glooms of waving trees,
　And sloping pastures speck'd with fleecy sheep.

———

ON A PAINTER.

When Laura appear'd, poor Apelles complain'd,
That his sight was bedimm'd, and his optics much pain'd ;
So his pallet and pencil the artist resign'd,
Lest the blaze of her beauty should make him quite blind.
But when fair Anne enter'd the prospect was changed,
The paints and the brushes in order were ranged ;
The artist resumed his employment again,
Forgetful of labor, and blindness, and pain ;
And the strokes were so lively that all were assured
What the brunette had injured the fair one had cured.
Let the candid decide which the chaplet should wear,
The charms which destroy, or the charms which repair.

TIMOTHY DWIGHT.

Timothy Dwight was born at Northampton, in Massachusetts on the 14th day of May, 1752. His father, Timothy
Dwight, was a merchant liberally educated, and the proprie-
tor of a considerable estate ; and is described by the biogra-
phers of his illustrious son as " a man of sound understanding,
of fervent piety, and of great purity of life." His mother—
the third daughter of Jonathan Edwards, a name celebrated
alike in systems of philosophy, and systems of divinity—was in
many respects a remarkable woman, and to her early assiduity,
doubtless, more than to any other cause, must be ascribed his
subsequent celebrity. During the years of childhood, his education was conducted almost exclusively by her, and in her
nursery.

In his twelfth year he was placed in the family of the Rev.
Enoch Huntington, of Middletown, a gentleman distinguished
for his classical attainments in an age when such attainments
were probably more valued, and more frequent among the
clergy of New England than they now are. He was admitted
a member of Yale College, at the age of thirteen years.
Owing partly to personal misfortunes, and partly to the inau-

spicious circumstances of the institution, his studies were for two years in a great measure interrupted. For the two remaining years his application was such as has been seldom surpassed by any person so early in life. He commenced Bachelor of arts in 1769.

After two years spent in the superintendance of the classical school in New Haven, he was chosen tutor in Yale College, and immediately entered on the duties of that office. In this new station he soon exhibited those peculiar talents which eminently qualified him for the high place which he afterwards filled with honor to himself, and with usefulness to his country. His colleagues in office, of whom JOHN TRUMBULL was one, were men of a kindred spirit with himself. These men, by their united efforts, inspired as they were, with the enthusiasm of genius, soon effected a decided change in the literary character of the institution. For many years previous, the study of the classics, and of mathematical and metaphysical sciences had been pursued with great zeal. The period of the tutorship of Dwight, which included the six years from 1771, to 1777—is regarded as an era in the history of Yale College. A better standard of superiority, and a more liberal course of study were adopted. English literature became an object of attention. Rhetoric and oratory were cultivated. And so devoted were the attentions of Dwight to the improvement of his class, that he not only carried them through, and far beyond the usual studies, but was at the pains of addressing to them a series of lectures on style and composition, similar in plan to the lectures of Blair, which had not then come before the public. His instructions generally at that time were of the same character which they afterwards possessed when from the chair of the President he taught, for twentytwo years, as many successive classes of the young citizens of independent and republican America. The first class of his pupils entered on their Bachelor's degree a year before the declaration of independence. Yet at that time he, in common with other men of enlarged and powerful minds, had formed the noble and prophetic conception of what this country was to be, and of what it will be in the ages yet to come. In teaching then, as well as afterwards, he regarded his pupils as destined to sustain the various duties of citizens, and to bear up the honors of a great republic. The consequence was, that all his instructions had a peculiarly practical cast and bearing. He endeavored to impress on his pupils distinct notions of the scenes in which they were to act, and of the responsibilities which they must sustain. " You should by no means consider yourselves," said he, " as members of a small neighborhood, town, or colony only, but as being concerned in laying the foundation of American greatness. Your wishes, your designs, your labors are not to be confined by the narrow bounds of the present age, but are to comprehend succeeding generations, and to be pointed to immortality. You are to act, not like inhabitants of a village, nor like beings of an hour, but like citizens of a world, and like candidates for a name that shall survive the conflagration."

During this period of his life, he attempted to join with the severest study a system of abstemiousness which, as he thought, might prevent the necessity of bodily exercise. This system he followed till he had nearly destroyed his life. Another consequence of his close and unremitting application was the impairing of his eyesight—a calamity under which he suffered to the end of his life.

In March, 1777, he married Miss Mary Woolsey, daughter of Benjamin Woolsey, Esq. of Long Island. In September following he relinquished his connexion with the college ; and soon after accepted a chaplaincy in the continental army. It is one of the most remarkable circumstances in the history of the revolutionary war, and one which strikingly illustrates the deep and universal enthusiasm of the nation, that not a few of the clergy, eminent alike for piety and talents, went forth from their homes, and from the solitude of sacred study, to animate the army by their exhortations, and by their prayers to call down upon it the blessings of heaven. Mr Dwight on joining the army found himself indeed in circumstances entirely unlike his previous course of life ; but the power and versatility of his genius, and the enthusiasm with which he shared with all around him, proved adequate to the exigency. The soldiers of the brigade with which he was connected, were mostly farmers of Connecticut, who had left only for a season their firesides, and their hereditary acres, and the churches in which they had been wont from infancy to worship.

His reputation in the army was high. Several patriotic songs from his pen acquired a wide popularity, particularly with the soldiers. His "Columbia" is at this day among our best and most popular national songs.

After a single year thus spent, his father's death compelled him to resign his office. For the five succeeding years, he resided at Northampton with his mother, assisting her in the support and education of her numerous family. During this period he directed the cultivation of the paternal estate, (of which he relinquished his share in favor of his mother and her other children,) superintended the education of his young brothers and sisters, and preached on Sundays to vacant congregations in the vicinity. Not forgetting his favorite employment in which he was destined to be more widely and eminently useful than perhaps any other individual who ever lived, he established an Acadamy at Northampton which speedily attained a great share of public favor. Yale College being at this time, as it often had been during his own tutorship, in a dispersed and broken state, owing to the danger of its maritime situation, a part of one of the classes placed themselves under his tuition, and were conducted by him through the course of college study.

During his residence at Northampton, he was twice chosen to represent that town in the legislature of Massachusetts. This was at a time when many questions of great importance, arising from the revolutionary condition of society, were to be settled by legislative authority. In these circumstances he exhibited such political wisdom and integrity, and such parliamentary talents, as gained for him great confidence. He was earnestly solicited by his friends, to devote himself to public life. In particular he was requested to become a condidate for a seat in Congress. But he could not be persuaded to abandon the work to which he had now devoted himself. He esteemed the sphere which is occupied by a minister of Christianity, as more exalted and more desirable than any other station. In 1783 he was ordained pastor of the church and congregation in Greenfield, a parish of Fairfield, in Connecticut.

For twelve years his life was occupied with the labors of a country pastor. But such a man could not be withdrawn from public attention. His fame as a preacher, as a scholar, and as a man of splendid talents, was continually increasing. Extensively acquainted with distinguished men, himself an object of attraction almost equally to friends and to strangers, and by disposition and habit, hospitable even beyond the well-known hospitality of New England, his house was a place of almost constant resort.

The annual pittance of a country minister, was inadequate to the expenses of his family, and this circumstance, conspiring with his previous course of life, led him to establish here, as he had done at Northampton, an Academy for the liberal education of youth. He was soon surrounded by pupils from every part of the country; and in the course of the twelve years which were thus spent, he is said to have instructed more than one thousand scholars.

He became President of Yale College in 1795. His labors and his usefulness in this station are well known. He came to the Presidency at a critical moment. The institution was impoverished. The state, at that time, as at almost all other times, refused its patronage. No private munificence was afforded to enlarge its means of usefulness. The prosperity, and indeed the existence of the institution was at stake. Amid all these embarrassments, he succeeded. A system of kind and parental, yet vigorous discipline was immediately introduced, under which the college has been uniformly distinguished for its decorum to this hour. The college became more popular. The Legislature of the state, condescended to bestow upon it some appropriations of uncertain value, from which a considerable amount was ultimately realized.

The number of students was increased; new buildings were provided for their accommodation; the apparatus and library were enlarged; additional professorships were established, and the President soon gathered around him a body of instructers to whose talents and industry combined with his own, it is to be ascribed that the institution is now, in numbers and popularity, if not in resources, one of the first among the American Universities.

As President, Dr Dwight was charged with the direct instruction of the senior class. How well he performed this work, how he delighted his pupils by the eloquence and variety of his instructions ; how he won their confidence, and their admiration ; how he secured for himself their warmest and kindest affections; with what paternal feelings he advised them individually, entering into all their plans, and understanding as if by intuition all their difficulties and embarrassments ; and how intimate and enduring was the tie by which he and they were mutually connected—hundreds now living, can tell.

In addition to his duties as President, he sustained the Professorship of Divinity. In this office, he preached in the college Chapel twice every Sunday. One of the sermons every week was in the course of systematic lectures on Theology, which has been published since his death, and has obtained a popularity unprecedented for a work of that description. In discharging the duties of this department, he also conducted the studies of the Theological class, and was, as the Professor of Divinity has always been till within a short time past, their sole instructer.

After his accession to the Presidency, his course of life was remarkably uniform. Forty weeks of each year, he was confined by his official duties. The remaining twelve weeks were generally spent in excursions through almost every part of the Northern states. The vast amount of local, historical, and statistical information, which he was able thus to collect, has been published since his death under the title of "Travels in New England and New York." The transactions of the Connecticut Academy, several of the literary and religious periodicals of his time, and his frequent occasional publications, anonymous and avowed, testify to his industry, and to the richness and energy of his mind.

Twenty years had thus passed away, and he had never been once detained from his pulpit by sickness or by any other cause. At the age of sixtythree his constitution, notwithstanding so many years of sedentary toil, was unimpaired. The same manly frame, and noble and commanding aspect, the same indefatigable activity, the same powerful intellect, the same splendid imagination which had distinguished him at forty, still remained. But in February 1816, he was attacked by the disease under which he died. For twelve weeks he endured an agony which a constitution less powerful could not have so long sustained. After this, he gained a partial relief, and the hope of his recovery was indulged. He again entered his pulpit, and recommenced the course of his labors. But the disease was not removed. His employments were unremitted till within four days of his death, which took place on the 11th day of January 1817, in the sixtyfifth year of his age.

The poetical works of Dr Dwight, are The Conquest of Canaan, in eleven books. The Triumph of Infidelity. Greenfield Hill, in seven parts. Watts's Psalms with additions and emendations, and some miscellaneous pieces.

The Conquest of Canaan is a regular epic, founded on that portion of Scripture history to which the title refers. It was commenced in early youth, and finished when the writer was in his twentythird year. Soon after, in 1775, it was proposed for publication, and more than three thousand subscribers gave their names for the encouragement of the design. Unfortunately, owing to the state of the country, it was withheld from the press for ten years longer. Thus, when it was at last given to the public, although it had undergone no material alteration, it was regarded not as the production of youthful genius, trying its wings by long any daring flights, nor as the work of a mind immature in judgment or in strength, and from which, therefore, nothing perfect ought to be expected,—but rather as the most elaborate effort of an author renowned for splendid faculties and thoroughly disciplined.

In the same light has it been generally regarded to this hour. And as the reputation of its author has been continually spreading and swelling, this work has been held in less and less esteem, and is now rarely mentioned, save when some witling, rejoicing in the weak efforts of genius, refers to the epic of Dwight as an illustration of the "*Nemo omnibus horis sapit.*" Yet the poem is not without its merits. If we regard it as written by a youth, before his twentyfourth year, it is abundant with the marks of genius. The smoothness of its versification, the distinctness and beauty of many descriptive passages, and its occasional flights of sublimity, indicate a mind which by culture might have attained no moderate sphere of poetical excellence. It is copious, indeed, in faults, but they are mostly the faults of youth. A turgid versification, and the perpetual recurrence of favorite expressions, and favorite rhymes, may be laid to the charge of every youthful poet; and are generally remedied by practice in composition and by the exercise of maturer judgment. The characters are wanting in individuality : they are not sufficiently distinguished from each other by their separate traits : they resemble too much the "*fortemque Gyan fortemque Cloanthum*" of Virgil. But who would expect of an academic stripling, that acquaintance with human nature, and that creative skill in the conception of character, which are among the last attainments of genius? The propriety of local circumstances and national character is violated. The narrative is too much broken up by long and commonplace discussions that have little connexion with the progress of the action. And finally though the poem has a formal unity in respect to time and place and action, it is wanting in that unity which consists in fastening the attention of the reader to one object, and in leaving on his mind one deep impression. For all these faults in the poem of a young man, we can easily make allowance. But the case is altered in a measure, when we reflect that though the poem was written by a young man within the walls of a college, it was revised and finished by one of years and discretion, who had been long familiar with the groves of Academus, and the fountains of sweet song, and long versed in the ways of the world ; by one who had been a scholar and a teacher, a chaplain in the tented field, a politician in the halls of legislation, and a pastor in the quiet country.

Greenfield Hill is rather a collection of poems than one connected work. For though the several parts have a slight relation to the general title, each part is in itself a separate performance. Portions of it were written expressly in imitation of the manner of some popular British poets. Thus " The Prospect," imitates Thomson ; " The Flourishing Village " is a beautiful counterpart to the masterpiece of Goldsmith ; " The Destruction of the Pequods," in versification and style, is modeled after the " Minstrel " of Beattie ; and "The Clergyman's advice to the Villagers "—one of the simplest and truest, and most beautiful of ethical poems—is in the manner of Edward Moore. In every part of the work, we see not only maturity and strength of mind, superadded to melody of verse and power of imagination, but every proof that the author feels himself at home, and is employed in just that class of subjects in which his genius is best fitted to excel.

The " Triumph of Infidelity," is a satire occasioned by the publication of Dr Chauncey's work on Universal Salvation. In its style it resembles the strong and hearty invective of Juvenal, more than the playful ridicule of Horace. It is not without obvious faults. Its topics of sarcasm are sometimes trite, and it occasionally expresses, perhaps too freely, the author's contempt of individuals. This poem was published anonymously, and has not been numbered with his works in any biography of the author hitherto published.

His edition of Watts contains thirtythree psalms written by himself. Some of these are superior and favorite specimens of a kind of poetry in which true excellence is uncommon.

Respecting the poems of Dwight generally, it may be said, that while they cannot claim for him the praise which is rendered only to a few exalted names, they rise in merit far above the average level of that mass of compositions which constitutes as a body, the poetry of the English language.

THE DESTRUCTION OF THE PEQUODS.

Ah me! while up the long, long vale of time,
Reflection wanders towards the eternal vast,
How starts the eye, at many a change sublime,
Unbosom'd dimly by the ages pass'd!
What mausoleums crowd the mournful waste!
The tombs of empires fallen! and nations gone!
Each, once inscribed, in gold, with "Aye to last,"
Sate as a queen; proclaim'd the world her own,
And proudly cried, "By me no sorrows shall be known."

Soon fleets the sunbright form, by man adored.
Soon fell the head of gold, to time a prey;
The arms, the trunk, his cankering tooth devour'd;
And whirlwinds blew the iron dust away.
Where dwelt imperial Timur?—far astray,
Some lonely-musing pilgrim now inquires;
And, rack'd by storms, and hastening to decay,
Mohammed's mosque foresees its final fires;
And Rome's more lordly temple day by day expires.

As o'er proud Asian realms the traveller winds,
His manly spirit, hush'd by terror, falls;
When some deceased town's lost site he finds,
Where ruin wild his pondering eye appals;
Where silence swims along the moulder'd walls,
And broods upon departed grandeur's tomb.
Through the lone, hollow aisles sad echo calls,
At each low step; deep sighs the breathing gloom,
And weeping fields, around, bewail their Empress's doom.

Where o'er an hundred realms, the throne uprose,
The screech-owl nests, the panther builds his home;
Sleep the dull newts, the lazy adders doze,
Where pomp and luxury danced the golden room.
Low lies in dust the sky-resembled dome;
Tall grass around the broken column waves;
And brambles climb, and lonely thistles bloom:

The moulder'd arch the weedy streamlet laves,
And low resound beneath, unnumber'd sunken graves.

Soon fleets the sun-bright form, by man adored;
And soon man's demon chiefs from memory fade.
In musty volume, now must be explored,
Where dwelt imperial nations, long decay'd.
The brightest meteors angry clouds invade;
And where the wonders glitter'd, none explain.
Where Carthage, with proud hand, the trident sway'd,
Now mud-wall'd cots sit sullen on the plain,
And wandering, fierce, and wild, sequester'd Arabs reign.

In thee, O Albion! queen of nations, live
Whatever splendors earth's wide realms have known;
In thee proud Persia sees her pomp revive;
And Greece her arts; and Rome her lordly throne:
By every wind, thy Tyrian fleets are blown;
Supreme, on fame's dread roll, thy heroes stand;
All ocean's realms thy naval sceptre own;
Of bards, of sages, how august thy band!
And one rich Eden blooms around thy garden'd land.

But O how vast thy crimes! through heaven's great year,
When few centurial suns have traced their way;
When southern Europe, worn by feuds severe;
Weak, doting, fallen, has bow'd to Russian sway;
And setting glory beam'd her farewell ray;
To waste, perchance, thy brilliant fields shall turn;
In dust, thy temples, towers, and towns decay;
The forest howl, where London's turrets burn;
And all thy garlands deck thy sad, funereal urn.

Some land, scarce glimmering in the light of fame,
Sceptred with arts, and arms (if I divine)
Some unknown wild, some shore without a name,
In all thy pomp, shall then majestic shine.
As silver-headed Time's slow years decline,
Not ruins only meet the inquiring eye:
Where round yon mouldering oak vain brambles twine,
The filial stem, already towering high,
Ere long shall stretch his arms, and nod in yonder sky.

Where late resounded the wild woodland roar,
Now heaves the palace, now the temple smiles;
Where frown'd the rude rock, and the desert shore,

Now pleasure sports, and business want beguiles,
And commerce wings her flight to thousand isles;
Culture walks forth ; gay laugh the loaded fields ;
And jocund labor plays his harmless wiles ;
Glad science brightens; art her mansion builds ;
And peace uplifts her wand, and heaven his blessing yields.

O'er these sweet fields, so lovely now, and gay,
Where modest nature finds each want supplied,
Where home-born happiness delights to play,
And counts her little flock, with household pride,
Long frown'd, from age to age, a forest wide :
Here hung the slumbering bat; the serpent dire
Nested his brood, and drank the impoison'd tide ;
Wolves peal'd, the dark drear night, in hideous choir ;
Nor shrank the unmeasured howl from Sol's terrific fire.

No charming cot imbank'd the pebbly stream ;
No mansion tower'd, nor garden teem'd with good ;
No lawn expanded to the April beam ;
Nor mellow harvest hung its bending load ;
Nor science dawn'd ; nor life with beauty glow'd ;
Nor temple whiten'd, in the enchanting dell ;
In clusters wild, the sluggish wigwam stood ;
And, borne in snaky paths the Indian fell
Now aim'd the death unseen, now scream'd the tiger-yell.

E'en now, perhaps, on human dust I tread,
Pondering, with solemn pause, the wrecks of time ;
Here sleeps, perchance, among the vulgar dead,
Some chief, the lofty theme of Indian rhyme,
Who loved ambition's cloudy steep to climb,
And smiled, death, dangers, rivals, to engage ;
Who roused his followers' souls to deeds sublime,
Kindling to furnace heat vindictive rage,
And soar'd Cæsarean heights, the Phœnix of his age.

In yon small field, that dimly steals from sight,
(From yon small field these meditations grow,)
Turning the sluggish soil, from morn to night,
The plodding hind, laborious, drives his plough,
Nor dreams, a nation sleeps his foot below.
There, undisturbed by the roaring wave,
Released from war, and far from deadly foe,
Lies down, in endless rest, a nation brave,
And trains, in tempests born, there find a quiet grave.

Oft have I heard the tale, when matron sere
Sung to my infant ear the song of wo;
Of maiden meek, consumed with pining care,
Around whose tomb the wild-rose loved to blow:
Or told, with swimming eyes, how, long ago,
Remorseless Indians, all in midnight dire,
The little, sleeping village, did o'erthrow,
Bidding the cruel flames to heaven aspire,
And scalp'd the hoary head, and burn'd the babe with fire

Then, fancy-fired, her memory wing'd its flight,
To long-forgotten wars, and dread alarms,
To chiefs obscure, but terrible in fight,
Who mock'd each foe, and laugh'd at deadliest harms,
Sydneys in zeal, and Washingtons in arms.
By instinct tender to the woes of man,
My heart bewildering with sweet pity's charms,
Through solemn scenes, with nature's step, she ran,
And hush'd her audience small, and thus the tale began.

" Through verdant banks where Thames's branches glide,
Long held the Pequods an extensive sway;
Bold, savage, fierce, of arms the glorious pride,
And bidding all the circling realms obey.
Jealous, they saw the tribes, beyond the sea,
Plant in their climes; and towns, and cities, rise;
Ascending castles foreign flags display;
Mysterious art new scenes of life devise;
And steeds insult the plains, and cannon rend the skies."

   *   *   *   *   *

" The rising clouds the savage chief descried,
And, round the forest, bade his heroes arm;
To arms the painted warriors proudly hied,
And through surrounding nations rung the alarm.
The nations heard; but smiled, to see the storm,
With ruin fraught, o'er Pequod mountains driven
And felt infernal joy the bosom warm,
To see their light hang o'er the skirts of even,
And other suns arise, to gild a kinder heaven."

"Swift to the Pequod fortress Mason sped,
Far in the wildering wood's impervious gloom;
A lonely castle, brown with twilight dread;
Where oft the embowel'd captive met his doom,
And frequent heaved, around the hollow tomb,

Scalps hung in rows, and whitening bones were strew'd;
Where, round the broiling babe, fresh from the womb,
With howls the Powaw fill'd the dark abode,
And screams, and midnight prayers, invoked the evil god.

"There too, with awful rites, the hoary priest,
Without, beside the moss-grown altar, stood,
His sable form in magic cincture dress'd,
And heap'd the mingled offering to his god,
What time, with golden light, calm evening glow'd,
The mystic dust, the flower of silver bloom,
And spicy herb, his hand in order strew'd;
Bright rose the curling flame; and rich perfume
On smoky wings upflew, or settled round the tomb.

"Then, o'er the circus, danced the maddening throng,
As erst the Thyas roam'd dread Nysa round,
And struck, to forest notes, the ecstatic song,
While slow, beneath them, heav'd the wavy ground.
With a low, lingering groan, of dying sound,
The woodland rumbled; murmured deep each stream;
Shrill sung the leaves; all ether sigh'd profound;
Pale tufts of purple topp'd the silver flame,
And many color'd forms on evening breezes came.

"Thin, twilight forms; attired in changing sheen
Of plumes, high tinctured in the western ray:
Bending, they peep'd the fleecy folds between,
Their wings light rustling in the breath of May.
Soft hovering round the fire, in mystic play,
They snuff'd the incense, waved in clouds afar,
Then, silent, floated toward the setting day;
Eve redden'd each fine form, each misty car;
And through them faintly gleam'd, at times, the western star.

"Then (so tradition sings,) the train behind,
In plumy zones of rainbow'd beauty dress'd,
Rode the Great Spirit, in the obedient wind,
In yellow clouds slow sailing from the west.
With dawning smiles, the God his votaries bless'd,
And taught where deer retired to ivy dell;
What chosen chief with proud command to invest,
Where crept the approaching foe, with purpose fell,
And where to wind the scout, and war's dark storm dispel.

"There on her lover's tomb, in silence laid,
While still, and sorrowing, shower'd the moon's pale beam,

At times, expectant, slept the widow'd maid,
Her soul far wandering on the sylph-wing'd dream.
Wafted from evening skies, on sunny stream,
Her darling youth with silver pinions shone ;
With voice of music, tuned to sweetest theme,
He told of shell-bright bowers, beyond the sun,
Where years of endless joy o'er Indian lovers run.

" But now no awful rites, nor potent spell,
To silence charm'd the peals of coming war ;
Or told the dread recesses of the dell,
Where glowing Mason led his bands from far :
No spirit, buoyant on his airy car,
Control'd the whirlwind of invading fight :
Deep died in blood, dun evening's falling star
Sent sad o'er western hills its parting light,
And no returning morn dispersed the long, dark night.

" On the drear walls a sudden splendor glow'd,
There Mason shone, and there his veterans pour'd.
Anew the hero claim'd the fiends of blood,
While answering storms of arrows round him shower'd,
And the war-scream the ear with anguish gored.
Alone, he burst the gate ; the forest round
Re-echoed death ; the peal of onset roar'd,
In rush'd the squadrons ; earth in blood was drown'd ;
And gloomy spirits fled, and corses hid the ground.

" Not long in dubious fight the host had striven,
When, kindled by the musket's potent flame,
In clouds, and fire, the castle rose to heaven,
And gloom'd the world, with melancholy beam.
Then hoarser groans, with deeper anguish, came ;
And fiercer fight the keen assault repell'd :
Nor e'en these ills the savage breast could tame ;
Like hell's deep caves, the hideous region yell'd,
Till death, and sweeping fire, laid waste the hostile field."

THE FARMER'S ADVICE TO THE VILLAGERS.

Not long since lived a farmer plain,
Intent to gather honest gain,
Laborious, prudent, thrifty, neat,
Of judgment strong, experience great,

In solid homespun clad, and tidy,
And with no coxcomb learning giddy,
Daily, to hear his maxims sound,
The approaching neighbors flock'd around ;
Daily they saw his counsels prove
The source of union, peace, and love,
The means of prudence, and of wealth,
Of comfort, cheerfulness, and health :
And all, who follow'd his advice,
Appear'd more prosperous, as more wise.

Wearied, at length, with many a call,
The sage resolved to summon all :
And gathering, on a pleasant Monday,
A crowd, not always seen on Sunday,
Curious to hear, while hard they press'd him,
In friendly terms, he thus address'd 'em.

" My friends, you have my kindest wishes ;
Pray think a neighbor not officious,
While thus, to teach you how to live,
My very best advice I give.

" And first, industrious be your lives ;
Alike employ'd yourselves, and wives :
Your children, join'd in labor gay,
With something useful fill each day.
Those little times of leisure save,
Which most men lose, and all men have ;
The half days, when a job is done ;
The whole days, when a storm is on.
Few know, without a strict account,
To what these little times amount :
If wasted, while the same your cost,
The sums, you might have earn'd, are lost.

"Learn small things never to despise :
You little think how fast they rise.
A rich reward the mill obtains,
Though but two quarts a bushel gains :
Still rolling on its steady rounds,
The farthings soon are turn'd to pounds.

" Nor think a life of toil severe :
No life has blessings so sincere.
Its meals so luscious, sleep so sweet,
Such vigorous limbs, such health complete,

A mind so active, brisk, and gay,
As his, who toils the livelong day.
A life of sloth drags hardly on ;
Suns set too late, and rise too soon ;
Youth, manhood, age, all linger slow,
To him, who nothing has to do.
The drone, a nuisance to the hive,
Stays, but can scarce be said to live ;
And well the bees, those judges wise,
Plague, chase, and sting him, till he dies.
Lawrence, like him, though saved from hanging,
Yet every day deserves a banging.

"Let order o'er your time preside,
And method all your business guide.
Early begin, and end, your toil ;
Nor let great tasks your hands embroil.
One thing at once, be still begun,
Contrived, resolved, pursued, and done.
Hire not, for what yourselves can do ;
And send not, when yourselves can go ;
Nor, till tomorrow's light, delay
What might as well be done today.
By steady efforts all men thrive,
And long by moderate labor live ;
While eager toil, and anxious care,
Health, strength, and peace, and life impair.

" What thus your hands with labor earn,
To save, be now your next concern.
Whate'er to health, or real use,
Or true enjoyment, will conduce,
Use freely, and with pleasure use ;
But ne'er the gifts of heaven abuse :
I joy to see your treasured stores,
Which smiling plenty copious pours ;
Your cattle sleek, your poultry fine,
Your cider in the tumbler shine,
Your tables, smoking from the hoard,
And children smiling round the board.
All rights to use in you conspire ;
The laborer 's worthy of his hire.
Ne'er may that hated day arrive,
When worse yourselves, or yours, shall live
Your dress, your lodging, or your food,
Be less abundant, neat, or good ;
Your dainties all to market go,
To feast the epicure, and beau ;

But ever on your tables stand,
Proofs of a free and happy land.

"Yet still, with prudence, wear, and taste;
Use what you please, but nothing waste:
On little, better far to live,
Than, poor and pitied, much survive.
Like ants, lay something up in store,
Against the winter of threescore.
Disease may long your strength annoy;
Weakness and pain your limbs destroy;
On sorrow's bed your households lie;
Your debtors fail, your cattle die;
Your crops untimely seasons kill,
And life be worn with many an ill.

*　　*　　*　　*　　*　　*

"'T is folly in the extreme, to till
Extensive fields, and till them ill.
The farmer, pleased, may boast aloud
His bushels sown, his acres plough'd;
And, pleased, indulge the cheering hope,
That time will bring a plenteous crop.
Shrew'd common-sense sits laughing by,
And sees his hopes abortive die;
For, when maturing seasons smile,
Thin sheaves shall disappoint his toil.
Advised, this empty pride expel;
Till little, and that little well.
Of taxing, fencing, toil, no more,
Your ground requires, when rich, than poor;
And more one fertile acre yields,
Than the huge breadth of barren fields.

*　　*　　*　　*　　*　　*

"When first the market offers well,
At once your yearly produce sell.
A higher price you wait in vain,
And ten times lose, where once you gain.
The dog, that at the shadow caught,
Miss'd all he had, and all he sought.
Less, day by day, your store will grow,
Gone, you scarce know or when, or how;
Interest will eat, while you delay,
And vermin steal your hopes away.
In parcels sold, in ways unknown,
It melts, and, unobserved, is gone.
No solid purpose driblets aid,
Spent, and forgot, as soon as paid:

The sum, a year's whole earnings yield,
Will pay a debt, or buy a field.

*   *   *   *   *   *   *

"Neat be your farms : 't is long confess'd,
The neatest farmers are the best.
Each bog, and marsh, industrious drain,
Nor let vile balks deform the plain ;
No bushes on your headlands grow,
Nor briars a sloven's culture show.
Neat be your barns ; your houses neat ;
Your doors be clean ; your court-yards sweet ;
No moss the sheltering roof inshroud ;
No wooden panes the window cloud ;
No filthy kennel foully flow ;
Nor weeds with rankling poison grow :
But shades expand, and fruit-trees bloom,
And flowering shrubs exhale perfume.
With pales your garden circle round ;
Defend, enrich, and clean the ground :
Prize high this pleasing, useful rood,
And fill with vegetable good.

"With punctual hand your taxes pay,
Nor put far off the evil day.
How soon to an enormous size,
Taxes, succeeding taxes, rise !
How easy, one by one, discharged !
How hardly, in the mass enlarged !
How humbling the intrusive dun !
How fast, how far, the expenses run !
Fees, advertisements, travel, cost,
And that sad end of all, the post !
This gulf of swift perdition flee,
And live, from duns and bailiffs free.

"In merchants' books, from year to year,
Be cautious how your names appear.
How fast their little items count !
How great, beyond your hopes, the amount !
When shelves, o'er shelves, inviting stand,
And wares allure, on either hand ;
While round you turn enchanted eyes,
And feel a thousand wants arise,
(Ye young, ye fair, these counsels true
Are penn'd for all, but most for you,)
Ere fancy lead your hearts astray,

Think of the means you have to pay;
What wants are nature's; fancy's what;
What will yield real good, when bought;
What certain, future means you find,
To cancel contracts, left behind;
What means to make the first of May
To you and yours a welcome day.

"To you, let each returning spring
That day of certain reckoning bring;
All debts to cancel, books t' adjust,
And check the wild career of trust.
From frequent reckonings friendship grows,
And peace, and sweet communion, flows.

*   *   *   *   *   *

"With steady hand your household sway,
And use them always to obey.
Always their worthy acts commend;
Always against their faults contend;
The mind inform; the conscience move;
And blame, with tenderness, and love.
When round they flock, and smile, and tell
Their lambkin sport, and infant weal,
Nor foolish laugh, nor fret, nor frown;
But all their little interests own;
Like them, those trifles serious deem,
And daily witness your esteem:
Yourselves their best friends always prove,
For filial duty springs from love.
Teach them, with confidence t' impart,
Each secret purpose of the heart:
Thrice happy parents, children bless'd,
Of mutual confidence possess'd!
Such parents shall their children see
From vice, and shame, and anguish, free.

*   *   *   *   *   *

"How blest this heaven-distinguish'd land!
Where schools in every hamlet stand;
Far spread the beams of learning bright,
And every child enjoys the light.
At school, beneath a faithful guide,
In teaching skill'd, of morals tried,
And pleased the early mind to charm
To every good, from every harm,
Learn they to read, to write, to spell,
And cast accompts, and learn them well:

For, on this microscopic plan,
Is form'd the wise and useful man.
Let him a taste for books inspire ;
While you, to nurse the young desire,
A social library procure,
And open knowledge to the poor.
This useful taste imbibed, your eyes
Shall see a thousand blessings rise.
From haunts and comrades vile secure,
Where gilded baits to vice allure,
No more your sons abroad shall roam,
But pleased, their evenings spend at home ;
Allurements more engaging find,
And feast, with pure delight, the mind.
The realms of earth their thoughts shall scan,
And learn the works and ways of man ;
See, from the savage, to the sage,
How nations ripen, age by age ;
How states, and men, by virtue rise ;
How both to ruin sink, by vice ;
How through the world's great prison-bounds,
While one wide clank of chains resounds,
Men slaves, while angels weep to see,
Some wise, and brave, and bless'd, are free.
Through moral scenes shall stretch their sight ;
Discern the bounds of wrong and right ;
That loathe ; this love ; and, pleased, pursue
Whate'er from man to man is due ;
And, from the page of heaven derive
The motives, and the means, to live.

    *   *   *   *   *   *

    " In this new world, life's changing round
In three descents, is often found.
The first, firm, busy, plodding, poor,
Earns, saves, and daily swells, his store :
By farthings first, and pence, it grows ;
In shillings next, and pounds, it flows ;
Then spread his widening farms, abroad ;
His forests wave ; his harvests nod ;
Fattening, his numerous cattle play,
And debtors dread his reckoning day.
Ambitious then t' adorn with knowledge
His son, he places him at college ;
And sends, in smart attire, and neat,
To travel, through each neighboring state ;
Builds him a handsome house, or buys,
Sees him a gentleman, and dies.

"The second, born to wealth, and ease,
And taught to think, converse, and please,
Ambitious, with his lady-wife,
Aims at a higher walk of life.
Yet, in those wholesome habits train'd,
By which his wealth and weight were gain'd,
Bids care in hand with pleasure go,
And blends economy with show.
His houses, fences, garden, dress,
The neat and thrifty man confess.
Improved, but with improvement plain,
Intent on office, as on gain,
Exploring, useful sweets to spy,
To public life he turns his eye.
A townsman first ; a justice soon ;
A member of the house anon ;
Perhaps to board, or bench, invited,
He sees the state, and subjects, righted ;
And, raptured with politic life,
Consigns his children to his wife.
Of household cares amid the round,
For her, too hard the task is found.
At first she struggles, and contends ;
Then doubts, desponds, laments, and bends ;
Her sons pursue the sad defeat,
And shout their victory complete ;
Rejoicing, see their father roam,
And riot, rake, and reign, at home.
Too late he sees, and sees to mourn,
His race of every hope forlorn,
Abroad, for comfort, turns his eyes,
Bewails his dire mistakes, and dies.

"His heir, train'd only to enjoy,
Untaught, his mind or hands t' employ,
Conscious of wealth enough for life,
With business, care, and worth, at strife,
By prudence, conscience, unrestrain'd,
And none, but pleasure's habits, gain'd,
Whirls on the wild career of sense,
Nor danger marks, nor heeds expense.
Soon ended is the giddy round ;
And soon the fatal goal is found.
His lands, secured for borrow'd gold,
His houses, horses, herds, are sold.
And now, no more for wealth respected,
He sinks, by all his friends neglected ;

Friends, who, before, his vices flatter'd,
And lived upon the loaves he scatter'd.
Unacted every worthy part,
And pining with a broken heart,
To dirtiest company he flies,
He gambles, turns a sot, and dies.
His children, born to fairer doom,
In rags, pursue him to the tomb.

   " Apprenticed then to masters stern,
Some real good the orphans learn ;
Are bred to toil, and hardy fare,
And grow to usefulness, and care ;
And, following their great-grandsire's plan,
Each slow becomes a useful man.

*   *   *   *   *   *

   " But should contentions rise, and grudges,
Which call for arbitrating judges,
Still shun the law, that gulf of woe,
Whose waves without a bottom flow ;
That gulf, by storms for ever toss'd,
Where all, that 's once afloat, is lost ;
Where friends, embark'd, are friends no more,
And neither finds a peaceful shore :
While thousand wrecks, as warnings, lie,
The victims of an angry sky.

   " Each cause let mutual friends decide,
With common-sense alone to guide :
If right, in silent peace be glad ;
If wrong, be neither sour, nor sad :
As oft you 'll find full justice done,
As when through twenty terms you 've run ;
And when, in travel, fees, and cost,
Far more than can be won, is lost.

   " Learn, this conclusion whence I draw.
Mark what estates are spent in law !
See men litigious, business fly,
And loungers live, and beggars die !
What anger, hatred, malice fell,
And fierce revenge their bosoms swell!
What frauds, subornings, tamperings rise !
What slanders foul! what shameful lies!
What perjuries, blackening many a tongue !
And what immensity of wrong !

Where peace and kindness dwelt before,
See peace and kindness dwell no more!
Ills to good offices succeed,
And neighbors bid each other bleed!

" Esop, the merry Phrygian sage,
Worth half the wise men of his age,
Has left to litigants a story,
Which, with your leave, I 'll set before you.

" ' The bear and lion on the lawn,
Once found the carcase of a fawn.
Both claim'd the dainty; neither gave it;
But each swore roundly he would have it.
They growl'd; they fought; but fought in vain ;
For neither could the prize obtain ;
And, while to breathe they both retreated,
The lawyer fox came in, and ate it.' "

*   *   *   *   *

Thus spoke the sage. The crowd around,
Applauding, heard the grateful sound ;
Each, deeply musing, homeward went,
T' amend his future life intent ;
And, pondering past delays, with sorrow,
Resolved he would begin tomorrow.

———

COLUMBIA.

Columbia, Columbia, to glory arise,
The queen of the world, and the child of the skies!
Thy genius commands thee; with rapture behold,
While ages on ages thy splendors unfold.
Thy reign is the last, and the noblest of time,
Most fruitful thy soil, most inviting thy clime ;
Let the crimes of the east ne'er encrimson thy name,
Be freedom, and science, and virtue thy fame.

To conquest and slaughter let Europe aspire ;
Whelm nations in blood, and wrap cities in fire ;
Thy heroes the rights of mankind shall defend,
And triumph pursue them, and glory attend.
A world is thy realm: for a world be thy laws,
Enlarged as thine empire, and just as thy cause ;
On freedom's broad basis, that empire shall rise,
Extend with the main, and dissolve with the skies.

Fair Science her gates to thy sons shall unbar,
And the east see thy morn hide the beams of her star.
New bards, and new sages, unrivall'd shall soar
To fame unextinguish'd, when time is no more;
To thee, the last refuge of virtue designed,
Shall fly from all nations the best of mankind;
Here, grateful to heaven, with transport shall bring
Their incense, more fragrant than odors of spring.

Nor less shall thy fair ones to glory ascend,
And genius and beauty in harmony blend;
The graces of form shall awake pure desire,
And the charms of the soul ever cherish the fire;
Their sweetness unmingled, their manners refined,
And virtue's bright image, instamp'd on the mind,
With peace, and soft rapture, shall teach life to glow,
And light up a smile in the aspect of woe.

Thy fleets to all regions thy power shall display,
The nations admire, and the ocean obey;
Each shore to thy glory its tribute unfold,
And the east and the south yield their spices and gold.
As the day-spring unbounded, thy splendor shall flow,
And earth's little kingdoms before thee shall bow:
While the ensigns of union, in triumph unfurl'd,
Hush the tumult of war, and give peace to the world.

Thus, as down a lone valley, with cedars o'erspread,
From war's dread confusion I pensively stray'd—
The gloom from the face of fair heaven retired;
The winds ceased to murmur; the thunders expired;
Perfumes, as of Eden, flow'd sweetly along,
And a voice, as of angels, enchantingly sung:
" Columbia, Columbia, to glory arise,
The queen of the world and the child of the skies."

THE CRITICS.

A FABLE.

'T is said of every dog that's found,
Of mongrel, spaniel, cur, and hound,
That each sustains a doggish mind,
And hates the new, sublime, refined.
'T is hence the wretches bay the moon,
In beauty throned at highest noon,

Hence every nobler brute they bite,
And hunt the stranger-dog with spite ;
And hence, the nose's dictates parrying,
They fly from meat to feed on carrion.
'T is also said, the currish soul
The critic race possesses whole ;
As near they come, in thoughts and natures,
As two legg'd can, to four legg'd creatures ;
Alike the things they love and blame,
Their voice, and language, much the same.

The muse this subject made her theme,
And told me in a morning dream.
Such dreams you sages may decry ;
But muses know they never lie.
Then hear, from me, in grave narration,
Of these strange facts, the strange occasion.

In Greece Cynethe's village lay,
Well known to all, who went that way,
For dogs of every kindred famed,
And from true doggish manners named.
One morn, a greyhound pass'd the street ;
At once the foul-mouth'd conclave met,
Huddling around the stranger ran,
And thus their smart review began.
" What tramper," with a grinning sneer
Bark'd out the clumsy cur, " is here ?
No native of the town, I see ;
Some foreign whelp of base degree.
I 'd show, but that the record 's torn,
We true Welsh curs are better born.
His coat is smooth ; but longer hair
Would more become a dog by far.
His slender ear, how straight and sloping !
While ours is much improved by cropping."

" Right," cried the blood-hound, " that straight ear
Seems made for nothing but to hear ;
'T is long agreed, through all the town,
That handsome ears, like mine, hang down ;
And though his body 's gaunt and round,
'T is no true rawboned gaunt of hound.
How high his nose the creature carries !
As if on bugs, and flies, his fare is ;
I 'll teach this strutting stupid log,
To smell 's the business of a dog."

"Baugh-waugh!" the shaggy spaniel cried,
"What wretched covering on his hide!
I wonder where he lives in winter;
His straight, sleek legs too, out of joint are;
I hope the vagrant will not dare
His fledging with my fleece compare.
He never plunged in pond or river,
To search for wounded duck and diver;
By kicks would soon be set a skipping,
Nor take one half so well a whipping."

"Rat me," the lap-dog yelp'd, "through nature,
Was ever seen so coarse a creature?
I hope no lady's sad mishap
E'er led the booby to her lap;
He'd fright Primrilla into fits,
And rob Fooleria of her wits;
A mere barbarian, Indian whelp!
How clownish, countryish, sounds his yelp!
He never tasted bread and butter,
Nor play'd the petty squirm and flutter;
Nor e'er, like me, has learn'd to fatten,
On kisses sweet, and softest patting."

"Some parson's dog, I vow," whined puppy;
"His rusty coat how sun-burnt! stop ye!"
The beagle call'd him to the wood,
The bull-dog bellowed, "Zounds! and blood!"
The wolf-dog and the mastiff were,
The muse says, an exception here;
Superior both to such foul play,
They wish'd the stranger well away.

From spleen the strictures rose to fury,
"Villain," growl'd one, "I can't endure you."
"Let's seize the truant," snarl'd another,
Encored by every foul-mouth'd brother.
"'T is done," bark'd all, "we'll mob the creature,
And sacrifice him to ill nature."

The greyhound, who despised their breath,
Still thought it best to shun their teeth.
Easy he wing'd his rapid flight,
And left the scoundrels out of sight.

Good Juno, by the ancients holden
The genuine notre-dame of scolding,

Sat pleased, because there 'd such a fuss been,
And in the hound's place wish'd her husband ;
For here, even pleasure bade her own,
Her ladyship was once outdone.
"Hail, dogs," she cried, "of every kind !
Retain ye still this snarling mind,
Hate all that 's good, and fair, and new,
And I 'll a goddess be to you.

"Nor this the only good you prove ;
Learn what the fruits of Juno's love.
Your souls, from forms, that creep all four on,
I 'll raise, by system Pythagorean,
To animate the human frame,
And gain my favorite tribe a name.
Be ye henceforth (so I ordain)
Critics, the genuine curs of men.
To snarl be still your highest bliss,
And all your criticism like this.
Whate'er is great or just in nature,
Of graceful form, or lovely feature ;
Whate'er adorns the enobled mind,
Sublime, inventive, and refined ;
With spleen, and spite, for ever blame,
And load with every dirty name.
All things of noblest kind and use,
To your own standard vile reduce,
And all in wild confusion blend,
Nor heed the subject, scope, or end.
But chief, when modest young beginners,
'Gainst critic laws, by nature sinners,
Peep out in verse, and dare to run,
Through towns and villages your own,
Hunt them, as when yon stranger dog
Set all your growling crew agog ;
Till stunn'd, and scared, they hide from view,
And leave the country clear for you."

This said, the goddess kind caressing,
Gave every cur a double blessing.
Each doggish mind, though grown no bigger,
Henceforth assumed the human figure :
The body walk'd on two, the mind
To four still chose to be confined ;
Still creeps on earth, still scents out foes,
Is still led onward by the nose ;
Hates all the good, it used to hate,
The lofty, beauteous, new, and great ;

The stranger hunts with spite quintessent,
And snarls, from that day to the present.

———

THE WORSHIP OF THE GIBEONITES.

Now o'er the hills red streams began to burn,
And bursting splendors usher'd in the morn;
With living dyes the flowers all beauteous glow'd,
O'er the glad fields etherial odors flow'd;
The forest echoed with a boundless song,
And rising breezes pour'd the strains along.
Adorn'd with green before the palace lay
A spacious square, and smiled upon the day.
Here, ere the dawn the kindling skies illumed,
Or opening flowers the fragrant gales perfumed,
Of every age, a vast, assembled train
Pour'd from the lofty domes, and fill'd the plain.
High in the midst two sacred altars shone,
Adorn'd with honors to their God, the Sun.
This, deck'd with art, and bright in royal pride,
With sable gore the quivering victim dyed:
On that, gay flowers in rich profusion lay,
And gales of Eden bore their sweets away.
Here, white with age, in snowy vesture dress'd,
Aradon stood, their monarch, and their priest;
Red in his hand a torch refulgent shone,
And his fix'd countenance watch'd the rising sun.
When first the flaming orb, with glorious rays,
Roll'd o'er the hills, and pour'd a boundless blaze;
Charmed at the sight, the monarch stretch'd his hand,
And touch'd the tributes with the sacred brand;
Through freshen'd air perfumes began to rise,
And curling volumes mounted to the skies.
Thrice to the earth the raptured suppliants bow'd,
Then struck the lyre, and hymn'd the rising god.
" O thou, whose bursting beams in glory rise,
And sail, and brighten, through unbounded skies!
The world's great Parent! heaven's exalted King!
Sole source of good! and life's eternal Spring!
All hail, while cloth'd in beauty's endless ray,
Thy face unclouded gives the new-born day!
" Above all scenes is placed thy heavenly throne;
Ere time began, thy spotless splendor shone;
Sublime from east to west thy chariot rolls,
Cheers the wide earth, and warms the distant poles;

Commands the vegetable race to grow,
The fruit to redden, and the flower to blow.
This world was born to change : the hand of Time
Makes, and unmakes the scenes of every clime.
The insect millions scarce the morn survive ;
One transient day the flowery nations live ;
A few short years complete the human doom ;
Then pale death summons to the narrow tomb.
Lash'd by the flood, the hard rocks wear away ;
Worn by the storm, the lessening hills decay ;
Unchanged alone is thine exalted flame,
From endless years to endless years the same ;
Thy splendors with immortal beauty shine,
Roll round the eternal heavens, and speak thy name divine.
    "When thy bright throne, beyond old ocean's bound,
Through nether skies pursues its destined round,
Lost in the ascending darkness, beauty fades ;
Through the blank field, and through the woodland, spreads
A melancholy silence. O'er the plain
Dread lions roam, and savage terrors reign.
    "And when sad autumn sees thy face retire,
And happier regions hail thy orient fire,
High in the storm imperious winter flies,
And desolation saddens all the skies.
But when once more thy beam the north ascends,
Thy light invigorates, and thy warmth extends ;
The fields rejoice, the groves with transport ring,
And boundless nature hails the sky-born spring.
    "Nor even in winter's gloom, or night's sad reign,
Darts the warm influence of thy beams in vain.
    " Beyond the main some fairer region lies,
Some brighter isles beneath the southern skies,
Where crimson war ne'er bade the clarion roar,
Nor sanguine billows dyed the vernal shore :
No thundering storm the day's bright face conceals,
No summer scorches, and no frost congeals ;
No sickness wastes, no grief provokes the tear,
Nor tainted vapors blast the clement year.
Round the glad day-star endless beauties burn,
And crowned with rainbows, opes the imperial morn ;
A clear unbounded light the skies display,
And purple lustre leads the the changing day.
O'er conscious shades, and bowers of soft repose,
Young breezes spring, and balmy fragrance blows,
The fields all wanton in serenest beams,
Wake fairer flowers, and roll diviner streams ;

Through the long vales aerial music roves,
And nobler fruitage dyes the bending groves.
"Through spotless nations as the realm refined,
Thy influence there sublimes the immortal mind;
Its active pinions swift through nature roam,
Lose the low world, and claim a nobler home.
Their limbs, of endless life, with glory crown'd,
New youth improves, and growing charms surround:
On the bless'd shore thy splendors love to shine,
And raise thy sons each hour, to raptures more divine."
Thus ceased the sound: the harp's melodious strain
Join'd the glad hymn, and charm'd the listening train;
A sparkling joy each speaking face display'd,
While light expanding lessen'd every shade.

BATTLE BEFORE THE WALLS OF AI.

Now near the burning domes, the squadrons stood,
Their breasts impatient for the scenes of blood:
On every face a deathlike glimmer sate,
The unbless'd harbinger of instant fate.
High through the gloom, in pale and dreadful spires,
Rose the long terrors of the dark red fires;
Torches, and torrent sparks, by whirlwinds driven,
Stream'd through the smoke, and fired the clouded heaven.
As oft tall turrets sunk with rushing sound,
Broad flames burst forth, and swept the etherial round,
The bright expansion lightened all the scene,
And deeper shadows lengthen'd o'er the green.
Loud through the walls that cast a golden gleam,
Crown'd with tall pyramids of bending flame,
As thunders rumble down the darkening vales,
Roll'd the deep solemn voice of rushing gales:
The bands admiring gazed the wondrous sight,
And expectation trembled for the fight.
At once the sounding clarion breath'd alarms;
Wide from the forest burst the flash of arms;
Thick gleam'd the helms; and o'er astonish'd fields,
Like thousand meteors, rose the flame-bright shields.
In gloomy pomp, to furious combat roll'd
Ranks sheath'd in mail, and chiefs in glimmering gold;
In floating lustre bounds the dim-seen steed,
And cars, unfinish'd, swift to cars succeed;
From all the host ascends a dark red glare,
Here in full blaze, in distant twinklings there;
Slow waves the dreadful light; as round the shore
Night's solemn blasts with deep concussion roar,

So rush the footsteps of the embattled train,
And send an awful murmur o'er the plain.
   Tall in the opposing van, bold Irad stood,
And bade the clarion sound the voice of blood.
Loud blew the trumpet on the sweeping gales,
Rock'd the deep groves, and echo'd round the vales :
A ceaseless murmur all the concave fills,
Waves through the quivering camp, and trembles o'er the
      hills.
   High in the gloomy blaze the standards flew ;
The impatient youth his burnish'd falchion drew ;
Ten thousand swords his eager bands display'd,
And crimson'd terrors danced on every blade.
With equal rage, the bold, Hazorian train
Pour'd a wide deluge o'er the shadowy plain ;
Loud rose the song of war ; loud clanged the shields ;
Dread shouts of vengeance shook the shuddering fields ;
With mingled din, shrill, martial music rings,
And swift to combat each fierce hero springs.
So broad, and dark, a midnight storm ascends,
Bursts on the main, and trembling nature rends ;
The red foam burns, the wat'ry mountains rise,
And deep unmeasured thunder heaves the skies ;
The bark drives lonely ; shivering and forlorn,
The poor, sad sailors wish the lingering morn :
Not with less fury rush'd the vengeful train ;
Not with less tumult roar'd the embattled plain.
Now in the oak's black shade they fought conceal'd ;
And now they shouted through the open field ;
The long, pale splendors of the curling flame
Cast o'er their polish'd arms a livid gleam ;
An umber'd lustre floated round their way,
And lighted falchions to the fierce affray.
Now the swift chariots 'gainst the stubborn oak
Dash ; the dark earth re-echoes to the shock.
From shade to shade the forms tremendous stream,
And their arms flash a momentary flame.
Mid hollow tombs, as fleets an airy train,
Lost in the skies, or fading o'er the plain ;
So visionary shapes, around the fight,
Shoot through the gloom, and vanish from the sight ;
Through twilight paths the maddening coursers bound,
The shrill swords crack, the clashing shields resound.
There, lost in grandeur, might the eye behold
The dark red glimmerings of the steel and gold,
The chief, the steed, the nimbly rushing car,

And all the horrors of the gloomy war.
Here the thick clouds, with purple lustre bright,
Spread o'er the long, long host and gradual sunk in night;
Here half the world was wrapp'd in rolling fires,
And dreadful valleys sunk between the spires.
Swift ran black forms across the livid flame,
And oaks waved slowly in the trembling beam:
Loud rose the mingled noise ; with hollow sound,
Deep rolling whirlwinds roar, and thundering flames resound.

As drives a blast along the midnight heath,
Rush'd raging Irad on the scenes of death ;
High o'er his shoulder gleam'd his brandish'd blade,
And scatter'd ruin round the twilight shade.
Full on a giant hero's sweeping car
He pour'd the tempest of resistless war ;
His twinkling lance the heathen raised on high,
And hurl'd it, fruitless, through the gloomy sky ;
From the bold youth the maddening coursers wheel,
Gash'd by the vengeance of his slaughtering steel :
'Twixt two tall oaks the helpless chief they drew ;
The shrill car dash'd ; the crack'd wheels rattling flew ;
Crush'd in his arms, to rise he strove in vain,
And lay unpitied on the dreary plain.

EVENING AFTER A BATTLE.

Above tall western hills, the light of day
Shot far the splendors of his golden ray ;
Bright from the storm with tenfold grace he smiled,
The tumult softened, and the world grew mild.
With pomp transcendent, robed in heavenly dyes,
Arch'd the clear rainbow round the orient skies ;
Its changeless form, its hues of beam divine,
—Fair type of truth and beauty's—endless shine
Around the expanse, with thousand splendors rare ;
Gay clouds sail'd wanton through the kindling air ;
From shade to shade, unnumber'd tinctures blend ;
Unnumber'd forms of wond'rous light extend :
In pride stupendous, glittering walls aspire,
Graced with bright domes, and crown'd with towers of fire,
On cliffs cliffs burn ; o'er mountains mountains roll :
A burst of glory spreads from pole to pole :
Rapt with the splendor, every songster sings,
Tops the high bough, and claps his glistening wings :

With new born green, reviving nature blooms,
And sweeter fragrance freshening air perfumes.
   Far south the storm withdrew its troubled reign ;
Descending twilight dimm'd the dusky plain ;
Black night arose ; her curtains hid the ground :
Less roar'd, and less, the thunder's solemn sound ;
The bended lightning shot a brighter stream,
Or wrapp'd all heaven in one wide, mantling flame ;
By turns, o'er plains, and woods, and mountains, spread
Faint, yellow glimmerings, and a deeper shade.
   From parting clouds, the moon outbreaking shone,
And sate, sole empress, on her silver throne ;
In clear, full beauty, round all nature smiled,
And claim'd o'er heaven and earth, dominion mild ;
With humbler glory, stars her court attend,
And bless'd, and union'd, silent lustre blend.

PROCESSION OF ISRAELITISH VIRGINS TO MEET THE RE-
TURNING ARMY.

   The sun declined ; besmear'd with dust and blood,
Slow o'er the plain the wearied squadrons trod ;
When fair as Phosphor leads the morning train,
Dress'd in new beams, and beauteous from the main ;
Crown'd with white flowers, that breath'd a rich perfume,
And clothed in loveliness of gayest bloom,
Rose in soft splendor Caleb's youngest pride,
A thousand maidens following at her side.
In snow white robes of flowing silk array'd,
First of the virgins walk'd the blushing maid ;
Her long, dark hair loose floated in the wind ;
Her glowing eyes confess'd the etherial mind ;
A wreath of olive flourish'd in her hand ;
A silver lyre obey'd her soft command ;
With sounds harmonious rang the warbled strings,
And thus the maids, and thus Selima sings.
  " Who comes from Ai, adorn'd with gay attire,
Bright as the splendor of the morning fire ?
Fair as the spring, ascends the lovely form,
And dreadful as the blaze that lights the storm !
Ye maids, with flowerets strew the conqueror's way,
Strike the loud harp, and sing the dreadful day ! "
   To Irad's steps the matchless fair one came,
Her breast quick panting, and her cheeks on flame ;

Her beauteous hand the verdant crown display'd;
Graceful he bow'd, and placed it on his head.
Slow to her train the trembling fair withdrew,
The charm'd youths following with a moveless view.
So, wing'd with light, and dress'd in strange array,
The mantling glory of the rising day,
With sweet complacence, such as angels show
To souls unprison'd from this world of woe,
Parted soft smiling from our general sire
Some bright-eyed virtue, of the heavenly choir,
Far in the solar walk, with wondrous flight,
The form celestial lessen'd on his sight.

LAMENTATION OF SELIMA FOR THE DEATH OF IRAD.

Canst thou forget, when, call'd from southern bowers,
Love tuned the groves, and spring awaked the flowers,
How, loosed from slumbers by the morning ray,
O'er balmy plains we bent our frequent way?
On thy fond arm, with pleasing gaze, I hung,
And heard sweet music murmur o'er thy tongue;
Hand lock'd in hand, with gentle ardor press'd,
Pour'd soft emotions through the heaving breast,
In magic transport heart with heart entwined,
And in sweet languors lost the melting mind.
'T was then, thy voice, attuned to wisdom's lay,
Show'd fairer worlds, and traced the immortal way;
In virtue's pleasing paths my footsteps tried,
My sweet companion, and my skilful guide;
Through varied knowledge taught my mind to soar,
Search hidden truths, and new-found walks explore:
While still the tale, by nature learn'd to rove,
Slid, unperceived, to scenes of happy love.
Till weak, and lost, the faltering converse fell,
And eyes disclosed what eyes alone could tell;
In rapturous tumult bade the passions roll,
And spoke the living language of the soul.
With what fond hope, through many a blissful hour,
We gave the soul to fancy's pleasing power;
Lost in the magic of that sweet employ
To build gay scenes, and fashion future joy!
We saw mild peace o'er fair Canaan rise,
And shower her pleasures from benignant skies.
On airy hills our happy mansion rose,
Built but for joy, nor room reserved for woes.

Round the calm solitude, with ceaseless song,
Soft roll'd domestic ecstacy along :
Sweet as the sleep of innocence, the day,
By raptures number'd, lightly danced away :
To love, to bliss, the union'd soul was given,
And each, too happy! ask'd no brighter heaven.
Yet then, even then, my trembling thoughts would rove,
And steal an hour from Irad, and from love,
Through dread futurity all anxious roam,
And cast a mournful glance on ills to come.
"Hope not, fond maid," some voice prophetic cried—
"A life, thus wafted down the unruffled tide :
Trust no gay, golden doom, from anguish free,
Nor wish the laws of heaven reversed for thee.
Survey the peopled world ; thy soul shall find
Woes, ceaseless woes, ordain'd for poor mankind.
Life's a long solitude, an unknown gloom,
Closed by the silence of the dreary tomb.

"For soon, ah soon shall fleet thy pleasing dreams ;
Soon close the eye, that, bright as angel's, beams
Grace irresistible. To mouldering clay
Shall change the face, that smiles thy griefs away :
Soon the sweet music of that voice be o'er,
Hope cease to charm, and beauty bloom no more :
Strange, darksome wilds, and devious ways be trod,
Nor love, nor Irad, steal thy heart from God."

And must the hours in ceaseless anguish roll?
Must no soft sunshine cheer my clouded soul?
Spring charm around me brightest scenes, in vain?
And youth's angelic visions wake to pain?
Oh come once more, with fond endearments come ;
Burst the cold prison of the sullen tomb ;
Through favorite walks, thy chosen maid attend ;
Where well known shades for thee their branches bend :
Shed the sweet poison from thy speaking eye ;
And look those raptures, lifeless words deny !
Still be the tale rehearsed, that ne'er could tire ;
But, told each eve, fresh pleasure could inspire :
Still hoped those scenes, which love and fancy drew ;
But, drawn a thousand times, were ever new !

Again all bright shall glow the morning beam ;
Again soft suns dissolve the frozen stream :
Spring call young breezes from the southern skies,
And, clothed in splendor, flowery millions rise.
In vain to thee—no morn's indulgent ray
Warms the cold mansion of the slumbering clay.

No mild etherial gale, with tepid wing,
Shall fan thy locks, or waft approaching spring :
Unfelt, unknown, shall breathe the rich perfume,
And unheard music wave around thy tomb.
A cold, dumb, dead repose invests thee round ;
Still as a void, ere nature form'd a sound.
O'er thy dark region, pierced by no kind ray,
Slow roll the long, oblivious hours away.
In these wild walks, this solitary round,
Where the pale moon-beam lights the glimmering ground,
At each sad turn, I view thy spirit come,
And glide, half seen, behind a neighboring tomb ;
With visionary hand, forbid my stay,
Look o'er the grave, and beckon me away.

DAVID HUMPHREYS.

DAVID HUMPHREYS was the son of a clergyman, of Derby in Connecticut, and was born at that place in 1753. He entered Yale College in 1767, where he formed an acquaintance with Dwight and Trumbull. He went into the army on the breaking out of the war, and in 1778 was attached to General Putnam's staff, with the rank of Major. In 1780 he was made a Colonel, and aide-de-camp to Washington, in whose family he continued till the end of the war, enjoying the full confidence and friendship of the Commander in Chief. When the army was disbanded, and Washington had resigned his commission, Colonel Humphreys accompanied him in his retirement to Virginia.

In 1784 he was appointed Secretary to the legation for concluding treaties with foreign powers, and sailed for Europe where he passed two years, principally at Paris and London. On his return in 1786, he was chosen to represent his native town in the Connecticut legislature, and shortly after appointed by Congress to the command of a body of troops raised in New England, for the western service. While occupied in this business he resided for the most part at Hartford, and associated with Trumbull, Barlow and Hopkins in the literary and political writings which engaged their attention at that period. In 1788 his corps being broken up, his commission expired, and he made a journey to General Washington at Mount Vernon, and remained there till the organization of the federal government, when he attended the President to New York. He remained in his family till 1790. At this time he was nominated ambassador to Portugal, and in 1791 sailed for Lisbon, being the first American minister to that country. He subsequently received the additional appointment of minister plenipotentiary to the court of Madrid, and during the discharge of these duties, concluded treaties of peace with the government of Tripoli and Algiers. He remained abroad till 1802, and after his return lived principally in his native state, without taking any share in public measures except receiving the command of the veteran volunteers of Connecticut in 1812, with the rank of General. He died at New Haven, February 21st, 1818, at the age of 65.

Colonel Humphreys attracted much notice by his first poem, "An Address to the Armies of the United States of America," written in 1782, in the bustle of the camp, for the patriotic purpose of inspiring his brethren in arms with courage and perseverance in the struggle. This piece had a great popularity. It was published in England, and translated into French by the Marquis de Chastellux, the friend and fellow soldier of Humphreys. His other works are, A Poem on the Happiness of America, A Poem on the future Glory of the United States, A Poem on the Industry of the United States, A Poem on the Love of Country, A Poem on the death of Washington, and a few small pieces. Besides these, he was the Author of a life of General Putnam, and a translation of the French tragedy, The Widow of Malabar.

The poetry of Humphreys displays considerable talent, but the sameness in the character of the subjects which he has adopted throughout his different pieces, gives it an air of monotony which materially detracts from the interest we feel in going over his volume. Either of his larger performances, will give a fair specimen of his general manner and merits.

His conceptions are elevated, his sentiments noble and warm with patriotic zeal, and his versification correct and harmonious.

YE martial bands! Columbia's fairest pride!
To toils inured, in dangers often tried—
Ye gallant youths! whose breasts for glory burn,
Each selfish aim and meaner passion spurn:
Ye who, unmoved, in the dread hour have stood,
And smiled, undaunted, in the field of blood—
Who greatly dared, at freedom's rapturous call,
With her to triumph, or with her to fall—
Now brighter days in prospect swift ascend;
Ye sons of fame, the hallow'd theme attend;
The past review; the future scenes explore,
And heaven's high king with grateful hearts adore!
    What time proud Albion, thundering o'er the waves,
Frown'd on her sons, and bade them turn to slaves—
When, lost to honor, virtue, glory, shame,
When nought remain'd of Britain but the name—
The parent state—a parent now no more—
Let loose the hirelings of despotic power,
Urged to keen vengeance their relentless ire,
And hoped submission from their sword and fire.
As when dark clouds, from Andes' towering head,
Roll down the skies, and round the horizon spread,
With thunders fraught, the blackening tempest sails,
And bursts tremendous o'er Peruvian vales:
So broke the storm on Concord's fatal plain;
There fell our brothers, by fierce ruffians slain—
Inglorious deed! to wild despair then driven,
We, suppliant, made our great appeal to heaven.
Then the shrill trumpet echoed from afar,
And sudden blazed the wasting flame of war;
From State to State swift flew the dire alarms,
And ardent youths, impetuous, rush'd to arms:
"To arms" the matrons and the virgins sung,
To arms, their sires, their husbands, brothers sprung.
No dull delay—where'er the sound was heard,
Where the red standards in the air appear'd,
Where, through vast realms the cannon swell'd its roar,
Between the Acadian and Floridian shore.

Now join'd the crowd, from their far distant farms,
In rustic guise, and unadorn'd in arms :
Not like their foes, in tinsel trappings gay,
And burnish'd arms that glitter'd on the day ;
Who now advanced, where Charlestown reared its height,
In martial pomp, and claim'd the awful sight;
And proudly deem'd, with one decisive blow,
To hurl destruction on the routed foe.
Not so—just heaven had fix'd the great decree,
And bade the sons of freemen still be free ;
Bade all their souls with patriot ardor burn,
And taught the coward, fear of death to spurn ;
The threats of danger and of war to brave,
To purchase freedom, or a glorious grave.
Long raged the contest on the embattled field ;
Nor those would fly, nor these would tamely yield—
Till Warren fell, in all the boast of arms,
The pride of genius and unrivall'd charms,
His country's hope!—full soon the gloom was spread :
Oppress'd with numbers, and their leader dead,
Slow from the field the sullen troops retired ;
Behind, the hostile flame to heaven aspired.

The imperious Britons, on the well-fought ground,
No cause for joy or wanton triumph found,
But saw with grief their dreams of conquest vain,
Felt the deep wounds, and mourn'd their veterans slain.

Nor less our woes.   Now darkness gather'd round;
The thunder rumbled, and the tempest frown'd ;
When lo! to guide us through the storm of war,
Beam'd the bright splendor of Virginia's star.
O first of heroes, fav'rite of the skies,
To what dread toils thy country bade thee rise !
"Oh raised by heaven to save the invaded state !"
(So spake the sage long since thy future fate,)
'T was thine to change the sweetest scenes of life
For public cares—to guide the embattled strife ;
Unnumber'd ills of every kind to dare,
The winter's blast, the summer's sultry air,
The lurking dagger, and the turbid storms
Of wasting war, with death in all his forms.
Nor aught could daunt.   Unspeakably serene,
Thy conscious soul smiled o'er the dreadful scene.

The foe then trembled at the well-known name ;
And raptured thousands to his standard came.
His martial skill our rising armies form'd ;
His patriot zeal their generous bosoms warm'd :
His voice inspired, his godlike presence led,
The Britons saw, and from his presence fled,

Soon reinforced from Albion's crowded shore,
New legions came, new plains were drenched in gore ;
And scarce Columbia's arm the fight sustains,
While her best blood gush'd from a thousand veins.
Then thine, O Brown! that purpled wide the ground,
Pursued the knife through many a ghastly wound.
Ah hapless friend! permit the tender tear
To flow e'en now, for none flowed on thy bier,
Where cold and mangled, under northern skies,
To famish'd wolves a prey thy body lies ;
Which erst so fair and tall in youthful grace,
Strength in thy nerves, and beauty in thy face,
Stood like a tower, till struck by the swift ball ;
Then what avail'd (to ward the untimely fall)
The force of limbs, the mind so well inform'd,
The taste refined, the breast with friendship warm'd,
(That friendship which our earliest years begun)
Or what the laurels that thy sword had won,
When the dark bands from thee, expiring, tore
Thy long hair mingled with the spouting gore?
Nor less, brave Scammel, frown'd thine angry fate,
(May deathless shame that British deed await!)
On York's famed field, amid the first alarms,
Ere yet fair victory crown'd the allied arms,
Fell chance betray'd thee to the hostile band,
The hapless victim of the assassin hand!
Lo! while I tell the execrable deed,
Fresh in his side the dark wound seems to bleed ;
The small red current still for vengeance cries,
And asks, "Why sleeps the thunder in the skies?"
On him, ye heavens, let all your vengeance fall,
On the curst wretch who wing'd the insidious ball.
But thou, blest shade, be sooth'd! be this thy praise,
Ripe were thy virtues, though too few thy days!
Be this thy fame, through life of all approved,
To die lamented, honor'd, and beloved.

   And see, far south, where yonder hearse appears,
An army mourning, and a land in tears!
There Laurens, passing to an early tomb,
Looks like a flower, just withering in its bloom.
Thy father's pride, the glory of our host!
Thy country's sorrow, late thy country's boast !
O Laurens! generous youth! twice hadst thou bled ;
Could not the ball with devious aim have sped ?
And must thy friends, now peace appears so near,
Weep the third stroke that cuts a life so dear ;
That blots the prospect of our rising morn,

And leaves thy country, as thy sire, forlorn?
Companions loved! long as the life-blood flows,
Or vital warmth in this fond bosom glows,
While there I cherish your remembrance dear,
Oft will I drop the tributary tear.
    But what avails to trace the fate of war
Through fields of blood, and paint each glorious scar?
Why should the strain your former woes recall,
The tears that wept a friend or brother's fall,
When by your side first in the adventurous strife,
He dauntless rush'd, too prodigal of life?
Enough of merit has each honor'd name,
To shine, untarnish'd, on the rolls of fame;
To stand the example of each distant age,
And add new lustre to the historic page:
For soon their deeds, illustrious, shall be shown
In breathing bronze, or animated stone,
Or where the canvass, starting into life,
Revives the glories of the crimson strife.
    Ye sons of genius, who the pencil hold,
Whose master strokes, beyond description bold,
Of other years and climes the history trace,
Can ye for this neglect your kindred race?
Columbia calls—her parent voice demands
More grateful offerings from your filial hands.
And soon some bard shall tempt the untried themes,
Sing how we dared, in fortune's worst extremes;
What cruel wrongs the indignant patriot bore,
What various ills your feeling bosoms tore,
What boding terrors gloom'd the threat'ning hour,
When British legions, arm'd with death-like power,
Bade desolation mark their crimson'd way,
And lured the savage to his destined prey;
When fierce Germania her battalions pour'd,
And rapine's sons, with wasting fire and sword,
Spread death around: where'er your eyes ye turn'd,
Fled were the peasants, and the village burn'd.
How did your hearts for others' sufferings melt!
What torturing pangs your bleeding country felt!
What! when you fled before superior force,
Each succor lost, and perish'd each resource!
When nature, fainting from the want of food,
On the white snow your steps were mark'd in blood!
When through your tatter'd garbs you met the wind,
Despair before, and ruin frown'd behind!
When nought was seen around, but prospects drear,
The insulting foe hung dreadful on your rear,

And boastful ween'd, that day to close the scene,
And quench your name, as though it ne'er had been.
   Why, Britian, raged thy insolence and scorn?
Why burst thy vengeance on the wretch forlorn?
The cheerless captive to slow death consign'd,
Chill'd with keen frost, in prison glooms confined;
Of hope bereft, by thy vile minions curst,
With hunger famish'd, and consumed with thirst,
Without one friend—when death's last horror stung,
Roll'd the wild eye, and gnaw'd the anguish'd tongue.
   Why, Britain, in thy arrogance and pride,
Didst thou heaven's violated laws deride,
Mock human misery with contemptuous sneers,
And fill thy cup of guilt with orphan's tears?
The widow's wailing, and the wretch's groan,
Rise in remembrance to the eternal throne,
While the red flame, through the broad concave driven,
Calls down the vengeance of insulted heaven.
And didst thou think, by cruelty refined,
To damp the ardor of the heaven-born mind,
With haughty threats to force the daring train
To bow, unnerved, in slavery's galling chain;
Make countless freemen—then no longer free,
Shrink at thy frown, and bend the servile knee?
And couldst thou dream? then wake, dissolve thy charms,
Roused by their wrongs, see desperate hosts in arms!
No fear dismays, nor danger's voice appals,
While kindred blood for sacred vengeance calls:
Their swords shall triumph o'er thy vaunted force,
And curb the conqueror in his headlong course.
   What spoils of war, thy sons, Columbia, claim'd!
What trophies rose, where thy red ensigns flamed!
Where the great chief, o'er Delaware's icy wave,
Led the small band, in dangers doubly brave;
On high designs, and ere the dawning hour,
Germania's veterans own'd the victor's power;
Or on the muse's plain, where round thy tomb,
O gallant Mercer! deathless laurels bloom;
Or where, anon, in northern fields renown'd,
The tide of slaughter stain'd the sanguine ground;
When the bold freemen, gathering from afar,
Foil'd the proud foe, and crush'd the savage war:
On that brave band their country's plaudit waits,
And consecrates to fame the name of Gates.
Nor less the valor of the impetuous shock,
Which seized the glorious prize on Hudson's rock,

Where Wayne, e'en while he felt the whizzing ball,
Pluck'd the proud standard from the vanquish'd wall.
Now turn your eyes, where southern realms are seen,
From ruin rescued by the immortal Greene:
See toils of death, where many a hero bleeds,
Till rapid victory to defeat succeeds.
On numerous plains, whose streams, unknown to song,
Till this great era, roll'd obscure along,
Their names shall now, to fame familiar grown,
Outlast the pile of monumental stone.
Or see on fair Virginia's strand arise,
The column pointing to the favoring skies,
Inscribed with deeds the federate arms have done,
And graved with trophies from Britannia won:
Here stand the conquering bands: the vanquish'd throng
Through the long lines in silence move along:
The stars and lilies, here in laurels drest,
And there, dark shrouds the banner'd pride invest:
These twice twelve banners once in pomp unfurl'd,
Spread death and terror round the southern world:
In various colors from the staff unroll'd,
The lion frown'd, the eagle flamed in gold;
Hibernia's heart, reluctant, here was hung,
And Scotia's thistle there spontaneous sprung:
These twice twelve flags no more shall be display'd,
Save in the dome where warlike spoils are laid;
Since, where the fathers in high council meet,
This hand has placed them prostrate at their feet.
    So beam the glories of the victor band!
And such the dawning hope that cheers our land!
Since Gallia's sire, intent on cares of state,
Sublimely good, magnanimously great!
Protector of the rights of human kind,
Weigh'd the dread contest in his royal mind,
And bade his fleets o'er the broad ocean fly,
To succor realms beneath another sky!
Since his blest troops, in happiest toils allied,
Have fought, have bled, have conquer'd by your side:
The mingled stream, in the same trench that flow'd,
Cements the nations by their heroes' blood,
    Yet still, Columbians, see what choice remains,
Ignoble bondage and inglorious chains,
Or all the joys which liberty can give,
For which you dare to die, or wish to live.
On the drawn sword your country's fate depends:
Your wives, your children, parents, brothers, friends,
With all the tender charities of life,
Hang on the issue of the arduous strife.

To bolder deeds, and victory's fierce delights,
Your country calls, and heaven itself invites.
Charm'd by their potent voice, let virtue's flame,
The sense of honor, and the fear of shame,
The thirst of praise, and freedom's envied cause,
The smiles of heroes, and the world's applause,
Impel each breast, in glory's dread career,
Firm as your rock-raised hills, to persevere.
   Now the sixth year of independence smiles,
The glorious meed of all our warlike toils ;
Auspicious power, with thy broad flag unfurl'd,
Shed thy stern influence on our western world !
With thy congenial flame our hearts inspire,
With manly patience and heroic fire,
The rudest shock of fortune s storm to bear :
Each ill to suffer ; every death to dare ;
To rush undaunted in the adventurous van,
And meet the Britons, man opposed to man ;
With surer aim repel their barbarous rage ;
Shield the poor orphan, and the white-hair'd sage ;
Defend the matron, and the virgin's charms,
And vindicate our sacred rights with arms.
This the great genius of our land requires,
This the blest shades of our illustrious sires,
This the brave sons of future years demand,
Cheers the faint heart, and nerves the feeble hand ;
This sacred hope, that points beyond the span
Which bounds this transitory life of man,
Where glory lures us with her bright renown,
The hero's triumph, and the patriot's crown ;
The fair reward to suffering virtue given,
Pure robes of bliss, and starry thrones in heaven.
   Changed are the scenes ; now fairer prospects rise,
And brighter suns begin to gild our skies,
The exhausted foe, his last poor effort tried,
Sees nought remain, save impotence and pride :
His golden dreams of fancied conquest o'er,
(And Gallia thundering round his native shore,
Iberia aiding with Potosi's mines,
While brave Batavia in the conflict joins)
Reluctant turns, and, deep involved in woes,
In other climes prepares for other foes.
   Anon, the horrid sounds of war shall cease,
And all the western world be hush'd in peace :
The martial clarion shall be heard no more,
Nor the loud cannon's desolating roar :

No more our heroes pour the purple flood,
No corse be seen with garments roll'd in blood ;
No shivering wretch shall roam without a shed ;
No pining orphans raise their cry for bread ;
No tender mother shriek at dreams of woe,
Start from her sleep, and see the midnight foe ;
The lovely virgin, and the hoary sire,
No more behold the village flame aspire,
While the base spoiler, from a father's arms,
Plucks the fair flower, and riots on its charms.

E'en now, from half the threaten'd horrors freed,
See from our shores the lessening sails recede :
See the red flags, that to the wind unfurl'd,
Waved in proud triumph round the vanquish'd world,
Inglorious fly ; and see their haggard crew,
Despair, rage, shame, and infamy pursue.

Hail, heaven-born peace ! thy grateful blessings pour
On this glad land, and round the peopled shore :
Thine are the joys that gild the happy scene,
Propitious days, and festive nights serene ;
With thee gay pleasure frolics o'er the plain,
And smiling plenty leads thy prosperous train.

Then oh, my friends ! the task of glory done,
The immortal prize by your bold efforts won :
Your country's saviours, by her voice confess'd,
While unborn ages rise and call you blest—
Then let us go where happier climes invite,
To midland seas, and regions of delight ;
With all that 's ours, together let us rise,
Seek brighter plains and more indulgent skies ;
Where fair Ohio rolls his amber tide,
And nature blossoms in her virgin pride ;
Where all that beauty's hand can form to please,
Shall crown the toils of war with rural ease.
The shady coverts and the sunny hills,
The gentle lapse of ever-murmuring rills,
The soft repose amid the noon-tide bowers,
The evening walk among the blushing flowers,
The fragrant groves that yield a sweet perfume,
And vernal glories in perpetual bloom,
Await you there ; and heaven shall bless the toil,
Your own the produce, as your own the soil.

No tyrant lord shall grasp a thousand farms,
Curse the mild clime, and spoil its fairest charms :
No blast severe your ripening fields deform,
No volleyed hail-stones, and no driving storm :
No raging murrain on your cattle seize,

And nature sicken with the dire disease.
But golden years, anew, begin their reigns,
And cloudless sunshine gild salubrious plains.
Herbs, fruits and flowers shall clothe the uncultured field,
Nectareous juice the vine and orchard yield;
Rich dulcet creams the copious goblets fill,
Delicious honey from the trees distil;
The garden smile, spontaneous harvests spring,
The valleys warble, and the woodlands ring.
　　Along the meads, or near the shady groves,
There sport the flocks, there feed the fattening droves;
There strays the steed, through bloomy vales afar,
Who erst moved lofty in the ranks of war.
　　There, free from envy, cankering care and strife,
Flow the calm pleasures of domestic life:
There mutual friendship soothes each placid breast,
Blest in themselves, and in each other blest.
From house to house the social glee extends,
For friends in war, in peace are doubly friends:
Their children taught to emulate their sires,
Catch the warm glow, and feel the kindred fires,
Till by degrees the mingling joys improve,
Grow with their years, and ripen into love:
Nor long the blushing pair in secret sigh,
And drink sweet poison from the love-sick eye;
Blest be their lot, when in his eager arms
The enamor'd youth folds the fair virgin's charms;
On her ripe lip imprints the burning kiss,
And seals with hallow'd rites the nuptial bliss.
Then festal sports the evening hours prolong,
The mazy dance and the sweet warbling song:
Then each endearment wakes the ravish'd sense
To pure delights and raptures most intense:
And the pleased parent tells his listening son,
What wondrous deeds by him in youth, were done.
No sights of woe, no torturing fears annoy
The sweet sensation of the heart-felt joy:
Nor shall the savages of murderous soul,
In painted bands dark to the combat roll,
With midnight orgies, by the gloomy shade,
On the pale victim point the reeking blade;
Or cause the hamlet, lull'd in deep repose,
No more to wake, or wake to ceaseless woes:
For your strong arm the guarded land secures,
And freedom, glory, happiness, are yours!
　　So shall you flourish in unfading prime,
Each age refining through the reign of time;

A nobler offspring crown the fond embrace,
A band of heroes, and a patriot race :
Not by soft luxury's too dainty food,
Their minds contaminated with their blood :
But like the heirs our great forefathers bred,
By freedom nurtured, and by temperance fed ;
Healthful and strong, they turn'd the virgin soil,
The untamed forest bow'd beneath their toil :
At early dawn they sought the mountain chase,
Or roused the Indian from his lurking place ;
Curb'd the mad fury of those barbarous men,
Or dragg'd the wild beast struggling from his den :
To all the vigor of that pristine race,
New charms are added, and superior grace.
  Then cities rise, and spiry towns increase,
With gilded domes, and every art of peace.
Then cultivation shall extend his power,
Rear the green blade, and nurse the tender flower ,
Make the fair villa in full splendors smile,
And robe with verdure all the genial soil.
Then shall rich commerce court the favoring gales,
And wondering wilds admire the passing sails ;
Where the bold ships the stormy Huron brave,
Where wild Ontario rolls the whitening wave,
Where fair Ohio his pure current pours,
And Mississippi laves the extended shores.
  Then oh, blest land ! with genius unconfined,
With polish'd manners, and the illumined mind,
Thy future race on daring wing shall soar,
Each science trace, and all the arts explore ;
Till bright religion beckoning to the skies,
Shall bid thy sons to endless glories rise.
  As round thy climes celestial joy extends,
Thy beauties ripen, and thy pomp ascends ;
Farther and farther still, thy blessings roll,
To southern oceans and the northern pole ;
Where now the thorn, or tangled thicket grows,
The wilderness shall blossom as the rose ;
Unbounded deserts unknown charms assume,
Like Salem flourish, and like Eden bloom.
  And oh, my heaven ! when all our toils are past,
Crown with such happiness our days at last :
So rise our sons, like our great sires of old,
In freedom's cause, unconquerably bold ;
With spotless faith, and morals pure, their name
Spread through the world, and gain immortal fame.

And thou Supreme! whose hand sustains this ball,
Before whose nod the nations rise and fall,
Propitious smile, and shed diviner charms
On this blest land, the queen of arts and arms;
Make the great empire rise on wisdom's plan,
The seat of bliss, and last retreat of man.

———

THE MONKEY WHO SHAVED HIMSELF AND HIS FRIENDS.

A FABLE.

A MAN who own'd a barber's shop
At York, and shaved full many a fop,
A monkey kept for their amusement;
He made no other kind of use on 't—
This monkey took great observation,
Was wonderful at imitation,
And all he saw the barber do,
He mimic'd straight, and did it too.
It chanced in shop, the dog and cat,
While friseur dined, demurely sat,
Jacko found nought to play the knave in,
So thought he 'd try his hand at shaving.
Around the shop in haste he rushes,
And gets the razor, soap, and brushes;
Now puss he fix'd (no muscle miss stirs)
And lather'd well her beard and whiskers,
Then gave a gash, as he began—
The cat cry'd "waugh!" and off she ran.
Next Towser's beard he try'd his skill in,
Though Towser seem'd somewhat unwilling:
As badly here again succeeding,
The dog runs howling round and bleeding.
Nor yet was tired our roguish elf;
He 'd seen the barber shave himself;
So by the glass, upon the table,
He rubs with soap his visage sable,
Then with left hand holds smooth his jaw,—
The razor in his dexter paw;
Around he flourishes and slashes,
Till all his face is seam'd with gashes.
His cheeks despatch'd—his visage thin
He cock'd, to shave beneath his chin;

Drew razor swift as he could pull it,
And cut, from ear to ear, his gullet.*

MORAL.

Who cannot write, yet handle pens,
Are apt to hurt themselves and friends.
Though others use them well, yet fools
Should never meddle with edge tools.

LEMUEL HOPKINS.

DR LEMUEL HOPKINS was born at Waterbury, in Connecticut, June 19th, 1750. His father was a farmer in easy
circumstances, and while he reared all his children to the
labor of the field, took care to bestow upon them a good education. Dr Hopkins is said to have been determined to the
study of physic when young, by observing the gradual decline of some of his connexions, who were sinking under a
consumption. This inclination to medical pursuits was
strengthened by the circumstance of a hereditary predisposi-
tion to the same disorder which existed in the family. His
education, it seems, had not been classical, and having resolved upon the medical profession, he applied himself to Latin
and other preliminary studies, and after proper qualification,
placed himself under the care of a physician in Wallingford.
He began regular practice in Litchfield, about the year 1776,
and was for a short time in the American army as a volunteer.
About 1784, he removed to Hartford. Here he passed the
rest of his life, devoted to the labors of a physician, and man
of letters. He fell a victim, we are told, to the exercise of an

---

* Humphreys had completed this fable with the exception of the last couplet,
and made several attempts to give it that pointed finish which he desired, but
could not succeed. He then went with it to the author of M'Fingal, and told
him his difficulty. Trumbull took the piece and read it aloud; then looking upward with that keen glance for which his eye was remarkable, added without
pausing—

" Drew razor swift as he could pull it,
And cut from ear to ear his gullet. "

improper remedy in his own case, occasioned by his dread of a pulmonary complaint. He died on the 14th of April, 1801.

Dr Hopkins was a physician of great skill and reputation. His memory was so retentive, that he would quote every writer he had read, whether medical or literary, with the same readiness that a clergyman quotes the Bible. In his labors for scientific purposes, he was indefatigable. The Medical Society of Connecticut is indebted to him as one of its founders. In his person he was tall, lean, stooping and long-limbed, with large features and light eyes, and this uncouth appearance, added to a great eccentricity of manner, rendered him at first sight a very striking spectacle.

In his literary character he was eminent among the distinguished writers of the place where the most of his life was spent. Trumbull, Barlow, Humphreys, Dwight and others, were his associates, and the two first with Hopkins wrote the Anarchiad. He also had a hand in The Echo, The Political Greenhouse, and many satirical poems of that description, in which he had for his associates, Richard Alsop, Theodore Dwight, and a number of others. Besides these, there are a few short pieces which were written by him exclusively.

The Anarchiad was published in portions in the Connecticut Magazine, during the year 1786, and 1787. It is a political satire, referring to the state of the country at the period immediately preceding the adoption of the federal constitution. The American states were at that time loosely connected, each pursuing its own separate policy, without any regard for the plans of the other members of the confederacy, or the general welfare of the country. This led to embarrassments in the public affairs, which by the instrumentality of factious and violent persons, occasioned great disorders. Against the promoters of these political troubles, the Anarchiad is pointed. The poem is represented in the introduction as having been discovered in digging among the ancient aboriginal fortifications in the western country, and by the aid of vision and prophecy, it is made to bear on modern events. A strain of grave moral expostulation is mixed up with satirical touches in a very able manner. Dr Hopkins suggested the plan of the work, and has always borne the credit of having written the most striking passages. Its authorship being more closely connected with his name than any other, the extracts from the poem are given under the present head.

"In visions fair, the scenes of fate unroll,
And Massachusetts opens on my soul.
There Chaos, Anarch old, asserts his sway,
And mobs in myriads blacken all the way :
See Day's stern port, behold the martial frame
Of Shays' and Shattuck's mob-compelling name :
See the bold Hampshirites on Springfield pour,
The fierce Tauntonians crowd the alewife shore.
O'er Concord fields, the bands of discord spread,
And Worcester trembles at their thundering tread :
See from proud Egremont, the woodchuck train
Sweep their dark files, and shade with rags the plain.
Lo, the court falls ; the affrighted judges run,
Clerks, lawyers, sheriffs, every mother's son.
The stocks, the gallows, lose the expected prize,
See the jails open, and the thieves arise.
Thy constitution, Chaos, is restored ;
Law sinks before thy uncreating word ;
Thy hand unbars the unfathom'd gulph of fate,
And deep in darkness whelms the new born state.

    *   *   *   *   *   *

Bow low, ye heavens, and all ye lands draw near,
The voice prophetic of great Anarch hear !
From eastern climes, by light and order driven,
To me, by fate, this western world was given ;
My standard rear'd, the realm imperial rules,
The last asylum for my knaves and fools.
Here shall my best and brightest empire rise,
Wild riot reign, and discord greet the skies.
Awake, my chosen sons, in folly brave,
Stab independence, dance o'er freedom's grave ;
Sing choral songs, while conquering mobs advance,
And blot the debts to Holland, Spain, and France ;
Till ruin come, with fire and sword and blood,
And men shall ask, where your republics stood ?
    Thrice happy race ! how bless'd are discord's heirs !

Bless'd while they know what anarchy is theirs;
Bless'd while they feel, to them alone 'tis given
To know no sovereign, neither law nor heaven.
From all mankind by traits peculiar known,
By frauds and lies distinguish'd for mine own,
Wonder of worlds! like which to mortal eyes,
None e'er have risen, and none e'er shall rise!
　　Lo, the poor Briton, who, corrupted, sold,
Sees God in courts, or hears him chink in gold,
Whose soul proud empire oft has taught to stray,
Far as the western world and gates of day;
Though plagued with debts, with rage of conquest curst,
In rags and tender-acts he puts no trust;
But in the public weal, his own forgets,
Finds heaven for him who pays the nation's debts;
A heaven like London his fond fancy makes
Of nectar'd porter and ambrosial steaks.
　　Not so, Columbia, shall thy sons be known,
To prize the public weal above their own;
In faith and justice least, as last in birth,
Their race shall grow a by-word through the earth:
Long skill'd to act the hypocritic part,
Grace on the brow, and knavery at the heart,
Perform their frauds, with sanctimonious air,
Despise good works, and balance sins by prayer.
Forswear the public debt, the public cause,
Cheat heaven with forms, and earth with tender-laws,
And leave the empire, at its latest groan,
To work salvation out by faith alone.
　　Behold the reign of anarchy begun,
And half the business of confusion done.
From hell's dark caverns, discord sounds alarms,
Blows her loud trump, and calls my Shays to arms;
O'er half the land the desperate riot runs,
And maddening mobs assume their rusty guns.
From councils feeble, bolder faction grows,
The daring corsairs, and the savage foes;
O'er western wilds the tawny bands, allied,
Insult the state of weakness and of pride;
Once friendly realms, unpaid each generous loan,
Wait to divide, and share them for their own.
　　Now sinks the public mind; a deathlike sleep
O'er all the torpid limbs begins to creep;
By dull degrees, decays the vital heat,
The blood forgets to flow, the pulse to beat.
The powers of life, in mimic death withdrawn,

Closed the fix'd eyes with one expiring yawn;
Exposed in state to wait the funeral hour,
Lie the pale relics of departed power,
While conscience harrowing up their souls with dread,
Their ghost of empire stalks without a head.
　　No more stands forth to check the rising feud,
Their great defender of the public good.
Retired, in vain his sighs their fate deplore;
He hears, unmoved, the distant tempest roar:
No more to save a realm dread Greene appears,
Their second hope, prime object of my fears:
Far in the south, from his pale body riven,
The deathful angel wings his soul to heaven.
　　Here shall I reign, unbounded and alone,
Nor men, nor demons shake my baseless throne;
Till comes the day—but late oh may it spring—
When their tumultuous mobs shall ask a king;
A king in wrath shall heaven, vindictive, send,
And my confusions and my empire end."
　　With arms where bickering fires innumerous shine,
Like the torn surface of the midnight brine;
In sunbright robes, that dazzled as he trod,
The stature, motion, armor of a god,
Great Hesper rose—the guardian of the clime—
O'er shadowy cliffs he stretch'd his arms sublime,
And check'd the Anarch old—" Malicious fiend,
Eternal curses on thy head descend!
Heaven's daring purpose can thy madness mar,
To glut thine eyes with ruin, death and war!
I know thee, Anarch, in thy cheerless plight,
Thou eldest son of Erebus and Night!
Yes, bend on me thy brows of hideous scowl,
Roll thy wild eyeballs, like the day-struck owl;
In Zion blow the trump, resound it far;
Fire the red beacons of intestine war;
Yet know for this, thyself to penance call'd,
Thy troops in terrors, their proud hearts appall'd.
Even Shays, that moment when eternal night
Rolls darkening shadows o'er his closing sight,
Shall feel, 't were better on a plank to lie,
Where surging billows kiss the angry sky;
'T were better through a furnace fiery red,
With naked feet on burning coals to tread;
Than point his sword, with parricidious hand,
Against the bosom of his native land.
　　" Where is the spirit of bold freedom fled?
Dead are my warriors, all my sages dead?

Is there—Columbia bending o'er her grave—
No eye to pity, and no arm to save?
 " Sister of freedom, heaven's imperial child,
Serenely stern, beneficently mild,
Bless'd independence, rouse my sons to fame,
Inspire their bosoms with thy sacred flame!
Teach, ere too late, their blood-bought rights to prize,
Bid other Greenes and Washingtons arise!
Teach those who suffer'd for their country's good,
Who strove for freedom, and who toil'd in blood,
Once more in arms to make the glorious stand,
And bravely die, or save their natal land.
 " Yes, they shall rise, terrific in their rage,
And crush the factions of the faithless age:
Bid law again exalt the impartial scale,
And public justice o'er her foes prevail:
Restore the reign of order and of right,
And drive thee, howling, to the shades of night."

*   *   *   *   *   *

Ye sires of nations, call'd in high debate,
From kindred realms, to save the sinking state,
A boundless sway on one broad base to rear—
My voice paternal claims your lingering ear;
O'er the wide clime my fostering cares extend,
Your guardian genius and your deathless friend.
 When splendid victory on her trophied car,
Swept from these shores the last remains of war,
Bade each glad state, that boasts Columbia's name,
Exult in freedom and ascend to fame,
To bliss unbounded stretch their ardent eyes,
And wealth and empire from their labor rise,
My raptured sons beheld the discord cease,
And soothed their sorrows in the songs of peace.
 Shall these bright scenes, with happiest omens born,
Fade like the fleeting visions of the morn?
Shall this fair fabric from its base be hurl'd,
And whelm in dust the glories of the world?
Will ye, who saw the heavens tempestuous lower,
Who felt the arm of irritated power,
Whose souls distending with the wasting flood,
Prepared the firm foundations, built in blood,
By discord seized, will ye desert the plan?
The unfinish'd Babel of the bliss of man?
 Go search the field of death, where heroes, lost
In graves obscure, can tell what freedom cost.
Though conquest smiled; there slain amid the crowd,

And plung'd promiscuous with no winding shroud,
No friendly hand their gory wounds to lave,
The thousands moulder in a common grave,
Not so thy son, oh Laurens! gasping lies,
Too daring youth, war's latest sacrifice ;
His snow-white bosom heaves with writhing pain,
The purple drops his snow-white bosom stain ;
His cheek of rose is wan, a deadly hue
Sits on his face, that chills with lucid dew.—
There Warren, glorious with expiring breath,
A comely corse, that smiles in ghastly death :
See Mercer bleed, and o'er yon wintry wall,
'Mid heaps of slain, see great Montgomery fall !

Behold those veterans worn with want and care,
Their sinews stiffen'd, silver'd o'er their hair,
Weak in their steps of age, they move forlorn,
Their toils forgotten by the sons of scorn;
This hateful truth still aggravates the pain,
In vain they conquer'd, and they bled in vain.
Go then, ye remnants of inglorious wars,
Disown your marks of merit, hide your fears,
Of lust, of power, of titled pride accused,
Steal to your graves dishonor'd and abused.

For see, proud faction waves her flaming brand,
And discord riots o'er the ungrateful land ;
Lo, to the north a wild adventurous crew
In desperate mobs the savage state renew ;
Each felon chief his maddening thousands draws,
And claims bold license from the bond of laws ;
In other states the chosen sires of shame,
Stamp their vile knaveries with a legal name ;
In honor's seat the sons of meanness swarm,
And senates base, the work of mobs perform,
To wealth, to power the sons of union rise,
While foes deride you and while friends despise.

Stand forth, ye traitors, at your country's bar,
Inglorious authors of intestine war ;
What countless mischiefs from their labors rise !
Pens dipp'd in gall, and lips inspired with lies !
Ye sires of ruin, prime detested cause
Of bankrupt faith, annihilated laws,
Of selfish systems, jealous, local schemes,
And union'd empire lost in empty dreams :
Your names expanding with your growing crime,
Shall float disgustful down the stream of time,
Each future age applaud the avenging song,
And outraged nature vindicate the wrong.

Yes there are men, who, touch'd with heavenly fire,
Beyond the confines of these climes aspire,
Beyond the praises of a tyrant age,
To live immortal in the patriot page ;
Who greatly dare, though warning worlds oppose,
To pour just vengeance on their country's foes.
  And lo ! the etherial worlds assert your cause,
Celestial aid the voice of virtue draws ;
The curtains blue of yon expansion rend :
From opening skies heroic shades descend.
See, robed in light, the forms of heaven appear,
The warrior spirits of your friends are near ;
Each on his steed of fire (his quiver stored
With shafts of vengeance) grasps his flaming sword :
The burning blade waves high, and, dipp'd in blood,
Hurls plagues and death on discord's faithless brood.
  Yet what the hope ? the dreams of congress fade,
The federal union sinks in endless shade,
Each feeble call, that warns the realms around,
Seems the faint echo of a dying sound,
Each requisition wafts in fleeting air,
And not one state regards the powerless prayer.
  Ye wanton states, by heaven's best blessings cursed,
Long on the lap of fostering luxury nursed,
What fickle frenzy raves, what visions strange,
Inspire your bosoms with the lust of change ?
And frames the wish to fly from fancied ill,
And yield your freedom to a monarch's will ?
  Go view the lands to lawless power a prey,
Where tyrants govern with unbounded sway ;
See the long pomp in gorgeous state display'd,
The tinsel'd guards, the squadron'd horse parade ;
See heralds gay with emblems on their vest,
In tissued robes tall beauteous pages drest ;
Where moves the pageant, throng unnumber'd slaves,
Lords, dukes, and princes, titulary knaves
Confusedly shine, the purple gemm'd with stars,
Sceptres, and globes, and crowns, and rubied cars,
On gilded orbs the thundering chariots roll'd,
Steeds snorting fire, and champing bitts of gold,
Prance to the trumpet's voice—while each assumes
A loftier gait, and lifts his neck of plumes.
High on the moving throne, and near the van,
The tyrant rides, the chosen scourge of man ;
Clarions, and flutes, and drums his way prepare,
And shouting millions rend the conscious air ;

Millions, whose ceaseless toils the pomp sustain,
Whose hour of stupid joy repays an age of pain.
   From years of darkness springs the regal line,
Hereditary kings by right divine;
'T is theirs to riot on all nature's spoils,
For them with pangs unblest the peasant toils,
For them the earth prolific teems with grain,
Theirs, the dread labors of the devious main,
Annual for them the wasted land renews
The gifts oppressive, and extorted dues,
For them when slaughter spreads the gory plains,
The life-blood gushes from a thousand veins,
While the dull herd, of earth-born pomp afraid,
Adore the power that coward meanness made.
Let Poland tell what woe returning springs,
Where right elective yields the crown to kings!
War guides the choice—each candidate abhorr'd
Founds his firm title on the wasting sword,
Wades to the throne amid the sanguine flood,
And dips his purple in the nation's blood.
   Behold, where Venice rears her sea-girt towers,
O'er the vile crowd proud oligarchy lowers;
While each Aristocrat affects a throne,
Beneath a thousand kings the poor plebeians groan.
   Nor less abhorr'd the certain woe that waits
The giddy rage of democratic states;
Whose popular breath, high blown in restless tide,
No laws can temper, and no reason guide;
An equal sway their mind indignant spurns,
To wanton change the bliss of freedom turns,
Led by wild demagogues the factious crowd,
Mean, fierce, imperious, insolent and loud,
Nor fame nor wealth nor power nor system draws,
They see no object and perceive no cause,
But feel by turns, in one disastrous hour,
Th' extremes of license and th' extremes of power.
   What madness prompts, or what ill-omen'd fates,
Your realm to parcel into petty states?
Shall lordly Hudson part contending powers?
And broad Potomac lave two hostile shores?
Must Allegany's sacred summits bear
The impious bulwarks of perpetual war?
His hundred streams receive your heroes slain?
And bear your sons inglorious to the main?
Will states cement by feebler bonds allied?
Or join more closely as they more divide?

Will this vain scheme bid restless factions cease?
Check foreign wars or fix internal peace?
Call public credit from her grave to rise?
Or gain in grandeur what they lose in size?
In this weak realm can countless kingdoms start
Strong with new force in each divided part?
While empire's head, divided into four,
Gains life by severance of diminish'd power?
So when the philosophic hand divides
The full grown polypus in genial tides,
Each sever'd part, inform'd with latent life,
Acquires new vigor from the friendly knife,
O'er peopled sands the puny insects creep,
Till the next wave absorbs them in the deep.
  What then remains? must pilgrim freedom fly
From these loved regions to her native sky?
When the fair fugitive the orient chased,
She fix'd her seat beyond the watry waste;
Her docile sons (enough of power resign'd,
And natural rites in social leagues combined,)
In virtue firm, though jealous in her cause,
Gave senates force and energy to laws,
From ancient habit local powers obey,
Yet feel no reverence for one general sway,
For breach of faith no keen compulsion feel,
And feel no interest in the federal weal.
But know, ye favored race, one potent head,
Must rule your states, and strike your foes with dread,
The finance regulate, the trade control,
Live through the empire, and accord the whole.
  Ere death invades, and night's deep curtain falls,
Through ruin'd realms the voice of Union calls;
Loud as the trump of heaven through darkness roars,
When gyral gusts entomb Caribbean towers,
When nature trembles through the deeps convulsed,
And ocean foams from craggy cliffs repulsed,
On you she calls! attend the warning cry,
" Ye live united, or divided die."

ON A PATIENT KILLED BY A CANCER QUACK.

    HERE lies a fool flat on his back,
    The victim of a cancer quack;
    Who lost his money and his life,
    By plaister, caustic, and by knife.

The case was this—-a pimple rose,
South-east a little of his nose ;
Which daily redden'd and grew bigger,
As too much drinking gave it vigor ;
A score of gossips soon ensure
Full threescore different modes of cure ;
But yet the full-fed pimple still
Defied all peticoated skill ;
When fortune led him to peruse
A hand-bill in the weekly news ;
Sign'd by six fools of different sorts,
All cured of cancers made of warts ;
Who recommend, with due submission,
This cancer-monger as magician ;
Fear wing'd his flight to find the quack,
And prove his cancer-curing knack ;
But on his way he found another,—
A second advertising brother:
But as much like him as an owl
Is unlike every handsome fowl ;
Whose fame had raised as broad a fog,
And of the two the greater hog :
Who used a still more magic plaister,
That sweat forsooth, and cured the faster.
This doctor view'd, with moony eyes
And scowl'd-up face, the pimple's size ;
Then christen'd it in solemn answer,
And cried, " this pimple 's name is cancer.
But courage, friend, I see your 're pale,
My sweating plaisters never fail ;
I 've sweated hundreds out with ease,
With roots as long as maple trees ;
And never fail'd in all my trials—
Behold these samples here in vials !
Preserved to show my wondrous merits,
Just as my liver is—in spirits.
For twenty joes the cure is done—"
The bargain struck, the plaister on,
Which gnaw'd the cancer at its leisure,
And pain'd his face above all measure.
But still the pimple spread the faster,
And swell'd, like toad that meets disaster.
Thus foil'd, the doctor gravely swore,
It was a right-rose cancer sore ;
Then stuck his probe beneath the beard,
And show'd him where the leaves appear'd ;
And raised the patient's drooping spirits,

By praising up the plaister's merits.—
Quoth he, "The roots now scarcely stick—
I'll fetch her out like crab or tick;
And make it rendezvous, next trial,
With six more plagues, in my old vial."
Then purged him pale with jalap drastic,
And next applied the infernal caustic.
But yet, this semblance bright of hell
Served but to make the patient yell;
And, gnawing on with fiery pace,
Devour'd one broadside of his face—
"Courage, 'tis done," the doctor cried,
And quick the incision knife applied:
That with three cuts made such a hole,
Out flew the patient's tortured soul!

 Go, readers, gentle, eke and simple,
If you have wart, or corn, or pimple;
To quack infallible apply;
Here's room enough for you to lie.
His skill triumphant still prevails,
For death's a cure that never fails.

THE HYPOCRITE'S HOPE.

BLEST is the man, who from the womb,
 To saintship him betakes,
And when too soon his child shall come,
 A long confession makes.

When next in Broad Church-alley, he
 Shall take his former place,
Relates his past iniquity,
 And consequential grace;

Declares how long by Satan vex'd,
 From truth he did depart,
And tells the time, and tells the text,
 That smote his flinty heart.

He stands in half-way-covenant sure;
 Full five long years or more,
One foot in church's pale secure,
 The other out of door.

Then riper grown in gifts and grace,
 With every rite complies,

And deeper lengthens down his face,
   And higher rolls his eyes.

He tones like Pharisee sublime,
   Two lengthy prayers a day,
The same that he from early prime,
   Has heard his father say.

Each Sunday perch'd on bench of pew,
   To passing priest he bows,
Then loudly 'mid the quavering crew,
   Attunes his vocal nose.

With awful look then rises slow,
   And prayerful visage sour,
More fit to fright the apostate foe,
   Then seek a pardoning power.

Then nodding hears the sermon next,
   From priest haranguing loud ;
And doubles down each quoted text,
   From Genesis to Jude.

And when the priest holds forth address,
   To old ones born anew,
With holy pride and wrinkled face,
   He rises in his pew.

Good works he careth nought about,
   But faith alone will seek,
While Sunday's pieties blot out
   The knaveries of the week.

He makes the poor his daily prayer,
   Yet drives them from his board :
And though to his own good he swear,
   Through habit breaks his word.

This man advancing fresh and fair,
   Shall all his race complete ;
And wave at last his hoary hair,
   Arrived in deacon's seat.

There shall he all church honors have,
   By joyous brethren given—
Till priest in funeral sermon grave,
   Shall send him straight to heaven.

PHILIP FRENEAU.

Mr Freneau is, we believe, a descendant of the French protestants who came to this country upon the revocation of the Edict of Nantes. Of the precise period and place of his birth we are ignorant. He received his education at Princeton College, in New Jersey, where he was graduated in 1771, and was associated with Hopkinson in certain political writings published in Philadelphia during the revolution. After the federal government was established, he occupied a station in the Secretary of State's office, and also conducted a newspaper in Philadelphia for several years. These employments he finally relinquished for commercial pursuits, in the course of which, he made voyages to several parts of the world.

We had always been accustomed to hear this gentleman spoken of as deceased, and a late writer in one of our most distinguished literary journals has classed him among the departed poets. But on making inquiries respecting him a few months since, we learned that he was still living near Middletown Point in New Jersey. We hope he regrets the very splenetic tone of the letter which he took the trouble to write about us on the occasion.

The principal part of Mr Freneau's poetical effusions were published in a large volume in 1795. This book contains a greater variety than any volume of poetry by a single hand which we have ever seen. Many of the pieces have uncommon merit, and exhibit a degree of talent which would have enabled the author to take a high rank among our native bards. Mr Freneau's poetry however, has been neglected. Had he published less, he would have found more readers. His volume presented a miscellany of about three hundred different pieces, and a miscellany of such a size is apt to discourage a common reader. He has not managed all the subjects he has undertaken with an equal degree of success, but he writes in general with an unaffected ease and sprightliness, and displays a truly poetical warmth and exuberance of fancy.

THE DYING INDIAN.

" On yonder lake I spread the sail no more!
Vigor, and youth, and active days are past—
Relentless demons urge me to that shore
On whose black forests all the dead are cast:
Ye solemn train, prepare the funeral song,
For I must go to shades below,
Where all is strange, and all is new;
Companion to the airy throng,
　　What solitary streams,
　　In dull and dreary dreams,
All melancholy, must I rove along!

To what strange lands must Shalum take his wa　:
Groves of the dead departed mortals trace;
No deer along those gloomy forests stray,
No huntsmen there take pleasure in the chase,
But all are empty unsubstantial shades,
That ramble through those visionary glades;
　　No spongy fruits from verdant trees depend:
　　　　But sickly orchards there
　　　　Do fruits as sickly bear,
And apples a consumptive visage shew,
And wither'd hangs the whortle-berry blue.
　　Ah me! what mischiefs on the dead attend!
Wandering a stranger to the shores below,
Where shall I brook or real fountain find?
Lazy and sad deluding waters flow—
Such is the picture in my boding mind!
　　　　Fine tales indeed, they tell
　　　　Of shades and purling rills,
　　　　Where our dead fathers dwell
　　　　Beyond the western hills,
But when did ghost return his state to shew;
Or who can promise half the tale is true?

I too must be a fleeting ghost—no more—
None, none but shadows to those mansions go;
I leave my woods, I leave the Huron shore,
　　For emptier groves below!
　　Ye charming solitudes,
　　Ye tall ascending woods,

Ye glassy lakes and prattling streams,
  Whose aspect still was sweet,
  Whether the sun did greet,
Or the pale moon embraced you with her beams—
  Adieu to all!
To all, that charm'd me where I stray'd,
The winding stream, the dark sequester'd shade;
  Adieu all triumphs here!
  Adieu the mountain's lofty swell,
  Adieu, thou little verdant hill,
  And seas, and stars, and skies—farewell,
  For some remoter sphere!

Perplex'd with doubts, and tortured with despair,
Why so dejected at this hopeless sleep?
Nature at last these ruins may repair,
When fate's long dream is o'er, and she forgets to weep.
Some real world once more may be assign'd,
Some new born mansion for th' immortal mind!
Farewell, sweet lake; farewell surrounding woods,
To other groves, through midnight glooms, I stray,
Beyond the mountains, and beyond the floods,
  Beyond the Huron bay!
Prepare the hollow tomb, and place me low,
My trusty bow and arrows by my side,
The cheerful bottle, and the ven'son store;
For long the journey is that I must go,
Without a partner, and without a guide."

He spoke, and bid the attending mourners weep:
Then closed his eyes, and sunk to endless sleep!

THE WILD HONEYSUCKLE.

Fair flower, that dost so comely grow,
Hid in this silent, dull retreat,
Untouch'd thy honey'd blossoms blow,
Unseen thy little branches greet:
  No roving foot shall find thee here,
  No busy hand provoke a tear.

By Nature's self in white array'd,
She bade thee shun the vulgar eye,
And planted here the guardian shade,
And sent soft waters murmuring by;

Thus quietly thy summer goes,
Thy days declining to repose.

Smit with those charms, that must decay,
I grieve to see your future doom;
They died—nor were those flowers less gay,
The flowers that did in Eden bloom;
    Unpitying frosts, and autumn's power
    Shall leave no vestige of this flower.

From morning suns and evening dews
At first thy little being came:
If nothing once, you nothing lose,
For when you die you are the same;
    The space between is but an hour,
    The frail duration of a flower.

THE MAN OF NINETY.

To yonder boughs that spread so wide,
Beneath whose shade soft waters glide,
    Once more I take the well known way;
With feeble step and tottering knee
I sigh to reach my white-oak tree,
    Where rosy health was wont to play.

If to the shades, consuming slow,
The shadow of myself, I go,
    When I am gone, wilt thou remain!—
From dust you rose, and grew like me;
I man became, and you a tree,
    Both natives of one grassy plain.

How much alike, yet not the same!—
You could no kind protector claim;
    Alone you stood, to chance resign'd:
When winter came, with blustering sky,
You fear'd its blasts—and so did I,
    And for warm suns in secret pined.

When vernal suns began to glow,
You felt returning vigor flow,
    Which once a year new leaves supplied;
Like you, fine days I wish'd to see,
And May was a sweet month to me,
    But when November came—I sigh'd.

If through your bark some ruffian arm
A mark impress'd, you took th' alarm,
  And tears awhile I saw descend ;
Till nature's kind maternal aid
A plaister on your bruises laid,
  And bade your trickling sorrows end.

Like you, I fear'd the lightning's stroke,
Whose flame dissolves the strength of oak,
  And ends at once this mortal dream ;—
You saw, with grief, the soil decay
That from your roots was torn away;
  You sigh'd—and cursed the stream.

With borrow'd earth, and busy spade,
Around your roots new life I laid,
  While joy revived in every vein ;
(The care of man shall life impart—)
Though nature owns the aid of art,
  No art, immortal, makes her reign.

How much alike our fortune—say—
Yet, why must I so soon decay,
  When thou hast scarcely reach'd thy prime—
Erect and tall, you joyous stand ;
The staff of age has found my hand,
  That guides me to the grave of time.

Could I, fair tree, like you resign,
And banish all these fears of mine,
  Gray hairs would be no cause of grief;
Your blossoms die, but you remain,
Your fruit lies scatter'd o'er the plain—
  Learn wisdom from the falling leaf.

As you survive by heaven's decree,
Let wither'd flowers be thrown on me,
  Sad compensation for my doom,
While winter-greens and withering pines,
And cedars dark, and barren vines,
  Point out the lonely tomb.

The enlivening sun that burns so bright,
Ne'er had a noon without a night,
  So life and death agree ;

The joys of man by years are broke—"
'T was thus the man of ninety spoke.
   Then rose, and left his tree.

———

THE INDIAN STUDENT : OR, FORCE OF NATURE.

From Susquehanna's farthest springs,
Where savage tribes pursue their game,
(His blanket tied with yellow strings,)
A shepherd of the forest came.

Not long before, a wandering priest
Express'd his wish with visage sad—
" Ah, why (he cried) in Satan's waste,
Ah, why detain so fine a lad ?

" In white man's land there stands a town,
Where learning may be purchased low—
Exchange his blanket for a gown,
And let the lad to college go."

From long debate the council rose,
And viewing Shalum's tricks with joy,
To Cambridge Hall, o'er wastes of snows,
They sent the copper-color'd boy.

One generous chief a bow supplied,
This gave a shaft, and that a skin ;
The feathers, in vermilion dyed,
Himself did from a turkey win :

Thus dress'd so gay, he took his way
O'er barren hills, alone, alone !
His guide a star, he wander'd far,
His pillow every night a stone.

At last he came, with foot so lame,
Where learned men talk heathen Greek,
And Hebrew lore is gabbled o'er,
To please the muses,—twice a week.

Awhile he writ, awhile he read,
Awhile he conn'd their grammar rules—
(An Indian savage so well bred
Great credit promised to the schools.)

Some thought he would in law excel,
Some said in physic he would shine;
And one that knew him passing well,
Beheld in him a sound divine.

But those of more discerning eye,
Even then could other prospects show,
And saw him lay his Virgil by,
To wander with his dearer bow.

The tedious hours of study spent,
The heavy moulded lecture done,
He to the woods a hunting went,
Through lonely wastes he walk'd, he run.

No mystic wonders fired his mind;
He sought to gain no learn'd degree,
But only sense enough to find
The squirrel in the hollow tree.

The shady bank, the purling stream,
The woody wild his heart possess'd,
The dewy lawn, his morning dream
In fancy's gayest colors drest.

" And why," he cried, " did I forsake
My native wood for gloomy walls;
The silver stream, the limpid lake
For musty books, and college halls.

" A little could my wants supply—
Can wealth and honor give me more ;
Or, will the sylvan god deny
The humble treat he gave before?

" Let seraphs gain the bright abode,
And heaven's sublimest mansions see—
I only bow to Nature's God—
The land of shades will do for me.

"These dreadful secrets of the sky
Alarm my soul with chilling fear—
Do planets in their orbits fly,
And is the earth, indeed, a sphere?

"Let planets still their course pursue,
And comets to the centre run—
In him my faithful friend I view,
The image of my God—the sun.

"Where nature's ancient forests grow,
And mingled laurel never fades,
My heart is fix'd and I must go
To die among my native shades."

He spoke, and to the western springs,
(His gown discharged, his money spent,
His blanket tied with yellow strings,)
The shepherd of the forest went.

———

THE HURRICANE.

Happy the man who, safe on shore,
Now trims, at home, his evening fire;
Unmoved, he hears the tempests roar,
That on the tufted groves expire:
Alas! on us they doubly fall,
Our feeble bark must bear them all.

Now to their haunts the birds retreat,
The squirrel seeks his hollow tree,
Wolves in their shaded caverns meet,
All, all are bless'd but wretched we—
Foredoom'd a stranger to repose,
No rest the unsettled ocean knows.

While o'er the dark abyss we roam,
Perhaps, whate'er the pilots say,
We saw the sun descend in gloom,
No more to see his rising ray,
But buried low, by far too deep,
On coral beds, unpitied, sleep!

But what a stange, uncoasted strand
Is that, where fate permits no day—
No charts have we to mark that land,
No compass to direct that way.
What pilot shall explore that realm,
What new Columbus take the helm?

While death and darkness both surround,
And tempests rage with lawless power,
Of friendship's voice I hear no sound,
No comfort in this dreadful hour—
What friendship can in tempests be,
What comfort on this troubled sea?

The bark, accustom'd to obey,
No more the trembling pilots guide ;
Alone she gropes her trackless way,
While mountains burst on either side—
Thus, skill and science both must fall ;
And ruin is the lot of all.

THE FIVE AGES.

THE reign of old Saturn is highly renown'd
For many fine things that no longer are found,
Trees always in blossom, men free from all pains,
And shepherds as mild as the sheep on their plains.

In the midland equator, dispensing his sway,
The sun, they pretended, pursued his bright way,
Not rambled, unsteady, to regions remote,
To talk, once a year, with the *crab* and the *goat*.

From a motion like this, have the sages explain'd,
How summer for ever her empire maintain'd ;
While the turf of the fields by the plough was unbroke,
And a house for the shepherd, the boughs of an oak.

Yet some say there never was seen on this stage
What poets affirm of that innocent age,
When the brutal creation from bondage was free,
And men were exactly what mankind should be.

But why should they labor to prove it a dream?—
The poets of old were in love with the theme,

And, leaving to others mere truth to repeat,
In the regions of fancy they found it complete.

Three ages have been on this globe, they pretend;
And the fourth, some have thought, is to be without end;
The first was of gold—but a fifth, we will say,
Has already begun, and is now on its way.

Since the days of Arcadia, if ever there shined
A ray of the first on the heads of mankind,
Let the learned dispute—but with us it is clear,
That the era of paper was realized here.

Four ages, however, at least have been told,
The first is compared to the purest of gold—
But, as bad luck would have it, its circles were few,
And the next was of silver—if Ovid says true.

But this, like the former, did rapidly pass—
While that which came after was nothing but brass—
An age of mere tinkers—and when it was lost,
Hard iron succeeded—we know to our cost.

And hence you may fairly infer, if you please,
That we're nothing but blacksmiths of various degrees,
Since each has a weapon, of one kind or other,
To stir up the coals, and to shake at his brother.

Should the Author of nature reverse his decree,
And bring back the age we're so anxious to see,
Agreement alas!—you would look for in vain,
The *stuff* might be changed, but the *staff* would remain.

The lawyer would still find a client to fleece,
The doctor, a patient to pack off in peace,
The parson, some hundreds of hearers prepared,
To measure his gifts by the length of his beard.

Old Momus would still have some cattle to lead,
Who would hug his opinions, and swallow his creed—
So it's best, I presume, that things are as they are—
If iron's the meanest—we've nothing to fear.

EPISTLE TO A GAY YOUNG LADY WHO WAS MARRIED TO A DOATING OLD DEACON.

THUS winter joins to April's bloom,
Thus daisies blush beside a tomb,
Thus, fields of ice o'er rivers grow,
While melting streams are found below.

How strange a taste is here display'd—
Yourself all light, and he all shade!
Each hour you live you look more gay,
While he grows uglier every day!

Intent upon celestial things,
He only Watts or Sternhold sings ;—
You tune your chord to different strains,
And merrier notes attract the swains.

Ah Harriot! why in beauty's prime
Thus look for flowers in Greenland's clime ;
When twenty years are scarcely run
Thus hope for spring without a sun!

THE INDIAN BURYING GROUND.

IN spite of all the learn'd have said,
I still my old opinion keep ;
The posture that we give the dead,
Points out the soul's eternal sleep.

Not so the ancients of these lands—
The Indian, when from life released,
Again is seated with his friends,
And shares again the joyous feast.

His imaged birds, and painted bowl,
And ven'son, for a journey dress'd,
Bespeak the nature of the soul,
Activity, that knows no rest.

His bow, for action ready bent,
And arrows, with a head of stone,
Can only mean that life is spent,
And not the finer essence gone.

'Thou, stranger, that shalt come this way,
No fraud upon the dead commit—
Observe the swelling turf, and say,
They do not lie, but here they sit.

Here still a lofty rock remains,
On which the curious eye may trace
(Now wasted, half, by wearing rains)
The fancies of a ruder race.

Here still an, aged elm aspires,
Beneath whose far projecting shade
(And which the shepherd still admires)
The children of the forest play'd!

There oft a restless Indian queen
(Pale Shebah, with her braided hair)
And many a barbarous form is seen
To chide the man that lingers there.

By midnight moons, o'er moistening dews,
In vestments for the chase array'd,
The hunter still the deer pursues,
The hunter and the deer, a shade!

And long shall timorous fancy see
The painted chief, and pointed spear,
And Reason's self shall bow the knee
To shadows and delusions here.

———

TO THE MEMORY OF THE BRAVE AMERICANS UNDER GENERAL GREENE, IN SOUTH CAROLINA, WHO FELL IN THE ACTION OF SEPTEMBER 8, 1781.

At Eutaw springs the valiant died :
Their limbs with dust are covered o'er—
Weep on, ye springs, your tearful tide ;
How many heroes are no more !

If in this wreck of ruin, they
Can yet be thought to claim a tear,
O smite thy gentle breast, and say
The friends of freedom slumber here !

Thou, who shalt trace this bloody plain,
If goodness rules thy generous breast,
Sigh for the wasted rural reign ;
Sigh for the shepherds, sunk to rest!

Stranger, their humble graves adorn ;
You too may fall, and ask a tear :
'T is not the beauty of the morn
That proves the evening shall be clear.

They saw their injured country's wo ;
The flaming town, the wasted field ;
Then rush'd to meet the insulting foe ;
They took the spear—but left the shield.

Led by thy conquering genius, Greene,
The Britons they compell'd to fly :
None distant view'd the fatal plain,
None grieved, in such a cause to die.

But, like the Parthian, famed of old,
Who, flying, still their arrows threw ;
These routed Britons, full as bold,
Retreated, and retreating slew.

Now rest in peace our patriot band ;
Though far from nature's limits thrown,
We trust, they find a happier land,
A brighter sunshine of their own.

———

PORT ROYAL.

Here, by the margin of the murmuring main,
While her proud remnants I explore in vain,
And lonely stray through these dejected lands
Fann'd by the noon-tide breeze on burning sands,
Where the dull Spaniard once possess'd these shades,
And ports defended by his palisades—
Though lost to us, Port Royal claims a sigh,
Nor shall the muse the unenvied verse deny.
    Of all the towns that graced Jamaica's isle,
This was her glory, and the proudest pile,
Where toils on toils bade wealth's gay structures rise,
And commerce swell'd her glory to the skies :
St Jago, seated on a distant plain,

Ne'er saw the tall ship entering from the main,
Unnoticed streams her Cobra's margin lave,
Where yon tall plantains shade her glowing wave,
And burning sands, or rock-surrounded hill
Confess its founder's fears—or want of skill.

While o'er these wastes with wearied step I go,
Past scenes of death return, in all their wo,
O'er these sad shores, in angry pomp he pass'd,
Moved in the winds, and raged with every blast—
Here, opening gulphs confess'd the Almighty hand,
Here, the dark ocean roll'd across the land,
Here, piles on piles an instant tore away,
Here, crowds on crowds in mingled ruin lay,
Whom fate scarce gave to end their noon-day feast,
Or time to call the sexton, or the priest.
Where yon tall bark, with all her ponderous load,
Commits her anchor to its dark abode,
Eight fathoms down, where unseen waters flow,
To quench the sulphur of the caves below:
There midnight sounds torment the sailors ear,
And drums and fifes play drowsy concerts there,
Sad songs of wo prevent the hour of sleep,
And fancy aids the fiddlers of the deep;
Dull Superstition hears the ghostly hum,
Smit with the terrors of the world to come.

What now is left of all your boasted pride!
Lost are those glories that were spread so wide,
A spit of sand is thine by heaven's decree,
And wasting shores that scarce resist the sea:
Is this Port Royal on Jamaica's coast,
The Spaniard's envy, and the Briton's boast!
A shatter'd roof o'er every hut appears,
And mouldering brick work prompts the traveller's fears;
A church, with half a priest, I grieve to see,
Grass round its door, and rust upon its key!—
One only inn with tiresome search I found
Where one sad negro dealt his beverage round;—
His was the part to wait the impatient call,
He was the landlord, post-boy, pimp, and all;
His wary eyes on every side were cast,
Beheld the present, and revolved the past,
Now here, now there, in swift succession stole,
Glanced at the bar, or watch'd the unsteady bowl.

No sprightly lads or gay bewitching maids
Walk on these wastes, or wander in these shades;
To other shores past times beheld them go,
And some are slumbering in the caves below;

A negro tribe but ill their place supply,
With bending back, short hair, and downcast eye ;
A swarthy race lead up the evening dance,
Trip o'er the sands and dart the alluring glance :
A feeble rampart guards the unlucky town,
Where banish'd tories come to seek renown,
Where worn out slaves their bowls of beer retail,
And sunburnt strumpets watch the approaching sail.
  Here (scarce escaped the wild tornado's rage,)
Why sail'd I here to swell my future page !
To these dull scenes with eager haste I came
To trace the relics of their ancient fame,
Not worth the search !—what domes are left to fall,
Guns, gales, and earthquakes shall destroy them all—
All shall be lost !—though hosts their aid implore,
The Twelve Apostles shall protect no more,
Nor guardian heroes awe the impoverish'd plain ;
No priest shall mutter, and no church remain,
Nor this palmetto yield her evening shade,
Where the dark negro his dull music play'd,
Or casts his view beyond the adjacent strand,
And points, still grieving, to his native land,
Turns and returns from yonder murmuring shore,
And pants for countries he must see no more.
  Where shall I go, what Lethe shall I find
To drive these dark ideas from my mind !
No buckram heroes can relieve the eye,
And George's honors only raise a sigh—
  Ye mountains vast, whose heights the heaven sustain,
Adieu, ye mountains, and fair Kingston's plain,
Where nature still the toils of art transcends—
In this dull spot the enchanting prospect ends :
Where burning sands are wing'd by every blast,
And these mean fabrics but entomb the past ;
Where want, and death, and care, and grief reside,
And threatening moons advance the imperious tide,
Ye stormy winds, awhile your wrath suspend ;
Who leaves the land, a bottle, and a friend,
Quits this bright isle for yon blue seas and sky,
Or even Port Royal quits—without a sigh !

ELIJAH FITCH.

ALL we know of this writer, is that he was a clergyman, and died at Hopkinton, in Massachusetts, December 16th, 1788, in the 43d year of his age. He wrote a poem in blank verse, called The Beauties of Religion, and a short piece entitled The Choice. These were published at Providence, the year after his death.

THE BEAUTIES OF RELIGION.

THE pencil dipp'd in various hues, to paint
Great nature's works, affords a sweet repast.
The mind with pleasing views of God is fill'd,
His beauteous works more beautiful appear,
Which captivate the heart the more they 're view'd,
And imitation gives more perfect charms.
On fancy's wings ascend the Aonian mount,
And let thy pencil sketch the landscape wide ;
Paint the Castalian fount, rising from foot,
Meandering thence through many a flowery mead,
Blooming with violet and jessamine.
On this side paint a row of lofty elms,
Waving with negligence their branching arms ;
On that let rows of spruce and evergreens
Extend through country villages and towns,
With birds of every kind perch'd on their boughs.
Paint cities then extending on the banks,
Whose thousand glittering spires dazzle the morn ;
And on the placid waves make boats descend
With streamers gay, and with their silken sails,
Swell'd with Favonian breeze, the breath of eve.
Fields next with growing harvests paint,
And verdant pastures, fill'd with flocks and herds ;
And far beyond, a rising wood of pine,
And cedar, ash and maple, oak and fir,
With shade o'er shade, as in a theatre,
Till topmost boughs are lost among the clouds.
A lively green to southward make appear,
Sloping far distant to the ocean broad,
Where lofty ships ride on the foaming main.
Far to the north, over a valley huge,

Let the sight end abrupt, 'midst rocks and trees:
Paint nature here dress'd in her negligee,
A sylvan scene, with virgin tresses crown'd;
Nor let luxuriant fancy go behind
Luxuriant nature in her wild disports.
To westward then a winding path, with trees
Of goodliest shade, and bowers by nature form'd,
From whence a gliding stream may be discern'd;
Now roaring down a horrid crag, and then
With gentle murmurs wind along the glade.
Paint sweet-brier hedges to perfume the air,
With pinks and roses strow the eglantine,
And crown it with the lily's graceful head.
Above let golden orange, nectarine,
With cherry, plumb and peach, apple and pear,
Bend branches low, tempting the hand to pluck.
Along the ground let all the charming race
Of berries creep;—and then this motto place:
" Fair works of nature are the works of God,
And God in all his beauteous works is seen."

SARAH PORTER,

Of Plymouth in New Hampshire, wrote a small volume containing The Royal Penitent, and David's Lamentation over Saul and Jonathan, published at Concord in 1791. The first of these is founded upon a portion of the history of King David, and shows a very respectable talent for versification.

THE ROYAL PENITENT. PART II.

Death's angel now, commission'd by the Lord,
O'er the fond infant holds the fatal sword;
From the dread sight the frantic father turns,
And, clad in sackcloth, in his chamber mourns;
The monitor, within the royal breast,
That long had slept, now roused at length from rest,
Holds forth a mirror to the aching sight,

Seizes the mind that fain would take its flight—
Bids it look in:—and first, Uriah stood,
Arm'd for the fight, as yet unstain'd with blood ;
Courage and care were on his brow combined,
To show the hero and the patriot join'd :—
Next, pale and lifeless, on his warlike shield,
The soldiers bore him from the bloody field.
" And is it thus ? (the Royal mourner said)
" And has my hand perform'd the dreadful deed ?
Was I the wretch that gave thee to the foe,
And bade thee sink beneath the impending blow ?
Bade every friend and hero leave thy side ?—
Open, O earth ! and in thy bosom hide
A guilty wretch who wishes not to live ;
Who cannot, dares not, ask for a reprieve ;
So black a crime just Heaven will not forgive !
Justice arrests thy coming mercy, Lord—
Strike then, O strike, unsheath thy dreadful sword :
Accursed forever be the hated day,
That led my soul from innocence astray ;
O may the stars, on that detested hour,
Shed all their influence with malignant power,
Darkness and sorrows jointly hold their reign,
When time, revolving, brings it round again.
Ye injured ghosts, break from the silent tomb,
In all the fearful pomp of horror come,
Breathe out your woes, and hail the dreadful gloom.
Why does not injured Israel now arise,
Proclaim my madness to the avenging skies,
Hurl quick the sceptre from my bloody hand,
While marks of infamy my forehead brand ?
No time shall e'er the dreadful act conceal—
No tongue shall fail its horrors to reveal—
Eternity, upon its strongest wing,
Shall bear the deeds whence all my sorrows spring.
Unhappy man !—ah ! whither shall I turn ?
Like Cain, accurst, must I for ever mourn ?
On beds of silk in vain I seek repose—
Uriah's shade forbids my eyes to close ;
No bars exclude him—to no place confined,
Eager he still pursues my flying mind :
Not all the crowd that bow at my approach,
Nor guards that thicken round the gilded couch,
Can with their arms, or martial air, affright,
Or drive the phantom from my wearied sight.
Whene'er I view the diamond's varied rays,

That grace my robes, or on my sceptre blaze,
Uriah still, reflected from the stone,
Points at his wounds, and shows me what I 've done.
Could all the gold that lies on India's coast,
Could all the gems its num'rous quarries boast,
Bribe peace a moment to this aching heart,
How freely with the glitt'ring store I 'd part.
Black, heavy thoughts, ah ! what a num'rous train !
I feel your stings unpitied, yet complain.
Thou gallant hero, say, where art thou now ?
Gone, gone for ever ! sunk beneath my blow !—
Of my uplifted arm, my dire command,
Fell Ammon's sword was wielded by my hand !
When the fierce battle glow'd with hottest rage,
Where all the mighty, arm to arm engage,
Where frightful death his various forms put on,
You met the terror of his dreadful frown.—
As some huge tree, whose tow'ring threats the sky,
While deep in earth its roots embosom'd lie,
Mocks at the warring winds, and proudly dares
The tempest's force, nor once destruction fears :
So, unappall'd, the glorious leader stood,
Though torn with wounds, and cover'd o'er with blood ;
O'er hills of slaughter'd foes he makes his way—
His sword, from Ammon, gain'd the doubtful day :
Yet, while aloft the Hebrew standard flies,
And vict'ry shouts to echoing earth and skies,
The lifeless hero, stretch'd upon the shield,
With countless wounds is borne from off the field.
Once, how he shone amidst the gazing throng,
Who praised his courage as he pass'd along !
On thy firm brow, what beaming splendor shone !
By thy bold arm, how strengthen'd was my throne !
And shall thy murd'rer crown thy head with bays,
And dare thy godlike virtues thus to praise ?
From cruel fate, ah ! whither shall I run ?—
Capricious lust !—thou hast my soul undone !
Drawn on by impious passion, I pursued
The flying fair, and oft my suit renew'd ;
The humble suppliant, and the haughty lord,
By turns put on, no ray of hope afford ;—
She heard at length, but with an obdurate ear—
And still Uriah draws the pitying tear.
O happy day ! when, blest with Eglah's charms,
I woo'd no other beauty to my arms ;
No court's licentious joys did then molest

My peaceful mind, nor haunt my tranquil breast.
A glitt'ring crown! thou poor, fantastic thing!
What solid satisfaction canst thou bring?—
Once, far removed from all the toils of state,
In groves I slept—no guards around me wait:
Oh! how delicious was the calm retreat!—
Sweet groves! with birds and various flowers stored,
Where nature furnish'd out my frugal board;
The pure, unstained spring, my thirst allay'd;
No poison'd draught, in golden cups convey'd,
Was there to dread.—Return, ye happy hours,
Ye verdant shades, kind nature's pleasing bowers—
Inglorious solitude, again return,
And heal the breast with pain and anguish torn.
   Oh! sweet content! unknown to pomp and kings,
The humble rest beneath thy downy wings;
The lowly cottage is thy loved retreat—
In vain, thou 'rt courted by the rich and great—
In vain, the miser seeks thee in his gold—
In vain, each day the glitt'ring store is told;
Thou art not there: in vain the ambitious sigh,
And seek the joys that still before them fly:
The merchant's ship all treasures brings but thee—
You from his anxious bosom ever flee:
For thee, the sailor tempts the boist'rous main,
And hopes to find thee in his dear-bought gain:
For thee, the hero mounts his iron car,
And hopes to find thee when return'd from war.
Their hopes are vain.—Who wish with thee to dwell,
Must seek the rural shade, or lonely cell:
The Gods themselves delight in verdant groves,
And shield from harm the innocence they love.—
Witness, the day, my youthful arm withstood
The foaming bear:—the monarch of the wood,
With open jaws appear'd, and crested mien,
But in a moment by my hand was slain:
Safe from their teeth I snatch'd the destined prey,
And bore it harmless in my arms away.—
Witness, the day, Gath's lordly champion came,
With haughty strides, and cursed Jehovah's name;
Though in my hand nor sword nor spear were found,
This vast unwieldly bulk lay stretch'd upon the ground.
Beloved by Heaven, nought had I then to fear—
Twice I escaped from Saul's emitted spear,
By malice thrown; and, free from danger, stand,
Hid in the hollow of th' Almighty's hand;—

His darling then I was ; who, mighty God !
Sink now beneath the terrors of thy rod.
Dispel those thick, dark clouds, this boist'rous wind,
That tears the soul, and harrows up the mind ;
Oh ! let thy mercy, like the solar ray,
Break forth and drive these dismal clouds away ;
Oh ! send its kind enliv'ning warmth on one,
Who sinks, who dies, beneath thy dreadful frown :
Thus fares the wretch at sea, by tempests tost—
Sands, hurricanes, and rocks, proclaim him lost ;
With eager eyes he views the peaceful shore,
And longs to rest where billows cease to roar :—
Of wanton winds and waves I 've been the sport—
Oh ! when shall I attain the wish'd for port ?
Or might I bear the punishment alone,
Nor hear the lovely infant's piteous moan ;—
My sins upon the dying child impress'd,
The dreadful thought forbids my soul to rest.
In mercy, Lord, thy humble suppliant hear—
Oh ! give the darling to my ardent prayer !—
Cleanse me from sin—oh ! graciously forgive—
Blest with thy love, oh ! let thy servant live :
Thy smiles withdrawn, what is the world to me ?
My hopes, my joys, are placed alone on thee :
Oh ! let thy love, to this desponding heart,
One ray, at least, of heavenly love impart."

WILLIAM MOORE SMITH

WAS the eldest son of the Rev. William Smith, D. D. the
first Provost of the Philadelphia College. He was born in
Philadelphia, on the first of June, 1759, and was educated at
the college in that city, where he was graduated with distinction at an early age. On leaving college he studied law, and
continued the practice of this profession with honor and profit
until the close of the last century, when he received an agency for the settlement of British claims in America, included
within the sixth article of Jay's treaty. The adjustment of

his agency obliged him to make a voyage to England in 1803, and on his return to his native country the following year, he retired from business to a country residence near Philadelphia, where he continued to reside until his death, which occurred on the 12th of March, 1821. He was a polished scholar, and retained his classical knowledge until the time of his death. In his retirement he read much, and his mind was literally a storehouse of learning. Possessed of a powerful memory, he was a living index to what had passed and still was passing in the world, and yet the writings of his early days alone entitle him to notice here, as he was not ambitious of literary distinction. In 1785, he published a small volume of poems, which was republished in London the following year. He wrote much on the politics of the times, but these papers have passed into oblivion, with the incidents which gave them birth and interest.

THE FALL OF ZAMPOR.

A PERUVIAN ODE.

Now ruin lifts her haggard head
    And madly staring horror screams!
O'er yonder field bestrew'd with dead,
    See, how the lurid lightning gleams!

Lo! 'mid the terrors of the storm,
    From yonder black brow'd cloud of night,
The mighty Capac's dreadful form
    Bursts forth upon my aching sight!

But ah! what phantoms, fleeting round
    Give double horrors to the gloom,
Each pointing to the ghastly wound
    That sent him, shroudless to the tomb!

On me they bend the scowling eye;
    For me their airy arms they wave!
Oh! stay—nor yet from Zampor fly,
    We'll be companions in the grave!—

Dear victims of a tyrant's rage!
  They 're gone !—each shadowy form is fled,
Yet soon these hoary locks of age
  Shall low as theirs in dust be laid !

Thou faithless steel, that harmless fell
  Upon the haughty Spaniard's crest,
Swift to my swelling heart, go tell
  How deep thou'st pierced thy master's breast.

But shall curst Spain's destroying son,
  With transport smile on Zampor's fate ?
No ere the deed of death be done
  The tyrant's blood shall glut my hate.

Yon forked flash with friendly glare
  Points where his crimson'd banners fly,
Look down, ye forms of fleeting air,
  I yet shall triumph ere I die!

He spoke—and like a meteor's blaze
  Rush'd on th' unguarded Spaniard's lord ;
Around his head the lightning plays—
  Reflected from his brandish'd sword :

" Great Capac nerve the arm of age,
  And guide it swift to Garcia's breast,
His pangs shall all my pangs assuage,
  His death shall give my country rest.

Ye powers who thirst for human blood
  Receive this victim at your shrine ! "
Aghast the circling warriors stood
  Nor could prevent the chief's design.

" 'T is Garcia's crimson stream that flows,
  'T is Zampor hurls him to his fate—
The author of my country's woes
  Now sinks the victim of my hate."

From Garcia's breast the steel he drew
  And sheathed it deep within his own—
" I come, ye gods of lost Peru,"
  He said—and died without a groan.

ODE TO MEDITATION.

Oн ! thou, who lov'st to dwell
Within some far sequester'd cell,
Unknown to Folly's noisy train,
Untrod by Riot's step profane,
Meek Meditation ! silent maid,
To thee my votive verse be paid ;
To thee, whose mildly pleasing power
Could check wild youth's impetuous flight,
And in affection's gloomy night
Could soothe the " torturing hour,"
   To thee the strains belong ;
But say, what powerful spell,
What magic force of song
Can lure thy solemn steps, to my uncultured bower

By night's pale orb, beneath whose ray
With thee thy Plato oft would stray ;
By the brilliant star of morn
That saw thee bend o'er Solon's urn ;
By all the tears you shed
When Numa bow'd his languid head ;
By the mild joys that in thy breast would swell,
When Antonine, by grateful realms adored,
Majestic Rome's immortal lord,
Would leave the toils, the pomp of state,
The crimson splendors of the victor's car,
The painful pleasures of the great,
The shouts of triumph, and the din of war,
In Tiber's hallowed groves with thee to dwell.

But ah !—on Grecian plains no more
Exists the taste for ancient lore,
For from oppression's scourge the muses fled ;
And Tiber's willow'd banks along
Where Maro pour'd the classic song,
Grim superstition stalks with giant tread.

Yet can Columbia's plains afford
The magic spell, the potent word ;—
A spell to charm thy sober ear,
A name to thee, to freedom dear !—
   By the soft sigh that stole o'er Schuylkill's wave,

When he around whose urn
Dejected nations mourn,
Immortal Franklin sunk into the grave ;
By his thoughts, by thee inspired ;
By his works by worlds admired ;
By the tears by science shed,
O'er the patriot's dying head ;
By the voice of purest fame
That gave to time his deathless name,
By these, and every powerful spell,
Oh ! come meek nymph, with me to dwell.

The garland weave for Franklin's head,
Wreaths of oak from Runnymead,
Where the British barons bold
Taught their king in days of old,
To tremble at insulted Freedom's frown,
And venerate the rights her children deem'd their own.
For he, like them, intrepid rose
Against insulted Freedom's foes,
Fix'd the firm barrier 'gainst oppression's plan,
And dared assert the sacred rights of man !

And in the wreath, which Freedom's hand shall twine
To deck her champion's ever honor'd shrine,
The victor's laurel shall be seen
In folds of never-dying green ;
The muses too, shall bring
Each flow'ret of the spring,
Wet with the beamy tears of morn ;
And there with all her tresses torn,
    What time meek twilight's parting ray
· Sinks lingering in nights dun embrace,
    Pale-eyed Philosophy shall stray
In hopes his awful form to trace,
Hovering on some pregnant cloud,
From whence, while thunders burst aloud,
From whence, while through the trembling air
In lurid streams the lightnings glare,
His rod her head she 'll wave around,
And lead the harmless terrors to the ground.

But, should milder scenes than these
Thy sober, pensive bosom please,
We 'll seek the dark embrowning wood

That frowns o'er broad Ohio's flood,
And while amid the gloom of night
No twinkling star attracts the sight;
And while beneath, the sullen tide
Shall in majestic silence glide,
We 'll listen to the notes of wo,
By echo borne from plains below,
Where Genius droops his laurel'd head,
And Honor mourns a Clymer dead.

Thou sullen flood, whose dreary shore
Has oft been stain'd with streams of gore,
Ah! never did a meeker tear
　Impearl thy banks from Virtue's eye ;
Ah! never did thy breezes bear
　A purer breath than Clymer's sigh.
Ye plains that saw sedition wave
　Her impious banners to the wind,
With you the youth has found his grave,
　To you is virtue's friend consign'd ;
Yet still, as each succeeding race
　Through time to fate shall pass away,
Ah! never shall your sods embrace
　A dearer pledge than Clymer's clay.

Oft o'er the spot that wraps his head
Shall Pity's softest tears be shed,
There Friendship's sacred form shall come
To strow with flowers his Clymer's tomb,
And while the queen of night shall shroud
Her beams behind some threatening cloud ;
And while the western mountain's brow
The star of eve shall sink below ;
And while the consecrated ground
Mute Melancholy stalks around,
There, Meditation, shalt thou find
A scene to suit thy sober mind,
There Fancy's hand shall form the cell
In which thou long shalt love to dwell,
And undisturbed by wild sedition's tread,
Muse o'er the virtues of the silent dead.

———

LAMPOON.

So very deaf, so blind a creature,
As Delia, ne'er was seen in nature.
Blind to each failing of a friend,
But ever ready to commend ;
Yet not to failings blind alone,
Blind to each beauty of her own.
  So very deaf, that if around
A thousand shrill-toned tongues should sound,
With scandal tipt, good names to tear,
A single word she would not hear ;
Or, if, by chance, amidst a crowd,
Some antiquated maid, so loud,
Against a youthful fair should rail,
That deafness' self must hear the tale :
Her comprehension is so slow,
A single word she would not know ;
Or did she know, so weak her brain,
That scandal's tale it can't contain.
Yet these are trifles, when compared
To things that all the town has heard,
For though so stupid, deaf and blind,
The greatest charge is left behind ;
The faults of nature, I'd forgive,
But she's the greatest thief alive.
In earliest youth, the cunning chit
Had pilfer'd Hermes of his wit !
Within a deep embowering wood,
A hoary hermit's cottage stood ;
There as Minerva once retired,
To seek the sage herself inspired,
While all around was wrapt in night,
Save the pale student's glimmering light,
She came with worse than burglar's tread,
And filch'd the helmet from her head !
She robb'd the Graces of their charms,
And off she ran with Cupid's arms.
She stole the queen of beauty's zone,
And made Diana's smiles her own ;
Nor does she ever spend a day
But what she steals some heart away ;
E'en while I write this hasty line,
I feel, I feel she's stealing mine.
Yes—stupid, deaf and blind's the creature,
And yet the greatest thief in nature.

JOHN D. M'KINNON

WROTE a volume entitled Descriptive Poems, containing picturesque views of the state of New York. It was published at New York, in 1802.

THE MOHAWK.

THE morn now glittering on the sandy brows
Of Alba's sloping city, westward spreads
A canopy of azure o'er the woods
And smiling lakes. The Mohawk's Falls we seek ;
And, turning to the rich and fragrant vales
That westward wind, approach the fractured steep,
In hoarse and silver fountains, where he pours
His urn amongst the far resounding rocks.
   Let Science tell the mighty cause that erst
The mountain fabric's horizontal base
Upturning, gave the roaring waters vent
Along their lacerated bed, slate-paved,
And branching to the Hudson ; while the muse,
With humbler views, the cataract admires,
In streams of foam, where, glancing down
The precipice, it widens to a gulf,
And amphitheatre of quarried rocks,
Their sylvan brows with spiral cedars set,
Or coppice crown'd ; and issuing through the vale,
With pleasing murmur steals along the shrubs
And shadowy elms.—Here, where the Mohawk gazed,
And wonder'd at th' abode vortiginous
Of his tremendous father, in the rocks
And flood impassable, see Art pervades
E'en Nature's ruins, with aspiring hand
Stretch'd o'er the torrent's foam, the rifted banks
Uniting, with such works as Rome, when throned
On nations, wrought. Across a giddy pile
Of wood the horseman now pursues his way,
Succeeded by the length'ning herd and swains
In slow procession, while beneath them roars
The headlong river. Leaving now the Falls,
With all their grander lineaments, behind,
We pass along the peaceful Mohawk's shore,

And trace the vale where'er the fruitful stream,
Meandering from the west, the distant hills
Receding designate. In front a width
Of richest intervale, our champaign route,
Within the smiling scenes of husbandry,
Far westward leads. Beneath its willowy banks
The fertilizing stream glides down the vale,
Now intersecting in an equal course, and now
Inclining to the north ; now south it laves
The sidelong hills' ascent ; then winding off,
Sleeps, high embower'd, within the spreading growth
Of pensive elms that tower luxuriant o'er
The elders, and with hanging plane trees mix
Their graceful limbs and interwoven shade.
As frequent thus the silent stream escapes
The traveller's eye incurious, while it lurks
In silence by, hoarse murmurs wake his ear
At intervals, as o'er the rapid shoals
The obstructed water fluctuating shoots
Among the broken rocks. The antique fronts
We gain, wrapt in Batavian gloom of sheds
And intermingled trees, where Corlear first,
Advancing from the sandy desert, fix'd
His dwelling on the margin of the still
And sable river. Academic Peace
And Meditation now consign the spot
To future Science. Here the dusty road
Forsaking for the verdant turf, we scent
The fragrance of the evening, and survey
The shore, enamor'd of its pensive scenes.
Harmonious, tranquil, which thy genius, Claude,
Taught by the sober Fancies, had confess'd her own.
Amidst the shade suspended o'er the vale,
The mirror of the Mohawk's tide reflects
A varied tapestry : the vivid green
Of willows interwove—the plane tree's hoar
And dappled waist—the pensive, sombre elm,
Queen of the Flats, her hanging robes diffuse
And graceful. Fronting in perspective dim,
A range of mountain, from the Kaatskill's loins
Projected, in a promontory falls
Sublime in distant grandeur on the shore ;
While through its horizontal firs, the west,
Still beaming with effulgence, dyes the stream
With ardent yellow. Night, contemplative,

Now drops her veil. How pleasing 't is to trace,
Upon the map of Time, the varied scenes
Of this revolving world; some nearly lost
In dim Oblivion's haze—some living yet
Upon the tablet of the memory—
And some in letter'd annals of the past!
   The Flats, that stretching west,   *   *
*   *   *   yield their rich increase
Of yellow harvests to the spacious barns,
*   *   sustain'd a sullen growth of wood,
And through the unchronicled domain of Day
Lay in tranquility and solitude ;
Till first the roving Huron glanced across,
Quick as his arrow that pursued the deer ;
And, hailing in the lonely chace his devious mate,
With shoutings wild, beside Schoharie's brooks,
Or Canajohary's echoing cliffs,
First broke the silence of the wilderness.
The houseless pair, encamping then, unstripp'd
The beech's yellow stem, and cased their walls
Of clay, or matted boughs; purloining yet,
Unconscious of their distant arrow's wing,
The squirrel of his life, or pheasant, clothed
With dappled feathers to his heels.   Then came
Some friend or kinsman, with his toiling wife,
Their quiver'd boys and dog ; and huts soon join'd
To huts, had form'd society, and taught,
By stationary life's progressive arts,
Its hard-earn'd comforts.   But eternal laws,
Employing man's own vengeance as the means
To bring abortion on his works, forbade.
Some hostile tribe, with carnage unappeased,
Lean, wandering, with invidious eyes beheld
Their haunts, and lurk'd in ambush near their huts ;
Then fell on them defenceless ; in a night
Up-rooted all their works, and half their race
Destroy'd.   Th' industrious colonists were chased,
Unshelter'd, through the woods, and left behind
No relic but their scalps.   The Mohawks next
And firm confederate friends, unused to war,
And studious of ignoble tillage, lash'd
By fierce oppressors from their homes, traced out
On Caughnawaga's meads, or 'neath Caroga's pines,
Their rude encampments.   Hate and dark design,
Though stifled, kindling in their vengeful hearts
Infuriate love of arms.   Their origin,

And whence their wild forefathers stray'd,
No annals tell; whether inclining toward
The peaceful ocean, where the sun at eve,
Upon the shining mountains lights his fires,
On Arathbuscaw's hungry shores, and where
The arctic circle girds the piny rocks
And lakes, in vast congeries round them spread;
Or southward from th' illimitable plain
Depastured by erratic buffaloes,
Where, hovering round the herds, th' Assinipoils
Upon their tongues and marrowy haunches feast.
Where'er the roving ancestors were born,
'T was here their spirited and martial sons
First sung the war-song—here on frequent spots
Which now the dwarfish oak and pine o'erspread,
And where the sumach scatters on the lap
Of autumn, azure-cheek'd, its pinnated
And scarlet leaves, once stood their huts; 't was here
Their arrows first they sharpen'd, to transfix
The Adirondac tyrants, seated round
The blanketed and tawny sachems smoked
In council, or the yelling bands, inspired
Like frantic Bacchanals, with fierce grimace,
And gesture fiend-like, beat the war dance: here,
By vengeance nursed, they raised a flame,
That, from the ocean to Machibon's gate,
Spread conflagration through the woods. The foe,
Unconscious of their strength, secure, remote,
And unsuspecting, till he heard the shrieks
Of savage fury, and the warriors bald,
Besmear'd with ochre, issued from their haunts,
Flinging their brandish'd tomahawks, with eyes
Red as the crouching panther's. None escaped,
Resisting or resistless, from their blows.
The aged sire struck lifeless on his seat;
The panting bosom gored, that press'd the babe
It nourish'd. Devastation swept o'er all
The scene, and stain'd the ruin'd stage with blood.
Rejoicing then, the victors to their vales,
Renown'd for empire, march'd with the acclaim
Of triumph: every proud and valiant hut
Was nail'd with bleeding scalps; and tribes remote
Gave tributary homage to the Wolf,
The Turtle and the Bear. The fosse still marks
Their castle's range, and in the lonely woods,
In hieroglyphics, still remain their boasts

Of conquest, and their graves.   Next Ceres came,
With German reapers in her train, and strow'd
Her harvests on the furrow'd width of flats.
Press'd by her golden sandals, we admire
The soil fructiferous, and scenes dress'd out
By smiling industry, that now reigns o'er
The wild demesnes of war.   Pursuing west
The sinuating stream within its vales
Of lengthening meadows, insulated oft
With steep ascent, we reach the rising ground
Of aromatic pines, where, jutting south,
The elevated shore confronting meets
Schoharie's stony creek.   The opening hills
Unfold its distant course, far in the blue
And mountainous horizon lost.   A rich
And flourishing expanse of vale then leads
Beyond the confluent waters, through the meads,
From Caughnawaga to a stately ridge
Of mountain granite, piled in lofty tiers,
Aerial, strutting in the scene.   Here stopp'd
The prospect of our level course ——We pause
In contemplation on the massy ribs
Developed, that maintain our earthly stage,
Till, length, the opening flats unfold the tower
And shapely roofs of Palatine—its plain
And intervening fields with herbage spread,
Or crested corn ; while sloping woodlands topp'd
With soaring pines, the Mohawk's bushy verge
O'ershadow, and the eye contemplative
In admiration fix.   Where is the mind
That honors truth, and in this transient day
Of perishable nature, 'mid the scoffs
And turmoil of a selfish world, would still
Preserve serene and animate the brows
Of virtuous sentiment, that does not seek
In rural peace a refuge from its sighs ?
What though ambition wear a crown—the fangs
Of avarice be fill'd with gold—esteem
And dear-bought wealth enrich the tongue that wins
By syren eloquence ; yet happier he,
Whom, in his valleys, ringing with the axe,
The setting sun forsakes, amidst the works
Of growing settlement.   Delightful cares !
That, in perspective of the future, charm
Beyond the plaudits of ephemeron praise.
How bless'd the prospect, to behold, each hour,

Increasing all around, expansive life
And happiness—their rapid progress urged
By ardent toil, invigorate by hope!
Though none here revel on the silken couch
Of zoneless pleasure, Friendship still may dwell
With Peace and Love, more sweet than is the voice
Of Fame, when from Parnassus she proclaims,
In melodies that vibrate betwixt heaven
And earth, her hero's actions. But, renew'd
Our journey, we pursue the mountain's stony edge,
Where the Caroga issues from the wild
And desert heights, in elevated range
Of sylvan tops far northward stretch'd, and where,
Below, its cataract pours down the hoarse
Canadian creek; till, rising in our front,
The mountains close, where once, perhaps, their rocks,
In one unbroken chain, the Mohawk's mass
Of waters, o'er the German flats and plains
Of Herkimer, suspended in a broad
Primeval lake, till, issuing through the strait's
Disjointed pass, and roaring granite rocks,
The lake, descending, left its reedy bounds,
And bed of slime, exhaling to the sun.

*   *   *   *   *   *

And now the airy Flats we pass, their church,
Litigious hall, and taverns, and approach
The gloomy shade of dark continuous wood,
That runs high westward to the Mohawk's fount.
Unbroken here the waste—half settled here
The towering trees on new-born fields recline—
Disorder'd, hewn, the venerable stems
And branching limbs surround their parent trunks,
That in the blackening conflagration still
Survive, and to the scythe of Time alone,
That levels all things, yield: a sturdy few
Yet standing, girdled by the fatal knife,
In slow destruction waste, upon their sprays
And airy summits quench'd the vital lymph;
In wintry desolation group'd, they pine
'Midst summer's genial solstice. Thriving near,
Their comrades flourish; tall, columnar bass,
With fluted shafts aspiring; oaks that stretch
Their vigorous arms; the hemlock, sombre topp'd
The yellow birch, her silken boddice half
Unlaced; and maple, delicately seam'd.

Athwart the solemn woods, of vast extent,
Stem beyond stem, in series infinite,
With vaulting foliage shadow'd as we pass,
The lively sun oft darts his influence;
And, 'midst the humid trees, an open square,
The hospitable roof of logs rough hewn,
Excorticate reveals. Aside, empaled,
The garden flourishes with roseate flowers;
And at the door the children gambol near;
Their lily-featured mother still intent
On busy cares domestic; while the sire
Along the echoing causeway drives his kine,
Or plies his axe far sounding.
              Thus, beloved
And happy scenes! a pensive wanderer,
I have trod your wilds, enamor'd much
Of Nature in her simplest guise, though sunk
At heart, and anxious to forsake the world
And all its vain, deceitful blandishments.
When these solicitous and weary eyes
Are closed through many a summer's reign, your vales
Shall flourish, each succeeding year shall yield
New stores of wealth, and future ages bless
The works, the zeal, the wisdom of the past.

SAMUEL LOW

Is the author of a collection of poems, in two volumes, published at New York in 1800.

WINTER.

"How changed, how fallen" now the landscape lies,
Which late with beauty's image bless'd our eyes;
Loved summer scenes, ah! whither have ye fled?
Ye short-lived charms, no sooner loved than dead!
Dear rural prospects, once with verdure graced,
But now by Winter's blighting touch laid waste;

Fair objects, that on mortal sense could pour
Delights, that glad man's torpid sense no more;
Once all your charms, with ever new delight,
In swift succession rose upon my sight;
With secret rapture often have I gazed
On Nature's gifts, and Nature's Author praised;
When genial showers enrich'd the teeming earth,
And vernal warmth gave vegetation birth,
Then throbb'd my heart, by Winter's blast unchill'd,
And speechless feelings through my bosom thrill'd;
Or when the fervor of a summer sun
Matured what Spring's creative power had done;
Or recent Autumn's yellow fields appear'd,
And health and hope the rustic owner cheer'd;
When bounteous harvests well repaid his toil,
And various plenty made the country smile;
When every wish indulgent Nature crown'd,
And shed her gifts exuberant around,
Enraptured I beheld,—the hours were spent
In warm acknowledgment and calm content.
While thus I call to mind enjoyments past,
And with them Winter's dreary scenes contrast,
On evanescent good while mem'ry dwells,
The gloomy retrospect my bosom swells;
Desponding images my thoughts employ,
The wreck of beauty, and the death of joy:
Dismantled earth inspires the soul with dread—
Loved Summer's scenes! ah, wherefore have ye fled?
    Long gath'ring vapors now to clouds increased,
Surcharged with frosty stores, involve the east:
Bleak Eurus there prepares his chilling blasts,
A weight of snow the burthen'd air o'ercasts;
Of keener cold and piercing frosts I sing,
Engend'ring in the air, which soon will cling
Fast hold on all beneath, which soon will throw
A robe of whiteness over all below:
Stern Winter, now confirm'd, in wrath impends;
With all his gloomy ensigns he descends;
For, lo! he gives the ripen'd mischief birth,
And shakes his vapory produce on the earth:
'T is come, dread Winter's hoary badge is come,
And bids the earth prepare to meet its doom.
By Eurus driven through the sluggish air,
The shower, minute and light, flies wavering there;
But soon, o'er all the atmosphere dispersed,
Creation in its bosom lies immersed:

Perpetual driving snow obscures the skies,
Commixing heaven and earth while thus it flies;
The spreading ruin overwhelms the plains,
And dazzling whiteness over nature reigns;
Its weight oppressive swells the hills, and lo!
Beneath accumulating heaps of snow,
How yonder trees, with drooping branches, stand
In white array, a venerable band!
How close the fleecy shroud to earth adheres!
How uniform the boundless scene appears!
Wide and more wide the spotless waste prevails,
Till aching vision at the prospect fails;
Till the spent gale an ermine mantle flings
O'er all this sublunary scene of things.
Nor have the clouds spent all their downy store,
But on the earth a frozen deluge pour:
Still more collecting, unexhausted still,
Though subtile flakes each lurking fissure fill,
And every vale exalts itself a hill.
Meanwhile the cattle shun the whelming waste,
With quicken'd speed for shelter home they haste,
Mournful, and ruminating as they go,
And shaking from their sides the cumb'rous snow:
Arrived at home, the dumb expecting band,
For entrance, near their hovels shivering stand;
The lowing kine the milker's hand intreat,
And oft the call importunate repeat;
Son'rous and long resounds the lowing strain;
The hills reponsive bellow back again.
There too the fleecy tribe their pittance crave,
Which once the herbage wild spontaneous gave;
And clam'rous bleat for their accustom'd meal,
Which cold made scant, and now thick snows conceal.
There chanticleer the storm undaunted braves,
Proud o'er the feather'd throng his plumage waves;
He spurns the snow, the blast he does not reck,
But, crowing shrill, exalts his glossy neck.
The steed rears graceful there his tow'ring size,
With head erect he gazes on the skies,
And prances wild, and snuffs the chilling air,
And neighs, impatient for the owner's care:
Nor long the helpless brutes his succor ask,
Soon, whistling, comes the peasant to his task;
Them large supplies of provender to spare,
And house them safe is his assiduous care.
Next comes the thrifty milk-maid, early taught

To shun destructive sloth, which oft hath brought
Its slaves to want, to vice, disease and wo,
And all the num'rous evils mortals know ;
She comes to drain the kine ; industrious she,
Domestic work to ply ; with heartfelt glee,
She treads her native snow, she cheerly sings
Her simple rural strains, and with her brings
Her ample pails, pure as contiguous snow,
Which soon with copious streams of milk o'erflow.
Now, laden with the luscious spoil, she trips,
And, as she treads incautious, often slips:
The peasant too, returns in jocund mood ;
His herds, well housed, enjoy their sav'ry food ;
From cold and hunger free, they there abide,
Nor aught of comfort wish or know, beside.

But oft, devoid of such a friendly shield,
To savage winter's ruthless grasp they yield ;
The fleecy flocks are buried oft in snow,
And undiscover'd breathe in depths below ;
The anxious shepherd seeks his charge in vain,
And rambles joyless o'er the desert plain ;
But if he chance to find the smother'd race,
Their breath, that thaws the snow, denotes the place :
The lengthy hook he gladly then suspends,
By this the suff'rer, scarce alive, ascends ;
While those remain whom death the power denies
To make the snow-dissolving breath arise.

By hunger urged, the nimble-footed deer
O'er snow-crown'd heights pursues his swift career ;
The hapless brute by huntsmen's toils annoy'd,
Oft meets the fate he labors to avoid ;
A vale, replete with snow, betrays his steps,
Incautious in the fatal depth he leaps ;
In vain he struggles now himself to clear,
And panting, dreading, sees his foes draw near ;
They come, they wound, they slay the guiltless beast :—
Already fancy riots at the feast ;
Big tears hang trembling in his dying eyes,
Unmoved they hear the captive's piteous cries,
Exulting, grapple their expiring prey,
And, loud rejoicing, bear the prize away.

Nor yet contented with the lusty prize,
Insatiate man to meaner conquests flies :
He skirts the forest, and he beats the copse,
The hare and squirrel now invite his hopes :
In hollow trees, and burrows under ground,

He careful pries, and looks expectant round.
If now the parent hare hath left her haunt,
In quest of sustenance her offspring want,
The helpless young, in man's deep arts unskill'd,
To his perfidious stratagem must yield :
The dam, improvident of winter's store,
Now dubious roams abroad in search of more ;
And, spurr'd by pressing want, the snow disturbs,
To glean precarious food from wither'd herbs ;
But deadly guns her anxious search cut short,
Or traps insidious lie where game resort;
Or, if she shun these snares, a harder fate,
Severer evils her return await :
Her haunt she enters, but the hapless hare
Beholds nor mate, nor harmless offspring there,
And dies with cold, with hunger and despair.

 The fowler too the meads and woods explores ;
With his remorseless feats the country roars ;
With cautious step, and big with hope and fear,
He pauses now, and now approaches near,
And eyes the feather'd flock through all their flight,
Till on some tempting meadow they alight,
Within his reach ; then points, with steady hand,
The fatal engine to the heedless band ;
Swift from the tube escapes the leaden death,
That lays them prostrate, gasping out their breath ;
While others, startled at the ruthless deed,
Precipitate and wild, forsake the mead ;
But many, flying, meet the death they shun,
And swifter ruin leaves the murd'rous gun ;
Through yielding air it flies, with thund'ring sound,
And hurls its conquest on the blood-stain'd ground !

 On skates of wood the sons of Lapland go.
To hunt the elk o'er endless tracts of snow,
Nor heed the cavities which lurk below :
Upon the snow-topp'd surface far and wide,
Accoutred for the chase, they fearless slide ;
The huntsman, fleet and fierce as winter's wind,
Each moment leaves a length'ning space behind ;
Mad with desire his object he pursues,
Too late the beast his luckless fortune rues ;
The sanguine foe, with horizontal aim,
Darts instantaneous ruin to the game ;
Dextrous he manages the missile bow,
That lays his victim's branching antlers low ;
The deathful weapon cuts th' aerial space,
And crowns the triumph of the savage chase !

TO A VIOLET.

Though not the gaudy Tulip's drap'ry fine,
Yet thou, fair plant, canst Tyre's rich purple boast;
The beauty of the Amethyst is thine;
Thy neat and simple garb delights me most;
Unseen and shadowy forms, of tiny size,
Delicious dew-drops from thy surface sip,
Feast on thy charms their microscopic eyes,
And breathe thy sweets, as o'er thy leaves they trip.
Emblem of innocence and modest worth,
Who lov'st the eye of rude remark to shun,
Whose lovely, lowly form still tends to earth,
Unlike the flower which courts the mid-day sun;
Thou seem'st, sweet flow'ret, of his beam afraid;—
Thus merit ever loves and seeks the shade.

TO A SEGAR.

Sweet antidote to sorrow, toil and strife,
Charm against discontent and wrinkled care.
Who knows thy power can never know despair;
Who knows thee not, one solace lacks of life:
When cares oppress, or when the busy day
Gives place to tranquil eve, a single puff
Can drive even want and lassitude away,
And give a mourner happiness enough.
From thee when curling clouds of incense rise,
They hide each evil that in prospect lies;
But when in evanescence fades thy smoke,
Ah! what, dear sedative, my cares shall smother?
If thou evaporate, the charm is broke,
Till I, departing taper, light another.

TO THE GENIUS OF POETRY.

Genius of tuneful verse! inspired by whom,
Divine Mæonides in numbers first
Dawn'd on a world o'ercast with mental gloom,
And strains sublime to barb'rous Greece rehearsed;

Spirit of song! from whose Castalian fount
The Mantuan poet sweet instruction drew ;
With piercing ken to whose Aonian mount,
Once Albion's bards on eagle pinions flew ;
Though far aloof thy vot'ry stretch his wing,
That o'er no classic land presumes to soar,
Him hast thou taught in plaintive strains to sing,
To feel thy solace, and thy power adore ;
And, spite of envy's futile venom, thou
Hast placed a leaf of laurel on his brow.

BENJAMIN PRATT

Was born in Massachusetts in 1710, and graduated at Harvard College in 1737. He was for some time a lawyer in Boston, and became distinguished also as a politician, but though attached to the cause of freedom, he became obnoxious to the people by his exertions in favor of Governor Pownall. He was appointed Chief Justice of New York, and filled that office with ability and reputation. He projected a history of New England, and made a large collection of materials, but the work was arrested by his death, January 5th, 1763. The following lines were found among his papers.

DEATH.

Though guilt and folly tremble o'er the grave,
No life can charm, no death affright the brave.
The wise at nature's laws will ne'er repine,
Nor think to scan or mend the grand design
That takes unbounded nature for its care,
Bids all her millions claim an equal share.
Late in a microscopic worm confined,
Then in a prison'd fetus drown'd the mind ;
Now of the ape kind both for sense and size,

Man eats and drinks and propagates and dies.
Good God! if thus to live our errand here,
Is parting with life's trifles worth our fear ?
Or what grim furies have us in their power,
More in the dying than the living hour.
Ills from ourselves, but none from nature flow,
And virtue's road cannot descend to wo.
What nature gives, receive, her laws obey ;
If you must die tomorrow, live today.
The prior states thy mind has varied through
Are drown'd in Lethe where black waves pursue,
To roll oblivion o'er each yesterday,
And will tomorrow sweep thyself away.
But where ? no more unknown in future fate
Than your own end or essence in this state.
The past, the future and our nature hid,
Now comic and now tragic scenes we tread.
Unconscious actors : with a drama run
And act a part, but for a plot unknown.
We see their shapes, we feel ten thousand things,
We reason, act and sport on fancy's wings,
While yet this agent, this percipient lies
Hid from itself and puzzles all the wise.
In vain we seek, inverted eyes are blind,
And nature form'd no mirror for the mind.
Like some close cell whence art excludes the day,
Save what through optics darts its pencil'd ray,
And paints the lively landscape to the sight,
While yet the room itself is veil'd in night.
Nor can you find with all your boasted art,
The curious touch that bids the salient heart
Send its warm purple round the venal maze,
To fill each nerve with life, with bloom the face.
How o'er the heart the numbing palsies creep
To chill the carcase to eternal sleep.
'T is ours t' improve this life, not ours to know
From whence this meteor, when or where 't will go.
As o'er a fen when heaven 's involved in night,
An ignis fatuus waves its new-born light,
Now up, now down, the mimic taper plays
As varying Auster puffs the trembling blaze ;
Soon the light phantom spends its magic store,
Dies into darkness, and is seen no more.
Thus run our changes, but in this secure,
Heaven trusts no mortal's fortune in his power.
Nor hears the prayers impertinent we send

To alter fate, and providence to mend,
As well in judgment as in mercy kind,
God hath for both the fittest date design'd.
The wise on death, the fools on life depend,
From toils and pains some sweet reverse to find.
Scheme after scheme the dupe successive tries,
And never gains, but hopes to gain the prize.
From the delusion still he ne'er will wake,
But dream of bliss, and live on the mistake.
Thus Tantalus in spite the furies placed
Tortured and charm'd to wish, and yet accursed :
In every wish infatuate, dreads lest Jove
Should move him from the torments of his love
To see the tempting fruit and stream no more,
And trust his Maker on some unknown shore.
Death buries all diseases in the grave,
And gives us freedom from each fool and knave,
To worlds unknown it kindly wafts us o'er—
Come death, my guide, I'm raptured to explore.

JOSEPH LATHROP

Was born at Norwich in Connecticut, October 20th, 1731,
and graduated at Yale College in 1754, soon after which he
was settled in the ministry at Springfield, Massachusetts.   In
1793 he was chosen Professor of Theology in Yale College,
but declined the office.   He died December 31st, 1820, in his
90th year.   Several volumes of his sermons have been published.

THE EXISTENCE OF A DEITY.

When I lift up my wond'ring eyes,
And view the grand and spacious skies,
"There is a God!" my thoughts exclaim,
Who built this vast stupendous frame.

The sun by day with glorious light,
The moon with softer rays by night,
Each rolling planet, glowing star,
Wisdom and power divine declare.

The lightning's blaze, the thunder's roar,
The clouds, which wat'ry blessings pour,
The winter's frost, the summer's heat,
This pleasing, awful truth repeat.

The forest and the grassy mead,
Where wild beasts roam, or tame ones feed,
Corn, springing from the lifeless clod,
Confess the agency of God.

My body form'd with nicest art,
My heaving lungs, and beating heart,
My limbs, obsequious to my will,
Show forth my Maker's power and skill.

The various passions of the mind,
The powers of reason more refined,
Bold fancy's flight, each lively sense
Prove a supreme intelligence.

A God so great and always near,
Shall be the object of my fear;
His goodness, wisdom, truth, and love,
Shall my best passions ever move.

My care shall be, his sacred will
To understand and to fulfil:
His service shall my life employ,
His favor is my highest joy.

STEPHEN SEWALL

Was born at York in Maine, in 1734, and studied at Harvard College, where he received a degree in 1761. The following year he was appointed teacher, and afterward Professor of Hebrew in that institution. He retained this office with the reputation of the most accomplished classical scholar in the country, till 1785. He died in 1804. He was the author of a Hebrew Grammar, and a Chaldee and English Dictionary; the last is still in manuscript.

Professor Sewall was one of the authors of the Pietas et Gratulatio Collegii Cantabrigiensis, which we have mentioned in the life of Dr Church. Many of the Greek and Latin verses are by him, and two of the compositions in English.

ON THE DEATH OF GEORGE II.

Of cypress deign, celestial muse, to sing;
To plaintive numbers tune the trembling string,
    And soothe the gen'ral grief.—
    The voice of joy's no more,
    On Albion's sadden'd shore:
    He's gone—Britannia's royal chief!
    From the north to southern pole,
    From the farthest orient floods
    To Hesperia's savage woods,
    Swelling tides of sorrow roll:
    Nor wonder; all an ample share
Partook, through boundless climes, of his paternal care.

Whate'er the muse's mournful lays can do,
And more, blest shade! to thy loved name is due.
    Under thy gentle sway,
    Religion, heaven-born fair,
    In her own native air,
    Refulgent shone in golden day:
    Virtue, science, liberty,
    Blooming sisters, wreathed with bays,
    Grateful sung their patron's praise:
    Commerce, o'er the broad-back'd sea,

Extending far on floating isles,
Imported India's wealth, and rich Peruvian spoils.

Let Rome her Julius and Octavius boast;
What both at Rome, George was on Albion's coast.
    An olive-wreath his brow,
    Majestic, ever wore;
    Unless by hostile power
    Long urged, and then the laurel bough.
    Faithful bards, in epic verse,
    Vict'ries more than Julius won,
    And exploits, before undone,
    George the Hero, shall rehearse:
    While softer notes each tuneful swain
Shall breathe from oaten pipe, of George's peaceful reign.

But, ah! while on the glorious past we dwell,
Enwrapt in silken thought, our bosoms swell
    With pleasing ecstacy,
    Forgetful of our wo.
    —Shall tears forbear to flow?
    Or cease to heave the deep-fetch'd sigh?
    Flow, ye tears, forever stream;
    Sighs, to whisp'ring winds complain;
    Winds, the sadly-solemn strain
    Waft, and tell the mournful theme.
    But what, alas! can tears or sighs?
What could, has ceased to be; the spirit mounts the skies.

With sympathetic wo, thy noontide ray,
Phœbus, suspend; ye clouds, obscure the day;
    Her face let Cynthia veil,
    Thick darkness spread her wing,
    And the night-raven sing,
    While Britons their sad fate bewail.
    Sacred flood, whose crystal tide,
    Gently gliding, rolls adown
    Fast by, once, the blissful town,
    Thames! with pious tears supply'd,
    Swell high, and tell the vocal shore
And jovial mariner, their glory's now no more!

But stop, my plaintive muse: lo! from the skies
What sudden radiance strikes our wond'ring eyes?
    As had the lab'ring sun,
    From black and dismal shades,
    Which not a ray pervades,
    Emerging, with new lustre shone,

In the forehead of the east,
See the gilded morning star,
Of glad day the harbinger:
Sighing, now, and tears are ceased:
Still George survives ; his virtues shine
In him, who sprung alike from Brunswick's royal line.

JAMES BOWDOIN

Was born in Boston in 1727. He received his education at
Harvard College, and at an early period of life was appointed
to many public offices of importance. In 1775 he became
President of the Council of Massachusetts, and remained in
that station till the adoption of the State Constitution in 1780.
He was President of the Convention which formed the constitution of Massachusetts, and in 1785 and 1786, was Governor of the State. He died in 1790. He was a man of extensive literary attainments, and was honored with a Doctor's
degree from several European universities, and created a
member of the Royal Societies of London and Dublin. He
wrote much on philosophical subjects, and was a principal agent
in forming the American Academy of Arts and Sciences at
Boston. He was the first President of this institution, and
bequeathed it a valuable legacy.

Among his various pursuits he also cultivated poetry. He
contributed to the *Pietas et Gratulatio,* but his principal work
of this kind is an enlarged paraphrase of The Economy of
Human Life, published at Boston in 1759. He had a respectable talent as a versifier, though his poetry displays little inventive faculty.

WOMAN.

Nature, fair creature ! when she form'd thy mind,
Form'd thee a fit companion for mankind :

Not merely to excite love's genial fire;
And with a flood of joy to quench desire:
Nor wantonly to sport the hours away;
Nor, like a slave, man's lawless will obey;
But to assist him in life's num'rous toils;
To cheer him in misfortune with your smiles;
To soothe his breast when troubles overbear;
And with your love to recompense his care:
To raise his drooping spirits in distress;
And with your own promote his happiness.
But who is she whom every grace surrounds;
Whom every grace with all that's lovely crowns;
By nature form'd to touch a gen'rous breast;
By nature form'd to make man amply blest?
Yonder she walks along in virgin bloom:
And where she walks the rose's sweets perfume.
See from her presence fly ill-boding fear;
And every gloom before her disappear!
See innocence with cheerfulness combine,
Sit on her brow, and in her actions shine!
See modesty adorn her lovely cheek,
And in her language and behaviour speak!
See temp'rance in due bounds restrain desire;
And give a check to passion's lawless fire!
Humility and meekness, round her head,
Are as a crown of circling glory spread:
Discretion ripens with her growing years,
And on her brow in sceptred state appears:
When scandal tarnishes a rising name,
And throws from tongue to tongue her neighbor's fame,
Her soul disdains to spread the scandal round;
And, far from wid'ning, strives to heal the wound.
Unrival'd goodness warms her gen'rous breast;
And there—its native home—takes up its rest:
O'er her it bears so uncontroll'd a sway,
She thinks all nature does its laws obey:
She harbors no suspicion in her mind;
But judges by herself of all mankind.
These virtues, with a graceful freedom crown'd,
Spread far and wide her character around.
Among her virtues prudence bears the sway,
And shines abroad with a distinguish'd ray.
In all she does, it uniformly guides;
And o'er her conduct constantly presides.
Softness and love with a majestic mien,
Speak in her eye, and in her looks are seen.
Her tongue harmonious music warbles round;

And on her lips is honey's sweetness found.
Sacred to truth, and by its laws confined,
Her lips impart the language of her mind.
With a becoming grace her words appear ;
And, like her honest heart, are all sincere.
By custom and example undecoy'd,
With cheerful mind she keeps herself employ'd :
Each day's revolving sun her task renews ;
Nor does her hand the welcome task refuse :
To that—her mind so uniformly bends ;
To that, with so much constancy attends ;
That morning visits (destined to amuse ;
To talk of dress, laced waistcoats, and the news ;
To spread the scandal of the night before ;
And, that once done, prepare the way for more)
Ne'er interrupt the business of the day ;
Nor by their levity her mind betray :
Much less shall *rabbles,* which the sex debase,
Or *routs,* or *drums* her character disgrace.
By wisdom sway'd, she thus her hours employs ;
And thus employ'd, a tranquil mind enjoys :
A tranquil mind—that very far outweighs
The applause of crowds; and even her own just praise.
Thus fame from such a course of action springs ;
And bears her high upon its rapid wings ;
Thus fame, thus inward peace—so heaven ordains—
Flows from one source, and lasting strength obtains.

JOHN LOWELL

Was born at Newbury in 1744. He was educated at Harvard College, and soon rose to eminence as a lawyer. In 1761 he removed to Boston, and was chosen to various public offices. He was one of the Convention which formed the Constitution of Massachusetts, and in 1771 became a member of Congress. In 1782, he was appointed a Judge of the Court of Appeals, from the courts of Admiralty in the United States. On the establishment of the Federal Government, he was made a Judge of the United States Circuit Court. He died May 6, 1822. The following lines by him are from the *Pietas et Gratulatio.*

LINES.

No more let ancient times their heroes boast,
Since all their fame in George's praise is lost ;
Not Greece—her Alexanders ; Cæsars—Rome
For worth and virtue view our Monarch's tomb.
Restless ambition dwelt in Cæsar's mind,
He murder'd nations and enslaved mankind :
He found a gen'rous people great and free,
And gave them tyrants for their liberty.
The glorious Alexander, half divine,
Whose godlike deeds in ancient records shine,
Dropt his divinity at every feast ;
And lost the god and hero in the beast.
Sh^ll then our monarch be with these compared,
Or George's glory with a Cæsar shared :
No—we indignant spurn the unworthy claim :
George shines unrivall'd in the lists of fame :
For while he reign'd, each virtue, every grace
Beam'd from his throne, and sparkled in his face :
While justice, goodness, liberty inspired,
And Britain's freedom all his conduct fired.
His people's father was his highest boast ;
And in that name was all the sovereign lost.
Justice which left the world since Saturn's reign,
In him returning blest these realms again ;
Even rigid justice with compassion join'd,
Sweetly uniting in his generous mind.
But why should we on separate features dwell,
When the great picture does in each excel ?
No single virtues strike us with surprise ;
All come united to the admiring eyes.

PETER OLIVER,

Chief Justice of Massachusetts, was graduated at Harvard
College, in 1730. He afterwards resided in the county of
Plymouth, where he filled several public offices, and was
finally appointed Chief Justice. He was disliked by the
people for refusing to receive his salary from the Legislature,

instead of the King. Charges of treason against the colony were brought against him, and he left the country for England, where he resided the rest of his life. He received a degree of Doctor of Laws, from the University of Oxford, and possessed the reputation of being an able and intelligent writer. He died in 1791. He wrote a poem in blank verse, on the death of Josiah Willard, Secretary of the Province of Massachusetts Bay, from which we make the following extract.

> Cease then the rapid tear, nor vainly urge
> The mournful gloom, erect the pensive eye
> To where the virtuous man is rank'd above ;
> See there the cloudless soul, unfetter'd, free
> From every terrene clog that here so late
> His flight retarded to the throne of God.
> See his exulting spirit, mounted high
> On wings of love celestial, basking full
> In the calm sunshine of the Deity.
> There, every tear wiped from his eyes, he views
> The rushing glories of the world of light,
> He drinks the stream of pleasure, pure, unmix'd,
> That flows incessant from the sacred fount :
> His ears delighted with angelic harps,
> He tunes his own, and joins the sacred choir :
> The odors from the golden tree of life,
> Which fill all heaven with fragrance, he inhales,
> And feels, enraptured, all those joys that flow
> From converse with the Godhead, face to face.

WILLIAM LADD.

WILLIAM LADD was born at Newport, Rhode Island, in 1755. Of the history of his youth we know no more than that his parents were poor, though of reputable character, and that he manifested an early love of study. He became a physician, and had just entered upon the world, with good success and flattering prospects, when a strange peculiarity of events gave a sudden and remarkable turn to his destiny.

His life is marked with a character of singularity, for it real-
izes the dreams of romance, and presents as striking a case
of ill-starred love as ever furnished a theme for the novelist
or poet.

Ladd possessed by nature a warm susceptible heart, and a
lively fancy. His early days were passed amid privations,
but his exuberant spirits and imaginative turn of mind made
amends for this lack of the gifts of fortune, and secured him
enjoyments in his penury. He became attached to poetry,
first as an amusement, and afterwards as a solace and refuge
from the troubles and mortifications which beset him. His
warm fancy, and quick susceptibility of feeling, kindled this
attachment into enthusiasm, and carried him into a dreaming
state of existence. His imagination reposed in regions of
sunshine and bliss, and pictured every scene in glowing colors.
He lived in an ideal world. When he first entered upon his
professional studies, this romantic delirium was somewhat
sobered away, but an incident revived it in its full ardor.
He formed an attachment which was not requited. It was
towards a lady whose feelings were directly the reverse of
his own. She had good sense, and a sober, well regulated
mind ; but constitutionally frigid and unimaginative, she had no
sympathy with the rapturous flights and paroxysms of her
enthusiastic lover. It does not appear that his person or
general character was objectionable in her eyes, but she took
alarm at his passionate manner of wooing, and the fervid and
soaring tone of his aspirations : these belonged to a refinement of feeling which she could not comprehend, or did not
relish. Our bard made the most zealous and persevering
attempts to win her favor, but she viewed him with an eye of
distrust. She was no poet,—no admirer of the muses; she
could not feel the fire of inspiration,—could not respond to the
emotions kindled by the glowing temperament of the man
who sought her love. To her, it was extravagance, and
frantic excess. Notwithstanding the earnestness and sincerity with which he pressed his suit, she repelled his addresses constantly and firmly. It appears strange that an

object, whose feelings and taste were so widely different from his own, should have so strongly attracted his regard; but either he had not a true conception of her character, or the violence of his love caused him to disregard the dissimilarity in their minds. It is indeed affirmed, that he was not violently enamored at first, but that his passion grew by being repelled, and that he no sooner found his object unattainable, than, with the disposition so natural to men, to value highly whatever is beyond their reach, he exalted her in imagination into a being of transcendent excellence, and his susceptible heart was kindled with a most intense flame. The more firmly the lady repulsed him, the more vehemently did he urge his addresses. He could not believe that a passion so ardent and sincere as that which he felt, could fail to move the heart of his mistress, and the coldness with which she steadily met his protestations of love, only caused a persuasion that he was not fervent and earnest enough. He found her inaccessible, and his solicitation hopeless; but desperate as his case was, he continued his assiduities, and occupied his mind with this romantic and unfortunate passion to the last hour of his existence.

In the prosecution of his hopeless suit, he called to his aid the powers of his muse. He committed his woes to verse, and the lady was annoyed with a multitude of poetical epistles, in which the strength of his affection, and the keen fine-toned sensibility of his feelings, are most eloquently displayed. In common cases, we are inclined to doubt the sincerity of that passion which can vent itself in the artificial and labored utterance of verse; and Doctor Johnson has declared, that a man who courts his mistress in rhyme, deserves to lose her. But the truth of our poet's grief is not to be doubted. A convincing earnestness marks every line that he utters. The unhappiness under which he was suffering is depicted in language too earnest to allow us to believe it a fiction. There is a tone of deep, sincere feeling in these outpourings of his sorrow, that must have come from the heart. He called these epistles, 'The Letters of Arouet to Amanda.' The lady continued inexorable, and Ladd becoming weary of so much ineffectual endeavor, yet not at all cooled in his passion, resolved to tear himself from his beloved Amanda, with the hope that absence and new objects would exert their usual influence in estranging his mind from the griefs which preyed upon his repose. He accordingly sailed for South Carolina, intending to remain there and practise his profession, but though at a distance from the object which had aroused his passion, it lived on with undiminished force ; absence could not weaken it. Amanda became the wife of another ; our poet received the information—he could no longer hope, but he loved still.

In 1786 he became engaged in a newspaper controversy, in Charleston, upon some political matter. This led to a personal misunderstanding, and a challenge was sent him, and accepted. A duel was fought, and Ladd received a wound which was not considered dangerous ; but this unhappy man was languishing in despair, and had become weary of life. He refused all medical aid, and a mortification ensued. He died in his thirtythird year.

A collection of his writings was published at Charleston in 1786, with the title of ' The Poems of Arouet.' It is said this volume contains but a small portion of his best Poems, and that the most of his epistles to Amanda are now lost. Those which remain show his poetical talent in a favorable and striking manner. They are written with the full energy of feeling, and are marked with none of the stale conceits, and worn-out figures of common love ditties, but come gushing from the heart in a strain of deep, poignant, and undissembled sorrow. His other poems are not so impressive, for they want the fervor and heartfelt earnestness of his epistles, but they have ease, and liveliness of fancy. We are told that his volume was hastily compiled, and probably there are many of his pieces still extant, which are not included in it, as it was published soon after his death, at a distance from the region where he had passed the most of his days. Should any of these remains be discovered, we think their publication would be a

service to the literature of the country, as well as a justice to
the character of a person whose talents and misfortunes conspire to make him a signal object of interest.

AROUET TO AMANDA.

ONCE more, dear maid, the wretched Arouet writes;
His pen obedient, as his heart indites;
These lines may haply waste your precious time,
And his loathed writings may be deem'd a crime.
Thou say'st that friendship can afford a cure
To the deep wounds, the sorrows I endure;
The generous thought with rapture I pursue—
It must be lovely, for it comes from you.
But O how poor is friendship to express
"The soul-felt pang of exquisite distress."
Once I was happy—blest with native ease,
A friend could cheer me, and a book could please;
But now no joys from books or friendship flow,
Not one poor respite to my load of wo.
Did not you, dearest, see my fond distress,
Beyond all power of language to express?
The whirling thought, the swift impassion'd kiss,
Delirium sweet and agony of bliss.
How have I listen'd when your accents broke,
And kiss'd the air that trembled as you spoke.
Death, friendly Death will soon relieve my pain,
Long sure he cannot be implored in vain.
When to my sight the monarch of the tomb
Shall rise terrific and pronounce my doom;
Will then Amanda, ah! she will, I trust,
Pay the last tribute to my clay-cold dust:
Will sighing say, here his last scene is o'er,
Who loved as mortal never loved before.
Dear, matchless maid! that kind concern display'd,
Would sweetly soothe my melancholy shade.
O'er my lone tomb O yield that sad relief;
Breathe the soft sigh and pour out all your grief;
Or shed one tear in pity as you pass,
And just remember that your Arouet was.

REMONSTRANCE OF ALMASA ALLICAWN, WIFE OF ALMAS
ALLICAWN, TO WARREN HASTINGS.

It was said that Warren Hastings, having taken the husband of this lady, one
of the eastern princes, prisoner, agreed to save his life for a ransom, and that he
took the ransom and put the king to death.

My subjects slaughter'd, my whole kingdom spoil'd ;
My treasures wasted and my husband slain.
O say, vile monster ! art thou satisfied ?
Hast thou, rapacious brute ! sufficient wealth ?
Hastings ! my husband was your prisoner—
The wealth of kingdoms flew to his relief;
You took the ransom, and you broke your faith.
Almas was slain—'t was perjury to your soul ;
But perjury 's a little crime with you.
In souls so black, it seem'd almost a virtue.
Say, cruel monster ! art thou thirsting still
For human gore ? O may'st thou ever thirst,
And may the righteous gods deny thee water
To cool thy boiling blood, inhuman wretch !
And, bloody ruffian ! thou must go where Almas
Sits on a throne of state, and every hour
He stabs an Englishman, and sweetly feasts
Upon his bloody heart and trembling liver.
Yet, Hastings, tremble not, for thou art safe,
Yes, murderer ! thou art safe from this repast:
A heart polluted with ten thousand crimes,
Is not a feast for Almas, he will pluck
That savage heart out of its bloody case,
And toss it to his dogs ; wolves shall grow mad
By feeding on thy murderous carcase.   More,
When some vile wretch, some monster of mankind,
Some brute like thee, perhaps thy relative,
Laden with horrid crimes without a name,
Shall stalk through earth, and we want curses for him,
We'll torture thought to curse the wretch, and then,
To damn him most supreme, we'll call him *Hastings*.

———

THE WAR HORSE.

PARAPHRASE FROM JOB.

Again the Almighty from the whirlwind broke,
And thus to Job, in stern continuance, spoke :

" Didst thou the horse with strength unequall'd mould,
Whose lofty neck the writhen thunders fold ?
And canst thou make the intrepid courser fly,
When steely dangers glitter in his eye ?

" See all around him spreads the flamy cloud,
Spurn'd from his nostrils, while he snorts aloud,
Trembling with vigor, how he paws the ground,
And hurls the thunder of his strength around !
Behold ! he pants for war, and scorning flight,
Collects his strength and rushes to the fight.

" When clouds of darts a sable horror spread,
And the full quiver rattles o'er his head:
To him no dread the sound of battle bears,
The clash of armor and the strife of spears ;
But o'er his neck his waving mane reclined,
Spreads to the gale and wantons in the wind :
He spurns the field, fierce, terrible, and strong,
And rolls the earth back as he shoots along.

" Lo ! where the strife the distant warriors wage,
The neighing courser snuffs the sanguine rage ;
While roaring trumpets and the dire affray
Provoke his laughter on that dreadful day ;
More loud he snorts, more terrible he foams,
When nearer still the storm of battle comes;
And mingling roars are dreadful on the heath,
In shouts of victory, and groans of death."

RETIREMENT.

HAIL, sweet retirement, hail !
Best state of man below,
To smooth the tide of passions frail,
And bear the soul away from scenery of wo.
When, retired from busy noise,
Vexing cares and troubled joys,
To a mild serener air,
In the country we repair :
Calm enjoy the rural scene,
Sportive o'er the meadows green:
When the sun's enlivening ray
Speaks the genial month of May,

Lo ! his amorous, wanton beams
Dance on yonder crystal streams ;
In soft dalliance pass the hours,
Kissing dew-drops from the flowers,
While soft music through the grove,
Sweetly tunes the soul to love.
And the hills harmonious round
Echo with responsive sound ;
There the turtle-dove alone,
Makes his soft, melodious moan ;
While from yonder bough 't is heard,
Sweetly chirps the yellow-bird :
There the linnet's downy throat
Warbles the responsive note ;
And to all the neighboring groves,
Robin Redbreast tells his loves.
  There, Amanda, we might walk,
And of soft endearments talk ;
Or anon we 'd listen, love,
To the gently-cooing dove.
In some sweet, embowering shade,
Some fair seat by nature made,
I my love would gently place,
On the tender woven grass :
Seated by thy lovely side,
Oh, how great would be my pride !
While my soul should fix on thine,
Oh the joy to call thee mine !
  For why should doves have more delight,
Than we, my sweet Amanda, might ?
And why should larks and linnets be
More happy, lovely maid, than we ?
  There the pride of genius blooms,
There sweet contemplation comes :
There is science, heavenly fair,
Sweet philosophy is there ;
With each author valued most,
Ancient glory, modern boast.
There the mind may revel o'er
Doughty deeds of days of yore ;
How the mighty warriors stood,
How the field was dyed in blood,
How the shores were heap'd with dead,
And the rivers stream'd with red ;
While the heroes' souls on flame,
Urged them on to deathless fame.

Or we view a different age
Pictured in the historic page—
Kings, descending from a throne ;
Tyrants, making kingdoms groan,
With each care to state allied,
And all the scenery of pride.
Or perhaps we'll study o'er
Books of philosophic lore ;
Read what Socrates has thought,
And how godlike Plato wrote ;
View the earth with Bacon's eyes ;
Or, with Newton, read the skies ;
See each planetary ball,
One great sun attracting all:
All by gravitation held,
Self-attracted, self-repelled :
We shall cheat away old time,
Passing moments so sublime.
Hail, sweet retirement, hail !
Best state of man below,
To smooth the tide of passions frail,
And bear the soul away from scenery of wo.

WHAT IS HAPPINESS ?

'T is an empty, fleeting shade,
By imagination made :
'T is a bubble, straw, or worse
'T is a baby's hobby-horse :
'T is two hundred shillings clear ;
'T is ten thousand pounds a year :
'T is a title, 't is a name ;
'T is a puff of empty fame ;
Fickle as the breezes blow ;
'T is a lady's yes or no !
And when the description's crown'd,
'T is just no where to be found.
    Arouet shows, I must confess,
Says Delia, what is happiness ;
I wish he now would tell us what
This self-same happiness is not.
    What happiness is not ? I vow,
That, Delia, you have posed me now :
What it is not—stay, let me see—
I think, dear maid, 't is—not for me.

EDWARD CHURCH.

EDWARD CHURCH was a native of Boston, and brother to Dr Benjamin Church already spoken of. He was graduated at Harvard College in 1759. He became known as a writer in the early part of the revolutionary contest, and at a period before this had exercised his pen to some effect; for we have been informed that he assisted his brother in the composition of many of his poems. When the federal constitution was adopted, Church, as we are given to understand, expected an office, in which hope being disappointed, he gave vent to his spleen in a satirical poem called The Dangerous Vice *********, meaning the Vice President John Adams, the person whom he imagined had hindered his advancement. His philippics however were not confined to a single object, but branched out into a harsh and bitter invective against the officers of the government generally, and the members of the Order of Cincinnati. Some years afterward he obtained the appointment of Consul for the United States at Lisbon. More of his history we are not acquainted with.

The satire above referred to, is the only considerable work which he is known to have published. It shows no mean talent in that species of writing, and if we could sympathise with the excited feelings of the satirist, we should involuntarily pay him the credit of our admiration for his eloquence. But from the motives which prompted his indignation, he fails to arouse us to any feeling correspondent with his own. His individual pique is too apparent. The satire is pointed, caustic, and spirited, but we never forget that it is vindictive and exaggerated.

THE DANGEROUS VICE *********.

BEHOLD the Merchant! once with plenty bless'd,
Whom fortune favor'd, and whom friends caress'd;
Who with rich dainties his loved offspring fed,

And quaff'd enjoyments from the fountain head ;
Whose stores were full, whose flagons running o'er,
And every smiling year was adding more ;
Yet nobly all for liberty resign'd,
For equal liberty with all mankind.
Behold him now ! from his possessions hurl'd,
Stripp'd by a faithless and ungrateful world ;
Reluctant forced from clime to clime to roam,
To earn a pittance for his starving home ;
Or—if at home— to want and misery driven,
Looks round—and wonders at the ways of Heaven.
By foes, by country robb'd—by treaty sold—
A poor, dependent slave when he is old—
Of credit, prospects, friends, and hope bereft,
And nought but family, and feelings left ;
Beggar'd, forgotten, and despondent grown,
He lives a stranger, and he dies unknown.

    See the poor soldier ! maim'd and seam'd with scars,
His hard-earn'd wages in his country's wars,
His crazy carcase tott'ring to a fall,
Propt by a crutch, or by some friendly wall,
Or hobbling on to some sequester'd spot,
Muses in vain on man's unequal lot ;
Arrived—he rests him on the humble ground,
To soothe the anguish of a smarting wound :
When lo ! a witness of his toils appears,
Who on his breast the pendent eagle* bears ;
The houseless vet'ran lifts his misty eyes,
Descries the badge—then mutters to the skies—
" Scars are the badges which poor soldiers wear,
Who for their thankless country bravely dare."

    *   *   *   *

Ape not the fashions of the foreign great
Nor make your betters at your levees wait,
Resign your awkward pomp, parade and pride,
And lay that useless etiquette aside ;
The unthinking laugh, but all the thinking hate
Such vile, abortive mimicry of state ;
Those idle lackeys, sauntering at your door,
But ill become poor servants of the poor ;
Retrench your board, for e'en the guests who dine,
Have cause to murmur at your floods of wine ;
Think not to bribe the wise with their own gold,
Though fools by flimsy lures should be cajoled ;
Places on places multiply to view,

*The badge of the order of the Cincinnati.

Creation on creation, ever new;
Therefore in decent competence to live,
Is all that you can ask, or justice give:
An humbler roof—could Madam condescend—
But heaven forbid I should the sex offend!
The chariot, too—pray who can live without,
And keep distinguished from the rabble rout?
All genteel people deem it a reproach
To go to plays, balls, routs, in hackney coach;
And as to walking—'t is so vulgar now—
Ladies have left it off, and scarce know how.
Women, I grant, are frequent in the street,
But real ladies, Sir, you 'll rarely meet.

But who art thou, who durst advice intrude,
So very prudent, and so very rude?
Take back thy niggard counsel, nor presume
O'er our bright sunshine to diffuse thy gloom;
Heads of Departments should be amply paid:
Places for this sole purpose have been made:
All are not like old Cincinnatus now,
To take up their old trades, or dirty plough.

     ＊   ＊   ＊   ＊

Ye would-be titled! whom, in evil hour—
The rash, unthinking people clothed with power,
Who, drunk with pride, of foreign baubles dream,
And rave of a COLUMBIAN DIADEM—
Be prudent, modest, moderate, grateful, wise,
Nor on your country's ruin strive to rise,
Lest great Columbia's awful god should frown,
And to your native dunghills hurl you down.

Ye faithful guardians of your country's weal,
Whose honest breasts still glow with patriot zeal!
The lawless lust of power in embryo quell,
The germe of mischief and first spawn of hell.
Within your sacred walls let virtue reign,
And greedy Mammon spread his snares in vain.
With unlick'd lordlings sully not your fame,
Nor daub our patriot with a lacker'd name.
O Washington! thy country's hope and trust!
Alas! perhaps her last, as thou wert first;
Successors we can find—but tell us where
Of all thy *virtues* we shall find the *heir?*

But if—which heaven avert!—we must have kings,
With all the curses the tiara brings,
Let us not frame the idol we adore,
But own the monster of some distant shore,

Bow to some foreign god, already grown,
Nor make a mongrel tyrant of our own,
To mimic monarchs, on his mimic throne :
Whom to equip with every gewgaw thing
Due to the proud regalia of a king,
Would beggar all his slaves of all their store,
And still the insatiate ape would gape for more.

    *   *   *   *

Speak boldly then—ye wise!—and act in season,
What but to think, tomorrow may be treason.
From small beginnings mighty mischief springs,
And soon the eaglet soars on eagle's wings.
Stifle the tyrant in his infant birth,
Or soon he 'll stalk a giant on the earth,
Tread on your necks, break all your barriers down,
Smile into life—and murder with a frown;
Disdain the balance, late the favorite theme,
And with his ponderous fiat kick the beam.
Dream not that homespun tyrants are the best,
Home-made or foreign, every king 's a pest,
Sent in God's wrath—O scatter not the seed,
Nor damn Columbia with a royal breed.
Great Washington! Columbia's prop and pride,
Her friend, her father, guardian god and guide;
If kings like thee could love, like thee could feel,
And know no wish but for their country's weal,
Or 'mongst the human race, if we could find,
Like thee to govern and to bless mankind ;
Then might Americans unblushing own
Such worth would *almost* sanctify a throne.

    *   *   *   *

Ye chosen people of the King of kings,
From whose behest your present being springs;
Who stamp'd this title on your federal birth,
Subjects in heaven—but citizens on earth;
Who gave you to possess these happy plains
Where peace and plenty dwell, and freedom reigns;
Freedom! the glorious prize—should ye resign,
Vengeance awaits you from the power divine;
Freedom! which heroes earn'd with their best blood,
And patriots bought with every other good ;
Freedom! which roused the Roman's honest zeal
Against his friend to lift the fatal steel,
Freedom! which those firm patriots deified,
Who in Rome's senate stabb'd the parricide.

Freedom! for fair Columbia bravely won
By the long toils of virtuous Washington,
Ne'er basely barter for a paltry crown,
"But piously transmit the blessing down."

SAMUEL EWING.

SAMUEL EWING was a resident of Philadelphia. We believe he was the son of Dr John Ewing, Provost of the
University of Pennsylvania. He is known as the author of
the Reflections in Solitude, a poem first published in the Port
Folio. He seems to have looked to Cowper for his model.
His poetry was the work of his early years, and though not
brilliant, has good qualities sufficient to recommend it to notice.

REFLECTIONS IN SOLITUDE.

To me, no heedless, listless looker on,
The idle fashions of a thoughtless race
Are pleasant. Though my feeble voice swell not
The hum of crowds, nor do I judge it wise
To mingle in their scenes, I do not yet
Forget my kind. Lull'd to tranquillity
By charms that Nature, in a kindly mood,
Grants, in profusion, to the lover-breath
Of youthful spring, I seek the grassy side
Of this clear brook. I deem it not unwise
To woo seclusion at the morning hour.
What place, along the hedge, the op'ning rose,
Peeps through the trembling dews, while all the wood
Rings with the varied strains of gratitude
That nature's children breathe, as flutt'ring light
From bough to bough, they make their duty, pleasure.
Driven, by a thankless world, to seek Content
In rural scenes, I sought and found her there.
With her it solaces me much to while,
In musings sweet, an idle hour away,
On gifts that God has lavish'd on mankind.

The last, the sweetest boon he gave to man,
Was Love. In Eden's bowers the cherub first
Was found. What hour uncoffin'd ghosts steal out,
To sit by new-made graves, or stand behind
The village matron's chair, to counterfeit
The clicking of the clock, or, yet more rude,
Tap at the window of the dreaming maid,
Or glide in winding-sheet across the room,
Borrowing the form that late her lover wore;
Upon a moon-beam, at such silent hour,
The boy descended, and, alighting soft,
Chose for his throne the mild blue eye of Eve.
On either pinion sat a fairy form
To guide the arrows, that, in wanton mood
The boy would hazard—This *Romance* was named,
And *Fancy*, that—One pluck'd, with busy hand,
Soft down from doves, and, artful, twined it round
The arrow's head, to hide from mortal eyes
The scorpion sting that barb'd the weapon's point.
While that, with syren smile, a mirror show'd
On whose smooth surface danced, in angel robes,
Perfection's form. And ever from that night,
The sportful twins attend the train of Love.
Thus was the garden, first by Adam's voice,
Call'd *Paradise*. And now what spot the boy
His transient visit pays, in wilderness
Or bower, or palace, or the lowly shed,
Man names it Paradise, nor errs he much
In such a name.
　　Though oft the side-long look,
The heavy sigh, that speaks the anxious doubt;
The flitting blush that lights the virgin's cheek;
The mind, abstracted from the present scene;
Eyes, idly fix'd unconscious on the hearth;
The trembling lip, and melancholy mien;
Though these, no dubious signs, proclaim the boy
The city's visitor, he yet prefers
To hold his court by moon-light, in the grove,
Or where the babbling brook winds through the wood,
Or where on shady side of sloping hill,
The green vine crawls, or where innum'rous boughs,
Raising each other's leaves just over head,
Keep the rude sun-beam from the lover's couch,
The grassy bank. Here Love his revels keeps,
While every breeze blows health, and every wind,
That sweeps the maiden's locks, and shows new charms,

Makes music sweeter than Apollo's lyre.
Sweet is the landscape, wild and picturesque,
To him, the youth, whose glowing fancy paints
The love-crown'd cottage as the seat of bliss!
Sweet is the forest's twilight gloom, and sweet
The May-morn ramble !   Sweet to pace along
The farm-boy's path, that, winding through the wood,
Leads to *variety*, within whose bounds
Alone is found the food that never cloys !
But sweeter far than brook, or walk, or wood,
Or May-morn ramble, or the evening stroll,
Far sweeter than imagination's stores,
The stolen interview with her he loves !
Sweet is the voice of Nature to his ear,
Long pain'd with list'ning to the tale of vice !
Sweet is the mock-bird's counterfeited note !
And sweet the murm'ring of the busy bee !
Sweet is the distant bell, at silent eve,
That guides the cow-boy where the cattle stray !
Sweet is the lengthen'd, still increasing sound,
Of horn that calls from meadows, wood, or field,
The weary lab'rer to his healthful meal !
The flute may cheat his melancholy mind
Of many a fancied ill, and as its strains
Float on the evening breeze, may gather mild
And mellowing influence to his greedy ear,
By mingling with the moonbeams !   Yet to him
No note so musical—no strain so sweet
As sighs that tell his fond—his doubting heart,
The love she would, but cannot hide from him !

ST GEORGE TUCKER.

THE Hon. St George Tucker was, we think, a Virginian.

STANZAS.

DAYS of my youth,
   Ye have glided away :
Hairs of my youth,
   Ye are frosted and gray :
Eyes of my youth,
   Your keen sight is no more :

Cheeks of my youth,
　Ye are furrow'd all o'er:
Strength of my youth,
　All your vigor is gone:
Thoughts of my youth,
　Your gay visions are flown.

Days of my youth,
　I wish not your recall:
Hairs of my youth,
　I 'm content ye should fall:
Eyes of my youth,
　You much evil have seen:
Cheeks of my youth,
　Bathed in tears have you been:
Thoughts of my youth,
　You have led me astray:
Strength of my youth,
　Why lament your decay?

Days of my age,
　Ye will shortly be past:
Pains of my age,
　Yet awhile ye can last:
Joys of my age,
　In true wisdom delight:
Eyes of my age,
　Be religion your light:
Thoughts of my age,
　Dread ye not the cold sod:
Hopes of my age,
　Be ye fix'd on your God.

J. HOPKINSON.

We have no knowledge of this author. The popular national ode which follows, appeared first, we believe, in Philadelphia.

HAIL COLUMBIA.

Hail Columbia! happy land!
　Hail ye heroes! heaven born band!
Who fought and bled in freedom's cause,
　And when the storm of war was gone,

Enjoy'd the peace your valor won.
　Let independence be our boast,
Ever mindful what it cost;
　Ever grateful for the prize,
Let its altar reach the skies.
　　Firm—united—let us be,
　　Rallying round our liberty;
　　As a band of brothers join'd,
　　Peace and safety we shall find.

Immortal patriots! rise once more;
　Defend your rights, defend your shore:
Let no rude foe, with impious hand
　Invade the shrine where sacred lies,
Of toil and blood the well-earn'd prize.
　　While offering peace, sincere and just,
　　In Heaven we place a manly trust,
　　That truth and justice will prevail,
　　And every scheme of bondage fail.

Sound, sound the trump of fame,
　Let Washington's great name
Ring through the world with loud applause,
　Let ev'ry clime to freedom dear,
Listen with a joyful ear.
　　With equal skill, and god-like power,
　　He govern'd in the fearful hour
　　Of horrid war; or guides, with ease,
　　The happier times of honest peace.

Behold the Chief, who now commands,
　Once more to serve his country stands—
The rock on which the storm will beat,
　But arm'd in virtue, firm and true,
His hopes are fix'd on Heaven and you.
　　While hope was sinking in dismay,
　　And glooms obscured Columbia's day,
　　His steady mind, from changes free,
　　Resolved on Death or Liberty.

RICHARD B. DAVIS

Was born in New York, August 21st, 1771. He studied at
Columbia College, but was too diffident to attempt any learned
profession, and chose the trade of his father, who was a car-

ver. In 1796 however, he was prevailed upon to become editor of The Diary, a daily paper in New York. He soon grew dissatisfied with the occupation, and gave it up at the end of the year. After this, he engaged in trade. In the autumn of 1799, the yellow fever prevailing in the city, he removed with his family to New Brunswick in New Jersey, but not before he had imbibed the disease. He died in his twentyeighth year. His poems were collected and published with a memoir in 1807.

TO A SLEEPING INFANT.

Sweet are thy slumbers, innocence, reclined
  On the fond bosom of maternal love;
  Calm as the lake whose waters gently move,
Wafting the spirit of the dying wind.
For thee affection wakes with pleasing care,
Delighted smiles, and breathes the fervent prayer.

Far different is sleep, when labor faints
  On his hard couch, when restless avarice quakes;
When from the scene of dread that conscience paints,
  Affrighted guilt with sudden horror wakes;
When from the eye of day misfortune shrinks,
And on his bed of thorns despondent sinks.

When night recalls the toilsome day of care,
  When hopeless love catches in short repose
Scenes that alike his aching bosom tear,
  Visions of shadowy bliss or real woes.

For dreams like these, and nights of anxious pain,
  Manhood thy peaceful slumbers must resign,
And all his boasted wisdom sigh in vain
  For the calm blessings of a sleep like thine.

THOU ART THE MUSE.

No genius lends its sacred fire
  To animate my song;
To me no heaven-presented lyre
  Or muse-taught verse belong.

She who first charm'd my soul to love,
　Inspired the tuneful breath ;
With love-instructed hand I wove
　For her the early wreath.

To her the softest strains I owe
　Who first inspired the flame ;
And sweetest shall the numbers flow,
　When graced with Emma's name.

———

TO EMMA.

I 've seen the loveliest roses blow
　That Hudson's verdant banks adorn ;
I 've seen the richest crimson glow
　That paints the smiling face of morn :

I 've listen'd while the evening gale,
　(Fraught with the sweets of many a flower,
Wafted sweet incense through the vale,
　And bless'd the contemplative hour.

Sweet tints the blushing rose adorn,
　And sweet the rays of morning shine
Sweet are the sounds by zephyrs borne,
　But sweeter charms, my fair, are thine.

The rose shall droop, its charms shall fade,
　Clouds shall obscure the brightest day ;
Music shall cease to bless the shade,
　And even *thy beauties* must decay :

But the bright flame that warms thy breast,
　Beams from those eyes, and tunes that tongue,
Virtue—shall ever shine confess'd,
　And ever claim my noblest song.